Law for Canadian Health Care Administrators

LAW FOR CANADIAN HEALTH CARE ADMINISTRATORS

J.J. Morris
B.A., M.A., L.L.B.

Butterworths
Toronto and Vancouver

Law for Canadian Health Care Administrators

October 1996

The Butterworth Group of Companies

Canada:
75 Clegg Road, MARKHAM, Ontario L6G 1A1
and
1721-808 Nelson St., Box 12148, VANCOUVER, B.C. V6Z 2H2

Australia:
Butterworths Pty Ltd., SYDNEY

Ireland:
Butterworth (Ireland) Ltd., DUBLIN

Malaysia:
Malayan Law Journal Sdn Bhd, KUALA LUMPUR

New Zealand:
Butterworths of New Zealand Ltd., WELLINGTON

Singapore:
Butterworths Asia, SINGAPORE

South Africa:
Butterworth Publishers (Pty.) Ltd., DURBAN

United Kingdom:
Butterworth & Co. (Publishers) Ltd., LONDON

United States:
Michie, CHARLOTTESVILLE, Virginia

Canadian Cataloguing in Publication Data

Morris, John J. (John Joseph), 1952-
Law for Canadian health care administrators

Includes index.
ISBN 0-433-39161-8

1. Medical care – Law and legislation – Canada.
I. Title.

KE3646.M67 1996 344.7'04 C96-931770-0
KF3821.M67 1996

Reprint #1, 1999.

For

Darcy, Deirdre, Nathan and Peter

Preface

The chief aim of health administrators is to manage the provision of first-rate patient care. A significant component of the health administrator's role, especially in recent years, however, has been to recognize and to deal with legal issues. Questions of consent to treatment, patient records and professional discipline are often directed to administrators by front line health-care workers. Boards of directors rely upon administrators to ensure that the operation of institutions complies with corporate bylaws and government legislation. Employment or labour law issues may be a frequent, if not daily, concern in some health-care facilities. Health administrators are expected to have ready answers to straightforward questions, or, where the issues are more complex, to consult legal counsel in a timely and cost-efficient way.

There has been a tremendous growth in the range of legal issues confronting health administrators. An increasing respect for patient confidentiality has given rise to strict legal obligations for health-care institutions and professionals. Whereas the enforced treatment of patients might, at one time, have been overlooked on the rationale that the treatment was humane and well-intentioned, recent jurisprudence has made it clear that such practices will not be countenanced by a court of law. The HIV-tainted blood scandal of the '80s and '90s resulted in numerous international investigations and inquiries, for example, the Krever Commission in Canada. New developments have generated a host of legal issues in the areas of patient rights, consent to treatment, health records, mental health and professional malpractice. Claims for civil compensation have rapidly increased. Health administrators cannot perform their duties competently unless they are familiar with legal developments in these areas.

Where, as is sometimes unavoidable, a health facility becomes involved in legal proceedings, the principal liaison between the legal system and the institution is likely to be a health administrator. Someone within the institution will be required to retain and instruct counsel. That person may be required to organize records, facilitate the investigation, provide support to staff, attend at court proceedings and make a full, in-depth report to the board of the particular institution. In some cases, board members will be directly involved in the legal process—for example, when the board of a public hospital is required by law to hold a hearing in relation to a physician's hospital privileges—and must be guided carefully through the complex statutory process.

This book is written for those who are involved in health administration in Canada and who, as part of that role, will from time to time encounter situations in which they must recognize and deal with legal issues. It attempts to orient basic legal principles, making them relevant to health care. This book will also be helpful to the lawyer who does not practise frequently in the health law field, but is asked to give advice to, or to represent, a health facility.

Although I have referred to cases and authorities and to numerous statutes and legal texts, I have tried to keep these references to a minimum, without excluding those references that some readers may wish to have in order to consult the source of the specific legal principle or the legislation of their own province or territory. Writing a text that deals with health law principles in different provinces and territories is no easy task. Although there are many similarities, there are also differences. In a number of chapters, where appropriate, the relevant legislation of a particular jurisdiction has been identified and cited for easy reference. It should go without saying that this text cannot be a substitute for qualified legal advice from experienced counsel. It should provide a basis, however, for recognizing legal issues in a timely way, dealing directly with those issues that are straightforward without incurring the expense of legal advice and eliminating the perplexity that sometimes arises in connection with legal proceedings.

Once again, as with my earlier book, *Canadian Nurses and the Law,* I am enormously grateful for the efforts of my legal assistant, Julie Ong, who has been tireless in ensuring that a busy legal practice was not jeopardized by the sometimes conflicting activities of book-writing. Lesley Slan, a law clerk and relatively new addition to our firm, has also helped in creating organization out of chaos. Martha Foote, of our firm's library, worked beyond the call of duty and demonstrated tremendous skill in locating citations, checking references, correcting footnotes and making numerous refinements that have improved the text significantly.

Without the dedicated assistance of a number of law students, some of whom are now lawyers, this book would still be in its conceptual states. I have been very fortunate in having the help of intelligent, hard-working individuals for whose contribution I will always be grateful. Joanna Rainbow, Kathy Church, Jasminka Kalajdzic, Cheryl Wooden, Kathleen Breedyk and Cindy Clarke have each assisted tremendously.

My colleagues at Borden & Elliot, and within our Health Law Group, have been as supportive of this project as they were with my earlier text. Rino Stradiotto, who heads our Health Law Group, was kind enough to review the chapter on Hospital Privileges. Eric Roher, a member of our Employment Law Group, reviewed the chapter on Employment and Labour Law. Colin White, Mike Boyce and Sandy Gow, of the Healthcare Insurance Reciprocal of Canada, offered comments and suggestions on the chapter on Malpractice and Institutional Liability. Having said that, any errors or inadequacies in the text are my own.

Finally, this book, as with most things in my life, would not have been possible if I did not have the support of an extremely talented and tenacious individual, my wife Julie. Aside from bearing a disproportionate share in raising four fabulous children and being a publisher in her own right, she is able to provide just the right measure of encouragement and admonishment to a sometimes reluctant author.

John J. Morris
Toronto, October 1996

Table of Contents

CHAPTER 1

Canadian Health Facilities

INTRODUCTION

Institutional health care is a recent phenomenon in the history of health care in Canada. In the nineteenth century, patients suffering from acute and chronic symptoms requiring medical attention were treated in their homes. Medical treatment tended to be less invasive and more palliative; the home was an appropriate setting for the type of treatment being provided. Medicine had not advanced technologically to the point where sophisticated equipment was used for the diagnosis and treatment of patients. Nursing services were supplied by family members or by someone paid directly by the patient. Hospitals consisted, for the most part, of small units which formed a part of a charitable or religious organization and were designed to provide accommodation for patients who were without homes or who were too poor to afford a private physician.[1]

Aside from the relative scarcity of hospitals and other health-care institutions, patients were reluctant to be admitted to institutions where they believed that the conditions they would be subjected to and the treatment they would receive were a poor alternative to treatment in their own homes.

> In those days (1867) it was with the greatest difficulty patients could be induced to go into a hospital. It was the popular belief that if they went in they would never come out alive. No records were kept. The clinical thermometer had not come into use; the patients had to look after themselves; fresh air was not thought necessary. Armies of rats disported themselves about the wards. Instruments were looked after by a man who assisted in the operating room and at post mortems in the dead house. Nothing was known of sepsis or antisepsis. Surgeons operated with dirty instruments and septic hands and wore coats which had been for years baptized with the blood of victims.[2]

---

1 See G.H. Agnew, *Canadian Hospitals, 1920 to 1970 — A Dramatic Half Century* (Toronto: University of Toronto Press, 1974), Chapter 1, Hospitals of the 1920's.

2 *Ibid.*, at 3.

Today, it is commonplace for patients to receive care and treatment in institutions rather than in their own homes. The number and nature of health facilities have mushroomed. Facilities are more specialized. In all provinces and territories there is a high degree of regulatory control exercised by government over public and private hospitals, psychiatric facilities, chronic-care facilities, nursing homes and other health-care institutions. Arguably, the most important role of the health administrator — aside from the general obligation to ensure the provision of high-quality health care — is to ensure compliance with the complex code of legal regulation which is likely to apply to the particular health care facility for which the administrator bears responsibility.

Provincial and Territorial Regulation

The provincial governments were charged in 1867 under the *British North America Act* (now the *Constitution Act*) with the "Establishment, Maintenance, and Management of Hospitals".[3] As a result, provincial governments, along with the territories, have passed a complex array of legislation governing the administration of various health facilities. The legislation includes such areas as

- the establishment and management of hospitals and other public health facilities;
- the licensing and management of nursing homes, chronic-care facilities and other privately owned and operated health facilities;
- the requirements for the continuous presence of professional care-givers such as doctors and nurses in health facilities;
- the criteria for allocation of capital grants and the continued funding of patients and services in health facilities;
- the provision for inspection on a regular basis by government-appointed inspectors;
- the construction, maintenance and physical environment of health-care facilities;
- the creation, confidentiality and retention of health records;
- the rights of patients and workers in health facilities;
- the procedures for accreditation and privileging of physicians.

---

[3] *Constitution Act, 1867* (U.K.), 30 & 31 Vict., c. 3, s. 92.

Public Hospitals and Other Types of Health Facilities

The hospital community in Canada consists of a wide variety of institutions. A distinction is drawn by Statistics Canada between general and special hospitals.[4] General hospitals provide care to people of all ages and genders and for all types of diseases. Some hospitals specialize in the care they provide. Thus, there are pediatric hospitals, maternity hospitals, rehabilitation hospitals and chronic-care hospitals. Psychiatric hospitals and tuberculosis hospitals are in special categories of their own.

There is also a distinction between private and public hospitals. Private hospitals, also known as proprietary hospitals, may be owned by individuals or private organizations. Although private hospitals are strongly linked to government through government supervision, they are often supported by private financing. Only a small percentage of Canada's hospital beds are contained in private hospitals.

Public hospitals are non-profit institutions. They range in size from small hospitals having fewer than 50 beds to large, general teaching hospitals having over 1,000 beds. Public hospitals, whether small or large, and whether operated by lay, religious or government bodies, are organized in corporate form. Most public hospitals are also general hospitals. All public hospitals are heavily dependent upon government funding. All provinces have enacted legislation that sets out certain standards and requirements for the operation of public hospitals.[5]

In 1990, there were 835 public hospitals in Canada providing general health care to patients. Of these, 777 were non-teaching hospitals and 58 were teaching hospitals. Together they accounted for 128,497 beds, 336,589 full-time staff and 3,391,854 admissions. The total operating cost for these hospitals was $18.5 billion, of which $12.2 billion was for salary and wages including the remuneration of medical staff.[6]

---

4 Statistics Canada, *Hospital Statistics, Preliminary Annual Report 1990-91* (Ottawa: Statistics Canada, Canadian Centre for Health Information, 1993).

5 Alberta: *Hospitals Act,* R.S.A. 1980, c. H-11; British Columbia: *Hospital Act,* R.S.B.C. 1979, c. 176; Manitoba: *Hospitals Act,* R.S.M. 1987, c. H120; New Brunswick: *Hospital Act,* S.N.B. 1992, c. H-6.1; Newfoundland: *Hospitals Act,* R.S.N. 1990, c. H-9; Nova Scotia: *Hospitals Act,* R.S.N.S. 1989, c. 208; Ontario: *Public Hospitals Act,* R.S.O. 1990, c. P.40; Prince Edward Island: *Hospitals Act,* R.S.P.E.I. 1988, c. H-10; Quebec: *An Act Respecting Health Services and Social Services,* R.S.Q. 1977, c. S-4.2; Saskatchewan: *Hospital Standards Act,* R.S.S. 1978, c. H-10.

6 *Hospital Statistics, supra* note 4.

Boards of Directors or Trustees

Most health facilities are non-profit corporations incorporated under provincial or territorial legislation. The objects and powers of the corporation are contained in letters patent or articles of incorporation. The body that bears the ultimate authority for the administration of the health-care corporation is a board of directors or trustees. The board is usually composed of members of the community, and in some cases, staff. Board members serve on a voluntary basis. Most board members are laypersons who have little practical experience in health care. Board members may be appointed because of their links in the community, their ability to raise funds from private sources or the high degree of knowledge and experience they can bring to the health facility from unrelated fields of endeavour.

In addition to the general role and responsibilities of directors in any incorporated entity, it is important that board members properly fulfil their function by recognizing that the public nature of a health facility means certain activities within the corporate structure are closely regulated by government, and that the onus for ensuring compliance falls, ultimately, upon the members of the board. In addition to duties imposed directly upon the board of the hospital, provincial legislation may set out a number of other duties designed to meet minimum standards for the provision of health services. Where minimum standards set out in the legislation are not met, and harm results to a patient, there is a risk of liability for the health facility and any health-care workers involved.

Traditionally, boards and administrators have placed great reliance upon the medical staff of a health facility in making decisions relating to the management and operation of the institution. The influence of physicians is sometimes greater than that of other health-care professionals working in the health facility, even though other health professionals may be greater in number (*e.g.*, nurses). In modern health facilities, the power and influence of other health professionals is growing. This is reflected in practice as well as in related health-care legislation.[7]

---

[7] *E.g.*, *Public Hospitals Act*, R.S.O. 1990, c. P.40, s. 12(1). In 1989, the Ontario government amended its hospital management regulation to require the participation of staff nurses and nurse managers in public hospital committees: Ont. Reg. 83/89. Following enactment of the regulation, the Ontario Nurses' Association brought an application to a judge for enforcement of nurses' rights at a particular hospital. The hospital had provided for the election of nurses to two budget committees, but not to a "fiscal advisory board" as required by the legislation. The Court held that the nurses were entitled to be elected to a fiscal advisory committee which would have direct access to the board of the hospital: *O.N.A. v. Toronto Hospital* (1989), 70 O.R. (2d) 389 (H.C.J.). Also, a number of

Despite the importance of having input from health-care professionals in the operation and management of the hospital, it must be recognized that ultimate authority rests with the board.

> A hospital is not unlike a machine. Each is built to carry out a certain function in a particular manner. Each requires materials, mechanics, maintenance and skilled operators. The design capacities built into the fabric of each predetermine their optimum work load. To press either beyond its optimum performance invites breakdown. It is the task of a Board of Governors to balance the operation of its hospital and tune it to that level of optimum performance permitted by its inherent limitations. The Board of Governors has the responsibility to determine the pace at which the facilities of its hospital will be operated, and to establish those staffing policies which satisfy the requirements of that operation.[8]

Circumstances may arise in which a government develops concerns in relation to the management and operation of a health facility. In some provinces, there is legislation which permits the appointment of a person who will assume the authorities and responsibilities of the board. In New Brunswick, a "trustee" may be appointed where the Minister of Health and Community Services forms the opinion that a public hospital board is "not functioning effectively" or is failing to comply with legislation that governs the conduct of the hospital. The trustee is "vested" with all "rights, powers, duties and responsibilities of the board".[9] In British Columbia, the Minister may appoint a "public administrator" to a hospital where it is "necessary in the public interest".[10] The public administrator may receive evidence about the "planning, construction or operation of the hospital"[11] and may be appointed to "manage the property and affairs of a hospital".[12] Upon the appointment of a public administrator to manage the property and affairs of the hospital, all board members cease to hold office unless otherwise ordered by the government.[13] In Ontario, the government is empowered

---

provinces have enacted legislation that gives a considerable degree of self-governance to all health professionals and which is likely, over time, to give increased authority and impact to a wide array of health professionals and render health facilities less deferential to physicians; see Chapter 3, Canadian Health Professions — Status and Discipline.

8 *Re Sheriton and North York General Hospital* (decision of the Hospital Appeal Board of Ontario, December 6, 1973), at 7; approved in *Board of Governors, Scarborough General Hospital and Schiller* (1974), 4 O.R. (2d) 201 (H.C.J.).

9 *Hospital Act*, S.N.B. 1992, c. H-6.1, s. 29(1).

10 *Hospital Act*, R.S.B.C. 1979, c. 176, s. 44(1).

11 *Ibid.*, s. 44(7)(c).

12 *Ibid.*, s. 44(4).

13 *Ibid.*, s. 44(6).

to appoint a "hospital supervisor" where it forms the opinion that the appointment is in the "best interest of the public".[14] The hospital board is bound to follow the advice or instructions of the hospital supervisor, and where it fails to do so, the hospital supervisor may act independently.[15]

Generally, board members of health facilities are shielded from direct liability by the corporation. There may, however, be common-law and statutory obligations for a board member or trustee, a breach of which may result in direct liability. A board member will be directly liable where he or she engages in conduct that is fraudulent or constitutes bad faith. A board member stands in a fiduciary relationship with the health facility and is required to act loyally, honestly and in good faith to achieve the mission of the health facility. Board members must avoid any situation in which self-interest and their duty to the institution come into conflict. If a board member has a direct or indirect interest in a matter which comes before the board, he or she has a duty to disclose that interest to the board when the matter is first discussed and on any future occasions. That board member must refrain from participating in any deliberations or voting in relation to the matter in which he or she has an interest. In some instances, the potential conflict of interest may be so significant that it will prevent the board member from participating meaningfully in many activities of the board, and will therefore necessitate a resignation.

A board member must exercise the care, diligence and skill that may be reasonably expected of a person having that board member's background, knowledge and experience. An accountant may be required to satisfy a higher standard of care with respect to financial matters than another board member without accounting expertise. On the other hand, board members, particularly where a large institution is involved, are entitled to rely upon the administrators and other staff of the institution to attend to day-to-day operations. Because most health facilities are operated on a not-for-profit basis, and funded entirely or almost entirely by government funds, board members of health facilities are in a position of public trust and must act accordingly.

Board members must exercise a reasonable standard in ensuring that the health facility complies with applicable laws, its letters patent or other incorporating document and its bylaws. If a board member disagrees with a proposed action or decision by the board, that board member should vote against the action or motion and ensure that the dissenting vote is recorded in the minutes. Individuals who are named as board members, but fail to attend meetings regularly or to make efforts to oversee the operation of the institution, may court direct legal liability. In some provinces, legislation has been enacted which expressly protects board

---

[14] *Public Hospitals Act*, R.S.O. 1990, c. P-40, s. 9(1).

[15] *Ibid.*, s. 9(6).

members from civil actions if they act "honestly and in good faith".[16] In Ontario, board members of public hospitals are protected from liability "for anything done or said in good faith in the course of a meeting, proceeding, investigation or other business".[17]

In addition to the common-law obligations of board members or trustees, there may be statutory obligations. In some jurisdictions, board members have direct liability, even after they have ceased to be board members, for such things as the failure to deduct, withhold, collect or forward amounts for federal and provincial income tax, unemployment insurance, Canada Pension Plan, retail sales tax and the Goods and Services Tax. Board members may also have direct personal liability for failure to ensure compliance with occupational health and safety legislation, and for violations of provincial employment standards legislation and federal and provincial environmental standards legislation.

An invitation to sit on the board of a public hospital or other health facility may be an honour, but it also imposes significant responsibilities. Where a board member exercises due diligence through familiarity with applicable legislation, ensuring that activities of the health facility are consistent with the goals and bylaws of the facility, and where he or she participates meaningfully in the activities of the board, direct liability can be avoided. To minimize the risk of exposure, the corporation may wish to offer an indemnity to board members as long as they have acted without fraud and in good faith. Insurance is also available to protect and indemnify board members.

Corporate Bylaws

Generally speaking, the activities of the board of directors, in governing the health-care corporation, will be regulated by a set of bylaws. Provincial statutes regulating public hospitals may specifically require the board of the hospital to enact bylaws governing the organization, management and operation of the hospital it controls.[18] These bylaws will conform generally to guide-lines stipulated by the minister responsible for the operation of hospitals in the province, or to general bylaws recommended by the Canadian Hospital Association or its provincial affiliate.

For example, public hospital legislation in the various provinces may require the hospital board to pass bylaws which relate to

---

[16] See, for example, *Hospital Act*, S.N.B. 1992, c. H-6.1.

[17] *Public Hospitals Act*, R.S.O. 1990, c. P-40, s. 13.

[18] *E.g.*, *Hospitals Act*, R.S.A. 1980, c. H-11, s. 28.

1. the development and implementation of an accident prevention policy within a hospital;
2. the appointment of an "administrator" who is responsible to the board and who is charged with administering the hospital in accordance with provincial legislation and the bylaws of the hospital;
3. the passage of bylaws for the internal administration and management of the hospital, including bylaws regulating the activities of the health-care personnel (*i.e.*, doctors and nurses), and the review of these bylaws at regular intervals;
4. the scheduling of regular meetings of medical staff;
5. the assurance that all orders for treatment are in writing and signed by the attending physician and that, upon admission of the patient, proper records are prepared, maintained and kept confidential;
6. the assurance that written consents be obtained in respect of certain medical procedures;
7. the installation of a system of accounting;
8. the designation of hospital wards as standard, private and semi-private;
9. the allocation of "gift" revenues for the specific purposes for which the gifts were made and the application of other revenues to projects that increase the productivity of the establishment;
10. the education and training of nurses and other hospital personnel.

The articles of incorporation and bylaws of the corporation, as enacted by the board, form the "constitution" of the institution. All activities by the board or by anyone employed by the corporation, in order to be valid, must conform to the incorporating documents and the bylaws. Ordinarily, the bylaws will contain provisions stating how the members of the board of directors are to be elected or appointed, what duties they will have, how these duties are to be carried out and when meetings will take place. The bylaws will cover basic financial aspects of the corporation's activities, such as banking, the maintenance of books and records, the appointment of an auditor for the corporation and the appointment of a treasurer. There may be provisions relating to conflicts of interest and confidentiality.

In most cases, the bylaws will also regulate (and in doing so must conform to any governing provincial legislation) the appointment and supervision of medical staff, classes of medical staff, organization of the medical staff, and the organization of various departments throughout the hospital. Bylaws may provide for the establishment of such committees as the Medical Advisory Committee, Credentials Committee, Medical Records Committee, Infection Control Committee, Medical Audit Committee and Utilization Committee.

Hospital bylaws must be in accordance with any regulations prescribed under the public hospitals legislation and may be subject to the approval of the minister. In some instances, representative bodies, such as provincial hospital associations, will recommend model or prototype bylaws for adoption by health facilities. Considerable caution should be exercised in adopting such bylaws without input from experienced legal counsel familiar with the legal principles affecting the management of health facilities. The fact that a model or prototype bylaw has been developed and recommended by a committee or organization does not guarantee legal validity or ensure that it is best suited to the requirements of the particular health facility.[19]

Medical Advisory Committee

The legislation of most provinces provides for the establishment of a Medical Advisory Committee in a public hospital. Various titles for this body are adopted in the relevant legislation: "Medical Advisory Committee"; "Medical Staff Review Committee"; "Hospital Standards Committee"; or "Advisory Management Committee". The Medical Advisory Committee is a committee of the hospital, made up primarily of staff physicians, established by the board under the bylaws and charged with advising the board in relation to medical issues. The duties of the Medical Advisory Committee may be broad or narrow, depending upon the nature of the institution and the empowering legislation and bylaws. In Ontario, the duties of the Medical Advisory Committee are broadly defined in the legislation. They include making recommendations to the board concerning

- applications for medical, dental or midwifery staff appointments and reappointments;
- the nature of the privileges to be granted to members of the medical, dental or midwifery staff;
- the bylaws respecting the medical, dental or midwifery staff;

---

[19] A prototype which has been developed for a large hospital may not be suited to a small hospital. For example, the Ontario Hospital Association developed a prototype bylaw to deal with the mid-term suspension of physician privileges. The prototype is in response to recommendations by that province's Hospital Appeal Board that hospitals have in place a bylaw to deal with mid-term suspensions. The prototype contains an extremely complex process to deal with emergent and non-emergent suspension of physician privileges. Aside from whether the complex nature of the process makes it difficult, in practice, to follow, it is clear that the prototype is not applicable, without modification, to small, community hospitals which may not have the various department heads and others who are mentioned in the prototype.

- the dismissal, suspension or restriction of hospital privileges of any member of the medical, dental or midwifery staff;
- the quality of medical, dental and midwifery care provided in the hospital; and
- the clinical and general rules respecting the medical, dental and midwifery staff as may be necessary in the circumstances.

The Medical Advisory Committee of a public hospital in Ontario has a statutory obligation to supervise the practice of medicine, dentistry and midwifery in the hospital, to appoint the members of the medical staff of all committees that are established by the board, to receive reports from the committees of the medical staff and to advise the board on any matter referred to it by the board.[20]

As a majority of the hospital board may often be composed of lay members, and as the board will in some instances be in the position of making decisions affecting medical care and practices in the hospital, the role of the Medical Advisory Committee is an important one. In some instances, the Medical Advisory Committee may be authorized by the board to reach and effect decisions of a medical nature without consultation with the board. In other instances, the board will consider recommendations made by the Medical Advisory Committee, but will reach the ultimate decision itself.

Provincial legislation relating to public hospitals may stipulate that the Medical Advisory Committee can only make "recommendations" in respect of certain subject matters (*e.g.*, the appointment of medical staff to the hospital) and that the ultimate decision must be left up to the board. In instances where a committee of the hospital has purported to "decide" an issue that must be decided by the board, the decision is invalid.[21] If a board places too great a reliance upon the Medical Advisory Committee and simply adopts a recommendation as if it were, *de facto*, a decision, without considering the issue on its merits, the decision of the board may be rendered invalid as well.[22] The operative principle is that the board of a hospital bears the ultimate responsibility and authority for any activity carried out by the hospital through its medical staff and employees. While certain bodies, committees or individuals within the hospital may exert considerable influence in guiding the activities of a hospital, no other entity within the hospital can supersede or abrogate the legal authority of the board.

---

20 R.R.O. 1990, Reg. 965, s. 7.

21 *Re Braun and Surrey Memorial Hospital*, January 23, 1989 (British Columbia Medical Appeal Board).

22 See R.W. Macaulay, *Practice and Procedure Before Administrative Tribunals* (Toronto: Carswell, 1988), Vol. 2, pp. 22-10.9-10.

QUALITY ASSURANCE

Aside from its day-to-day management of the corporation and its component parts, the administration of a health facility is also charged by law with ensuring that the medical care and treatment provided to patients meet an acceptable standard. In many instances, the provision of the appropriate standard of medical care and treatment will be within the domain of the health professionals administering treatment. Failure to provide the appropriate standard of treatment may result in disciplinary measures being taken against health personnel, and when that treatment results in harm to the patient, may result in civil or criminal proceedings. While primary responsibility for ensuring acceptable treatment rests with the health professional, the health facility may bear direct responsibility where it fails to make certain that safeguards are present to ensure that appropriate standards of treatment are being provided.[23]

In a number of jurisdictions in Canada, the provincial or territorial legislation governing the operation and management of health facilities sets out guide-lines and minimum requirements concerning many aspects of care and treatment within a hospital or other health facility. It is the responsibility of the board, through its management and health personnel, to ensure that these statutory criteria are met. Some provinces, such as Ontario, Alberta, Nova Scotia and Prince Edward Island, have enacted detailed standards regarding certain aspects of patient care in their public hospital legislation. In provinces where governments have enacted detailed legislation, the guide-lines are mandatory and any departure from the requirements contained in the legislation may provide a basis for civil liability against the hospital and those members of its staff who fail to comply with the legislation. Where governments have not legislated detailed guide-lines or standards, the absence of such legislation does not mean that a court will conclude, nonetheless, that similar guide-lines or standards should not apply.

Provincial legislation stipulating minimum standards and practices for patient treatment may be found in the following areas:

- the admission and discharge of patients, including which staff have the power to admit and discharge patients and the admitting and discharge procedure to be followed;[24]
- the preparation and maintenance of hospital records including the types of records to be compiled, by whom, time periods for retention of hospital records, access to medical records and considerations of confidentiality;[25]

---

[23] See Chapter 7, Malpractice and Institutional Liability.

[24] *E.g.*, Alta. Reg. 247/90, s. 9.

[25] *E.g.*, N.B. Reg. 92-84, ss. 20-24.

- prerequisites for surgical care including the execution by the patient of a written consent, mandatory work-ups prior to surgery and administration of anaesthesia; the necessity of assistance and consultation in respect of certain surgical procedures;[26]
- pathological examinations for certain types of tissue removed during surgery;[27]
- autopsies, notification of the coroner, the storage and removal of corpses;[28]
- treatment and isolation of patients suffering from infectious diseases;[29]
- guide-lines and restrictions in relation to the role of health personnel in the hospital including physicians, nurses, dentists and radiologists.[30]

In some provinces, special provision is made in relation to the quality and number of the health-care staff of a hospital. In Prince Edward Island, a hospital must have on duty

(a) during the period from midnight until eight o'clock in the forenoon, at least one registered nurse for each 50 patients or fraction thereof; and
(b) during the period from eight o'clock in the forenoon until midnight, at least one registered nurse for each 35 patients or fraction thereof.[31]

This represents a minimum requirement and does not relieve the hospital from the responsibility of having on duty at all times sufficient nursing staff to provide a level of nursing care to every patient in the hospital as is required for the patient's proper care and treatment.[32]

In Nova Scotia, the pharmacy or drug dispensary in a hospital must be under the "direction or advice of a pharmacist licensed under the *Pharmacy Act*".[33] In Alberta, the legislation stipulates that the "assistance of a second physician is required" for numerous complex surgical procedures that may "constitute a distinct hazard to life or health". The list includes 22 different operative procedures.[34] In New Brunswick, the "administration regulation" proclaimed pursuant to that province's *Hospital Act* simply states that the hospital "shall have qualified staff to provide the range of services approved by the Minister for each hospital".[35]

---

26 *E.g.*, E.C.574/76, ss. 48, 49 and 50.
27 *E.g.*, N.S. Reg. 16/79, s. 11.
28 *E.g.*, Alta. Reg. 247/90, ss. 25 and 26.
29 *E.g.*, *Hospital Standards Regulations, 1980*, Sask. Reg. 331/79, ss. 60-64.
30 *Ibid., passim.*
31 *Hospital Management Regulations,* E.C. 574/76, s. 16(2).
32 *Ibid.*, s. 16(1).
33 N.S. Reg. 16/79, s. 14.
34 Alta. Reg. 247/90, s. 20(3).
35 N.B. Reg. 92-84, s. 55(1).

In most provincial and territorial legislation, there is provision for inspections to be carried out by inspectors appointed by the branch of government responsible for health facilities. These inspectors are charged with ensuring that the facility is meeting the requirements set out in the legislation and that the care and treatment being provided is otherwise satisfactory.

Canadian Council on Hospital Accreditation

Traditionally, in Canada, the most intense scrutiny of the standards of health care being provided at health facilities has been carried out by a private agency called the Canadian Council on Health Services Accreditation (CCHSA). This umbrella organization comprises a number of organizations, including the Canadian Healthcare Association, the Canadian Medical Association, the Royal College of Physicians and Surgeons of Canada, the Canadian Nurses' Association and the Canadian College of Health Services Executives.

The CCHSA publishes, on an annual basis, standards for accreditation of health facilities in Canada. At present the vast majority of hospitals in Canada have been accredited. Non-accredited hospitals tend to be smaller hospitals in rural and outlying areas.[36] Accreditation takes place on a voluntary basis. While no province requires that a hospital be accredited, the accreditation process and any report on the hospital by the CCHSA will carry considerable weight in a provincial government's own evaluation of a hospital's performance.

In Alberta, a regulation passed pursuant to the *Hospitals Act* specifically provides that each hospital shall "strive to meet the standards for accreditation" established by the CCHSA.[37] In Nova Scotia, the equivalent regulation stipulates that a hospital must forward any report prepared by the CCHSA in relation to the hospital to the minister.[38]

Hospitals are surveyed by surveyors appointed by the CCHSA. For larger facilities, there will be several surveyors who, together, possess wide expertise. The surveyor or survey group will prepare a report and on the basis of this report, the CCHSA notifies the hospital of deficiencies found and of its decision on accreditation.[39] Standards are revised on an annual basis by the CCHSA. A survey will result in an examination of all elements of the administration, care and treatment within the facility. A facility will be required to meet certain standards in respect of the provision of health

---

36 L. Soderstrom, *The Canadian Health System* (London: Croom Helm, 1978), p. 32.

37 Alta. Reg. 247/90, s. 34(1).

38 N.S. Reg. 16/79, s. 9.

39 See Soderstrom, *supra* note 36, p. 32.

services, including goals and objectives, the organization and administration of the professional staff, direction and staffing practices, facilities, equipment and supplies, policies and procedures, care programme, education and quality assurance.[40]

Nursing Homes

A number of provinces have enacted special legislation for the regulation of nursing homes.[41] In other jurisdictions, nursing homes are regulated under umbrella legislation which applies to nursing homes and other residential-care facilities.[42] Nursing homes and similar facilities are monitored closely by provincial governments. For example, in Alberta, an owner or operator of a nursing home must enter into a contract with the provincial government;[43] nursing homes in that province are subject to the authority of district health boards[44] and the Minister of Health has the power to cancel the contract of a nursing home operator where there is conduct that may have a prejudicial effect on the "health, safety or well-being of residents".[45] In Ontario, an applicant may seek a hearing before the Nursing Homes Review Board where it is proposed that a licence not be issued or renewed or that a licence be revoked.[46] The term "nursing home" may be protected so that no one who does not hold a licence from the province can use the term "nursing home", or similar words, in connection with any premises.[47]

Like hospitals, the day-to-day operation and management of nursing homes and similar facilities is closely regulated. Regulations passed pursuant to nursing home legislation in Alberta typify provincial and territorial standards:

---

40 See Canadian Hospital on Health Services Accreditation, *Acute Care Standards, 1995*; *Small Health Facilities, 1994*; *Long Term Care Facilities I 1992* (Nursing Homes); *Long Term Care Facilities, 1992* (Chronic Care); *Mental Health (Psychiatric) Hospitals, 1992*; *Cancer Treatment Centres, 1995* (Ottawa: Canadian Council on Hospital Services Accreditation).

41 Alberta, Ontario, New Brunswick and Prince Edward Island.

42 For example, under Nova Scotia *Homes for Special Care Act*, R.S.N.S. 1989, c. 203, s. 2(1)(j), there is a definition of "nursing home", and a "building or place or part of a building or place" may be designated as a nursing home under s. 3(2).

43 *Nursing Homes Act*, S.A. 1985, c. N-14.1, s. 1.

44 *Ibid.*, s. 2.

45 *Ibid.*, s. 21.

46 *Nursing Homes Act*, R.S.O. 1990, c. N.7, s. 15(2).

47 *Nursing Homes Act*, S.N.B. 1982, c. N-11, s. 3(3).

- the appointment of an "administrator" whose "duty and responsibility" is the "day to day operation and management of the affairs of the nursing home";[48]
- the admission of a patient to a nursing home where there is a bed open and the appropriate assessment has been carried out by the assessment committee;[49]
- the preparation of an inventory for the personal property of each resident and to make this available on request to the resident or his or her personal representative;[50]
- the maintenance and retention of a record in relation to each resident which provides detailed documentation in relation to the resident's health condition, treatment, medications and other personal data;[51]
- the mandatory appointment of individuals to provide certain services to the residents; *i.e.*, a director of nursing; nursing and personal services staff; a registered dietician; a medical adviser, a pharmacist;[52]
- minimum levels of nursing and personal service staff per resident and minimum qualifications for the staff;[53]
- minimum requirements with respect to the number and timing of meals, the establishment of menus, the availability of nourishment outside mealtimes, the provision of meals for residents with special dietary needs;[54]
- the establishment and organization of "life enrichment services" which may involve religious services, shopping, and community activities;[55]
- frequent and regular intervention by medical and nursing personnel.[56]

In Ontario, the legislation also mandates

- the provision of such physical facilities as a nursing station on each floor,[57] an activity area[58] and minimum toilet facilities;[59]
- the reporting of harm or potential harm to a resident as a result of unlawful conduct, improper or incompetent treatment or care or neglect;[60]

---

48 Alta. Reg. 258/85, s. 1(b).
49 *Ibid.*, s. 5.
50 *Ibid.*, s. 8.
51 *Ibid.*, s. 11.
52 *Ibid.*, s. 12.
53 *Ibid.*, s. 14.
54 *Ibid.*, s. 15.
55 *Ibid.*, s. 16.
56 *Ibid.*, ss. 19 and 20.
57 R.R.O. 1990, Reg. 832, s. 12.
58 *Ibid.*, s. 17.
59 *Ibid.*, s. 20.
60 *Nursing Homes Act*, R.S.O. 1990, c. N.7, s. 25.

- the formation of a residents' council, the activities of which may include such things as advising residents respecting their rights and obligations and the rights and obligations of the licensee, mediating disputes between the residents and the licensee, advising the minister with respect to concerns or recommendations.[61]

In the absence of compliance with these and other statutory requirements, nursing home operators risk a loss of licence or prosecution by the government-regulating authority.

Other Health Facilities

There are many other types of health facilities regulated under provincial and territorial legislation. Some of these — such as psychiatric institutions in various provinces — are owned and operated by government. Others — clinics for elective cosmetic surgery, fertility clinics — may be owned and operated by private corporations, yet in most, if not all, cases, they are recipients of some degree of public funding and are subject to provincial regulation.

In British Columbia, "community care facilities" are governed by the *Community Care Facility Act.*[62] This statute regulates any health facility in the province that is not a public hospital or mental health facility. In effect, nursing homes, chronic-care facilities and other similar health facilities are governed by this legislation. Under the *Hospital (Auxiliary) Act*[63] the province may establish and maintain hospitals for patients who do not need the level of treatment provided in acute-care hospitals (*i.e.*, public hospitals).

In Alberta, the *Health Facilities Review Committee Act*[64] establishes a committee that has jurisdiction over public hospitals, nursing homes, senior citizens' homes and other government-operated health facilities. The committee has the power to investigate complaints and to inspect or visit health facilities. Hospitals for the treatment of cancer are specifically regulated under that province's *Cancer Programs Act.*[65]

In Saskatchewan, the *Hospital Standards Act* governs public hospitals for the treatment of acute-care patients, as well as nursing homes and other institutions established for the purpose of "diagnostic and treatment services

---

61 *An Act to amend certain Acts concerning Long-Term Care,* S.O. 1993, c. 2, s. 40.

62 R.S.B.C. 1979, c. 57.

63 R.S.B.C. 1979, c. 177, s. 1.

64 R.S.A. 1980, c. H-4.

65 R.S.A. 1980, c. C-1.

or either of them".[66] The *Housing and Special-care Homes Act*[67] defines a "special-care home" as a nursing home or other facility that provides supervisory, personal or nursing care. It specifically excludes facilities governed by the *Mental Health Act.*[68]

In Manitoba, the *District Health and Social Services Act*[69] applies to all facilities in which health services are provided, including public hospitals, personal-care homes, clinics and laboratories. In this province, health-care facilities are managed by districts established under the *Health Services Act.*[70] There is special legislation for "personal-care homes" in the form of the *Elderly and Infirm Persons' Housing Act*[71] and the Manitoba Care Facilities Regulation promulgated under the *Public Health Act.*[72] The *Private Hospitals Act*[73] in Manitoba covers private facilities such as maternity hospitals, medical or surgical hospitals and hospitals licensed for the care of alcoholic patients. Regulations passed pursuant to this statute govern such things as the criteria for admission to a private hospital, record-keeping requirements, reporting requirements, and the type of facility, equipment and supplies that must be maintained by the operator, despite the facility being private.

In Ontario, the government has passed legislation which has broad application to health facilities that are unregulated by other legislation. The *Independent Health Facilities Act*[74] requires the operator to be licensed by the provincial government and its regulations contain minimum standards for professional performance, record-keeping and confidentiality. No more private hospitals have been instituted in Ontario since 1973, but the few which continue to operate are governed by the *Private Hospitals Act.*[75]

In Quebec, the *Health Services and Social Services Act*[76] is compendium-style legislation which governs both public and private health facilities. It applies to hospital centres, social service centres, local community service centres and "reception centres".[77] The statute provides for the establishment of health and social service councils in various regions and for

---

66 R.S.S. 1978, c. H-10, s. 2.

67 R.S.S. 1978, c. H-13.

68 S.S. 1983, c. 11, s. 34(3).

69 R.S.M. 1987, c. H26.

70 R.S.M. 1987, c. H30.

71 R.S.M. 1987, c. E20.

72 R.S.M. 1987, c. P210.

73 R.S.M. 1987, c. P130.

74 R.S.O. 1990, c. I.3.

75 R.S.O. 1990, c. P.24.

76 R.S.Q. 1977, c. S-4.2.

77 "Reception centres" include facilities where in-patient, out-patient or home-care services are provided for persons who require supervised treatment, but do not include day-care centres, religious facilities or foster families.

administration of the councils. "Establishments" are required to prepare organizational plans describing the administrative structure of the establishment, including clinical departments and services and the number of health professionals required to carry out the plan. There are provisions dealing with the organization and appointment of boards of directors, the issuance of a "permit" by the minister for the operation of an establishment, as well as for the renewal, modification, suspension or cancellation of a permit. Regulations under the statute[78] classify establishments according to the type of care provided and regulate the organization of different departments within the facility.

In New Brunswick, recent legislation under the *Hospital Act*[79] establishes seven regional hospital corporations, each of which is responsible for all the hospital facilities within its boundaries. The statute contains provisions relating to the acquisition and use of property, and to the limitation period for actions against hospitals and employees or members of hospital boards. The *Nursing Homes Act*[80] governs the licensing and operation of nursing homes and similar chronic-care facilities. The minister may modify, revoke or refuse to renew a licence if the operator fails to meet certain standards. While the minister may review his decision, and in doing so change it, there is no appeal mechanism available.

Public hospitals in Newfoundland are governed by the *Hospitals Act.*[81] A hospital board may be constituted by the Lieutenant-Governor in Council. One board may manage more than one hospital. The Lieutenant-Governor in Council may also constitute Regional Hospital Boards to supervise and co-ordinate the work of a number of scheduled hospitals. The *Homes for Special Care Act*[82] and the *Private Homes for Special Care Allowances Act*[83] work in conjunction with several other pieces of provincial legislation to fund and regulate nursing homes and other chronic-care facilities.

In Nova Scotia, hospitals are regulated by the *Hospitals Act*[84] and regulations passed thereunder.[85] The regulations contain requirements relating to the preservation of tissues, the development and implementation of a safe work environment, the use of drugs and the contents and maintenance of medical records. The *Homes for Special Care Act*[86] pertains to nursing homes and other residential-care facilities. As in other provinces,

---

78 Regulation S-5, r. 3.01, O.C. 1320-84, 6 June 1984, G.O.Q. 1984. 2347, s. 2.
79 S.N.B. 1992, c. H-6.1.
80 S.N.B. 1982, c. N-11.
81 R.S.N. 1990, c. H-9.
82 R.S.N. 1990, c. H-5.
83 R.S.N. 1990, c. P-23.
84 R.S.N.S. 1989, c. 208.
85 N.S. Reg. 16/79.
86 R.S.N.S. 1989, c. 203.

licences are issued by the government and are subject to renewal, modification or cancellation.

In Prince Edward Island, a Hospital and Health Services Commission bears responsibility for the approval and monitoring of hospitals under the *Hospitals Act.*[87] Non-acute-care facilities are governed by the *Community Care Facilities and Nursing Homes Act.*[88] This Act establishes a Community Care Facilities and Nursing Homes Board that is required to ensure that the accommodation, care and nursing services are safe, of good quality and appropriate to the needs of the residents.

In the Northwest Territories, "health facilities", which include numerous types of treatment centres, but not tuberculosis hospitals and homes for the aged, are operated by Boards of Management. These boards have wide powers of management, control and operation under the *Territorial Hospital Insurance Services Act.*[89] If the government concludes that a facility is not being operated properly, however, a Public Administrator may be appointed. The Yukon's *Hospital Insurance Services Act*[90] contains similar broad provisions.

Relevant Legislation

Alberta

Co-ordinated Home Care Program Regulation, Alta. Reg. 239/85
Health Facilities Review Committee Act, R.S.A. 1980, c. H-4
Hospital District Regulations, Alta. Reg. 243/90
Hospitalization Benefits Regulation, Alta. Reg. 244/90
Hospitals Act, R.S.A. 1980, c. H-11
Nursing Homes Act, S.A. 1985, c. N-14.1
Nursing Homes Operation Regulation, Alta. Reg. 258/85
Nursing Homes Regulation, Alta. Reg. 232/85
Operation of Approved Hospitals Regulations, Alta. Reg. 247/90
Public Health Act, S.A. 1984, c. P-27.1

---

87 R.S.P.E.I. 1988, c. H-10.
88 R.S.P.E.I. 1988, c. C-13.
89 R.S.N.W.T. 1988, c. T-3.
90 R.S.Y. 1986, c. 85.

BRITISH COLUMBIA

Adult Care Regulations, B.C. Reg. 536/80
Community Care Facility Act, R.S.B.C. 1979, c. 57
Hospital Act, R.S.B.C. 1979, c. 176
Hospital Act Regulations, B.C. Reg. 289/73
Hospital District Act, R.S.B.C. 1979, c. 178

MANITOBA

Application for Grants Regulation, Man. Reg. 311/88R
Elderly and Infirm Persons' Housing Act, R.S.M. 1987, c. E20
Health Services Act, R.S.M. 1987, c. H30
Hospital Standards Regulation, Man. Reg. 453/88R
Hospitals Act, R.S.M. 1987, c. H120
Medical Nursing Unit Districts, Hospital Districts and Hospital Areas Regulation, Man. Reg. 455/88R
Private Hospitals Act, R.S.M. 1987, c. P130
Private Hospitals Regulation, Man. Reg. 58/93

NEW BRUNSWICK

Hospital Act, S.N.B. 1992, c. H-6.1
General Regulation, N.B. Reg. 92-84
Hospital Services Act, R.S.N.B. 1973, c. H-9
General Regulation, N.B. Reg. 84-167
Nursing Homes Act, S.N.B. 1982, c. N-11
General Regulation, N.B. Reg. 85-187

NEWFOUNDLAND

Homes for Special Care Act, R.S.N. 1990, c. H-S
Hospitals Act, R.S.N. 1990, c. H-9

NORTHWEST TERRITORIES

Medical Care Act, R.S.N.W.T. 1988, c. M-8
Territorial Hospital Insurance Services Act, R.S.N.W.T. 1988, c. T-3
Territorial Hospital Insurance Services Regulations, N.W.T. Regs. 274 and 275

Nova Scotia

Homes for Special Care Act, R.S.N.S. 1989, c. 203
General Regulations, N.S. Reg. 127/77
Hospitals Act, R.S.N.S. 1989, c. 208
General Regulations, N.S. Reg. 16/79

Ontario

Homes for the Aged and Rest Homes Act, R.S.O. 1990, c. H.13
General, R.R.O. 1990, Reg. 637
Homes for Retarded Persons Act, R.S.O. 1990, c. H.11
General, R.R.O. 1990, Reg. 635
Homes for Special Care Act, R.S.O. 1990, c. H.12
General, R.R.O. 1990, Reg. 636
Public Hospital Management Regulations, R.R.O. 1990, Reg. 965
Nursing Homes Act, R.S.O. 1990, c. N.7
General, R.R.O. 1990, Reg. 832
Private Hospitals Act, R.S.O. 1990, c. P.24
General, R.R.O. 1990, Reg. 937
Public Hospitals Act, R.S.O. 1990, c. P.40

Prince Edward Island

Hospital Management Regulations, E.C. 574/76
Hospitals Act, R.S.P.E.I. 1978, c. H-10

Quebec

Health Services and Social Services Act, R.S.Q. 1977, c. S-4.2
Hospital Centres (Appointment and Remuneration of Directors of Professional Services and Heads of Community Health Departments) Regulation, O.C. 2351-84
Organization and Management of Establishments Regulation, O.C. 1320-84

Saskatchewan

Hospital Standards Act, R.S.S. 1978, c. H-10
Hospital Standards Regulations, 1980, Sask. Reg. 331/79
Housing and Special-care Homes Act, R.S.S. 1978, c. H-13

Housing and Special-care Homes Regulations, Sask. Reg. 34/66
Union Hospital Act, R.S.S. 1978, c. U-2

Yukon

Health Act, S.Y. 1989-90, c. 36
Hospital Act, S.Y. 1989-90, c. 13
Hospital Insurance Services Act, R.S.Y. 1986, c. 85
Hospital Standards Regulations, Y.T. Reg. 130

CHAPTER 2

Canadian Health-Care Insurance

INTRODUCTION

Prior to the advent of health-care insurance, most patients in Canada were responsible for paying the cost of their own health care. Broadly speaking, this involved the cost of medical services received from health professionals, the use of hospitals and other health-care facilities and medication. To many patients, the cost of such medical treatment was not inconsiderable; patients were burdened with substantial and often unexpected expenses for medical treatment at times when they were least able to afford it. For lower-income groups, even elementary health care was beyond their means; individuals would be forced to forgo very basic treatment simply as a result of financial constraint. In some instances, physicians, institutions and other health-care professionals would be put in the position of having to provide treatment to individuals without fair remuneration for their services.

An insurance mechanism established by law for the payment of services is especially appropriate in the field of health care. Collectively, it is possible for society to pay for services individuals cannot afford. This is the theoretical basis for all insurance. Society is able to pool its resources in such a way that individuals who are ill will not be met suddenly with unexpected and substantial costs, but rather, will participate in a system whereby each individual contributes to a fund which is available to him or her in time of need. As a contributor, each patient is entitled to draw from the fund for the payment of health services as required. Certain individuals may draw from the fund on a frequent basis, while others may never place any significant reliance upon it. The essential benefit is the assurance to each individual that should health-care services be required, the collective resources of other members of society will be available to underwrite the costs of that individual's care.

The introduction of government assistance and regulation in the funding of health-care in Canada began in 1948 when the federal government introduced a programme of National Health Grants which provided funding for a wide variety of provincial health services including health planning, public health measures, hospital construction and professional medical training.[1] These were areas in which, generally speaking, the provincial governments exercised constitutional authority for health care.[2] However, there was still no comprehensive, government-sponsored plan to assist individual patients in paying for the cost of health-care services.

With the introduction of these grants, several provinces began to establish government-sponsored hospital and medical insurance plans. Over time, the federal and provincial governments combined to form a health insurance scheme in Canada which is available to all residents in all provinces.

Canada Health Act

Government health insurance in Canada is regulated by the federal *Canada Health Act*[3] (hereafter *CHA*) in conjunction with individual legislation of the various provinces. The Preamble to the *CHA* specifically recognizes the following conditions and objects for the legislation:

- that Canadians, through their system of insured health services, have made outstanding progress in treating sickness and alleviating the consequences of disease and disability among all income groups;
- that Canadians can achieve further improvements in their well-being through combining individual lifestyles that emphasize fitness, prevention of disease and health promotion with collective action against the social, environmental and occupational causes of disease, and that they desire a system of health services that will promote physical and mental health and protection against disease;
- that future improvements in health will require the cooperative partnership of governments, health professionals, voluntary organizations and individual Canadians;
- that continued access to quality health care without financial or other barriers will be critical to maintaining and improving the health and well-being of Canadians. . . .

The *CHA* establishes a method of providing federal funding assistance to the provinces for the payment of insured services in the health-care system. Under the federal legislation, the term "insured health services" is defined as:

---

1 Tyrus G. Fain, Ed., "National Health Insurance" in *Public Documents Series* (New York: R.R. Bowker Co., 1977), p. 188.

2 *Constitution Act, 1867* (U.K.), 30 and 31 Vict., c. 3, s. 91(7).

3 R.S.C. 1985, c. C-6.

> hospital services, physician services and surgical-dental services provided to insured persons, but does not include any health services that a person is entitled to and eligible for under any other Act of Parliament or under any Act of the legislature of a province that relates to workers' or workmen's compensation.[4]

The legislation commits the federal government to sharing the cost of a variety of insured health services that the federal government does not otherwise fund and that are not otherwise funded by the province. For example, the federal government, as part of its constitutional responsibility, provides health-care services to war veterans. Therefore, there is no need for a qualified war veteran to resort to provincial government-sponsored health-care insurance because the war veteran is already entitled to medical and hospital treatment funded directly by the federal government. Another exception where funding will not be provided through the *CHA* is that of health-care services provided to victims of industrial accidents under provincial workers' compensation legislation.[5]

In order to qualify for the federal contribution for insured services under the *CHA*, the provincial insurance scheme must operate according to the principles listed below.

1. Public Administration

It is a requirement that all provincial health-care insurance plans be administered and operated on a non-profit basis by a public authority appointed or designated by the government of the province.[6] The public authority's accounts and financial transactions are subject to audit in a manner similar to any branch of the provincial government.

2. Comprehensiveness

The health-care plan of the province must insure all insured health services provided by hospitals, medical practitioners, and, where applicable, similar or additional services rendered by other health-care practitioners.[7] This is an area that, in recent years, has been subject to controversy. The cost of health care in Canada correlates directly to the comprehensiveness of service. Some provinces have "de-listed" treatments considered non-essential;

---

4 *CHA*, s. 2.

5 See Chapter 9, Employment and Labour Relations Law, for a discussion of the law in this area.

6 *CHA*, s. 8.

7 *Ibid.*, s. 9.

these treatments are not covered by the provincial health insurance plan. Variation of coverage of treatment from province to province has an impact on universality, another principle of Canada's national health insurance. On the other hand, there are those who argue that there must be some limits on the types of services offered. They cite the experience of other jurisdictions in which controversial, experimental, highly expensive, or trivial treatments are not funded.[8] A "hospital" is defined in the *CHA* to include "any facility . . . that provides hospital care, including acute, rehabilitative or chronic care".[9] It, however, does not include hospitals or institutions "primarily for the mentally disordered" or facilities that provide nursing-home care, intermediate care, adult residential care or comparable services for children.

The term "hospital services" is defined in the legislation and designates a list of services to be provided to in-patients or out-patients of a hospital "if the services are medically necessary for the purpose of maintaining health, preventing disease or diagnosing or treating an injury, illness or disability". The listed services include accommodation and meals, nursing services, diagnostic procedures, medication, and the use of operating facilities and equipment, radiotherapy and physiotherapy facilities.[10]

3. Universality

The provincial health insurance plan must entitle all insured persons in the province to the insured health services provided under the plan on uniform terms and conditions.[11] In some instances, provinces have attempted to reduce the cost of health care by redefining the meaning of "insured persons" to exclude recent immigrants to Canada, Canadian "snowbirds" vacationing south of the border and others who are perceived to have a more transient link to the province.

---

8 See "Canadian Health Ministers are Preparing to Impose User Fees", *Toronto Star*, July 13, 1995, A17; this article cites the "Oregon Experience" in which, as a result of state-wide hearings, 565 procedures were listed for which the state government would pay. These procedures included transplants (except for patients with liver cancer), hip replacements and neo-natal care. However, treatment for the common cold, viral hepatitis or a viral sore throat are not covered on the ground that these conditions improve on their own and do not require proactive medical treatment.

9 *CHA*, s. 2.

10 *Ibid.*, s. 2.

11 *Ibid.*, s. 10.

4. Portability

Provincial health insurance plans must be designed so that residents who move from province to province, or who are absent temporarily from their province, remain eligible for insured health services.[12] Independent actions by some provinces have impaired the operation of the portability principle in Canada. For example, the fee schedule for physicians in Quebec is substantially lower than the fee schedule for physicians in Ontario. Although Quebec has signed an agreement guaranteeing the portability of insured services provided by doctors, it has refused to pay the higher rates of Ontario and the other provinces, except in limited circumstances.[13]

5. Accessibility

The provincial plan must provide insured health services on a basis that "does not impede or preclude, either directly or indirectly whether by charges made to insured persons or otherwise, reasonable access to those services by insured persons".[14] The collection by some provinces of premiums or payroll taxes to fund the health insurance system has been criticized as regressive in nature and for placing a heavy burden on large numbers of people with low or modest incomes.[15] Even though premium assistance may be available for some individuals, this method of collection may offend the accessibility principle.

Each province has enacted legislation providing funding for medical and institutional health-care services in conjunction with the federal government. The federal and provincial legislation constitutes a unique national medicare system which is extremely progressive in comparison with the international scene. In California, where a large percentage of residents have no health-care insurance of any kind, extensive consultation with Canadian health officials has produced draft legislation that closely mirrors the Canadian medicare system.[16]

---

12 *Ibid.*, s. 11.

13 See *Health, healthcare and medicare*, a report by the National Council of Welfare (Ottawa: Ministry of Supply and Services Canada, 1990).

14 *CHA*, s. 12(a).

15 *Health, healthcare and medicare, supra* note 13, pp. 55-62.

16 "Health care system for poor collapsing, Californians say", *The Globe and Mail*, January 4, 1988, A12.

ELIGIBILITY

Eligibility is based upon residency. Individuals who have been resident in a province for a certain duration are entitled to membership in the provincial plan. Tourists, transients, students from outside the province and individuals visiting residents of the province, who are not themselves resident in the province, do not qualify. Residents who go abroad, but who are only temporarily absent from their province, continue to be eligible for coverage for health-care treatment received abroad.

FEDERAL FUNDING

In Canada, government-sponsored health insurance plans are administered by the individual provinces and territories. The federal government plays its most significant role in the plan through its financial contribution.

Traditionally, the Government of Canada has contributed approximately 50 per cent of the net operating costs of the provincial plans both in respect of hospital and medical services. For the purposes of calculating the federal contribution, a formula is employed which favours poorer provinces. The effect of the formula is that less thrifty provinces or territories will receive a lower contribution from the federal government than will more efficient provinces or territories. In recent years, the federal government's contribution has dropped. It has been suggested that if the federal government's contribution continues to drop at the same rate as in recent years, there will be no transfer payments to some provinces by the year 2,000.[17]

In funding the cost of hospital and other designated health-care facility services the federal contribution is restricted to operating costs. In calculating the contribution, any amounts spent on land or buildings or for the depreciation of land and buildings are excluded. As a result, health-care facilities in the various provinces, and by extension, the provincial governments, have exclusive responsibility for the financing of construction and renovation of facilities. The federal contribution does, however, take into account expenses incurred by health-care facilities as a result of wear and tear on furniture and equipment.

The important responsibility of purchasing updated equipment and treatment facilities in hospitals rests exclusively with individual provinces. Not surprisingly, this is a weighty financial obligation having the potential to leave many hospitals and health facilities with insufficient financial

---

[17] *Funding health and higher education: danger looming,* a report by the National Council of Welfare (Ottawa: Ministry of Supply and Services, 1991).

resources for day-to-day operation, and in some cases, with insufficient resources to ensure that buildings, facilities and equipment remain up-to-date and available for the use of patients seeking treatment.[18]

Provincial Funding

In some provinces, residents become members of the provincial health insurance plan by paying (or having paid on their behalf) a "premium" or a "tax" that entitles the resident to the provision of insured health services. In other provinces, the province's share of the cost of the plan is funded exclusively from the general revenues of the province and there is no requirement that residents pay into the plan specific sums or "premiums" targeted to the funding of the plan itself.

In provinces where the plan is structured on the basis of "premiums", subsidies are available to individuals who can demonstrate reduced income or financial difficulties. Generally, premium assistance is available to individuals who have been resident in the province for a certain length of time and who can show taxable income that does not exceed certain minimum limits. In some instances, residents, such as senior citizens, are eligible for complete premium exemption regardless of their level of income.

It should be noted that even in a province where residents are required to pay a premium for the entitlement of insured health services, premium assistance and premium exemption regulations, along with the sometimes extraordinary cost of modern health care, can result in a provincial government having to make substantial payments out of its general revenues to subsidize the provision of insured health services, because the premiums received by the provincial authority do not completely cover costs.

For example, in Ontario, in the fiscal year ending March 31, 1985, the Ontario Health Insurance Plan (OHIP) had revenues of $1.6 billion. Its expenditures, however, totalled $2.8 billion. Of approximately 8.9 million participants in OHIP, over 2.5 million individuals were receiving partial or full assistance from the provincial government.[19] In other words, although the federal legislation speaks of *insured* health services,[20] and although premiums form the conceptual base for the accumulation of funding in most provinces, in practice the Canadian medicare system more closely resembles a government-funded social programme than it does an insurance scheme.[21]

---

18 See *Federal-Provincial Fiscal Arrangements Act*, R.S.C. 1985, c. F-8, as amended.

19 Ontario Ministry of Health, *Annual Report 1984-85*, pp. 45-46.

20 *CHA*, s. 12(1)(b).

21 In 1989, the Ontario government modified its health insurance plan so that

Insured Services

The federal legislation requires each province to set out a tariff or system of authorized payments to individuals and institutions providing health-care services. To be qualified for payment under the provincial plan, a particular service is specifically included as an insured health service under the provincial legislation.

Schedules that identify insured health services are created by the province in consultation with such bodies as the Canadian Medical Association, the Canadian Hospital Association, the Canadian Nurses' Association and other health-care organizations. From time to time, schedules of insured health services are updated and revised.

In Ontario, for example, the provincial health insurance scheme provides coverage for services performed by duly licensed doctors in the province including:

- physician's services in the home, office, hospital or institution;
- services of specialists certified by the Royal College of Physicians and Surgeons of Canada;
- diagnosis and treatment of illness and injury;
- treatment of fractures and dislocations;
- surgery;
- administration of anaesthetics;
- x-rays for diagnostic and treatment purposes;
- obstetrical care, including pre-natal and post-natal care; and
- laboratory services and clinical pathology when ordered by and performed under the direction of a physician.[22]

In addition, the Ontario plan provides coverage for qualified patients who are treated at an approved health-care facility by a licensed physician. The plan covers the cost of hospital services when medically necessary and the diagnosis and treatment of illness or injury, on an in-patient or out-patient basis, for such areas as:

---

ordinary residents, who apply, are no longer required to pay premiums: *Health Insurance Act*, R.S.O. 1980, c. 197, s. 11 [am. 1989, c. 76, s. 41(2)] [now R.S.O. 1990, c. H.6, s. 11(3)].

22 Government of Ontario, "Select Committee on Company Law," *Fifth Report on Accident and Sickness Insurance* (Legislative Assembly of Ontario, 1981), p. 16. © Queen's printer for Ontario, 1981. Reproduced with permission.

Some physician's services are not insured, such as telephone advice at the patient's request, renewal of a prescription by telephone, completion of various forms, documentation and associated medical assessments, some patient-related interviews and discussions with other professionals at the patient's request. A physician may choose to offer patients a block payment plan whereby the patient

- standard ward accommodation;
- necessary nursing services, when provided by the hospital;
- laboratory and x-ray diagnostic procedures;
- use of operating and delivery rooms, anaesthetics and surgical supplies;
- use of radiotherapy facilities;
- services rendered by any person paid by the hospital.[23]

A similar array of physician and health-care services are insured in other provinces. Specific reference should be made to the legislation of each province.

In addition to the cost of physician health-care services, provincial health insurance plans may provide limited coverage for such areas as:

- ambulance services;
- chiropractic and physiotherapy treatment;
- certain types of cosmetic surgery;
- certain types of dental and orthodontic treatment;
- certain types of optometric services.

As some services are not covered by the provincial plans, the patient is personally responsible for those costs. These services may include private or semi-private accommodation, charges for dental care not received in a hospital or other approved health-care facility, private-duty nursing fees, cosmetic surgery and acupuncture.

Extra-Billing and User Fees

The contribution of the federal government to the provision of medical services has been complicated by the fact that for a lengthy period following the introduction of a programme of national health insurance, physicians

---

is charged a flat yearly fee for all uninsured services. The payment is based on the average number of services used in the previous year. In s. 1(1) of O. Reg 857/93 under the *Medicine Act, 1991*, S.O. 1991, c. 30, the Ontario government changed the definition of professional misconduct to include the receipt of block payments. This regulation was challenged in *Szmuilowicz v. Ontario (Minister of Health)* (1995), 24 O.R. (3d) 204 (Div. Ct.), where it was ruled that block payments are permitted as long as physicians offer this payment option in accordance with the guide-lines established by the College of Physicians and Surgeons.

[23] *Ibid.*, p. 17.

and hospitals were permitted to "opt out" of the plan. Until fairly recently, in most jurisdictions there was no legal prohibition against physicians and hospitals charging patients a fee exceeding the fee schedules set by the individual provinces in conjunction with the federal government.

In recent years, controversy has arisen between the federal government and the various provinces over whether or not certain "extra billing" practices engaged in by physicians have resulted in a breach of the "accessibility" requirement of the *CHA*.

Before the advent of government health insurance, physicians generally were paid on a fee-for-service basis. In other words, physicians were paid by their patients for their services on the basis of a fee set by the physician. There is no strong tradition in Canada of physicians being paid by salary or through some other mechanism that pooled their services. As private insurance schemes were introduced in the late 1940s and in the 1950s, private insurers continued to pay physicians a fee for specific services provided to insured patients. Although there may have been a limit on the amount of fees the health-care market would bear in relation to a particular service, physicians continued to operate autonomously even though their fees were often paid through the intermediary of an insurer rather than by the patient. In constructing a national health insurance programme, the fee-for-service method of payment was retained. It appears to have been regarded as a beneficial arrangement for patients, physicians and governments.[24]

As noted, the *CHA* requires individual provinces to establish a tariff or system of payment for health-care services.[25] Aside from negotiations with professional bodies about the amounts that will form the tariff, the tariff undergoes constant revision to ensure that services that are medically necessary form a part of the tariff and those that are not medically necessary

---

[24] See Fain, *supra* note 1, pp. 191-201. In an effort to cut budgets, government officials have questioned whether the fee for service is the most effective method of payment. Recently, a new pilot project was announced in Ontario whereby patients will be asked to sign a contract with a group of physicians from whom they agree to receive all their non-emergency care. In return, that group of physicians must offer 24-hour care and telephone consultations. The group will receive a budget in relation to the number of patients signed up in their roster, adjusted for age and sex. The physicians will still be paid on a fee-for-service basis up to their maximum budget. The government may charge patients who receive discretionary services from physicians other than those with whom they have signed a contract. See, K. Toughill, "Patients May Pay Fees Under Reform Plan," *The Toronto Star* July, 19 1996, p. A9 and J. Coutts, "Ontario Minister Wants to Limit 'Doctor Hopping'" *The [Toronto] Globe and Mail,* July 19, 1996, p. A4.

[25] *CHA*, s. 12(1)(b).

do not. There is an incentive for individual provinces, beyond their own financial commitment, to ensure that the tariff is reasonable, as any federal contribution is reduced, by formula, to reflect the cost of insured services in a particular province in relation to all of the other provinces. As a result, provinces are penalized if the cost of insured services is more expensive on a *per capita* basis.

Under the originating federal legislation, it was possible for physicians and health-care facilities to charge patients fees that exceeded the provincial tariff. There was some disincentive to physicians who might choose to do this as, in doing so, they would be required to "opt out" of the health insurance system. While "opted-out" physicians were not prevented from receiving payment indirectly under the provincial plan, physicians would be required to seek payment directly from the patient, who, in turn, could seek to recover from the provincial government an amount in respect of the physician's fee not exceeding the amount set out in the tariff. From an administrative point of view, this was a significant disincentive, and as of 1975, in provinces where "opting out" was permitted, no more than 9 per cent of physicians had chosen to do so, with most provinces having an even lower percentage of opted-out physicians.[26]

In provinces where the practice of opting out and extra-billing remained permissible under the provincial legislation, controversy arose between the federal government and the provinces. From the federal point of view, the practice of extra-billing offended the principles of universality and accessibility and contravened the federal requirement that the provincial plan not

> impede or preclude, either directly or indirectly whether by charges made to insured persons or otherwise, reasonable access (to insured) services by insured persons;[27]

The introduction of revisions to the *CHA*, which were proclaimed April 17, 1984, meant that federal participation in any provincial health insurance plan would be reduced where it was permissible for physicians, or hospitals, to bill patients for fees or charges beyond the amounts authorized under the provincial health insurance plan. The *CHA* now stipulates that in order to "qualify" for a full cash contribution, no payments may be permitted by the province for "extra-billing" by physicians or for "user charges" by health facilities. Extra-billing is defined as

> billing for an insured health service rendered to an insured person by a medical practitioner or a dentist in an amount in addition to any amount

[26] See Fain, *supra* note 1, p. 205.

[27] *CHA*, s. 12(1)(a).

> paid or to be paid for that service by the health care insurance plan of a province;[28]

User charges are defined as

> any charge for an insured health service that is authorized or permitted by a provincial health care insurance plan that is not payable, directly or indirectly, by a provincial health care insurance plan, but does not include any charge imposed by extra-billing.[29]

In effect, in order for a province to qualify for the full federal contribution, physicians and health facilities within that province cannot charge for insured services outside of the government-sponsored health insurance scheme, except for certain limited exceptions contained in the legislation. Where extra-billing by doctors or user charges by health facilities continue, the federal government may deduct from the federal contribution an amount equal to the total amount charged by physicians or health facilities outside the provincial health insurance plan.

When the revisions to the *CHA* were first introduced, only in Quebec and British Columbia were doctors barred from receiving any payment from the provincial health insurance plan, either directly or indirectly, if they chose to opt out. In Nova Scotia, Alberta, Prince Edward Island, New Brunswick and Saskatchewan, physicians were permitted to extra-bill without the necessity of opting out of the provincial plan. In Manitoba, Newfoundland and Ontario, the provincial legislation, with minor variations, permitted physicians to opt out and then to recover a portion of their fee indirectly from the provincial plan. One of the provinces most significantly affected by the new federal position was the Province of Ontario. By 1981, for example, approximately 62 per cent of its anaesthetists had opted out, or, in other words, were charging patients a fee that exceeded the provincial tariff.[30]

In 1981, a Select Committee of the Ontario legislature had rejected specifically the rationale of extra-billing because of the committee's "concern" that fees charged outside of the provincial system would "deny reasonable access to insured services by insured persons".[31] Furthermore, the committee specifically rejected user fees as a means to control the cost of health-care services and expressed agreement with a recommendation made by an earlier committee appointed to study health-care financing:

---

28 *Ibid.*, s. 2.

29 *Ibid.*, s. 2.

30 From *Preserving Universal Medicare: A Government of Canada Position Paper*, Health Canada, 1983, p. 5. Excerpts reproduced with permission of the Minister of Supply & Services Canada, 1996.

31 *Fifth Report*, *supra* note 22, p. 247.

> The Committee recommends that user fees not be introduced into the health-care system of the Province and that the arguments for the use of such fees as a means of controlling utilization of services, of cost containment and of providing "reasonable compensation" to medical practitioners be rejected.[32]

In moving to reduce its contribution in provinces where the practice of extra-billing continued, the federal government likewise rejected the position advanced by physicians' groups that a ban on extra-billing would severely reduce the professional independence of physicians:

> Canada's system of Medicare has left physicians free to practise medicine on a fee for service basis unless they choose some form of salaried arrangement. They can practise anywhere they choose in any province in which they are licensed. At the same time, patients can choose any doctor they wish. Freedom of choice is a cornerstone of our Medicare system. The Government of Canada has no intention of changing any of this.
>
> Doctors are not obliged to participate in Medicare if they want to operate an entirely private practice. They can "opt out" and charge the patient directly, with or without extra-billing being involved. But the fact remains that the vast majority, nearly ninety per cent of Canada's more than 40,000 doctors are part of Medicare and accept provincial plan payments as payment in full.[33]

By 1985, the federal contribution to the provinces had been reduced by millions of dollars to reflect extra-billing. As a result, all provinces passed legislation prohibiting extra-billing and user fees so as to avoid deductions from the federal contribution to Medicare. In Ontario, for example, the *Health Care Accessibility Act*,[34] provides that physicians, dentists and optometrists who do not bill the provincial health insurance plan directly (*i.e.*, are "opted out") may not charge more than the amounts set out in the provincial health insurance tariff. A physician who does so may be charged with an offence under the *Health Care Accessibility Act*, and, if convicted, can be liable to a fine of $2,000 for the first offence and $2,000 for any subsequent offence.

Abuse of the Health Insurance System

As government is the major, if not only, source for the payment of physicians' fees for medical services, governments are able to develop very comprehensive and detailed statistics on the distribution of payments, the

---

32 *Ibid.*, p. 251.

33 *Preserving Universal Medicare*, *supra* note 30, p. 12.

34 R.S.O. 1990, c. H.3, s. 8.

number of claims being paid, the average cost per claim, the exact amount of the physician's income from the plan and a variety of other aspects of health care.[35] Consequently, provincial governments have at their disposal a very sophisticated basis upon which to assess the quantity and quality of medical services and are thereby able to detect abuses by both health practitioners and patients of the health insurance system. Abuses by health practitioners may be the subject-matter of an offence under provincial health insurance legislation and will also be considered ethical contraventions by the practitioner's own self-regulating professional body. Such contraventions could lead to suspension or termination of professional standing.

In *Re College of Physicians & Surgeons (B.C.) and Ahmad*,[36] the British Columbia College of Physicians and Surgeons found a physician to have engaged in unprofessional conduct in over-servicing patients for his own financial benefit. Similarly, in *Re Casullo and College of Physicians & Surgeons (Ont.)*,[37] proceedings were taken against a physician who had engaged in unprofessional conduct by ordering tests for patients in a laboratory in which he had a financial interest and where the cost of such tests was unreasonable and excessive. In *Idicula et al. v. College of Physicians & Surgeons (Alta.)*,[38] several physicians were suspended and fined by the college for having overbilled the Alberta Health Care Insurance Plan for services for which there was no entitlement to compensation. On appeal, however, the Alberta Court of Appeal withdrew the suspension and reduced the fine, as it was shown that the overbillings had resulted from a clerical error by an individual in the doctors' office. Although the physicians were reprimanded for having given inadequate instruction and supervision to the billing clerk, it was recognized that the extra-billing did not result from an intentional act by the physicians to deceive the provincial authorities.

Similar to the abuse of the health insurance system by health professionals is the potential for abuse of the system by patients. The continuation of extra-billing or user charges within a government-sponsored health insurance scheme has been advanced on the basis that these charges can limit the overall cost of the scheme by shifting a portion of health costs from government to individual recipients, discouraging "frivolous" or "unnecessary" use of health services by patients, impressing in recipients of health services a greater appreciation of the total costs involved, improving the quality of care provided to patients, and, during difficult financial times, assisting in the remuneration of health-care professionals.[39]

---

[35] See, *e.g.*, Ministry of Health of Ontario, *OHIP Practitioner Care Statistics*, 1984-1985 (Pre-Audit).

[36] [1973] 6 W.W.R. 412, 43 D.L.R. (3d) 381 (B.C.S.C.).

[37] (1973), 2 O.R. (2d) 261, 42 D.L.R. (3d) 43 (C.A.).

[38] (1987), 79 A.R. 181 (C.A.).

[39] Robin F. Badgley, *User Charges for Health Services: A Report of the Ontario Council of Health* (Toronto: The Council, 1979), p. 30.

The Future of National Health Insurance

Since the introduction of a national health insurance scheme in Canada, the cost of health-care services has increased dramatically. These rising costs have been employed as a further rationale for the retention of extra-billing and user charges.

> Some proponents of direct charges have claimed that [the] provinces can no longer afford to pay all of the costs of their current programs, and that user charges could be an added source of financing. We hear talk of "spiralling" health costs and the need to get government spending on health under control.[40]

In 1982, hospital expenditures in Canada increased by 17 per cent. From 1970 to 1981, there was an overall increase in expenditures of about 400 per cent, well in excess of the general inflation rate.[41] Nonetheless, in support of its opposition to extra-billing and user charges, the federal government asserted that while the cost of health-care services had increased dramatically over the past decade, health-care spending in Canada has been relatively constant as a component of national expenditures. Moreover, in comparison with other countries in the western world, in particular the United States, the increase in the cost of health-care services has been modest.[42]

It would appear that the most significant increase in the cost of health care in Canada does not arise from the cost of medical services supplied by physicians, but rather, from the cost of hospital services. During the seventies and eighties, hospital costs increased at an average rate of 15 per cent per annum and contributed more to the rise in health-care costs than any other health-care component.[43]

When extra-billing was banned in Ontario, the cost of physicians' services increased by $436 million in the next fiscal year. This increase represented an increase of 17 per cent over the previous fiscal year (more than three times the projected increase) and gave rise to the appointment of a joint committee of the Ontario government and the Ontario Medical Association to study the causes of spiralling health-care costs.[44]

---

40 *Ibid.*, p. 7.

41 *Preserving Universal Medicare, supra* note 30, p. 11.

42 *Ibid.*, p. 13.

43 L. Auer, *Canadian Hospital Costs and Productivity* (Ottawa: Economic Council of Canada, 1987), p. xi.

44 "Ontario Doctor Costs Jump by almost $500 Million", *The Globe and Mail*, February 4, 1988, A1.

The financial ability of governments to meet the costs imposed by the health-care insurance system has become an issue which threatens the system's viability.[45]

Other Forms of Health-Care Insurance

The advent of government-sponsored health insurance in Canada has not removed the need for other insurance schemes, both private and government-run, to supplement national health insurance. It should be understood that while the Canadian health insurance system provides a comprehensive basis for the provision of basic health-care services in the individual provinces, it does not finance all of the health-care needs of residents within the provinces.

For example, if provinces continue to permit extra-billing and user charges, despite the reduced federal contribution, residents (unless otherwise insured for such costs) will be responsible for paying these direct charges. Individuals who do not qualify for membership in the provincial health-care insurance plan, or who, for other reasons, choose not to enroll, will be responsible for the full cost of their own health-care services. Medications are not covered in most instances by provincial plans and there are a number of other areas for which patients will bear the financial responsibility unless private insurance is obtained. Private insurance is available to meet the cost of semi-private and private accommodation in hospital, nursing-home care, prescription drugs, dental care, health care outside of Canada, special duty nursing, etc.

---

[45] Another element threatening the system's viability is the possibility that the federal government will permit physicians to operate privately-funded clinics. The federal government has suggested that it may permit such clinics to operate if the province would ensure that all residents have reasonable access to medical care and that any private clinic would not receive government funding. The federal government would continually monitor the effect of such private clinics on the health-care insurance system and if it concluded that too many doctors were leaving the public system for higher incomes offered by private clinics, the government would take action to stop the flow of talent. Some experts have questioned whether these restrictions would succeed in preventing a two-tier system of health care. See M. Kennedy, "Ottawa May Allow Private Clinics Fees," *The Toronto Star*, September 24, 1995, p. A1.

There are other provincial statutes that supplement health-care expenses in certain situations. Workers' compensation legislation, in addition to providing income benefits to injured workers, provides comprehensive medical rehabilitation benefits to workers who are injured while on the job. Such coverage may provide health-care services, without charge, that are not covered under health insurance laws. In some provinces, medical and rehabilitation benefits are available to victims of motor-vehicle accidents through mandatory insurance legislation. Under federal legislation, health-care benefits, not otherwise available under provincial legislation, are made available to veterans who demonstrate a disability attributable to their military service.

There are also a great many health-care benefits provided through clinics, assistance programmes, hospitals for the chronically ill, senior citizens' homes, programmes for the disabled, visiting nurses, public health nurses, rehabilitation centres, etc. For the most part, these are services funded through the general revenues of the provinces or municipalities, which provide a variety of services, many relating to health care, and are available to qualified residents in the province.

Lastly, both federal and provincial governments allow taxpayers to deduct from taxable income certain medical expenses incurred in relation to themselves or disabled dependants. Also those provinces that have a provincial sales tax traditionally grant exemptions in respect of products that relate to health-care needs.

Relevant Legislation

Alberta

Alberta Health Care Insurance Act, R.S.A. 1980, c. A-24
Alberta Health Care Insurance Regulation, Alta. Reg. 216/81

British Columbia

Hospital Insurance Act, R.S.B.C. 1979, c. 180
Hospital Insurance Regulations, B.C. Regs. 16/58 and 25/61
Medical Service Act, R.S.B.C. 1979, c. 255
Medical Service Act Regulations, B.C. Reg. 144/68

Manitoba

Health Services Insurance Act, R.S.M. 1987, c. H35
Diagnostic Laboratories Regulation, Man. Reg. 94/86
Health Services Insurance Regulation, Man. Reg. 506/88R
Payments for Insured Medical Services Regulation, Man. Reg. 167/89

New Brunswick

Health Services Act, R.S.N.B. 1973, c. H-3
General Regulation, N.B. Reg. 84-115
Hospital Services Act, R.S.N.B. 1973, C. H-9
General Regulation, N.B. Reg. 84-167
Elimination of Authorized Charges Regulation, N.B. Reg. 86-74

Newfoundland

Hospital Insurance (Agreement) Act, R.S.N. 1990, c. H-7
Newfoundland Medical Care Insurance (Beneficiaries & Enquiries) Regulations 1973, Nfld. Reg. 331/78
Newfoundland Medical Care Insurance (Insured Services) Regulations, 1973 Nfld. Reg. 332/78
Newfoundland Medical Care Insurance (Physicians and Fees) Regulations, 1973 Nfld. Reg. 576/78

Nova Scotia

Health Services and Insurance Act, R.S.N.S. 1989, c. 197
Hospital Insurance Regulations, N.S. Reg. 11/58

Ontario

Health Insurance Act, R.S.O. 1990, c. H.6
General Regulation, R.R.O. 1990, Reg. 552

Prince Edward Island

Health Services Payment Act, R.S.P.E.I. 1988, c. H-2
General Regulations, R.R.P.E.I., E.C. 56/77

Hospital and Diagnostic Services Insurance Act, R.S.P.E.I. 1988, c. H-8
General Regulations, R.R.P.E.I., E.C. 539/63

Quebec

Health Insurance Act, R.S.Q. 1977, c. A-29
Regulation respecting the application of the Health Insurance Act, R.R.Q. 1981, c. 1981, c. A-29, r. 1
Health Insurance Board of Quebec Act (An Act respecting the Régie de l'assurance-maladie du Québec), R.S.Q. 1977, c. R-5
Regulation respecting the contributions to the Quebec Health Insurance Plan, R.R.Q. 1981, c. R-5, r. 1
Hospital Insurance Act, R.S.Q. 1977, c. A-28
Regulations respecting the application of the Hospital Insurance Act, R.R.Q. 1981, c. A-28, r. 1

Saskatchewan

Saskatchewan Health Insurance Act, R.S.S. 1978, c. S-21
Saskatchewan Hospitalization Act, R.S.S. 1978, c. S-23
Saskatchewan Hospitalization Regulations, Sask. Reg. 82/78
Saskatchewan Medical Care Insurance Act, R.S.S. 1978, c. S-29
Medical Care Insurance Beneficiary and Administration Regulations, R.R.S., c. S-29, Reg. 13
Medical Care Insurance Payment Regulations, R.R.S., c. S-29, Reg. 14

CHAPTER 3

Canadian Health Professions — Status and Discipline

INTRODUCTION

Most health care in Canada is carried out by health professionals, including doctors, nurses, psychologists, therapists, technicians and numerous other groups involved in the treatment of patients. The term "health profession" has been defined to mean a profession in which a person "exercises skill or judgment or provides a service related to the preservation or improvement of the health of individuals or the treatment or care of individuals who are injured, sick, disabled or infirm".[1] Generally, recognized health professionals in Canada are given exclusive rights, protected by law, to work in areas where they have specialized training and expertise. In theory, this establishes and identifies a standard of performance within each profession, thereby affording protection to the public from those not qualified to practise. There is continuous regulation and monitoring of those who are registered or licensed members of the profession. Unqualified individuals are prohibited from declaring themselves to be members of a particular profession or, in some cases, from practising skills which are identified as those of a particular profession.

Apart from any benefit to the public, laws that stipulate that only registered or licensed individuals can engage in a particular profession are also of direct benefit to the profession's members. The reputation of the profession may be enhanced and those who are members of the profession are part of an exclusive group. Such laws create a form of monopoly. Exclusivity may have a direct and beneficial effect on the incomes of a profession's members as competition is limited. There is a risk that professional bodies will become isolated and be perceived as protective of their own members and interests at the expense of patients. Health professions in Canada have an obligation to ensure that their members are performing in a competent and ethical manner. When members fail to comply with their professional obligations, the governing body of the

---

1 *Health Professions Act*, S.B.C. 1990, c. 50, s. 1.1

profession may impose penalties, including suspension or termination of professional status.

An essential role of health administrators is the management of health professionals within their institution. In some cases, the professional may be an employee of the health facility; in other cases, the professional may not be a direct employee, but may carry out professional activities within the facility for the benefit of patients. It is important that the goals and obligations imposed by the institution do not conflict with the goals and obligations of the profession. Where the conduct of a health professional offends or fails to comply with the standards of the profession, legal liability for the institution may result. Professional governing bodies may have the legal right to carry out investigations within the institution and to obtain copies of patient records as part of their investigations. Institutions have an obligation to co-operate. In some cases, administrators of health facilities may have a legal or statutory obligation to ensure that individuals employed by the institution are registered health professionals, or to report conduct that is unprofessional. Where a health professional practising within the institution is the subject of disciplinary proceedings, the institution may be an important source of evidence. Sometimes, disciplinary proceedings may result from patient complaints the institution considers unwarranted; in those cases, the institution may offer legal and moral support to the member.

Provincial Regulation

Legislation governing the conduct of health professionals in Canada is a matter of provincial and territorial jurisdiction.[2] Each province and territory has enacted legislation that establishes a system of professional self-regulation in which designated health professions are charged with organizing administrative bodies for identifying professional standards, establishing entry-to-practise criteria, licensing or registering members,[3] setting guide-lines for continuing education, and meting out discipline.

---

2 *Constitution Act, 1867* (U.K.), 30 & 31 Vict., c. 3, s. 91.

3 In some provinces, for certain professions, the ability to use a particular title, *i.e.*, registered nurse, is protected by the legislation. In those circumstances, the legislation does not prohibit others from carrying out activities associated with the particular profession, only from identifying himself or herself as a person who has been registered to carry out those activities. For other professions, the area of practice is protected by law, *i.e.*, physicians, and those not "licensed" as physicians are not only barred from using the term "physician" or "doctor" to describe themselves but also may not engage in the "practice" of medicine as identified by the standards of the profession.

In some provinces, each individual health profession is regulated by an independent, self-contained statute which sets out the basis for self-regulation.[4] For example, in Manitoba, there are specialized statutes regulating a number of health professions including doctors,[5] nurses,[6] physiotherapists,[7] chiropractors,[8] dentists,[9] optometrists,[10] psychologists,[11] respiratory therapists[12] and naturopaths.[13] Each statute, and the regulations thereto, contains the complete statutory code for regulation of the particular profession in that province.

Several provinces have "umbrella legislation" containing general provisions pertaining to all recognized health professionals within the province, as well as companion legislation relating to each profession.[14] For example, in British Columbia, the *Health Professions Act*[15] establishes a Health Professions Council which considers and evaluates whether it is "in the public interest" to have a health profession "designated" under the Act. Once designated, the health profession is bound by the provisions of the Act which require that a "College" be established which, in turn, may pass by-laws that establish requirements for registration, standards, limits or conditions of practice, standards of professional ethics, standards of education, requirements for continuing education, requirements for maintenance of professional liability insurance and a number of other matters integral to professional self-regulation.[16] Matters of professional discipline are handled by individual colleges according to a uniform code of procedure set out in the *Health Professions Act*. Companion legislation has been passed in relation to each designated health profession which creates and regulates the operation of individual colleges and matters that pertain to the individual profession.[17]

The legislation enacted in each province typically establishes the basic threshold of competence an applicant must meet in order to qualify as a

---

[4] Alberta, Saskatchewan, Manitoba, New Brunswick, Nova Scotia, Newfoundland and Prince Edward Island. The Yukon and Northwest Territories have similar statutory schemes.

[5] *Medical Act*, R.S.M. 1987, c. M90.5

[6] *Registered Nurses Act*, R.S.M. 1987, c. R40.6

[7] *Physiotherapists Act*, R.S.M. 1987, c. P65.7

[8] *Chiropractic Act*, R.S.M. 1987, c. C100.

[9] *Dental Association Act*, R.S.M. 1987, c. D30.

[10] *Optometry Act*, R.S.M. 1987, c. O70.

[11] *Psychologists Registration Act*, R.S.M. 1987, c. P190.

[12] *Registered Respiratory Therapists Act*, R.S.M. 1987, c. R115.

[13] *Naturopathic Act*, R.S.M. 1987, c. N80.

[14] British Columbia, Ontario, Quebec.

[15] *Supra* note 1, s. 18.

[16] *Ibid.*

[17] See Relevant Legislation at the end of this chapter.

member of the health profession. Generally, an applicant is entitled, as of right, to have his or her name entered upon the provincial register for the health profession upon meeting the basic educational and training criteria set out in the governing legislation. For example, in Alberta, s. 21 of the *Medical Profession Act*[18] provides that:

> 21. An applicant for registration who has not previously been registered in Part I of the Alberta Medical Register is qualified to be registered if the applicant
> (a) holds a certificate of registration from the Medical Council of Canada, and
> (b) has met the education and training requirements set out in the by-laws.

In other words, an applicant for registration is qualified to be registered as a physician in Alberta if he or she holds a degree in medicine, has satisfactorily served a period of post-graduate training or holds a certificate of registration from the Medical Council of Canada and has served the appropriate period of training following qualification in medicine.[19]

"Good character" is a common requirement of legislation governing professions throughout Canada; however, what is meant by "good character" is not defined. Although the requirement that members of the health profession be of good character is implicit in the legislation, a ruling by a profession's governing body, which purports to bar an applicant considered to be of bad character, leaves scope for a considerable divergence of opinion. This requirement would have to be interpreted rather restrictively so as not to offend human rights legislation either on the basis of discrimination or on the basis of simple fairness to the applicant. For example, past mental illness should not be considered as an impairment to one's character or reputation, and thereby, an obstacle to entering the profession.[20]

In most provinces, when an application for registration is refused by the governing body of the profession, the legislation expressly provides for an appeal or review process designed to ensure that the applicant is treated fairly. In Manitoba, the various statutes that regulate health professions specifically prohibit any applicant from being denied membership in a particular health profession because of race, nationality, religion, colour, sex, marital status, physical disability, age, source of income, family status, political belief, ethnic or national origin.[21] This provision recognizes a

---

18 R.S.A. 1980, c. M-12.

19 *Professional Statutes Amendment Act, 1994,* S.A. 1994, c. 27, s. 21.

20 *Hutton v. Law Society of Newfoundland* (1992), 102 Nfld. & P.E.I.R. 34, 96 D.L.R. (4th) 670 (Nfld. S.C.).

21 *I.e., Physiotherapists Act, supra* note 7, s. 7(5).

principle inherent in the health professions legislation of all provinces even if not expressly stated. All applicants for membership in the health professions must be treated fairly and any refusal of entry into the profession must be based upon a legitimate concern about the applicant's ability to provide competent and reliable health services.

Aside from any common-law obligation a health facility may have to ensure that health professionals working in the facility are properly qualified,[22] provincial or territorial legislation may impose a duty upon employers of health professionals to ensure that they are registered with the governing body of the profession. For example, in Manitoba there is a statutory responsibility for an employer of a health professional to ensure that, at the time of employment, the person is duly registered and holds an appropriate certificate.[23] If a health professional's employment is terminated for professional misconduct, incompetence or incapacity, the employer is obliged to report the matter to the profession's governing body and to provide a copy of that report to the individual whose employment was terminated.[24] In Ontario, there is an obligation to report even if the employer only *intended* to terminate the employment or to revoke the privileges of the health professional for reasons of professional misconduct, incompetence or incapacity, but did not do so because the health professional resigned or voluntarily relinquished his or her employment or privileges.[25]

Where a health professional in Manitoba holds conditional membership in a profession, it is an offence for any "person, institution, hospital or agency" to cause or knowingly permit the health professional to fail to comply with and to observe the conditions that have been imposed.[26] In Ontario, an employer in certain health facilities is obliged to take reasonable precautions to ensure that a health professional acting within the scope of his or her employment does not engage in conduct outside of that individual's scope of practice. Failure to do so will constitute an offence punishable by a fine of not more than $25,000.[27]

A provincial governing body may exercise control over the kind of facility in which a health professional may practise. In Alberta, under the *Medical Profession Act*,[28] a Medical Facility Assessment Committee may investigate and inspect the ownership and operation of diagnostic and

---

22 See Chapter 7, Malpractice and Institutional Liability.

23 *I.e., Physiotherapists Act, supra* note 7, s. 15.

24 *Ibid.*, s. 15(b).

25 *Regulated Health Professions Act, 1991*, S.O. 1991, c. 18, Sch. 2, s. 85.5(2).

26 *Physiotherapists Act, supra* note 7, s. 17.

27 *Regulated Health Professions Act, supra* note 25, s. 42.

28 R.S.A. 1980, c. M-12.

treatment facilities and the financial arrangements pertaining to them. If the committee concludes that a particular facility does not meet the required standards, it may order the diagnostic and treatment facility to cease operation until the standards are met. Further, it is considered "unbecoming conduct for a medical practitioner" to continue to see or to treat patients if the diagnostic or treatment facility does not have the approval of the governing body.[29]

Scope of Practice

In some jurisdictions, a health profession may be regulated by a system that does not protect the particular activities of the health profession from being practised by others, but protects only the right to identify one's self as a member of a particular health profession. For example, in Newfoundland, the *Psychologists Act*[30] provides for the registration of qualified applicants who will be considered "registered psychologists" under the statute. The Act further provides that "no person, unless registered or provisionally registered, may use the designation 'psychologist'". Someone who is unregistered as a psychologist but who holds himself or herself out to the public by title or description of services as a psychologist or a person who practises psychology is guilty of an offence under the statute. In effect, the title "psychologist" or "registered psychologist" is protected by the statute. The statute, however, does not prohibit individuals from engaging in activities or conduct associated with the practice of psychology, such as counselling and therapy, as long as the individual engaging in the practice does not identify himself or herself as a psychologist.

Recently, the tendency of government has been to enact legislation that safeguards not only the title or designation of the particular health profession but also the scope of practice. This has long been the case with legislation governing physicians. Traditionally, not only individuals who are not registered with the governing body for physicians have been prevented from holding themselves out as "physicians" or "doctors" but also unregistered members of the public have been prohibited from engaging in activities considered to be within the domain of the medical profession. In Newfoundland, for example, the legislation governing physicians protects the practice of medicine in a way in which the legislation governing psychologists does not. That province's *Medical Act*[31] provides

---

29 *Ibid.*, s. 93.

30 R.S.N. 1990, c. P-34.

31 R.S.N. 1990, c. M-4.

that, other than a person licensed under the statute, no person shall engage in the practice of medicine, hold himself or herself out as someone who is entitled to engage in the practice of medicine or use the name, title or description implying that he or she is licensed to practise medicine in that province.[32] In effect, the statute protects not only the designation of physician or doctor but also the right to engage in the practice of medicine.

In Ontario, the provincial government recently adopted an elaborate scheme for the regulation of health professionals and the delineation of the scope of practice for designated health professions in that province. Under the *Regulated Health Professions Act, 1991*,[33] 21 health professions are designated as "regulated professions". This represents a considerable increase from the five health professions that were regulated under the *Health Disciplines Act*.[34] As in British Columbia, there is companion legislation for each profession that defines that profession's "scope of practice". In addition, the *Regulated Health Professions Act* defines a number of treatments designated as "controlled acts", which include:

> 1. Communicating to the individual or his or her personal representative a diagnosis identifying a disease or disorder as the cause of symptoms of the individual in circumstances in which it is reasonably foreseeable that the individual or his or her personal representative will rely on the diagnosis.
> 2. Performing a procedure on tissue below the dermis, below the surface of a mucous membrane, in or below the surface of the cornea, or in or below the surfaces of the teeth, including the scaling of teeth.
>
> . . .
>
> 6. Putting an instrument, hand or finger,
>   i. beyond the external ear canal,
>   ii. beyond the point in the nasal passages where they normally narrow,
>   iii. beyond the larynx,
>   iv. beyond the opening of the urethra,
>   v. beyond the labia majora,
>   vi. beyond the anal verge, or
>   vii. into an artificial opening into the body.[35]

An individual who is not a member of a designated health profession is prohibited from engaging in a controlled act. If a health professional is authorized by the legislation governing that profession to perform one of

---

32 *Ibid.*, s. 30.

33 S.O. 1991, c. 18, Sch. 1.

34 R.S.O. 1990, c. H.4 [renamed the *Drug and Pharmacies Regulation Act, 1991*, Vol. 2, c. 18, s. 47(2)]: the professions regulated were medicine, dentistry, nursing, pharmacy and optometry.

35 *Supra* note 25, s. 27(2).

the controlled acts, he or she may perform the controlled act. For example, the *Medicine Act, 1991*[36] specifically allows a physician to communicate a diagnosis. On the other hand, if the scope-of-practice definition in the companion legislation governing the particular profession does not include the controlled act, the health professional is not permitted to carry out the controlled act unless delegated to do so by a health professional who is authorized to perform the controlled act and unless such delegation is in accordance with regulations proclaimed pursuant to the *Regulated Health Professions Act*. For example, the *Dental Hygiene Act, 1991*[37] does not permit dental hygienists to provide diagnoses. The *Regulated Health Professions Act* contemplates overlapping activities on the part of the various health professions and specifically allows for the expansion of each profession's scope of practice as health-care practices change and evolve. In effect, the new legislation does not license individuals to perform in an exclusive area of practice; rather, the legislation licenses certain *health-care activities* in which a health professional may engage, depending upon that individual's background, training, experience, abilities and professional designation.

The Ontario legislation establishes several administrative bodies to assist in the operation and enforcement of the Act. The Health Professions Regulatory Advisory Council advises the Minister of Health on whether unregulated professions should be regulated, or whether regulated professions should be unregulated. It suggests amendments or regulations to the legislation and matters concerning the quality assurance programmes which must be undertaken by the various professional colleges. The Health Professions Board has supervisory jurisdiction over individual colleges and may, in some cases, review decisions made by colleges. Each college must establish a number of statutory committees: an executive committee, a registration committee, a complaints committee, a discipline committee, a fitness-to-practise committee, a quality insurance committee and a patient-relations committee.

Most Canadian health professions, by their own bylaws or through the governing legislation, require their members to engage in continuing education to maintain and upgrade their skill levels. A health professional may be required to demonstrate that he or she has completed a certain number of courses, or a certain number of hours of continuing education, to obtain renewal of registration. Also, a health professional may be required to have practised his or her profession on a regular basis, and if he or she has not, he or she may be required to complete a refresher course or to engage in a more limited scope of practice as a condition of continuing registration.

---

36 S.O. 1991, c. 30.

37 S.O. 1991, c. 22.

Misconduct and Incompetence

Aside from establishing positive standards, which a health professional must meet in order to engage in the practice of the profession, most governing bodies have codes of professional conduct. A breach of the code by a member may result in disciplinary proceedings. In Saskatchewan, for example, a physician may be disciplined if engaged in conduct that is "unbecoming, improper, unprofessional or discreditable".[38] This type of conduct is more specifically defined to include conduct in which the physician:

(a) wilfully betrays a professional secret;
(b) abandons a patient in danger without cause and without giving him an opportunity to engage the services of another physician;
(c) knowingly gives a false certificate respecting birth, death, notice of disease or otherwise or respecting any matter relating to life insurance, health insurance or any other insurance;
(d) divides with another member, who is not a partner, any fees or moneys accruing to him as a medical practitioner without the patient's knowledge and consent;
(e) is addicted to the excessive use of intoxicating liquors or the excessive or habitual use of opiates, narcotics or habit-forming drugs;
(f) impersonates another licensed practitioner;
(g) employs in connection with his professional practice an assistant who is not registered under this Act or any other Act entitling him to provide services to the sick or injured or permits any such unregistered person:
    (i) to attend or treat patients or to perform operations on patients with respect to matters requiring professional discretion or skill; or
    (ii) by his presence or advice, assistance or co-operation, whether acting as an assistant or otherwise, to attend or treat any person for any ailment or to perform any operation on a patient with respect to any matter requiring professional discretion or skill; or who holds out any such unregistered person as a person qualified to practise in Saskatchewan;
(h) fails, after being served with a notice pursuant to this Act, to appear before the council, the discipline hearing committee, a preliminary inquiry committee, a competency committee, a competency hearing committee or a special committee appointed by the council for the purpose of interviewing him;
(i) performs for a patient a professional service that is not justifiable on any reasonable grounds;
(j) provides any professional service that, in the opinion of the discipline hearing committee, is in volume or, in relation to other professional services provided by him, not justifiable on any reasonable grounds;

---

[38] *Medical Profession Act, 1981*, S.S. 1980-81, c. M-10.1, s. 46.

(k) charges a fee or causes a fee to be charged for a service that he has not rendered;
(l) makes or permits false or misleading statements to be made in an account for payment for services rendered by him when he knew, or when under the circumstances it was reasonable to conclude that he knew, that the statements were false or misleading;
(m) violates any of the terms and conditions imposed by the council under this Act in connection with his practice;
(n) prescribes drugs for other than medical or therapeutic purposes;
(o) does or fails to do any act or thing where the discipline hearing committee considers that action or failure to be unbecoming, improper, unprofessional or discreditable; or
(p) does or fails to do any act or thing where the council has, by bylaw, defined that act or failure to be unbecoming, improper, unprofessional or discreditable.[39]

Similar codes of professional conduct are contained in legislation or bylaws for most health professions in Canada. Where a code of professional conduct has not been established, it is likely that the types of misconduct described in the Saskatchewan legislation would apply. Moreover, a code of professional conduct is not likely to be exhaustive; professional governing bodies have broad remedial powers, in some cases specifically supported by legislation, for identifying and disciplining conduct considered to be unprofessional. In Ontario, for example, each health profession's college is given authority, subject to the approval of the Lieutenant-Governor in Council, to make regulations that define "what constitutes a conflict of interest" and also that define "professional misconduct" in greater detail than is found in the governing statute for health professions in that province.[40]

In recent years, sexual abuse is an aspect of professional misconduct that has received considerable notoriety. It has been suggested that sexual abuse of patients or colleagues by certain members of the health professions is occurring at an extremely high and clearly unacceptable rate.[41] In Ontario, as part of its comprehensive reform of health professions legislation, the government has enacted provisions explicitly prohibiting any conduct that may be considered sexual abuse and imposing mandatory reporting obligations upon health professionals. Under the Ontario legislation, "sexual abuse" is defined as:

---

[39] *Ibid.*

[40] *Regulated Health Professions Act, supra* note 25, Sch. 2, s. 95(1), paras. 22, 24.

[41] College of Physicians and Surgeons of Ontario, *The Final Report of the Task Force on Sexual Abuse of Patients: An Independent Task Force Commissioned by the College of Physicians and Surgeons of Ontario* (Toronto: The College, 1991).

(a) sexual intercourse or other forms of physical sexual relations between the member and patient;
(b) touching, of a sexual nature, of the patient by the member; or
(c) behaviour or remarks of a sexual nature by the member towards the patient.[42]

Any registered health professional is obliged to report to the college if he or she has reasonable grounds, obtained in the course of practising the profession, to believe that another registered health professional has sexually abused a patient. Failure to report is an act of professional misconduct. The legislation specifically provides that a person who terminates the employment or revokes, suspends or imposes restrictions on the privileges of a member, or who dissolves a partnership or association with a member for reasons of professional misconduct, incompetence or incapacity, must report to the registrar of the particular college within 30 days.[43] Note the significance of the legislation to employers and health-care administrators. For certain defined activities of sexual abuse, the Act imposes a mandatory revocation of the health professional's certificate of registration.[44] The new legislation has raised a great deal of controversy, both in terms of its explicitness and in terms of what some perceive as a Draconian system based upon the principle of "zero tolerance". On the other hand, proponents of the legislation insist that it is necessary if the severe, long-standing problem of sexual abuse of patients is to be remedied.

The Complaint

The majority of discipline proceedings begin as complaints to the provincial governing body. Such complaints may come from patients, their families, other health professionals or administrators of health-care facilities.

Generally, investigation or review of a complaint by the governing body is mandatory, no matter how frivolous the complaint may appear. In Alberta, the "investigation chairman" is obliged to "review" any matter brought to his or her attention. Even where there has been no complaint, the chair

---

[42] *Regulated Health Professions Act, 1991*, *supra* note 25, s. 1(3).

[43] *Regulated Health Professions Amendment Act, 1993*, S.O. 1993, c. 37, s. 23.

[44] The defined activities are set out in s. 51(5) of Schedule 2:

i. sexual intercourse;
ii. genital to genital, genital to anal, oral to genital, or oral to anal contact,
iii. masturbation of the member by, or in the presence of, the patient,
iv. masturbation of the patient by the member,
v. encouragement of the patient by the member to masturbate in the presence of the member.

must conduct a review where a physician has been convicted of an offence punishable by more than one year's imprisonment, is alleged to be guilty of unbecoming or criminal conduct (whether in a professional capacity or otherwise), is alleged to be incapable or unfit to practise and may constitute a danger to the public, or is alleged to display a lack of skill or judgment.[45] In Prince Edward Island, the Complaints and Registration Committee considers and investigates complaints against physicians, but the complaint must consist of "a signed, written complaint" that has been filed with the Registrar.[46] In Ontario, a complaint must be investigated by the Complaints Committee of a college, but the complaint must be in writing or "recorded on a tape, film, disk or other medium".[47] Failure to convene the Complaints Committee before any disciplinary proceedings are taken may result in the disciplinary proceeding being quashed.[48]

Most governing bodies have extensive investigatory powers permitting them to enter a health facility, interview staff, and seize documents, including patient records. Ordinarily, investigations are carried out by officers or inspectors who are appointed by the governing body and empowered by the legislation to carry out the investigation. In British Columbia, an inspector may, without court order, inspect, observe or examine,

(a) the premises, the equipment and the materials used by a registrant to practise the designated health profession;
(b) the records of the registrant relating to the registrant's practice of the designated health profession and may copy those records;
(c) the practice of the designated health profession performed by or under the supervision of the registrant.[49]

Additional powers of investigation may be obtained by court order, which may include the seizure and removal of evidence relating to the investigation.[50] The obstruction or prevention of an investigation carried out by an inspector or officer is unlawful. In Ontario, it is an offence punishable by a fine of not more than $10,000 to "obstruct an investigator or withhold or conceal from him or her or destroy anything that is relevant to the investigation".[51] Failure to co-operate with the regulatory body's

---

45 *Medical Profession Act*, R.S.A. 1980, c. M-12, s. 36.

46 *Medical Act*, R.S.P.E.I. 1988, c. M-5, s. 33(6).

47 *Regulated Health Professions Act, 1991*, S.O. 1991, c. 18, Sch. 2.

48 *Bechamp v. Manitoba Assn. of Registered Nurses* (1994), 90 Man. R. (2d) 111, 109 D.L.R. (4th) 399 (Q.B.); revd (1994), 115 D.L.R. (4th) 287 (C.A.).

49 *Health Professions Act*, S.B.C. 1990, c. 50, s. 27(1).

50 *Ibid.*, ss. 28 and 29.

51 *Regulated Health Professions Act, supra* note 47, Sch. 2, ss. 76(3) and 93(2).

investigation of a complaint is grounds for a finding of professional misconduct.[52]

In a number of provinces, the complaint may be dealt with informally, often through the Complaints Committee. The Complaints Committee may meet with the complainant, the health professional who is the subject of the complaint and any other individuals who may have information. In some instances, the complaint may be resolved through informal means, for example, by an apology, if appropriate. In other circumstances, the Complaints Committee may determine that the complaint is without merit and may recommend that no further proceedings be undertaken. Where the complaint appears to have merit, the Complaints Committee may recommend that the complaint be dealt with by a discipline hearing.

A health professional whose conduct is the subject of a complaint must be given notice of the complaint and an opportunity to be heard. In *Kenney v. College of Physicians and Surgeons of New Brunswick*,[53] the president of the hospital's medical staff wrote to a physician expressing the hospital's concern with his competence and performance. A copy of the letter was sent to the college. The Registrar investigated the matter and had several conversations with the physician. The physician was then suspended by the college's Fitness-to-Practise Committee. The Court held that sending the college a copy of the letter sent to the physician fell short of constituting a statement identifying objectionable conduct that might be considered a complaint. Also, the college had failed to give the physician written notice of the complaint and had failed to allow him reasonable time to make an explanation. It was held that the college had no jurisdiction to suspend the physician.

Discipline Hearings

In all provinces, legislation governing the various health professions requires that a Discipline Committee or similar tribunal be formed for the purpose of hearing and deciding discipline proceedings against members. The Discipline Committee will be composed of members of the profession and may have lay members as well. The proceeding takes the form of a "hearing".

In some provinces, the legislation contains a detailed description of the procedure to be followed when a hearing is conducted. In Ontario, for

52 *Matthews v. Ontario (Board of Directors of Physiotherapy)* (1987), 61 O.R. (2d) 475n, 43 D.L.R. (4th) 478n (C.A.); also see *Artinian v. College of Physicians and Surgeons of Ontario* (1990), 73 O.R. (2d) 704 (Div. Ct.).

53 (1991), 120 N.B.R. (2d) 49, 85 D.L.R. (4th) 637 (C.A.).

example, the legislation provides that no person selected to sit on a discipline panel is to have taken part in the investigation of what is to be the subject-matter of the panel's hearing. Evidence against a member is not admissible at a hearing unless, at least ten days before the hearing, the member (or the member's counsel) is permitted to examine written or documentary evidence, review reports or written summaries of any expert evidence and have any witnesses who will testify at the hearing identified. The panel may, in its discretion, allow the introduction of evidence that is otherwise inadmissable and give directions to ensure that the member is not prejudiced. If a panel obtains legal advice during the course of the hearing, it must make that advice known to the parties. Hearings are open to the public, subject to an overriding power on the part of the panel to exclude the public if it is satisfied that a private hearing is necessary for reasons of public or private security or for other reasons in the public interest. Where the allegation against the member involves misconduct of a sexual nature, the panel may make an order that no person shall publish the identity of a witness or information that could disclose the identity of the witness. Oral evidence must be recorded and transcripts must be made available if requested.[54] Similar procedural protections are owed to any health professional in Canada who is subject to discipline, even if not specifically elaborated in a particular province's or territory's legislation.[55]

A Discipline Committee is a specialized tribunal considered to have "expertise" in judging matters of professional conduct and competence. The Discipline Committee is entitled to make a finding of professional misconduct or incompetence based upon its own judgment that there is sufficient evidence to conclude that the health professional's conduct has endangered, or is likely to endanger, a patient.[56] A health professional's conduct and skill must be judged in relation to the "welfare of the patient". It has been held that an allegation that there is a general lack of skill, knowledge or judgment is insufficient for a finding of professional misconduct or incompetence.[57] Where there is a competent body of professional opinion that supports a health professional's conduct in the face of criticism by other experts, there has not been clear, convincing and cogent evidence of professional misconduct.[58]

---

[54] *Regulated Health Professions Act*, *supra* note 47, Sch. 2, ss. 36-48.

[55] *Re Crandell and Manitoba Association of Registered Nurses* (1976), 72 D.L.R. (3d) 602, [1977] 1 W.W.R. 468 (Man. Q.B.).

[56] *Re Reddall and College of Nurses of Ontario* (1981), 33 O.R. (2d) 129, 123 D.L.R. (3d) 678 (Div. Ct.).

[57] *Re Singh and College of Nurses (Ont.)* (1981), 33 O.R. (2d) 92, 123 D.L.R. (3d) 713 (Div. Ct.).

[58] *Hallam v. College of Physicians and Surgeons of Ontario* (1993), 61 O.A.C. 143 (Div. Ct.).

A finding of incompetence must relate to the professional practice of the health professional. In *Re Crandell and Manitoba Association of Registered Nurses*,[59] the provincial governing body of nurses suspended a nurse for incompetence because she had difficulty in getting along with other staff members. The Court found that poor interpersonal skills should not deprive a nurse of registration unless those poor interpersonal skills resulted in risk of harm to patients. The suspension was set aside. The Court suggested that the nurse's inability to get along with other staff members was an obstacle to her employment in the *particular institution*, but that nursing employment might be available elsewhere that would not involve a significant level of interpersonal skills. In *Li v. College of Pharmacists of British Columbia*,[60] a complaint was made against a pharmacist on the ground that he had behaved in a rude and condescending manner. In concluding that the Discipline Committee had no authority to deal with the complaint, the Court stated:

> Regulating the personal idiosyncrasies of its members, including short temper, intemperate language, and rude behaviour is not, however, reasonably connected to any objective embodied in the legislation.[61]

It seems reasonable, however, that if the evidence demonstrates that the health professional's manners or demeanour is having a direct impact upon the operation of the health facility to the potential detriment of the patients, there would be grounds for professional discipline.

In *Re Brown and College of Nurses (Ont.)*,[62] an unreported decision referred to in *Re Matheson and College of Nurses of Ontario*,[63] the Court distinguished a discipline committee's right to scrutinize professional incompetence from its ability to scrutinize "administrative duties or the other responsibilities which do not relate directly to the adminstration of health care to a patient".[64] In other words, although the professional governing body is empowered to make findings and administer penalties for incompetent professional activities, its jurisdiction does not allow it to discipline a health professional for conduct that occurs in the context of administrative or management duties.

---

59 *Supra* note 55.

60 (1992), 70 B.C.L.R. (2d) 243 (S.C.); affd (1994), 95 B.C.L.R. (2d) 153, 116 D.L.R. (4th) 606 (C.A.).

61 *Ibid.*, at 619 (D.L.R.).

62 Unreported, August 20, 1979.

63 (1979), 27 O.R. (2d) 632, 107 D.L.R. (3d) 430 (Div. Ct.). Appeal dismissed on consent (1980), 28 O.R. (2d) 611, 111 D.L.R. (3d) 179 (C.A.).

64 *Ibid.*, at 635 (27 O.R.).

In *Re West and College of Nurses of Ontario*,[65] a nurse had been found guilty of professional misconduct by the College of Nurses of Ontario. After working in her profession for nearly five years, the nurse had obtained employment as a private investigator. One method of investigation she had employed was to pretend to be a member of a fictitious doctor's office staff in order to obtain access to confidential medical information. On appeal, the Ontario Divisional Court overturned a finding of professional misconduct by the college on the grounds that the nurse was "not engaged in the performance of nursing services" and that, therefore, her conduct was outside the jurisdiction of the college.

Traditionally, regulatory bodies have imposed significant restrictions upon health professionals who wish to advertize. Business promotion to attract patients or to promote certain kinds of treatment may seem, to some, to be inconsistent with the role of a health professional. It has been held that professional regulatory bodies do have the authority to limit the scope and nature of advertizing by health professionals. The authority, however, is limited to preventing irresponsible and misleading advertizing, not advertizing that serves the legitimate purpose of providing information to the public.[66]

INCAPACITATION

In addition to discipline proceedings that may arise as a result of complaints made about specific acts of incompetence or professional misconduct, proceedings may also be taken against a health professional who is considered to be incapacitated. For example, in British Columbia, an inquiry committee may, on its own motion, investigate a registrant for "a physical or mental ailment, an emotional disturbance or an addiction to alcohol or drugs that impairs his or her ability to practise the designated health profession".[67] In Ontario, the term "incapacitated" is defined to mean that:

> the member is suffering from a physical or mental condition or disorder that makes it desirable in the interest of the public that the member no longer be permitted to practise or that the member's practice be restricted.[68]

---

65 (1981), 32 O.R. (2d) 85, 120 D.L.R. (3d) 566 (Div. Ct.).

66 *Rocket v. Royal College of Dental Surgeons (Ontario)* (1990), 71 D.L.R. (4th) 68 (S.C.C.).

67 *Health Professions Act*, S.B.C. 1990, c. 50, s. 32(2)(e).

68 *Regulated Health Professions Act, 1991*, S.O. 1991, c. 18, Sch. 2, s. 1(1).

A finding of incapacity on the part of the health professional may result when there is drug or alcohol addiction, physical or mental illness, or a general determination by the disciplinary body that the professional skills of the individual in question have so deteriorated as to create a danger to patients. Findings of professional misconduct or incompetence most often relate to a specific occurrence or series of occurrences in which a health professional has failed to meet appropriate professional standards. Considerations of professional incapacity are often prospective in nature, and the disciplinary body must determine whether it is likely, in the future, that the particular individual will engage in unacceptable conduct as a health professional.

PENALTIES

Where the professional governing body, through its discipline committee, concludes that there has been professional incompetence or misconduct, or that the member suffers from incapacity, the profession is given jurisdiction in all provincial legislation to impose a penalty. The range of penalties available are:

(a) revocation of the health professional's membership in the professional body,
(b) suspension of the health professional's membership in the professional body for a specified period,
(c) imposition of limitations upon the areas of practice in which the health professional may engage,
(d) a requirement that the health professional engage in remedial education or training,
(e) a reprimand of the health professional and a record of the fact that the reprimand was made,
(f) imposition of a fine,
(g) an award of costs against the member for the cost of the legal proceedings.

There may be a combination of penalties imposed. For example, a health professional may be fined and also may receive a suspension. Or, the professional may receive a suspension until such time as he or she completes a retraining programme. Reference should be made to the legislation of a particular province or territory. In rare circumstances, professional misconduct may give rise to criminal law sanctions.[68a]

[68a] For example, in *R. v. Manjanatha* (1995), 131 Sask. R. 316, [1995] 8 W.W.R.

The penalty imposed must be fair and must conform to the relevant statute.[69] In *Mason v. Registered Nurses' Association (B.C.)*,[70] a nurse was found to have engaged in professional misconduct and the discipline committee decided that her nursing licence would be suspended indefinitely. On appeal to the British Columbia Supreme Court it was held that the penalty of "indefinite suspension" constituted a vague penalty that was not consistent with the provincial legislation.

In *Re Singh and College of Nurses (Ont.)*,[71] a nurse was suspended by the Discipline Committee pending specified retraining. The nurse appealed the penalty on the ground that it, as with the penalty in *Mason*, constituted an indefinite suspension. The Court held, however, that suspension pending retraining constituted a suspension for a "stated period" and denied the appeal.

Where a court, on appeal, concludes that the particular penalty imposed is inappropriate or unduly severe, it may intervene. In *Re Cunningham and College of Nurses of Ontario*,[72] the Discipline Committee had cancelled the registration of a nurse upon a finding of professional incompetence. The Ontario Divisional Court held that although the "findings did merit some discipline", the particular penalty imposed was inappropriate and the nurse was ordered to be reinstated.

101, 95 W.A.C. 316 (C.A.), an anaesthetist was disciplined by the College of Physicians and Surgeons and was charged with criminal negligence causing death when he left the operating room to make a personal telephone call shortly after a patient was given an anaesthetic. The nurses did not notice when the patient stopped breathing because one warning was inaudible and the other failed to work. The patient suffered oxygen deprivation causing irreversible brain damage. The college sentenced Dr. Manjanatha to a six-month suspension and imposed skill-upgrading requirements. The courts sentenced the doctor to six months in jail. The doctor argued that a jail term was excessive because he had been sufficiently deterred by the actions of the college and that he was not a danger to the public. The Court of Appeal disagreed and upheld the jail term.

69 In *Re Milstein and Ont. College of Pharmacy* (1978), 20 O.R. (2d) 283, 87 D.L.R. (3d) 392, 2 L. Med. Q. 297 (C.A.). The Ontario Court of Appeal commented that "The cancellation or revocation of a professional licence to practise is an extreme penalty and ought . . . to be reserved for the most serious cases." (at 290, O.R.). In *McKee v. College of Psychologists of British Columbia* (1994), 116 D.L.R. (4th) 555 (B.C. C.A.), the Court of Appeal referred the matter of penalty back to the college where a chambers judge had varied the penalty from a lifetime suspension to a two-year suspension, holding that the principles of sentencing in criminal cases were applicable.

70 [1979] 5 W.W.R. 509 (B.C.S.C.).

71 *Supra* note 57.

72 (1975), 8 O.R. (2d) 60, 56 D.L.R. (3d) 697 (Div. Ct.).

A penalty that requires a health professional to undergo a psychiatric assessment is an acceptable condition of reinstatement so long as the requirements of the assessment are specified with certainty and particularity.[73]

APPEAL

In most provinces there is a provision in the legislation for an appeal or a review of a decision by the Discipline Committee. The appeal may be to a court or to an appeal committee authorized to hear appeals from the Discipline Committee. Such appeals do not constitute re-hearings. In most cases, the appeal will be restricted to a review of transcripts of the testimony and documents that constituted the evidence before the Discipline Committee, in conjunction with the written reasons of the Discipline Committee. If the appeal tribunal finds that the decision reached by the Discipline Committee cannot be justified on the basis of the evidence, or is in some measure inappropriate, the decision of the Discipline Committee may be overturned or modified. While the health professional may be present at the appeal, it is unlikely that he or she would be given a further opportunity to testify or to call evidence. This fact highlights the importance of the original proceedings before the Discipline Committee.

An appeal proceeding before the court will be restricted to a review by the court of the decision of the Discipline Committee in conjunction with the evidence that was before the Committee. The court will rarely hear evidence on appeal unless the evidence is new evidence that was unavailable at the time of the proceedings before the Discipline Committee. Moreover, it should be recognized that a court, in dealing with an appeal from an administrative tribunal such as a professional Discipline Committee, is unlikely to second-guess that tribunal in areas where it considers the tribunal to have expertise, and will restrict its own review to legal issues as opposed to professional issues.[74] In other words, unless there has been manifest legal error in the discipline process, a court is unlikely to overturn or to modify the Discipline Committee's decision.

---

[73] *Brand v. College of Physicians and Surgeons of Saskatchewan* (1990), 86 Sask. R. 18, 72 D.L.R. (4th) 446 (C.A.).

[74] See *Re Reddall and College of Nurses of Ontario, supra* note 56.

Reinstatement

Most provincial statutes specifically provide for the restoration or reinstatement of a health professional to the provincial register where the health professional's registration has been suspended or revoked. Ordinarily, the governing body will consider such an application, upon notice to other members of the profession, and order reinstatement where the health professional is able to demonstrate that the problems that led to the suspension or revocation have been remedied and that he or she is likely to engage in acceptable practice in the future.

In *Wakeford v. College of Physicians and Surgeons of British Columbia,*[74a] a physician, with 13 years' experience specializing in obstetrics and gynaecology had his licence revoked upon a finding of sexual misconduct with female patients. He applied for reinstatement with the College of Physicians and Surgeons and, in 1994, was accepted pursuant to conditions imposed by the Council of the college. The physician sought judicial review of the Council's decision, arguing that the conditions imposed were too onerous and were intended to punish. The most contentious conditions were: a prohibition on accepting female patients unless referred by another medical practitioner — before accepting such a patient the physician was to confirm that the referring physician and patient were aware of the disciplinary action for sexual misconduct; all persons employed to assist with the physician's practice were to be informed by him that he had been found guilty of misconduct of a sexual nature; when attending a female patient, the physician was to be "chaperoned" by a nurse, physician or a person requested by the patient; and a notice by the Registrar of the requirement that a "chaperone" be present was to be placed in all private rooms in which female patients would be attended. In ruling against the physician, the Supreme Court of British Columbia decided that the Council was best equipped to decide what conditions were necessary to protect the public interest and that these conditions were reasonable in the circumstances.

Relevant Legislation

Alberta

Chiropractic Profession Act, S.A. 1984, c. C-9.1
Dental Mechanics Act, R.S.A. 1980, c. D-9

[74a] [1995] B.C.J. No. 1113 (B.C.S.C.).

Dental Profession Act, S.A. 1988, c. D-9.5
Health Disciplines Act, R.S.A. 1980, c. H-3.5
Medical Profession Act, R.S.A. 1980, c. M-12
Nursing Profession Act, S.A. 1983, c. N-14.5
Nursing Service Act, R.S.A. 1980, c. N-15
Occupational Therapy Profession Act, S.A. 1987, c. O-2.5
Opticians Act, R.S.A. 1980, c. O-8
Optometry Profession Act, S.A. 1983, c. O-10
Pharmaceutical Profession Act, S.A. 1988, c. P-7.1
Physical Therapy Profession Act, S.A. 1984, c. P-7.5
Podiatry Act, R.S.A. 1980, c. P-11
Psychiatric Nurses Association Act [rep. S.A. 1986, c. 18, s. 16]
Psychiatric Nursing Training Act [rep. S.A. 1986, c. 18, s. 16]
Psychology Profession Act, S.A. 1985, c. P-25.01
Registered Dietitians Act, S.A. 1983, c. R-10.0

British Columbia

Chiropractors Act, R.S.B.C. 1979, c. 50
Dental Technicians and Denturists Act, R.S.B.C. 1979, c. 91
Dentists Act, R.S.B.C. 1979, c. 92
Health Professions Act, S.B.C. 1990, c. 50
Medical Practitioners Act, R.S.B.C. 1979, c. 254
Naturopaths Act, R.S.B.C. 1979, c. 297
Nurses (Licensed Practical) Act, R.S.B.C. 1979, c. 300
Nurses (Registered) Act, R.S.B.C. 1979, c. 302
Nurses (Registered Psychiatric) Act, R.S.B.C. 1979, c. 301
Optometrists Act, R.S.B.C. 1979, c. 307
Pharmacists, Pharmacy Operations and Drug Scheduling Act, 1993, S.B.C. 1993, c. 62
Podiatrists Act, R.S.B.C. 1979, c. 330
Psychologists Act, R.S.B.C. 1979, c. 342

Manitoba

Chiropodists Act, R.S.M. 1987, c. C90
Chiropractic Act, R.S.M. 1987, c. C100
Dental Health Workers Act, R.S.M. 1987, c. D31
Denturists Act, R.S.M. 1987, c. D35
Licensed Practical Nurses Act, R.S.M. 1987, c. P100
Medical Act, R.S.M. 1987, c. M90
Naturopathic Act, R.S.M. 1987, c. N80

Occupational Therapists Act, R.S.M. 1987, c. O5
Optometry Act, R.S.M. 1987, c. O70
Physiotherapists Act, R.S.M. 1987, c. P65
Psychologists Registration Act, R.S.M. 1987, c. P190
Registered Dietitians Act, R.S.M. 1987, c. D75
Registered Nurses Act, R.S.M. 1987, c. R40
Registered Psychiatric Nurses Act, R.S.M. 1987, c. P170
Registered Respiratory Therapists Act, R.S.M. 1987, c. R115

New Brunswick

An Act to Incorporate the New Brunswick Guild of Dispensing Opticians, S.N.B. 1976, c. 68 [am. S.N.B. 1981, c. 87]
Chiropractic Act, S.N.B. 1958, c. 64
College of Psychologists Act, S.N.B. 1980, c. 61
Dental Technicians Act, 1957, S.N.B. 1957, c. 71
Denturists Act, S.N.B. 1986, c. 90 [am. S.N.B. 1990, c. 73; 1993, c. 72]
Dieticians Act, S.N.B. 1988, c. 75
Medical Act, S.N.B. 1981, c. 87 [am. S.N.B. 1989, c. 45; 1993, c. 76]
Medical Laboratory Technology Act, S.N.B. 1991, c. 67
Medical Radiation Technologists Act, S.N.B. 1981, c. 89
New Brunswick Dental Act, 1985, S.N.B. 1985, c. 73
Occupational Therapy Act, S.N.B. 1988, c. 76
Optometry Act, 1978, S.N.B. 1978, c. 73 [am. 1987, c. 75]
Pharmacy Act, S.N.B. 1983, c. 100
Physiotherapy Act, 1985, S.N.B. 1985, c. 74 [am. S.N.B. 1992, c. 97]
Podiatrists Act, S.N.B. 1983, c. 101
Registered Nurses Act, 1957, S.N.B. 1957, c. 82
Registered Nursing Assistants Act, S.N.B. 1977, c. 60

Newfoundland

Chiropractors Act, R.S.N. 1990, c. C-14
Dental Act, R.S.N. 1990, c. D-6
Denturists Act, R.S.N. 1990, c. D-7
Dieticians Act, R.S.N. 1990, c. D-23
Medical Act, R.S.N. 1990, c. M-4
Midwifery Act, R.S.N. 1990, c. M-11
Nursing Assistants Act, R.S.N. 1990, c. N-6
Occupational Therapists Act, R.S.N. 1990, c. O-4
Optometry Act, R.S.N. 1990, c. O-7
Pharmaceutical Association Act, 1994, S.N. 1994, c. P-12.1

Physiotherapy Act, R.S.N. 1990, c. P-13
Psychologists Act, R.S.N. 1990, c. P-34
Registered Nurses Act, R.S.N. 1990, c. R-9

Northwest Territories

Certified Nursing Assistants Act, R.S.N.W.T. 1988, c. C-2
Dental Auxiliaries Act, R.S.N.W.T. 1988, c. D-3
Dental Mechanics Act, R.S.N.W.T. 1988, c. D-2
Dental Profession Act, R.S.N.W.T. 1988, c. 33 (Supp.)
Medical Care Act, R.S.N.W.T. 1988, c. M-8
Medical Profession Act, R.S.N.W.T. 1988, c. M-9
Mental Health Act, R.S.N.W.T. 1988, c. M-10
Nursing Profession Act, R.S.N.W.T. 1988, c. N-4
Ophthalmic Medical Assistants Act, R.S.N.W.T. 1988, c. O-2
Optometry Act, R.S.N.W.T. 1988, c. O-3
Pharmacy Act, R.S.N.W.T. 1988, c. P-6
Psychologists Act, R.S.N.W.T. 1988, c. P-11

Nova Scotia

Chiropractic Act, R.S.N.S. 1989, c. 69
Dental Act, S.N.S. 1992, c. 3
Dental Technicians Act, R.S.N.S. 1989, c. 278
Denturist Act, R.S.N.S. 1989, c. 127
Medical Act, R.S.N.S. 1989, c. 278
Medical Radiation Technologists Act, R.S.N.S. 1989, c. 280
Medical Services Act, R.S.N.S. 1989, c. 281
Nursing Assistants Act, R.S.N.S. 1989, c. 319
Occupational Therapists Act, R.S.N.S. 1989, c. 321
Optometry Act, R.S.N.S. 1989, c. 328
Pharmacy Act, R.S.N.S. 1989, c. 343
Physiotherapy Act, R.S.N.S. 1989, c. 344
Professional Dietitians Act, R.S.N.S. 1989, c. 361
Psychologists Act, R.S.N.S. 1989, c. 368
Registered Nurses' Association Act, R.S.N.S. 1989, c. 391

Ontario

Chiropody Act, 1991, S.O. 1991, c. 20
Chiropractic Act, 1991, S.O. 1991, c. 21

Dental Hygiene Act, 1991, S.O. 1991, c. 22
Dental Technology Act, 1991, S.O. 1991, c. 23
Dentistry Act, 1991, S.O. 1991, c. 24
Denturism Act, 1991, S.O. 1991, c. 25
Dietetics Act, 1991, S.O. 1991, c. 26
Massage Therapy Act, 1991, S.O. 1991, c. 27
Medical Laboratory Technology Act, 1991, S.O. 1991, c. 28
Medical Radiation Technology Act, 1991, S.O. 1991, c. 29
Medicine Act, 1991, S.O. 1991, c. 30
Midwifery Act, 1991, S.O. 1991, c. 31
Nursing Act, 1991, S.O. 1991, c. 32
Opticianry Act, 1991, S.O. 1991, c. 34
Optometry Act, 1991, S.O. 1991, c. 35
Pharmacy Act, 1991, S.O. 1991, c. 36
Physiotherapy Act, 1991, S.O. 1991, c. 37
Psychology Act, 1991, S.O. 1991, c. 38
Regulated Health Professions Act, 1991, S.O. 1991, c. 18
Respiratory Therapy Act, 1991, S.O. 1991, c. 39

Prince Edward Island

Chiropractic Act, R.S.P.E.I. 1988, c. C-7
Dental Profession Act, R.S.P.E.I. 1988, c. D-6
Dieticians Act, S.P.E.I. 1994, c. 12
Licensed Nursing Assistants Act, R.S.P.E.I. 1988, c. L-10
Medical Act, R.S.P.E.I. 1988, c. M-5
Nurses Act, R.S.P.E.I. 1988, c. N-4
Occupational Therapists Act, S.P.E.I. 1994, c. 43 [as of Jan. 1/96 not yet proclaimed in force]
Optometry Act, R.S.P.E.I. 1988, c. O-6
Pharmacy Act, R.S.P.E.I. 1988, c. P-6
Physiotherapy Act, R.S.P.E.I. 1988, c. P-7
Psychologists Act, S.P.E.I. 1990, c. 49; R.S.P.E.I. 1988, c. P-27.1
Registered Occupational Therapists Act, R.S.P.E.I. 1988, c. R-9 [this Act to be repealed by S.P.E.I. 1994, c. 43 — as of Jan. 1/96 not yet proclaimed in force]

Quebec

Chiropractic Act, R.S.Q. 1977, C-16
Dental Act, R.S.Q. 1977, c. D-3
Denturologists Act, R.S.Q. 1977, c. D-4

Dispensing Opticians Act, R.S.Q. 1977, c. O-6
Hearing-Aid Acousticians Act, R.S.Q. 1977, c. A-33
Medical Act, R.S.Q. 1977, c. M-9
Nurses Act, R.S.Q. 1977, c. I-8
Optometry Act, R.S.Q. 1977, c. O-7
Pharmacy Act, R.S.Q. 1977, c. P-10
Podiatry Act, R.S.Q. 1977, c. P-12
Practice of Midwifery, within the Framework of Pilot Projects, R.S.Q. 1977, c. P-16.1
Professional Chemists Act, R.S.Q. 1977, c. C-15
Professional Code, R.S.Q. 1977, c. C-26
Radiology Technicians Act, R.S.Q. 1977, c. T-5

SASKATCHEWAN

Ancillary Dental Personal Education Act, R.S.S. 1978, c. A-20
Chiropody Profession Act, R.S.S. 1978, c. C-9
Chiropractic Act, 1994, S.S. 1994, c. C-10.1
Dental Care Act, R.S.S. 1978, c. D-4
Dental Profession Act, R.S.S. 1978, c. D-5.1 (Supp.)
Dental Technicians Act, R.S.S. 1978, c. D-6
Dental Therapists Act, S.S. 1980-81, c. D-6.1
Denturists Act, R.S.S. 1978, c. D-7
Licensed Practical Nurses Act, S.S. 1988-89, c. L-14.1
Medical Profession Act, 1981, S.S. 1980-81, c. M-10.1
Medical Radiation Technologists Act, S.S. 1983-84, c. M-10.2
Naturopathy Act, R.S.S. 1978, c. N-4
Ophthalmic Dispensers Act, R.S.S. 1978, c. O-5
Optometry Act, 1985, S.S. 1984-85-86, c. O-6.1
Osteopalmic Practice Act, R.S.S. 1978, c. O-7
Pharmacy Act, R.S.S. 1978, c. P-9
Physical Therapists Act, 1984, S.S. 1983-84, c. P-11.1
Professional Dietitians Act, R.S.S. 1978, c. P-28
Registered Nurses Act, 1988, S.S. 1988-89, c. R-12.2
Registered Occupational Therapists Act, R.S.S. 1978, c. R-13
Registered Psychiatric Nurses Act, S.S. 1993, c. R-13.1
Registered Psychologists Act, R.S.S. 1978, c. R-14

YUKON

Chiropractors Act, R.S.Y. 1986, c. 23
Dental Profession Act, R.S.Y. 1986, c. 42

Denture Technicians Act, R.S.Y. 1986, c. 43
Medical Profession Act, R.S.Y. 1986, c. 114
Mental Health Act, S.Y. 1989-90, c. 28
Nursing Assistants Registration Act, S.Y. 1987, c. 19
Optometrists Act, R.S.Y. 1986, c. 125
Pharmacists Act, R.S.Y. 1986, c. 131
Registered Nurses Profession Act, S.Y. 1992, c. 11

CHAPTER 4

Health Records

Introduction

Health administrators will not be involved in the day-to-day completion of records, but do need to be familiar with the system of record-keeping in their institutions. They must ensure that the system is followed by health practitioners working in the institution. Health practitioners have a general common-law obligation to keep treatment records and the quality of these records must meet a reasonable standard. Many of the statutes that regulate health professionals contain provisions that stipulate a minimum standard for record-keeping.

Health records are prepared to keep contemporaneous accounts of the care and treatment of patients. A health record is an important vehicle of communication among health providers participating in the patient's treatment. It gives providers from various disciplines the precise medical status of a patient. It immediately familiarizes hospital staff with the past medical history of a patient. It informs physicians treating a patient about the medications that have been prescribed and about the medications to which the patient may be allergic.

Health records may be used for other purposes. A patient or a patient's lawyer may require a copy of the record to establish the patient's condition while he or she was in the institution. A record may be subpoenaed to court to support or to contradict allegations of injuries sustained in an accident. Records may also be used to support or to contradict claims for workers' compensation, disability insurance, life insurance and similar claims. Patient records may be used for monitoring the cost of health care, analyzing health trends in the population and tracking down abuses.

The health record provides a retrospective account, sometimes on a minute-to-minute basis, of the health-care team's activities in treating a patient. Where the adequacy or propriety of treatment is under scrutiny — by a hospital committee, professional disciplinary body, or a court — the contents of the health-care record may be the most detailed and reliable evidence available.

The Use of Health Records in Legal Proceedings

Traditionally, courts have preferred the oral testimony of witnesses as the most reliable form of evidence. Witnesses are sworn to tell the truth. Their evidence can be tested by cross-examination and, where appropriate, rebutted by other oral evidence. Courts are reluctant to introduce into the proceedings any evidence that does not constitute sworn oral evidence on the ground that it may not constitute the "best evidence".

Written communications purporting to reflect the sworn evidence of a witness may be second-best compared to the sworn oral testimony of the actual witness. The written communication may be self-serving. It will not have been prepared at a time when the witness has "sworn to tell the truth". It will not be susceptible to cross-examination.

Nonetheless, courts have recognized that in certain circumstances a written record may be more reliable than a witness's personal recollection, especially when the witness is attempting to recall events that took place months or years earlier and that involve detailed facts and information that a witness ordinarily would not be able to recollect with accuracy. Accordingly, in court proceedings, as well as in proceedings before other tribunals, health records will be admitted into evidence where it can be established that the making of the record was contemporaneous with the occurrence of the events recorded and that the record was made as a part of a general system for recording the care and treatment of a patient.[1]

In a malpractice proceeding, where the management of the patient by a multitude of caregivers may be under scrutiny, the availability of a comprehensive written record is crucial in two respects:

1. It will assist the witnesses who were involved in the care of the patient to relate details of treatment, which might be difficult or impossible to recall after a period of months or years.
2. It will assist witnesses in persuading a court that their testimony is accurate and can be believed when that testimony is consistent with contemporaneous notations shown on the record.

Where the particular health practitioner who made the notation on the records is available, that individual may be required to testify orally, though the health record may form the basis for that individual's testimony by

[1] *Ares v. Venner*, [1970] S.C.R. 608, 14 D.L.R. (3d) 4, 12 C.R.N.S. 349. Most, if not all, provinces have now passed evidence legislation which permits the admission of health-care records into evidence on the basis that they qualify as "business records".

refreshing his or her memory. It is not unusual in a medical malpractice case for a witness, who treated the patient some years before, not to have any present recollection of the treatment. Such a witness must rely entirely upon the actual record in giving evidence. Where the individual who made the notation on the record is no longer available, the record itself may be evidence of the facts stated therein.

General Duty to Create and Maintain Records

As noted, many statutes regulating health professionals contain provisions requiring the health professional to create and maintain records of a particular kind and quality. In British Columbia, for example, rules made under the *Medical Practitioners Act*[2] set out the following minimum requirements for physician record-keeping:

> Members in practice shall keep:
> (a) a clinical record on each patient showing the patient's name and address and the date seen. For each time a patient is seen there must be enough information recorded to clearly explain why the patient came to see the physician and what the physician found out both from the history and from the physical examination. There must be a clear record of what investigations the physician ordered and a clear record of either a provisional diagnosis or a diagnosis made, and a clear record of the specifics of any treatment prescribed;
> (b) an account card or a ledger page or section with respect to each patient or the person upon whom the patient is dependent which shall show the date of service rendered, type of service, charge made, payments made and balance outstanding;
> (c) a day book, daily diary, appointment sheets or the like showing for each day the names of patients seen or treated or in respect of whom professional service is rendered.
> All such records shall be typed or legibly written in ink and kept in suitable systematic permanent forms such as books, binders, files, cards or folders for a period of not less than six years from the date of the last entry recorded, PROVIDED that in practices where computerized, mechanical or electronic record-keeping or accounting systems are used, the same shall be deemed sufficient if the information kept by such system can be reproduced promptly in written form if required and if the material so reproduced, either by itself or in conjunction with other records, constitutes an orderly and legible permanent record that would provide without delay the information required under (a), (b), and (c).

---

2 R.S.B.C. 1979, c. 254, s. 4(2).

> Members attending a patient in hospital shall promptly complete the medical records for which they are responsible.[3]

Health professionals in all provinces and territories have similar professional obligations depending upon the nature of their profession and practice. In Ontario, "[f]ailing to keep records as required" is an act of professional misconduct.[4]

Health professionals may, from time to time, delegate record-keeping to one another. A resident or intern may be directed by the staff physician to reduce an order to writing or to dictate an operative report. A nurse may write out a verbal order which is subsequently countersigned by the physician who made the order.

Health administrators should recognize that there is a professional obligation and common-law duty on all health practitioners to create and maintain good-quality records.[5] A failure by the institution to require conformance with these professional obligations may have ramifications for the institution as well as for the individual professionals. Institutional policies or protocols for record-keeping may include, by reference, the professional standards set out in the relevant legislation as a means for ensuring good-quality record-keeping in the institution.

Institutional Records

Many jurisdictions have enacted legislation setting out minimal requirements for record-keeping by health-care institutions. Section 15 of the regulation passed pursuant to the Nova Scotia *Hospitals Act*[6] provides that a "hospital shall maintain a record of the diagnostic and treatment services provided in respect of each in-patient and out-patient".[7] Section 16 of the regulation sets out the minimum components of the hospital record, which must contain at least the following:

> (a) full name of the patient, including all previous surnames, where applicable;
> (b) date of birth;
> (c) history of present illness;

---

3 Rules made under the *Medical Practitioners Act*, R.S.B.C. 1979, c. 254.

4 O. Reg. 799/93, ss. 1, 13, made under the *Nursing Act, 1991*, S.O. 1991, c. 32.

5 *McInerney v. MacDonald* (1990), 66 D.L.R. (4th) 736 (N.B.C.A.); affd (1992), 93 D.L.R. (4th) 415 (S.C.C.).

6 R.S.N.S. 1989, c. 208.

7 N.S. Reg. 16/79.

(d) history of previous illness;
(e) family history;
(f) physical examination;
(g) provisional diagnosis;
(h) orders for treatment;
(i) medical, nursing and other notes on the progress of the patient;
(j) condition on discharge;
(k) reports if any of
  (i) consultations;
  (ii) follow-up care;
  (iii) laboratory, radiological, and other diagnostic examinations;
  (iv) medical, surgical, obstetrical and other therapeutic treatment, including renal dialysis treatment;
  (v) operations and anaesthesia;
  (vi) the hospital autopsy report; and
(l) the final diagnosis;
(m) on decease of the patient in hospital, a copy of the death certificate under the Vital Statistics Act; and
(n) such other items as the board may prescribe.

The public hospitals legislation of Ontario provides that an admitting note clearly describing the reason for the admission of the patient and authenticated by a member of the medical or midwifery staff is to be entered in the medical record of the patient within 24 hours after admission.[8] The Ontario legislation also codifies a common practice, namely, that all orders for treatment must be in writing and signed by the "physician, dentist or midwife giving the order".[9] Alternatively, a physician, dentist or midwife may dictate an order by telephone to a "person designated by the administrator to take such orders"[10] but is obliged to "authenticate the order on the first visit to the hospital after dictating the order".[11]

In Alberta, the original or a copy of a record from another institution, which is "sufficiently recent to be relevant to the patient's current status", is to be included in the health record of the institution currently treating the patient.[12] The Alberta regulation even deals with a rule of record-keeping which may be more honoured in the breach: "[d]iagnostic and treatment service records shall be *legible*, accurate and complete" [emphasis added].[13] There may be a requirement that a record be completed "before

---

8 R.R.O. 1990, Reg. 965, s. 25.
9 R.R.O. 1990, Reg. 965, s. 24(1).
10 *Ibid.*, s. 24(2).
11 *Ibid.*, s. 24(3)(b).
12 Alta. Reg. 247/90, s. 13(3).
13 *Ibid.*, s. 13(6).

surgery on all elective cases and as soon as possible after surgery in emergency cases".[14]

There is similar legislation — though it may not be as detailed — in relation to other health-care institutions. For example, the New Brunswick *Nursing Homes Act*[15] provides that:

> An operator shall keep a complete and up-to-date record for each resident from the time of admission to the time of discharge and such record shall include
> (*a*) the standard admission form required by the regulations;
> (*b*) the admission medical and subsequent medical reports;
> (*c*) a comprehensive care plan;
> (*d*) physician's and dentist's notes and orders;
> (*e*) medication and treatment sheets;
> (*f*) nurse's notes;
> (*g*) activation and rehabilitation program progress reports and attendance records;
> (*h*) special dietary requirements or problems;
> (*i*) discharge sheets showing the date of discharge, the reason for discharge, the condition of the resident at the time of discharge, the address to which the resident has been discharged;
> (*j*) the type and amount of drugs accompanying the resident on discharge;
> (*k*) a recording of all valuables belonging to the resident, if the operator has undertaken to keep them in safe-keeping.[16]

In British Columbia, the *Continuing Care Act*[17] provides that operators of continuing-care facilities must permit an inspector "to inspect all records related to the provision of continuing care of current or former clients of the operator". In Manitoba, there is a regulation under the *Private Hospitals Act*[18] outlining the licensee's responsibility to maintain records, including their contents, deadlines for completion and storage requirements. In Nova Scotia, the *Homes for Special Care Act*[19] contains provisions that relate to the "records" in nursing homes and other chronic-care facilities. In Quebec, there are broad and detailed legislative provisions relating to a variety of health-care facilities in the province.[20] In Saskatchewan,

---

14 *Ibid.*, s. 18(3).

15 S.N.B. 1982, c. N-11, s. 14(1).

16 Section 10 of the regulation passed pursuant to the *Nursing Homes Act* also requires an operator of a nursing home to ensure that staff properly complete, in writing, an incident report and submit it to the administrator each time an incident or accident takes place that affects, or may affect, the health and safety of the residents or staff. N.B. Reg. 91-55, s. 5.

17 S.B.C. 1989, c. 2, s. 5(2).

18 Man. Reg. 58/93R, under *Private Hospitals Act*, R.S.M. 1987, c. P130.

19 R.S.N.S. 1989, c. 203.

20 See *An Act Respecting Health Services and Social Services*, R.S.Q. 1991, c. S-4.2, ss. 17-26.

regulations under the *Housing and Special-Care Homes Act*[21] require that the records kept for "guests" admitted to a home include an admission record and a medical and social assessment. Additional records may also be required from health practitioners where there is "intensive personal or nursing care". In the Northwest Territories and the Yukon, a "hospital authority" must ensure that a complete medical record is prepared and maintained.[22]

In some jurisdictions, the relevant legislation may refer to a medical, hospital or patient record, but does not set out the basic requirements. This does not relieve the institution or its health professionals from compiling records which meet the ordinary standard of care exercised by similar institutions.

Where an institution formulates bylaws or policies in relation to record-keeping, care should be taken to ensure that these bylaws or policies conform to the relevant legislation in the jurisdiction. Where there is a conflict, the legislation will apply. Internal bylaws or policies of the institution that are inconsistent with legislation are likely to result in a negative inference about the quality of record-keeping within the institution.

Quality of Record-Keeping

An inadequate or incomplete record may have an impact upon patient care. In legal proceedings where the standard of patient care is at issue, it is difficult to overstate the importance a good-quality record will have in demonstrating that the care provided was of a reasonable standard. In a malpractice proceeding, the record may carry more weight than any other evidence because the health professionals whose conduct is under scrutiny will typically place great reliance upon the record when giving oral evidence.

It is not unusual for a malpractice proceeding to reach trial five years or more after the events that gave rise to the action. In many instances, the care providers had no inkling at the time of treatment that their actions would give rise to a claim. A physician or nurse may not discover that his or her conduct has become the subject of a complaint until months or years after the conduct of which the patient complains. It will be difficult to recall events precisely in the absence of accurate health records. The contemporaneous recording of information at the time that the events took place is likely to be received as more credible and objective evidence

---

[21] Sask. Reg. 34/66, s. 9.

[22] Regulation 275, under the *Territorial Hospital Insurance Services Act*, R.R.N.W.T. 1980, as amended; Regulation 130 under the *Hospital Insurance Service Ordinance*, R.R.Y. 1977.

than the retrospective viewpoint of a witness or defendant whose recollections may be perceived as coloured by the lawsuit.

Health-care records admitted as evidence in a court of law will be scrutinized closely. Discrepancies, inaccuracies or omissions will be used to discredit the records and the witness who relies upon them. It is essential that health records be compiled in an accurate, timely and professional manner.

An institution should require that information obtained or actions taken by staff be recorded at the time of occurrence or as shortly thereafter as possible. Failure to do so may lead to an inference that the record is inaccurate. Common sense dictates that the longer the period between the event and the recording of it, the more likely the occurrence of error. Records made a considerable time after an occurrence may be influenced, inadvertently, by subsequent events.

Entries on the record should be made in chronological order. Failure to do so may place the accuracy of the record in doubt. An entry that is out of order may appear to have been placed there as an afterthought, or worse, as an alteration. Such an entry will not satisfy the criterion of contemporaneity. Where an entry has been forgotten or must be added out of order for some other reason, the entry should be dated and signed, indicating both the time of entry and the time the event itself occurred. This will avoid a suspicion of falsification. Spaces for later entries should never be left in the chart. Similarly, subsequent notations should never be added between the lines or in the margins. Late entries should be clearly marked as such.

The record should show the pertinent facts clearly and objectively. Opinions or judgments should appear only when supported by sufficient documented information. For example, a notation that the "patient is depressed" by itself may be considered incomplete and possibly inaccurate. A court would wish to know what observations or information were relied upon to justify this conclusion. It is doubtful that any witness can recall these details several years after the events in question unless they have been recorded in the health-care record.

The required frequency or extent of charting will be determined by the condition of the patient, generally-accepted standards of care within the profession, applicable policies and procedures within the institution and any medical orders in the patient's chart. Care given or significant occurrences should be recorded. It may also be important to chart routine activities or events. In legal proceedings such charting will constitute evidence that the care and treatment of the patient was proceeding smoothly and without incident. Health practitioners often refer to the practice of "charting by exception". Such a practice should be employed cautiously, if at all. A patient's chart with routine observations and events recorded may be very valuable in demonstrating that the preceding care was adequate and that a rapidly declining condition or sudden event could not have been anticipated or prevented.

The Ontario case of *Kolesar v. Jeffries*[23] concerned the death of a patient who was confined to a Stryker frame following back surgery. The hospital chart contained no record of nursing observations or activities during the eight hours preceding the discovery that the patient had died. The trial judge stated:

> On a ward with a great many patients the medical record becomes the common source of information and direction for patient care. If kept properly it indicates on a regular basis the changes in the patient's condition and alerts staff to developing dangers. And it is perhaps trite to say that if the hospital enforced regular entries during each nursing shift, a nurse could not make the entry until she had first performed the service required of her. In Kolesar's case the absence of entries permits of the inference that nothing was charted because nothing was done.[24]

The hospital was found liable in negligence for Mr. Kolesar's death. The Court found that the ward was inadequately staffed and that the patient did not receive proper care.

In other circumstances the absence of entries on the chart may lead to a different conclusion than the one reached in *Kolesar*. In *Ferguson v. Hamilton Civic Hospitals*,[25] a patient became a quadriplegic after undergoing an angiogram. Mr. Justice Krever commented:

> While on the subject of nursing care, this is an appropriate place to say that, although invited so to find, I reject the submission that the absence of any nurse's entry in the nurses' record forming part of the hospital chart between 1:30 p.m. and 3:30 p.m. on June 27, 1973, is an indication of a failure in care on the part of the attending nurses. I infer that there was no observable change during that period that justified being recorded. With relation to nurses' notes this case is distinguishable from *Kolesar v. Jeffries* . . . in which [it was] held that where there is a positive duty on the part of a nurse to perform a physical act, the absence in the nurses' record of any reference to the performance of the act justifies the inference that the act was not performed. In the absence of any evidence that good nursing practice requires the making of a note every time a nurse attends to observe a patient, even

---

23 (1974), 9 O.R. (2d) 41, 59 D.L.R. (3d) 367 (H.C.J.); varied on other grounds (1976), 12 O.R. (2d) 142, 68 D.L.R. (3d) 198 (C.A.); affd on other grounds (*sub nom. Joseph Brant Memorial Hospital v. Koziol*), [1978] 1 S.C.R. 491, 15 N.R. 302 (*sub nom. Kolesar v. Joseph Brant Memorial Hospital*), 77 D.L.R. (3d) 161, 2 C.C.L.T. 170.

24 *Ibid.*, at 47-48 (9 O.R.).

25 (1983), 40 O.R. (2d) 577, 144 D.L.R. (3d) 214, 23 C.C.L.T. 254 (H.C.J.); affd (1985), 50 O.R. (2d) 754, 18 D.L.R. (4th) 638, 33 C.C.L.T. 56 (C.A.).

> when there is no observable change in the patient's condition, it would be extending that principle too far to apply it to routine inspections of the patient by the nurses.[26]

In effect, the frequency and content of charting activities requires balancing. Although it may be important to chart some routine, unexceptional events and treatment, this does not mean that every health-care activity must be recorded.

Corrections to the health record should be made in an honest and forthright manner. Notations that have been erased or obliterated may suggest that the record-keeper has something to hide. An error should be corrected by drawing a straight line through the mistake so that it remains legible. The error should be initialled, and the reader's attention should be directed to the corrected entry. The new entry should include the date, time and the writer's signature.

Accuracy of the patient record is essential — for both medical and legal purposes. In the British Columbia case of *Meyer v. Gordon*,[27] an action was brought on behalf of an infant plaintiff who had sustained permanent brain damage as a result of hypoxia at birth. In reviewing relevant nursing notes the trial judge found:

> [A]ccording to Nurse Webb's note in the hospital record, the fetal heart rate was monitored and found to be normal. She noted that Mrs. Meyer's labour was "good labour" and that she was experiencing a dilation of the cervix of 3 cm. with contractions every two minutes which were strong. Nurse Webb did not note or record the duration of each contraction.
>
> She noted that the fetus was at "mid" station.[28]
>
> . . .
>
> When Nurse Webb conducted her examination of Mrs. Meyer shortly after 11:30 she omitted to ascertain Mrs. Meyer's obstetrical history and that her first labour and delivery had been a rapid one. Nurse Webb agreed on cross-examination that if she had taken the history of the rapid first labour she would have realized that she must watch Mrs. Meyer more closely than she did.
>
> Nurse Webb's evidence of her understanding of the significance of her measurements of 3 cm. dilatation at 11:30 was imprecise. I found her appreciation of the progress of Mrs. Meyer's labour to be inaccurate. She testified that when she conducted the first vaginal examination, she thought Mrs. Meyer was in "early" labour. But that description was not used on the chart. She described the labour as "good" labour. In her incident report (Ex. 31) she described the labour as "hard". On cross-examination she

---

26 *Ibid.*, at 602-03 (40 O.R.).

27 (1981), 17 C.C.L.T. 1 (B.C.S.C.).

28 *Ibid.*

> described the stage of labour as "active labour" requiring a fetal heart rate check every 15 minutes. . . .
>
> A further indication of her inexact approach was the use of the expression "mid" to describe the station or position of the fetus.[29]

Expert nursing witnesses in the case testified that the term "mid" was not specific enough to evaluate the progress of labour. The trial judge noted:

> . . . Nurse Webb omitted to record the specific duration of the contractions during her vaginal examination conducted shortly after 11:30. She merely designated the duration as "strong". She admitted that she "missed putting it in". She made no record of the effacement or character of the cervix. Yet she was aware that a determination of whether contractions were increasing, the extent or size of the cervical dilatation and the effacement or character of the cervix were important indications of the progress of labour and should be accurately recorded.[30]

Moreover, in addition to finding the record-keeping inadequate, alterations and additions to the record caused the trial judge to suspect that someone had tampered with the record.

> The hospital chart contains alterations and additions which compel me to view with suspicion the accuracy of many of the observations which are recorded.
>
> The chart also contains at least one entry which was discovered during this trial (in May 1980) to have been made after the fact. That also casts suspicion on the reliability of those who made the entries and undermines the accuracy of medical opinions based upon these entries and observations.[31]

The trial judge found that there was an entry on the record that was crucial. The entry had been inserted on the chart by Nurse Webb after the infant plaintiff had been sent to another hospital.

> This became apparent quite late during the trial when a copy of this page of the chart, which had accompanied the child when she was taken to Vancouver General Hospital, was introduced into evidence (Ex. 85). This copy of the page did not contain the interlineation contained in the original record of the Nurses' Notes. Nor did the copy (Ex. 85) contain the signatures of Nurse Thiessen and Nurse McAuley which appear at the foot of the entry made opposite the time 12:32.[32]

---

[29] *Ibid.*, at 11-12.

[30] *Ibid.*, at 12.

[31] *Ibid.*, at 15.

[32] *Ibid.*, at 17.

. . .

I have concluded that after Nurse Webb subsequently became aware that the child was in trouble and after the child had been taken to Vancouver General Hospital, Nurse McAuley noted the inadequacy of Nurse Webb's charting. She communicated her concern of this inadequacy to Nurse Webb and Nurse Webb then made the interlineated entry. It was not until she was faced with proof at the trial that the interlineated entry was made after the copy of the chart had gone to Vancouver General Hospital that she changed her evidence.[33]

The conduct of Nurse Webb was found to have contributed to the serious injuries sustained by the infant plaintiff at birth. Both Nurse Webb and the hospital were found liable.

Incident Reports

When unusual incidents occur within a health facility that place patients or staff at risk, an incident report must be completed. Generally, the report describes the incident, the surrounding events, any resulting injuries and the corrective action taken. The incident report does not ordinarily become part of the patient record. It is an internal document, the primary purpose of which is to provide data to the health-care institution so that it may monitor, from a risk-management and quality-assurance perspective, actual or potential sources of harm to individuals.[34]

Incident reports often involve patients and the incidents described may result in litigation. Where an incident report contains opinions or

---

[33] *Ibid.*, at 18.

[34] It should be noted that in at least one case, a court suggested that the incident report *should* form part of the "medical record". In *Fiege v. Cornwall General Hospital* (1980), 30 O.R. (2d) 691, 117 D.L.R. (3d) 152 (H.C.J.), the hospital, in a malpractice proceeding, took the position that the incident report should not form part of the medical record. Carruthers J. stated, however, that the "document should have formed part of the medical record because either it is a report of a 'physical examination', 'medical examination', or a 'progress note'. Reports of these examinations, by the provisions of s. 38, are required to be included in a patient's medical record." The decision focused on whether the hospital should have produced, prior to trial, a copy of the incident report and whether the hospital was entitled to claim privilege for it. It is not clear that the judge intended to suggest that the incident report should be kept with the patient chart or that it had any treatment purpose, only that unless there is a justifiable claim of privilege, the record must be produced if relevant to the particular proceeding.

accusations, it can be damaging to the health-care institution. It is sometimes arguable that an incident report is not admissible in court on the grounds that it is privileged or is confidential information. For example, if a court concludes that the incident report was made for the purpose of advising counsel about impending litigation, it may be considered privileged and, therefore, not admissible in court. In many cases, however, the incident report will be admitted into court as evidence. In *Levinson v. Royal Victoria Hospital*,[35] the Quebec Court of Appeal ruled that a patient who was injured while being treated in hospital was entitled to receive a copy of the incident report that had been prepared.

Consequently, incident reports, as well as the forms that are the basis for the report, should always be prepared with the possibility of litigation in mind. The report should contain accurate, concise, factual information and should be prepared by the person, or persons, who actually witnessed the events. Information obtained from the patient or from other individuals should be clearly identified as such. Opinions and judgments should be avoided when preparing these reports.

Computerized Record-Keeping

Legal obligations for record-keeping now include computerized records. Some jurisdictions have specifically amended their health legislation to cover situations in which the record is created, maintained or stored by computer. In Ontario hospitals, "every order for treatment" must be in "writing and shall be dated and authenticated by the physician, dentist or midwife giving the order".[36] Section 1 of Reg. 965 defines "writing" as including "an entry in a computer" and "authenticate" as identifying "oneself as the author of a document or a record by personal signature or by any other means authorized by the board" of the hospital. The regulation further provides:

> 34.—(1) Where in this Regulation or under by-laws of a hospital a notation, report, record, order, entry, signature or transcription is required to be entered, prepared, made, written, kept or copied, the entering, preparing, making, writing, keeping or copying may be done by such electronic or optical means or combination thereof as may be authorized by the board.
>
> (2) The board shall ensure that the electronic or optical means referred to in subsection (1) is so designed and operated that the notation, report, record, order, entry, signature or transcription is secure from loss, tampering, interference or unauthorized use or access.

---

35 Unreported, November 18, 1982 (Que. C.A.).

36 R.R.O. 1990, Reg. 965, s. 24(1).

The advent of computerized records and their use in health care raises legal issues in relation to confidentiality of patient records. Information systems that allow on-line access to health-care records may compromise a patient's right to privacy. The benefit of a computerized information system is the quick and easy access to patient records; however, if access is gained by third parties, even treatment-givers, without the patient's consent and against the patient's wishes, a breach of patient privacy rights may result in legal liability. The Ontario Ministry of Health has released a discussion paper contemplating wide-ranging legislation which would serve as a regulatory guide for the creation of, and access to, electronic information systems containing patient records.[37]

Retention of Records

Once a health-care record has been created it will be retained for a period of time. The retained record may be a reference source for future treatment of the patient, may be used as a source of data for teaching or research, may form the basis of an overall programme for quality control within the institution, may be a source of measuring the standard of treatment and care afforded by the hospital or its staff, and may be a source of evidence in disciplinary or legal proceedings that arise out of the care and treatment of the patient.[38]

Most provinces have passed health legislation setting out mandatory periods for retaining health records. In British Columbia, documents contained in the medical record of a patient in a public hospital are classified into "primary documents", "secondary documents" and "transitory documents". A transitory document is defined as:

> A document such as a diet report, graphic chart, departmental check-list or any other document which appears to be of no further value once the patient has been discharged from hospital.[39]

Although legislation may suggest that certain parts of the patient's record can be disposed of once the patient has been discharged from hospital,

---

[37] Ontario Ministry of Health, *Principles for Proposed Legislation on Health Care Information, Access and Privacy* (December, 1991); also, see D. Robinson, "A Legal Examination of Computerized Health Information" (1993), Vol. 14, No. 2, *Health Law in Canada* 40.

[38] See L.E. Rozovsky and F.A. Rozovsky, *The Canadian Law of Patient Records* (Toronto: Butterworths, 1984), pp. 34-44, for a comprehensive summary of the purposes for which retained records may be employed.

[39] B.C. Reg. 289/73, s. 13(1).

the administrator of the institution should look closely at documents being disposed of in this way. In some cases, check-lists or graphic charts, though not retained, may be an important part of the record should the care and treatment of the patient subsequently be called into question. Some institutions have developed "cardex" systems or "patient-care cards", used to monitor and record day-to-day care of the patient. In some cases, most of the treatment is charted by this method and progress notes and other portions of the chart are reduced proportionately. The notations are sometimes made in pencil and erased and rewritten as the patient's condition and treatment plan changes. In some institutions these notations are not considered part of the "record" and are not retained in the manner and for the period required by the governing legislation.

This method of record-keeping may be perceived as a means of complying with the relevant legislation while reducing the burden on the institution of retaining voluminous records. Where the quality of care becomes the subject of scrutiny, however, the institution may be hindered in demonstrating a reasonable standard of care if the detailed records that tracked the care of the patient are no longer available. If the most detailed record is considered "transitory", and is disposed of, the institution may find itself in difficult circumstances one or two years later. Even though the relevant legislation may not impose an obligation on the institution to retain certain types of records, it may, nonetheless, be in the best interests of the institution to identify those records that closely track the care and treatment of the patient and to retain them for a reasonable period of time. Furthermore, the characterization of records as non-permanent because of pencilled notations or for other reasons, may constitute a breach of the institution's statutory obligation to retain records. Whether a record is one that should be retained should depend on the purpose and content of the record and not upon the label applied to it.

Confidentiality of Records

The Supreme Court of Canada has held that it is a patient's right to have records or information regarding his or her treatment and health condition kept confidential.[40]

> It is, perhaps, not easy to exaggerate the value attached by the community as a whole to the existence of a competently trained and honourable medical profession; and it is just as important that patients, in consulting a physician,

---

[40] *Halls v. Mitchell*, [1928] S.C.R. 125, [1928] 2 D.L.R. 97.

> shall feel that they may impart the facts touching their bodily health, without fear that their confidence may be abused to their disadvantage.[41]

Because of the nature of modern medical treatment, health professionals, out of necessity, will have to communicate confidential information about a patient's condition and background to other personnel responsible for the care of the patient. In some instances, the information communicated will not be noteworthy. The revelation by a health professional to a third party that a patient has a gall bladder disorder, has undergone routine minor surgery or is being treated for high blood pressure is unlikely to raise any complaint by the patient. On the other hand, there may be situations where the patient's condition is of a much more sensitive nature and the patient may be very disturbed at having it divulged unless this was necessary for the purpose of his or her treatment.[41a] An example would be a patient afflicted with AIDS. If this condition were communicated to family members or an employer without the permission of the patient, it could result in harm to the patient, and consequently, in legal proceedings.

A breach of confidentiality may constitute an invasion of privacy, which is actionable at law.[42] A right to privacy includes not only a right to territorial or spacial privacy but also a right to privacy of information. The Supreme Court of Canada has commented:

> situations abound where the reasonable expectations of the individual that the information shall remain confidential to the persons to whom, and restricted to the purposes for which it is divulged, must be protected.[43]

Privacy has been defined as "the right of the individual to determine for himself when, how, and to what extent he will release personal information about himself".[44]

---

41 *Ibid.*, at 138 (S.C.R.).

41a In *Peters-Brown v. Regina District Health Board* (1995), 26 C.C.L.T. (2d) 316 (Sask. Q.B.), a hospital was found liable for breach of contract and negligence. A confidential list of patients requiring body fluid precautions was posted in an inner room in the Emergency Department in full view of police officers, ambulance workers and correctional officers who had access to the room. The plaintiff, a correctional officer who had been a patient at the hospital approximately eight years before, overheard her co-workers discussing her name in connection with the list. The Court concluded that the hospital should have employed a more secure method for recording such information, and further, that the list should have been kept up to date. The judge held that it was foreseeable that the release of the confidential information would cause harm to the plaintiff. There was a damage award of $5,000.

42 *Roth v. Roth* (1991), 9 C.C.L.T. (2d) 141 (Ont. Gen. Div.).

43 *R. v. Dyment* (1988), 55 D.L.R. (4th) 503, at 515 (S.C.C.).

44 *R. v. Duarte* (1990), 53 C.C.C. (3d) 1 (S.C.C.).

In some instances, an obligation may arise for health-care professionals to divulge particulars of a patient's condition even though this may be unauthorized by the patient. For example, in the case of *Tarasoff v. The Regents of the University of California*,[45] a student informed his psychologist that he was going to kill another student. The psychologist did not report this to anyone. After the student carried out his threat, the family of the deceased student brought an action against the psychologist and alleged that he should have taken steps to warn their son or the proper authorities. The psychologist argued that to do so would have breached the confidential relationship he had established with his patient. Nonetheless, the Supreme Court of California held that, despite the confidential nature of his relationship with his patient, the psychologist was under an obligation to inform the police of the danger so that appropriate steps could be taken. In circumstances where a patient may do harm to himself or herself or to others, an institution and its caregivers may be compelled to breach the more general obligation of confidentiality.

Specific legislation in most provinces obliges health professionals to disclose certain health-care information. For example, provincial highway traffic legislation may require physicians to notify government licensing authorities of any patient who may be suffering from a condition that makes it dangerous for that patient to drive. Likewise, legislation requires the mandatory reporting of births, deaths, stillbirths and suspected child abuse. Public health legislation may require health-care practitioners to report conditions such as venereal disease, tuberculosis, polio and, more recently, AIDS, to local health authorities. In some instances, failure to comply with the legislation can result in prosecution or civil proceedings.

In *Spillane v. Wasserman*,[46] two physicians were found negligent and therefore liable for damages caused by a patient whom the physicians had failed to report as required by the provincial *Highway Traffic Act*. A bicyclist had died after being hit by a truck proceeding through a red light. The driver had been treated over a period of years for idiopathic temporal lobe epilepsy. Both physicians testified that they did not believe that the driver was a danger to himself or to others and that his seizures were controlled by medication they had prescribed. The trial judge held, however, that they should have been aware of the frequency and type of the seizures, that they had failed to adequately monitor the patient's blood serum levels and that they had failed to comply with their statutory duty to report.

The legislation of some provinces specifically states that health-care records are to remain confidential except in certain specified instances. For example, the Nova Scotia *Hospitals Act* provides:

---

[45] 551 P.2d 334 (Cal. 1976).

[46] (1992), 13 C.C.L.T. (2d) 267 (Ont. Gen. Div.).

> The records and particulars of a hospital concerning a person or patient in the hospital or a person or patient formerly in the hospital shall be confidential and shall not be made available to any person or agency except with the consent or authorization of the person or patient concerned.[47]

In Alberta, the legislation governing the operation of nursing homes in that province stipulates that, subject to limited exceptions,

> no person in possession of any diagnosis, record or information relating to a resident shall divulge, release or disclose any diagnosis, record or information relating to the resident to any person without the written consent of the resident.[48]

In Newfoundland, a person who publishes or discloses information obtained from hospital records may be subject to a summary conviction and a fine not exceeding $500 or, in default of payment, to 30 days' imprisonment.[49] The legislation of other provinces contains similar sanctions.[50]

Generally, health professionals and others working in the health-care field are well-advised not to discuss or to disclose health-care information about a patient unless the communication is made for the express purpose of treating the patient. Although it is difficult to put into practice, avoidance of discussions or "gossip" among health facility personnel about patients and their respective conditions is desirable. If the need arises to disclose health-care information about a particular patient outside the clinical context, consideration should be given to consulting legal counsel.

A patient who commences a malpractice proceeding, or who involves an institution in some other type of legal proceeding, may be considered to have waived the right to confidentiality. In *General Accident Assurance Co. of Canada v. Sunnybrook Hospital*,[51] an issue arose whether legal counsel for

---

47 R.S.N.S. 1989, c. 208, s. 71(1).

48 Alta. Reg. 232/85, s. 12(1) under the *Nursing Homes Act*, S.A. 1985, c. N-14.1.

49 *Hospitals Act, 1971*, S.N. 1971, No. 81, s. 36(6) [en. S.N. 1977, c. 61, s. 6].

50 The Rozovskys note in *The Canadian Law of Patient Records*, *supra* note 38, pp. 82-83, that the 1980 Royal Commission of Inquiry into the confidentiality of health records in Ontario recommended that a statutory right be created to allow patients to sue health-care personnel who "unjustifiably disclosed" health information to third parties. They note that no legislation has yet been adopted by any of the provinces, though a number of provinces have specific legislation permitting an individual to commence a civil action for damages against anyone who violates his or her privacy. They also suggest that there is caselaw to support an argument that a breach of confidentiality constitutes negligence, that it falls below the standard of reasonable treatment, and that it may give rise to civil liability if the disclosure leads to harm.

51 (1979), 23 O.R. (2d) 513 (H.C.J.).

a hospital's insurer was entitled to production of the medical records of a patient without the patient's consent. The Court held that the hospital was entitled to permit its insurers or their solicitors to inspect and to make copies of the health records in question for the purpose of dealing with, or defending, a civil action. The judge held that the *Public Hospitals Act* of Ontario did not prevent the hospital from using the patient's medical record to defend the claim or action.

> I think that by making such claim or commencing such action the patient has opened up for inspection, examination, consideration and review by all persons properly interested in the claim or action, all relevant aspects of the patient's confinement and treatment while in the hospital, and this should include the patient's medical record. . . .[52]

In *Hay v. University of Alberta Hospital*,[53] a patient sued following heart surgery. He alleged that he had been prematurely discharged and had suffered an infection which weakened his heart. In the course of the litigation, the defence sought access to the records of other physicians who had treated the plaintiff over the years for the purpose of establishing the patient's pre-existing health history. The patient refused to allow access to any records beyond those dealing with the surgery that was the subject of the legal action. The Court ruled, however, that the patient could not use confidentiality as a bar to open disclosure in the lawsuit. The commencement of an action for damages constituted a waiver of any right to confidentiality in relation to records relevant to the issue of damages in the action.

Access to Health Records

A time-consuming and important aspect of the operation of a health-care institution is the processing of requests for access to health-care records. Institutions commonly receive requests from numerous sources: patients, relatives, lawyers, physicians, police, insurers, government agencies, other health care institutions, the Coroner's office, the Children's Aid Society, provincial health insurance agencies, professional regulatory bodies, etc. In some cases, parties seeking access have provisions in their enabling statutes allowing access for restricted purposes. For example, professional regulatory bodies may be granted access for the purpose of investigating a complaint. A provincial Children's Aid Society may have limited access for the purpose of caring for a ward or for investigating an allegation that a

---

[52] *Ibid.*, at 516.

[53] [1990] 5 W.W.R. 78 (Alta. Q.B.).

child is in need of protection. Health-care facilities must have clear and well-understood policies to ensure that access is granted only in circumstances authorized by law. The provision of access to unauthorized parties may result in legal liability or embarrassment for the institution. For example, police may wish to review records or to receive information from records in the course of investigating a crime, but such access should not be granted unless authorized by a warrant obtained from a judge or a justice of the peace.

Most health facilities are prepared to provide a patient with copies of the patient's own health-care record, at the patient's expense, upon presentation of a written authorization signed by the patient. In fact, contrary to the belief of some patients, the record belongs not to the patient, but to the hospital. It has been held that hospital records "are 'the property of the hospital and shall be kept in the custody of the administrator'".[54] In a number of provinces, this principle is codified by legislation.

In Ontario, the practice of providing the patient with a copy of his or her own record upon presentation of a signed authorization is prescribed by statute. The governing legislation specifically prohibits the hospital from permitting "any person to remove, inspect or receive information from medical records" except in limited circumstances.[55] The regulation does provide that a hospital "may permit . . . a person who presents a written request signed by . . . the patient"[56] to obtain a copy of the record. It should be noted that in requesting the release of psychiatric records, a clear authorization by the patient will not necessarily lead to release of the record.[57]

Most public hospitals legislation contains provisions governing access to patient records. The general rule is that patients are entitled to have access if they supply a written consent or authorization to the institution. In some instances, however, the right to access is restricted. For example, the Alberta *Hospitals Act* provides that a hospital board, the Minister of Health or a physician may

> (a.1) with the written consent of a patient or his guardian or without that consent if the patient is not mentally competent and does not have a guardian, divulge any diagnosis record or information relating to the patient to any person, if in the opinion of the person making the disclosure it is in the best interests of the patient to disclose the information.[58]

---

54 *Re Mitchell and St. Michael's Hospital* (1980), 29 O.R. (2d) 185, at 189, 112 D.L.R. (3d) 360, 19 C.P.C. 113 (H.C.J.).

55 R.R.O. 1990, Reg. 965, s. 22(1).

56 *Ibid.*, s. 22(6)(c).

57 See Chapter 5, Mental Health Law.

58 *Hospitals Act*, R.S.A. 1980, c. H-11, s. 40(5) as amended by S.A. 1988, c.M-13.1, s.55.

The Alberta statute does not define what is meant by "in the best interests of the patient". In fact, such a qualification conflicts with the developing common law and with statutes in other jurisdictions in which "competent" patients are given unlimited access to their health records. Although some mental health legislation restricts access to psychiatric records in situations where disclosure is likely to result in harm to the patient or to others, in a time when access to records is commonplace and consistent with the principle of openness and reduced paternalism in health care, a provision that can deny access on a basis as broad and imprecise as "the best interests of the patient" is difficult to justify.

In many instances, despite the general rule of confidentiality, health-care records, or information contained in those records, will be released to third parties. Circumstances in which access to health-care records may be authorized without the authority of the patient include the following:

1. where a court or other tribunal orders health-care records to be produced;[59]
2. where information from the record and particulars of a patient are furnished to a municipal official for the purpose of establishing a patient's entitlement to insured medical services;[60]
3. where a professional governing body requires access to the health-care records for the purpose of investigating a complaint;[61]
4. where such access is in the public interest, a person engaged in health or medical research may obtain access to the record for teaching purposes or for scientific research;[62]
5. where the patient is a member or ex-member of the Canadian Armed Forces, the Deputy Minister of Veterans' Affairs or his representative may obtain access to the record.[63]

Generally, the cost of providing a copy of the record should be borne by the patient or the person authorized to receive a copy of the record. Any charge must be reasonable. A charge that is punitive or that exceeds the actual cost to the institution may be viewed as an unreasonable obstacle to access. In some jurisdictions, the issue of cost may be dealt with directly in the governing statute. In British Columbia, the *Hospital Act* regulations[64] specifically state that a hospital board's obligation to provide access to

---

59 Sask. Reg. 331/79, s. 16.

60 *Hospitals Act*, R.S.N.S. 1989, c. 208, s. 71(6)(c).

61 R.R.O. 1990, Reg. 965, s. 22(3).

62 *Hospitals Act*, R.S.N. 1990, c. H-9, s. 35(4).

63 N.B. Reg. 84-212, s. 19(3)(j).

64 B.C. Reg. 289/73.

patient x-rays is subject to the patient paying "the costs of making and delivering a copy" of the x-ray. The "costs" would appear to include not only the cost of copying the x-ray but also reasonable overhead costs associated with making a copy.

In *McInerney v. MacDonald*,[65] a physician was ordered to provide a patient with a copy of all medical documentation in his possession, including documentation he had received from other physicians who were acting as consultants. The physician had resisted releasing the consultants' reports in the belief that it would be unethical to provide documents that were the property of other physicians. This position was rejected. Rather, it was held that the patient had a right to access all medical documents that involved her care and treatment and that were relied upon by her physician in providing such care and treatment, subject to a physician's conclusion that release of some, or all, of the record would be harmful to the patient or to others. Furthermore, the physician's discretion in this regard is subject to the supervising jurisdiction of the courts. The patient, however, was required to pay a legitimate fee for the preparation and reproduction of the information by the physician. The access did not extend to information in the physician's file that was outside the doctor-patient relationship. *McInerney* is supportive of the practice of most hospitals and other health-care facilities — the payment by the patient or other party who wishes to obtain access to the patient record.

In *Metropolitan Life Insurance Co. v. Fernnette*,[66] the Supreme Court of Canada dealt with an application by a life insurance company to obtain access to patient records of a deceased insured. The hospital took the position that there was no valid authorization from the insured as the authorization relied upon by the insurer had not been signed within 90 days of the request. The Supreme Court held that any authorization to access depended upon the wording of the authorization and that the record should be released unless the authorization was in some way ambiguous. A health facility's internal policy cannot restrict the right of a patient to authorize the access of the record to the patient or to others. It was clear that the deceased patient had authorized access to his insurer for the purpose of the insurer evaluating any claim under a life insurance policy. To the extent that the insurer's request for access was relevant to a claim under the insurance policy and to its evaluation of the entitlement to indemnity, the access was reasonable. In the circumstances, a requirement by the institution that the authorization be signed 90 days in advance of the request was not reasonable. In this case, the deceased patient had signed the authorization several years before the insurer requested access. In the particular facts of the case, however, it was

---

[65] (1990), 66 D.L.R. (4th) 736 (S.C.C.).

[66] [1992] 1 S.C.R. 647, 89 D.L.R. (4th) 653.

understandable that there was no recent authorization and that the patient had intended the authorization to apply even if presented by the insurer years after its execution.

In *Re Meyers and Wellesley Hospital*,[67] a patient had lapsed into a coma as a result of complications arising from childbirth. The patient's husband wished to obtain a copy of her hospital record for the purpose of evaluating the care received by his wife. The hospital took the position that the statutory regulation governing disclosure of patient records permitted access only to a patient, personal representative or to a parent or guardian, but not to a spouse. It was held that the husband obviously spoke for the comatose patient and disclosure was ordered. In *Halliday v. McCulloch*,[68] the Court set out a procedure for production of hospital records where a patient claimed privilege for some of the records. It is not within the exclusive purview of a health facility to decide what records are privileged. There is a distinction between patient records and other types of records. Nonetheless, in *Duras v. Welland General Hospital*,[69] a hospital was ordered to produce the personnel files of physicians who had been sued where such records were considered relevant to the issues in the action.

Peer Review and Quality Assurance Privilege

In some Canadian jurisdictions, there may be a privilege preventing the disclosure of documents or reports prepared for the purpose of quality assurance or the ongoing assessment and review of health-care professionals by their peers. In *Smith v. Royal Columbian Hospital*,[70] the plaintiff in a malpractice action sought production of all documents relating to an investigation conducted by the Credentials Committee of the hospital. The hospital took the position that the documents were privileged and that the release of the documents would compromise the hospital's ability to obtain frank and honest opinions about the physician's competence from the physician's colleagues. It was argued that the hospital's inability to conduct such an investigation on a confidential basis would compromise patient care. In that case, the Court accepted the hospital's claim for privilege on the ground that the interest in protecting the confidentiality of the inquiry process outweighed the public interest in having the particular documents disclosed.

---

[67] (1986), 57 O.R. (2d) 54 (H.C.J.).

[68] (1986), 1 B.C.L.R. (2d) 194 (C.A.).

[69] (1985), 51 O.R. (2d) 284 (S.C.).

[70] (1981), 123 D.L.R. (3d) 723 (B.C.S.C.).

In effect, there is a legal basis to suggest that an assurance of confidentiality, where there is an inquiry into the competence of a health professional, will strengthen the quality assurance and peer review process. If individuals or institutions are concerned that comments or criticisms may be disclosed at some future date, they may be less than candid. A privilege for quality assurance and peer review information may encourage more widespread and active participation in the review process by doctors and other health professionals and may strengthen quality assurance programmes which, ultimately, is in the best interest of patients.[71]

Several provinces have enacted legislation protecting peer review documents from being produced in evidence. For example, the Alberta *Department of Health Act*,[72] provides:

> 9.(1) A witness in an action, whether a party to it or not,
> (a) is not liable to be asked and shall not be permitted to answer any question as to any proceedings before a committee to which this subsection applies, and
> (b) is not liable to be asked to produce, and shall not be permitted to produce, any report, statement, memorandum, recommendation, document or information of, or made by or made to, a committee to which this subsection applies and that was used in the course of or arose out of any study, investigation, research or program carried on by a hospital or any such committee for the purpose of medical education or improvement in medical or hospital care or practice.

Some of the committees to which the legislation applies includes hospital tissue committees, hospital research committees, medical staff committees established for the purpose of studying or evaluating medical practice in a hospital and medical committees designated by the Minister of Health.

Hospital administrators should recognize that even in jurisdictions where there is such legislation, it is likely to be narrowly interpreted, as courts have continually made the concept of complete disclosure a high priority. In Ontario, however, there has been a specific rejection by the Office of the Attorney General for the enactment of such a provision on the ground that it is not necessary for the continued provision of quality care and is unfair to patients.

---

71 See Kevin P. Feehan, "Legal Access to Patient Health Records/Protection of Quality Assurance Activities" (1991), Vol. 12, No. 1, *Health Law in Canada* 3, at 7.

72 R.S.A. 1980, c. A-21, s. 9.

CHAPTER 5

Mental Health Law

INTRODUCTION

Special legal considerations apply to the treatment of patients suffering from conditions that affect their mental health. These considerations apply even where the patient is not being treated in a facility designated for the treatment of psychiatric patients. All provinces have passed legislation that sets out a statutory scheme for the treatment of the mentally ill. This legislation relates to the management of health facilities in which psychiatric patients are being treated, the voluntary or involuntary admission of psychiatric patients, the competence of psychiatric patients to consent to treatment, the retention and disclosure of psychiatric records, and the availability of legal remedies or review procedures for psychiatric patients who may wish to question the nature or propriety of their psychiatric care and treatment. This legislation applies to hospitals and to other health facilities that treat patients suffering from mental illness and is not exclusive to treatment of patients in institutions dedicated to psychiatric care.

The treatment of psychiatric patients raises legal issues that ordinarily do not arise in the treatment of other illnesses. The fact that patients are often detained against their will places a high priority on the protection of individual rights within the treatment facility.[1] Consequently, administrators and health professionals who work in the mental health field must be as sensitive to legal issues as they are to medical issues. Decisions about treatment of psychiatric patients will often receive a high degree of scrutiny from tribunals or boards charged under the provincial legislation with the review of such decisions. The question whether treatment is authorized by law may eclipse any question about the quality of the treatment administered and whether or not it was effective.

1 See Chapter 11, The Charter of Rights and Freedoms.

Provincial Mental Health Facilities

All provinces have established health facilities dedicated to the care and treatment of patients suffering from mental illnesses. In some cases, the facilities are owned and operated by the province. In other cases, they are separate corporate entities, managed independently by a board of trustees, though funded and regulated by the provincial government.[2] The legislation that applies to psychiatric patients being treated in provincial psychiatric facilities may also apply, expressly or by implication, to the treatment of patients in other health facilities where the care consists of treatment of the mentally ill. In some jurisdictions government may designate certain health facilities to be psychiatric units or psychiatric hospitals for the purpose of mental health legislation. The legislation may authorize the transfer of psychiatric patients to other health facilities for treatment not available in the psychiatric facility.

In British Columbia, for example, the legislation identifies certain provincial mental health facilities that are administered by a director.[3] The government is empowered to designate "a public hospital or a part of it" as a "psychiatric unit" to be administered by "the officer in charge".[4] In Prince Edward Island, the administrator of a public hospital to which a psychiatric patient is transferred is given the "powers . . . of an administrator of a psychiatric facility in respect of the custody and control of the patient".[5] In Saskatchewan, the *Mental Health Services Act*[6] defines a psychiatric "facility" to include a "psychiatric ward" and provides for the appointment of an "officer in charge" who will be "responsible for the administration" of that province's mental health legislation in the facility.[7]

British Columbia's *Mental Health Act* imposes certain obligations on the director or officer in charge. These include:

- ensuring that patients are provided with professional service, care and treatment appropriate to their condition;
- signing consent to treatment forms on behalf of patients;
- ensuring that appropriate standards are established and maintained;

---

2 In *McNamara v. North Bay Psychiatric Hospital* (1994), 110 D.L.R. (4th) 129, the Ontario Court of Appeal ruled that a mental health facility that was not a separate corporate body was not suable in its own name in the absence of legislation making it liable to a suit. The correct procedure was to name Her Majesty the Queen in Right of the Province of Ontario.

3 *Mental Health Act*, R.S.B.C. 1979, c. 256, s. 1.

4 *Ibid.*

5 *Mental Health Act*, R.S.P.E.I. 1988, c. M-6, s. 20.

6 S.S. 1984-85-86, c. M-13.1.

7 *Ibid.*, s. 8.

- ensuring that orders and directives of the Minister of Health are observed and performed.[8]

In effect, where a hospital or other health facility has been designated as a psychiatric facility or unit for the purpose of the provincial legislation, this will impose upon the administration of the designated facility a number of legal obligations applicable to the care and treatment of patients diagnosed as suffering from mental illness.

Where mentally ill patients in a health facility not designated for management or treatment of psychiatric patients are treated in a manner inconsistent with the provincial mental health legislation, this may result in legal sanction. For example, a patient who is refusing treatment and, as a result, may constitute a risk to himself or herself or to others, cannot be detained against his or her will in an undesignated nursing home simply because he or she is a patient. To comply with the law, the correct practice would be to have that patient referred to a physician who is familiar with the governing mental health legislation, and who can carry out, in a formal way, whatever certification and transfer procedure may be appropriate.

Involuntary Detention and Confinement

It is a well-accepted common-law principle that a patient who is sufficiently competent to understand the nature and to appreciate the consequences of his or her health condition can decide either to accept or to reject treatment.[9] Even a patient who is suffering from a condition that is likely to be fatal if untreated is permitted to exercise his or her own free will about whether or not treatment will be administered.[10] A physician or nurse who disregards the patient's wish and proceeds to administer treatment commits a battery and may be the subject of civil and criminal proceedings.[11] Likewise, if a patient wishes to discharge himself or herself from the hospital, even against medical advice, the patient's decision must be respected. Preventing a competent patient from leaving a health-care facility voluntarily may constitute the intentional tort of false imprisonment.[12]

---

[8] *Supra* note 3, s. 8.

[9] *Marshall v. Curry*, [1933] 3 D.L.R. 260, at 266, 60 C.C.C. (N.S.) 136 (N.S.S.C.).

[10] *Malette v. Shulman* (1990), 72 O.R. (2d) 417 (C.A.); *Nancy B. v. Hôtel-Dieu de Québec*, [1992] R.J.Q. 361 (C.S.).

[11] *Mulloy v. Sang*, [1935] 1 W.W.R. 714 (Alta. C.A.).

[12] *Burke v. Efstathianos* (1961), 27 D.L.R. (2d) 518, 34 W.W.R. 337 (Man. C.A.); *Ketchum v. Hislop* (1984), 54 B.C.L.R. 327 (S.C.).

In the mental health setting, however, a patient's right to accept or refuse treatment may be subordinated to other concerns. Provincial mental health legislation, in restricted situations, allows health-care providers to detain patients for the purpose of examination and diagnosis, to admit and to confine patients against their will, and in some provinces, to forcibly administer treatment to patients who are determined to be in need of it.

The underlying rationale of these legislative measures is based upon a societal desire to protect individuals whose decision-making abilities about their own care and treatment have been undermined by the disease itself. The legislation assumes that in certain situations a patient, or would-be patient, is affected by illness in such a way that he or she is incapable of making rational or concrete choices about treatment. In some instances, a patient may be subject to involuntary detention and treatment, not because of a concern that the patient will harm himself or herself, but because of a risk of harm to others.[12a] In Canada, when an individual demonstrates that he or she could be a danger to himself or herself or to others, possible involuntary detention and treatment is considered.

In most jurisdictions, the test for involuntary detention and confinement is two-fold; it requires both that the patient suffers from mental illness and that the patient is a danger to himself or herself or to others. The language varies from jurisdiction to jurisdiction. In Alberta, for example, a physician must certify that the patient is "suffering from a mental disorder" and is "in a condition presenting or likely to present a danger to himself or others" before involuntary admission to a psychiatric facility can be considered.[13] In British Columbia, a physician is required to certify that the patient requires "medical treatment" and "care, supervision and control"

[12a] In *Starnaman v. Penetanguishene Mental Health Centre* (1995), 24 O.R. (3d) 701, 100 C.C.C. (3d) 190 (C.A.), a pedophile with a long criminal record and a lengthy history of aggressive sexual misconduct directed primarily at young females was serving a prison sentence for uttering a death threat. A few days prior to his release the names and addresses of children and single mothers in the Kingston and Toronto areas were discovered in his cell. One of the doctors at the Mental Health Centre requested an assessment. The assessment was conducted by a staff psychiatrist and a certificate of involuntary admission was signed. The certificate was renewed on several occasions. The patient appealed the involuntary admission, but the Ontario Court of Appeal held that at the date of the review hearing the doctor had clearly established the criteria for involuntary admission. The patient also argued that his involuntary admission was a violation of ss. 7 and 12 of the *Canadian Charter of Rights and Freedoms*. These arguments were dismissed by the Court.

[13] *Mental Health Act*, S.A. 1988, c. M-13.1, s. 2. In addition to this medical diagnosis, two physicians must also certify that the patient is unsuitable for admission to a psychiatric facility other than as a formal (*i.e.*, involuntary) patient (s. 8).

in a mental health facility "for his own protection or for the protection of others".[14]

In some jurisdictions, involuntary detention and confinement criteria may go beyond the two-fold requirement of a mental disorder and risk of harm to the patient or to others. In Manitoba, a physician may make an application for the involuntary psychiatric assessment of a person suffering from a mental disorder where that disorder is likely to result in "substantial mental or physical deterioration of the person" and the person refuses to undergo a voluntary psychiatric assessment,[15] even though the physician cannot certify that the patient presents a likelihood of "serious harm" to the patient or to others. In Ontario, there is a similar criterion that may result in involuntary confinement, even in the absence of risk of "danger" or serious "harm" to the patient or to others, but the criterion is restricted to situations where the patient may sustain "imminent and serious physical impairment". It would seem that the likelihood of serious or substantial *mental* impairment, when coupled with the other criteria set out in the legislation, is insufficient to authorize involuntary detention in Ontario.[16]

In addition to a medical determination that an individual should be the subject of involuntary detention and confinement, most provincial statutes permit police officers or courts to apprehend and convey individuals to psychiatric facilities for the purpose of an examination by a physician where certain criteria are met. In British Columbia, for example, where a person is acting in a manner likely to endanger his or her own safety or that of others, and is apparently suffering from a mental disorder, a police

---

[14] *Mental Health Act*, *supra* note 3, s. 20(3).

[15] *Mental Health Act*, R.S.M. 1987, c. M110, s. 8(1).

[16] The *Mental Health Act*, R.S.O. 1990, c. M.7, s. 15(1), contains one of the most detailed set of criteria for involuntary commitment:

> (1) Where a physician examines a person and has reasonable cause to believe that the person,
>
> (a) has threatened or attempted or is threatening or attempting to cause bodily harm to himself or herself;
>
> (b) has behaved or is behaving violently towards another person or has caused or is causing another person to fear bodily harm from him or her ; or
>
> (c) has shown or is showing a lack of competence to care for himself or herself,
>
> and if in addition the physician is of the opinion that the person is apparently suffering from mental disorder of a nature or quality that likely will result in,
>
> (d) serious bodily harm to the person;
>
> (e) serious bodily harm to another person; or
>
> (f) imminent and serious physical impairment of the person,
>
> the physician may make application in the prescribed form for a psychiatric assessment of the person.

officer or constable is empowered to take that person into custody and to immediately convey that person to a physician who will assess him or her.[17] Likewise, in British Columbia, an application can be made to a provincial court judge to issue a warrant for the apprehension of a person and the subsequent "conveyance" and "admission" of that person to a psychiatric facility upon evidence that there is "good reason to believe that a person is a mentally disordered person and dangerous to be at large".[18]

Involuntary detention and commitment have been attacked in the courts as contrary to the *Canadian Charter of Rights and Freedoms.*[19] In the case of *Thwaites v. Health Sciences Centre Psychiatric Facility,*[20] the Manitoba Court of Appeal struck down provisions in that province's *Mental Health Act* permitting the detention of an individual for examination when a medical practitioner was of the opinion that the person should be confined. The Court determined that compulsory committal in those circumstances violated the *Charter's* guarantee of freedom from arbitrary detention or imprisonment. A revision of the offending section in the *Mental Health Act* was upheld by the Court in *Bobbie v. Health Sciences Centre.*[21] The Court stated that compulsory detention, even where authorized by statute, will be considered arbitrary under the *Charter* if the statute does not narrowly define the persons to whom it may be properly invoked and does not prescribe the conditions under which the person may be detained. The Court concluded, however, that the more precise definition of "mental disorder" contained in the revised legislation, combined with the introduction of objective criteria that had to be met before an involuntary admission certificate was completed, satisfied the requirements of the *Charter.* Although the applicant in *Bobbie* was deprived of his liberty under the *Charter,* the deprivation was *in accordance with the principles of fundamental justice.* The Court commended the legislature for its skill in balancing the rights of the individual with the protection of society as a whole when redrafting the legislation. In effect, although the rights of an individual suffering from a mental illness can be abrogated in limited circumstances, the abrogation is unlawful where the abrogating process is unlawful.

The Manitoba Court of Appeal has held that there was a breach of the *Mental Diseases Act*[22] when a woman was taken mistakenly to a psychiatric hospital, admitted without authority and held for 15 days.[23] In British

---

17 *Mental Health Act, supra* note 3, s. 24(1).

18 *Ibid.,* s. 24(2).

19 *Constitution Act, 1982,* being Schedule B to the *Canada Act 1982,* (U.K.), 1982, c. 11; see Chapter 11, The Charter of Rights and Freedoms.

20 [1988] 3 W.W.R. 217 (Man. C.A.).

21 [1989] 2 W.W.R. 153 (Man Q.B.).

22 R.S.M. 1954, c. 161.

23 *Burke v. Efstathianos, supra* note 12.

Columbia, in a more recent case, the plaintiff successfully sued for false imprisonment when she was incarcerated unlawfully in a mental institution and forcibly injected with prescribed drugs.[24]

CONTINUATION OF INVOLUNTARY STATUS

Because of the infringement of individual rights, which is, by necessity, associated with involuntary status, the legislation of all provinces contains provisions requiring the further verification of a patient's condition before involuntary status can be continued. In a number of provinces, the initial determination of involuntary status is only for observation and assessment; some further determination must be made before the individual is formally admitted.

For example, in Ontario, an initial determination of involuntary status is made during a "psychiatric assessment", at which time the patient is detained for that purpose. A person cannot be held under an application for assessment in a psychiatric facility for longer than 72 hours.[25] Upon the conclusion of the initial examination and assessment, the physician must release the person or obtain consent from the person for admission on a voluntary basis. In circumstances where the physician concludes that the patient should be admitted against his or her will, and that the necessary criteria for involuntary admission have been fulfilled, the physician must complete a "certificate of involuntary admission".[26] The physician completing the certificate of involuntary admission must be a physician other than the physician who completed the original application for psychiatric assessment.[27] An involuntary patient cannot be detained in a psychiatric facility in Ontario for more than two weeks under a certificate of involuntary admission, but must be made the subject of a series of renewal certificates requiring further examination and assessment of the patient's condition at stipulated intervals.[28]

The mental health legislation of each province and territory contains similar legislative safeguards requiring that a patient be assessed at regular intervals to determine whether or not the patient's condition is such that it continues to meet the criteria set out in the legislation for involuntary status. If the criteria are not met, or, in the alternative, if further

---

[24] *Ketchum v. Hislop, supra* note 12.

[25] *Mental Health Act, supra* note 16, s. 15(5)(b).

[26] *Ibid.*, s. 20(1)(c).

[27] *Ibid.*, s. 20(2).

[28] *Ibid.*, s. 20(4).

examinations and assessments are not undertaken, the patient's involuntary status is terminated.

Generally, the authority to detain and to admit a patient involuntarily is reserved to a physician. No other health practitioner is permitted to involuntarily detain and admit a patient. The decision must be based upon the physician's own observations and knowledge of the patient's condition, though it is not necessary that the patient be in the physical presence of the physician for the certificate of involuntary admission to be issued.[29] It has been suggested that the issuing of a certificate of involuntary admission by a physician, based upon information received over the telephone and without a face-to-face examination of the patient, is insufficient, but the Court was not required to rule on that point.[30] Most likely, any determination would depend upon the particular facts of the case and whether the physician had good reason to believe that the patient was suffering from a mental illness that gave rise to a risk of harm to the patient or to others.

Involuntary Detention Under the Criminal Code

In addition to involuntary detention and confinement under provincial mental health legislation, there is also legislation under the federal *Criminal Code*[31] that can result in the involuntary detention and confinement in psychiatric facilities of persons charged with criminal offences. A person charged with a criminal offence can be admitted to a provincial psychiatric facility in two situations. First, a determination may be made in the course of criminal proceedings that the accused is "unfit to stand trial".[32] In those circumstances a court may order, usually based upon medical and psychiatric evidence, that the accused be detained until he or she either is acquitted or becomes fit to stand trial. Recent amendments to the *Criminal Code* set out a complex code of procedure to protect the rights of accused persons in this situation. The accused is likely to be detained in a psychiatric facility in the province where the criminal proceedings are taking place. In theory, the accused can be detained indefinitely until he or she has recovered sufficiently to be considered fit to stand trial, though the *Criminal*

---

[29] *Geiger v. Dua*, unreported, December 20, 1994 (Ont. Gen. Div.).

[30] See *Cascone v. Rodney* (1981), 131 D.L.R. (3d) 593 (Ont. H.C.J.).

[31] R.S.C. 1985, c. C-46.

[32] *Ibid.*, s. 672.11.

Code mandates a continuing series of reviews to establish whether the accused's condition has changed.[33]

Second, a person also may be detained at a provincial psychiatric facility because of a finding, following a criminal trial, that the accused is "not criminally responsible on account of mental disorder".[34] Similarly, the accused will be held at an approved psychiatric facility for an indefinite period, subject to a continuing process of reviews in which the provincial review board determines whether continued custody is required by law.

Under provisions of the *Criminal Code*, which were repealed in 1991, a prisoner who was serving a sentence in a federal penal institution might be determined to be "insane, mentally ill, mentally deficient or feeble-minded" and placed in a psychiatric facility, rather than a prison, for safe-keeping.[35] The amendments to the *Code* contain no such provision, though this does not mean that a prisoner requiring care and treatment in a psychiatric facility cannot be transferred involuntarily from a penal institution. In *Khan v. St. Thomas Psychiatric Hospital*,[36] a prisoner opposed her transfer to a provincial psychiatric facility on the ground that she was already detained, in segregation for the most part, in a maximum security penitentiary, and that it could not be said that enforced custody in a psychiatric facility would prevent harm to others. It was suggested that the involuntary admission, in that case, was for the underlying purpose of involuntary treatment. The Court of Appeal disagreed, concluding that "[s]ince it is caused by a mental illness, her dangerousness may be more easily anticipated, gauged and assessed in a psychiatric facility than in a prison setting".[37]

Generally, once an individual has been ordered into custody at a provincial psychiatric facility pursuant to the *Criminal Code*, the individual is considered, for practical purposes, to be an "involuntary patient" within the facility. Unlike patients who have been detained and confined under provincial mental health legislation, and who can be released by medical personnel, an accused who has been detained and confined under the *Criminal Code* cannot be discharged from the facility without the authority of a court or a provincial review board.

---

33 For a thorough discussion of the law in this area and the review procedures that have been established see H.S. Savage and C. McKague, *Mental Health Law in Canada* (Toronto: Butterworths, 1987), Chapter 2, LGWs: The Unwarranted Warrants. The amendments to the *Criminal Code* since the publication of this text respond to some of the authors' criticisms.

34 *Criminal Code*, *supra* note 31, s. 672.54.

35 *Ibid.*, s. 618.

36 (1992), 7 O.R. (3d) 303 (C.A.).

37 *Ibid.*, 310.

TREATMENT OF INVOLUNTARY PATIENTS

In some provinces, little or no distinction is made between involuntary admission and involuntary treatment. Authority and responsibility for the treatment of psychiatric patients may be delegated by statute to the administrator of the psychiatric facility. For example, in British Columbia, the involuntary admission of a patient by the completion of two admission certificates gives the director of the provincial mental health facility the authority to sign consent-to-treatment forms for a patient in order to ensure that

> each patient in a Provincial mental health facility is provided with professional service, care and treatment appropriate to his condition and appropriate to the function of the Provincial mental health facility . . . .[38]

Where involuntary patients are given treatment authorized by the director, the treatment is "deemed to be given with the consent" of the patient.[39] The British Columbia legislation further provides that a patient held in a provincial mental health facility under the *Criminal Code* provisions relating to accused persons who are unfit to stand trial or who are not guilty on account of a mental disorder "shall receive care and psychiatric treatment appropriate to his condition as authorized by the director".[40] In effect, the British Columbia legislation suggests that the determination of involuntary status gives the facility and its health-care givers a right to administer treatment to the patient without that patient's consent. Other provinces, notably, New Brunswick, Newfoundland and Saskatchewan, have passed provisions that seem to have a similar effect.[41]

In Ontario, an involuntary patient retains the right to refuse treatment unless a finding is made that the patient is "incapable with respect to a treatment". Where an involuntary patient is not mentally competent, consent may be given or refused by a substitute decision-maker who has been authorized to do so.[42] Alternatively, a psychiatric review board may authorize specified psychiatric and other related medical treatment for a mentally incompetent patient if it is satisfied that:

---

38 *Mental Health Act,* R.S.B.C. 1979, c. 256, s. 8(1)(a).

39 *Ibid.*, s. 25.2.

40 *Ibid.*, s. 25.1.

41 *Mental Health Act,* R.S.N.B. 1973, c. M-10, s. 8; *Mental Health Act,* R.S.N. 1990, c. M-9, s. 5(1); *Mental Health Services Act,* S.S. 1984-85-86, c. M-13.1, s. 25(2). This legislation may be subject to review, and possibly declared invalid, if challenged under the *Charter.*

42 *Health Care Consent Act, 1996,* S.O. 1996, c. 2, Sch. A, s. 20.

> (b) . . . the mental condition of the patient will [not] improve or is [not] likely to improve without the specified psychiatric treatment;
> (c) . . . the anticipated benefit from the specified psychiatric treatment and other related medical treatment outweighs the risk of harm to the patient; and
> (d) . . . the specified psychiatric treatment is the least restrictive and least intrusive treatment that meets the requirements of clauses (a), (b) and (c).[43]

In Nova Scotia, as in Ontario, the legislation stipulates that an involuntary patient cannot be treated, if competent, without his or her consent. Where the patient is incompetent, there is provision for a relative or the public trustee to exercise a substitute consent.[44]

In Manitoba, every patient of a psychiatric facility has the right to refuse consent to psychiatric or other medical treatment except in urgent situations where immediate treatment is necessary or where a review board has authorized treatment against the expressed desire of the patient. That province's legislation requires that a physician, as soon as reasonably possible after admission, determine whether the patient is mentally competent to consent to psychiatric or medical treatment by considering

> (a) whether the patient understands
> (i) the condition for which the treatment or course of treatment is proposed,
> (ii) the nature and purpose of the treatment or course of treatment,
> (iii) the risks and benefits involved in undergoing the treatment or course of treatment, and
> (iv) the risks and benefits involved in not undergoing the treatment or course of treatment; and
> (b) whether the patient's ability to make treatment decisions is affected by his or her condition.[45]

If a determination is made by the health-care provider that the patient is competent to consent to or refuse treatment, treatment cannot be authorized without that patient's consent even though the refusal to accept treatment may be considered physically or mentally harmful to the patient.

It is interesting to note that in Alberta[46] there is a specific provision in the legislation to overturn the decision of the *competent* psychiatric patient. The attending physician may apply to a review panel to authorize the

---

43 *Mental Health Act,* R.S.O. 1990, c. M.7, s. 49(5).

44 *Hospitals Act,* R.S.N.S. 1989, c. 208, s. 54(2).

45 *Mental Health Act,* R.S.M. 1987, c. M110, s. 24(3).

46 *Mental Health Act,* S.A. 1988, c. M-13.1, s. 29.

giving of specified psychiatric treatment and other related medical treatment to an involuntary, but competent, patient where consent has been refused. The legislation empowers the review panel to "make an order that . . . treatment may be administered" if the proposed treatment would be in the "best interest" of the patient having regard to certain criteria set out in the legislation. The criteria relate to the likelihood of the patient improving with treatment, the weighing of risks involved in treatment and whether the treatment being proposed is the least intrusive treatment available in the circumstances.[47] The only mention made of the principle of the competent patient's right, under law, to refuse treatment is a provision which gives authority to the competent patient to object to psychosurgery.[48] The British Columbia, New Brunswick, Newfoundland, Saskatchewan and Alberta mental health statutes appear to treat psychiatric patients differently from other patients in that they purport to override the decision of a competent patient to reject treatment. In doing so, they may offend the equality rights set out in the *Charter*.

By contrast, the Ontario legislation, which also requires a determination of competency to be made in relation to a consent to treatment, restricts the role of the Consent and Capacity Board to the determination of capacity or incapacity, but does not give the board the authority to make decisions on behalf of incapable persons. In the latter case the decision must be made by a guardian of the person or an attorney for personal care who is authorized under the *Substitute Decisions Act, 1992* and who must act in a manner consistent with the wishes expressed by the patient, when competent, or if the patient's wishes are unknown, in the best interest of the patient.[49] In other words, a competent psychiatric patient, like any other patient, can refuse treatment, even if the health-care providers feel the refusal will have harmful consequences. The court has held that *parens patriae* jurisdiction cannot be invoked to abrogate the *Charter* rights of competent mentally ill patients, nor can it be invoked to authorize the medical treatment of an incompetent person who, while competent, had given instructions refusing to consent to the proposed treatment.[50] In *Re Howlett and Karunaratne*,[51] the Court held that the provisions of the Ontario *Mental Health Act*, which permitted the involuntary treatment of a mentally *incompetent* patient, did not infringe the patient's rights under the *Charter*.

---

47 *Ibid.*

48 *Ibid.*, s. 29(5).

49 *Substitute Decisions Act, 1992*, S.O. 1992, c. 30, s. 66, amended S.O. 1996, c. 2.

50 *Fleming v. Reid* (1991), 4 O.R. (3d) 74 (C.A.).

51 (1988), 64 O.R. (2d) 418 (Dist. Ct.).

Voluntary Status

A patient suffering from a mental illness may be admitted voluntarily to a psychiatric facility for the purpose of treatment, just as a patient may be admitted for treatment of any other type of illness, and he or she is no different from any other patient. The patient has an absolute right to refuse treatment and has an absolute right to discharge himself or herself, even against medical advice. The individual must be provided with sufficient information about any proposed treatment to enable him or her to give an informed consent.

In most jurisdictions, there is provision for voluntary patients to be considered for involuntary status. If a situation arises wherein a voluntary patient's conduct raises concern about whether or not the patient's condition meets the criteria for involuntary status, steps must be taken to have the patient examined in accordance with the procedures stipulated by the legislation before the patient can be treated as other than a voluntary patient.

In some jurisdictions special provisions in the governing legislation highlight the general obligation of administrators and health-care providers to safeguard the distinction between voluntary and involuntary patients. In British Columbia, a nurse in charge of a ward in a mental health facility must ensure that a voluntary patient can "communicate without delay to the director . . . any desire to leave".[52] The Manitoba legislation stipulates that a voluntary patient may leave the psychiatric facility at any time or refuse any treatment.[53] In the Yukon, the legislation states that a voluntary patient must be discharged "forthwith" if the patient so requests[54] and that an involuntary patient, whose status has been changed from involuntary to voluntary, must be "promptly informed" of his or her right to leave the facility.[55]

Competency

The question of competency can arise in a variety of settings. All provinces have passed legislation[56] providing for the appointment by the court of a

---

52 *Mental Health Act, supra* note 38, s. 19(2).

53 *Mental Health Act, supra,* note 45, s. 7(4).

54 *Mental Health Act,* S.Y. 1989-90, c. 28, s. 4(2).

55 *Ibid.*, s. 17(3).

56 Alberta: *Dependent Adults Act,* R.S.A. 1980, c. D-32; British Columbia: *Patients Property Act,* R.S.B.C. 1979, c. 313; Manitoba: *Mental Health Act, supra* note 45,

committee that is charged with the management of the affairs of a person who is found to be mentally incompetent.[57] Generally, these statutes give the committee control over the individual's estate. Historically, this type of legislation was intended to deal with financial aspects of the individual's estate, but its use has been broadened to include other areas. In the treatment of the mentally ill there is, sometimes, a presumption that mental illness can be equated with incompetence. This is not the case; a patient cannot be considered incompetent to make decisions about treatment, finances, personal hygiene or anything else simply because that patient suffers from a mental illness.

In Prince Edward Island, competency legislation has been used to allow a substitute consent to be given by the committee for treatment of the patient. In the 1983 case of *Re Casford*,[58] the Supreme Court of Prince Edward Island granted a provisional guardianship order to move a woman into an institutional setting where care and treatment could be administered. Her illness rendered her not only physically incapable of taking care of herself but also so "unreasonable and unco-operative" that it was extremely difficult for anyone to provide the care she required. The *Mental Health Act*[59] defined "a person in need of protection" as a person "who is suffering from such a disorder of the mind" that he or she requires supervision and control. Without explicitly declaring Mrs. Casford to be incompetent, the Court used the provisions of the Act to appoint a guardian and to provide her with personal care.

In Alberta, Saskatchewan and Ontario, legislation has been passed specifically for the purpose of authorizing substitute decisions for treatment. The Alberta *Dependent Adults Act* notes that:

---

ss. 56-79; New Brunswick: *Infirm Persons Act*, R.S.N.B. 1973, c. I-8; Newfoundland: *Mentally Disabled Persons' Estates Act*, R.S.N. 1990, c. M-10; Nova Scotia: *Incompetent Persons Act*, R.S.N.S. 1989, c. 218; Ontario: *Mental Incompetency Act*, R.S.O. 1990, c. M.9; Prince Edward Island: *Mental Health Act*, R.S.P.E.I. 1988, c. M-6, ss. 30-45; Saskatchewan: *Mentally Disordered Persons Act*, R.S.S. 1978, c. M-14; *Dependent Adults Act*, S.S. 1989-90, c. D-25.1.

See also Gerald B. Robertson, *Mental Disability and the Law in Canada*, 2nd ed. (Toronto: Carswell, 1994), Part I: Property and Personal Guardianship.

[57] This concept is best known as guardianship of the person, but some provinces use the term "committee" (pronounced com-mit-tée) of the person. Originally created in English law to deal with the management of the mentally incompetent individual's property, guardianship of the person has been criticized for its lack of clarity of basic issues, such as authority of the guardian.

[58] (1983), 43 Nfld. & P.E.I.R. 240, 127 A.P.R. 240 (P.E.I. S.C.).

[59] R.S.P.E.I. 1974, c. M-9, s. 2(n) [now R.S.P.E.I. 1988, c. M-6, s. 1(m)]: "person in need of guardianship".

> When the Court is satisfied that a person named in an application for an order appointing a guardian is
> (a) an adult, and
> (b) repeatedly or continuously unable
> (i) to care for himself, and
> (ii) to make reasonable judgments in respect of matters relating to his person
> the Court may make an order appointing a guardian.[60]

The Alberta legislation represents a departure from traditional mental incompetency statutes that authorize substitute decision-making. It is justifiably discriminating in its direction to grant limited guardianship permitting dependent adults to exercise independent judgment to the extent that they are capable of managing their own affairs. Compared to traditional incompetency legislation, this would appear to be an improved model for substitute decision-making.

A question of competency may arise in circumstances where there is concern about a person's capacity to handle his or her financial affairs, to enter into contracts, to make a will, to testify in court, to vote, to marry, to be a witness in a court proceeding or to instruct counsel. In those instances, courts may be compelled to make determinations about competency, often with the assistance of health-care personnel.

In *Clark v. Clark*,[61] Justin Clark, a resident at a government facility for the disabled, expressed a wish to participate in a residential placement programme, despite severe personal limitations resulting from cerebral palsy. His father, who opposed Justin's wish, applied to the Court to have him declared mentally incompetent. The judge, however, determined that Justin was mentally competent to make decisions about his own lifestyle and issued a declaratory order to that effect.

Review Procedures

In all Canadian jurisdictions, decisions about admission and treatment are subject to review by a board or tribunal appointed for that purpose. In some provinces, a patient who wishes to contest an involuntary admission may apply to the court. The Nova Scotia *Hospitals Act* provides:

> [A] person in a facility or the guardian of that person or his spouse or next of kin or the Public Trustee may, on five clear days notice in writing to the

60 *Supra* note 56, s. 6 [am. S.A. 1985, c. 21, s. 7]; also see *Dependent Adults Act, supra* note 56, and *Substitute Decisions Act, 1992*, S.O. 1992, c. 30, as amended.

61 (1982), 40 O.R. (2d) 383, 4 C.H.R.R. D/1187, 3 C.R.R. 342 (Co. Ct.).

> administrator of the facility, apply to the judge of the county court for the district in which the facility is situate for the discharge of the person on the ground that he is not suffering from a psychiatric disorder or is not a danger to his own safety or the safety of others.[62]

Upon such an application, the judge is required to review the evidence and records. The judge may require that the patient be examined by one or more medical practitioners. If the judge, upon considering the evidence, determines that the person should not be detained in the facility, the judge may grant a discharge.[63] Similarly, in British Columbia, involuntary patients may apply to the court for discharge.[64] In the other provinces, a review board is appointed to consider such an application.

The nature of the review will depend upon the particular jurisdiction. In New Brunswick and Prince Edward Island, review boards are required only to "conduct an investigation", but are not required to hold a hearing.[65] In Ontario, an application to the review board regarding an involuntary admission or a determination of incompetency will require a "hearing" at which the patient will be entitled to be represented by counsel, examine and cross-examine witnesses, have full access to the health-care records and exercise other procedural rights.[66] Furthermore, in some provinces where review boards are appointed, a party to proceedings before the review board is entitled to appeal the decision of the review board to the courts. The legislation in both New Brunswick and Prince Edward Island is silent on this point, but further redress by way of judicial review would be possible in either jurisdiction.

Patients' Rights

There is, by necessity, in the field of mental health law, a constant tug-of-war between the concepts of individual rights and involuntary care and treatment. Personal freedom favours autonomy of the person and the right of the individual to make choices about treatment that are respected by others. Conversely, the intrusion of the state through legislation mandating care and treatment that contravenes the expressed desire of

---

62 *Supra* note 44, s. 47(1).

63 *Ibid.*, s. 47(2).

64 R.S.B.C. 1979, c. 256, s. 27.

65 See H.S. Harvey and C. McKague, *Mental Health Law in Canada* (Toronto: Butterworths, 1987).

66 *Statutory Powers Procedure Act*, R.S.O. 1990, c. S.22.

the patient may be justified on the ground that the state has an interest in preventing individuals from harming themselves and others, particularly in situations where the individual's expressed desires may be a result of illness and not the result of rational processes.

This government intrusion has been based historically on two seemingly contradictory principles: the *parens patriae* power and the police power. The term *parens patriae* refers to society's interest in protecting the vulnerable. The concept has been used by government to support legislation mandating involuntary detention and admission. The police power has been used to uphold the traditional state interest in public order and welfare. Its primary goals have been to protect property and the physical safety of citizens, not the individual interests of the mentally disordered.

Treatment of psychiatric patients in the context of these two concepts can lead to difficult decisions for health-care providers. Statutory authority, which allows, in specific situations, compulsory detention, restraint and treatment, does not permit the unrestricted infringement of personal freedom. Several provincial statutes contain specific provisions that highlight the contradiction between personal freedom and compulsory treatment. In practice, however, the distinction will be one of judgment on the part of the individual caregiver and no exhaustive list of possible situations can be prepared.

Caregivers have an obligation to ensure that patients who are being detained involuntarily are not permitted to escape or be released without legal authority. Failure to fulfil that obligation may result in legal sanction. In British Columbia, a person commits an offence who

> (a) assists a patient to leave or to attempt to leave a Provincial mental health facility without proper authority;
> (b) does or omits to do an act to assist a patient in leaving or attempting to leave a Provincial mental health facility without proper authority; or
> (c) incites or counsels a patient to leave a Provincial mental health facility without proper authority.[67]

The fact that a patient is involuntarily detained, however, does not authorize care or treatment that is discriminatory or unfair. Involuntary patients must be treated like any other patient to the extent that their conditions and the security of the institution allow. In British Columbia, a person employed in a provincial mental health facility who "ill-treats, assaults or wilfully neglects a patient" is guilty of an offence punishable by fine or incarceration.[68] In Newfoundland, the *Mental Health Act* provides:

---

[67] *Mental Health Act, supra* note 64, s. 17(1).

[68] *Ibid*, s. 17(2).

> [i]f the administrator, medical director or an officer or other person employed in a treatment facility maltreats, abuses or neglects any patient, or obstructs patients from communication with the review board, such administrator, medical director, officer or other person is guilty of an offence and is liable on summary conviction to a penalty not exceeding $500, or in default, to imprisonment for a period not exceeding 6 months.[69]

The fact that a patient is a psychiatric patient does not allow the obstruction, censoring or interception of the patient's mail or other forms of communication. In Alberta, communication written by or to a patient in a facility shall not be "opened, examined or withheld", and "its delivery shall not be obstructed or delayed in any way by the board or a member of the staff of a facility".[70] It has been held, however, that a policy at a psychiatric facility requiring that mail be opened under the observation of staff is not in violation of a psychiatric patient's rights under the *Charter*.[71] The Alberta legislation provides that a patient may receive visitors during hours fixed by the board, unless a physician considers that a visitor would be "detrimental to the patient's health".[72] This provision is too broad, and of doubtful legal validity, if one accepts that a *competent* psychiatric patient should be able to refuse or accept treatment (and by extension, choose to refuse or accept visitors) even though it may be harmful to the patient's health. A lawyer acting for a patient in Alberta "may visit the patient at any time".[73]

In Nova Scotia, there are specific provisions relating to incoming and outgoing mail and telephone calls. Outgoing mail cannot be opened, examined, withheld, obstructed or delayed.[74] The administrator of a facility, however, may insist on being present at the opening of the mail and may remove "contents detrimental to the addressee or others, but not the correspondence itself". Such withholding can occur only where it is the opinion of a psychiatrist that failure to withhold the contents would be "detrimental" to the patient. Patients are permitted to make and to receive unmonitored telephone calls at reasonable times unless it is the opinion of a psychiatrist that it would be "detrimental" to the patient to permit such calls.[75] The legislation stipulates that patients shall be permitted to receive visitors at reasonable times and under reasonable circumstances.[76]

---

69 R.S.N. 1990, c. M-9, s. 20.

70 *Mental Health Act*, S.A. 1988, c. M-13.1, s. 15.

71 *Everingham v. Ontario* (1993), 100 D.L.R. (4th) 199 (Gen. Div.).

72 *Supra* note 70, s. 16(1).

73 *Ibid.*, s. 16(2).

74 *Hospitals Act*, R.S.N.S. 1989, c. 208, s. 70(1).

75 *Ibid*, s. 70(5).

76 *Ibid*, s. 70(6).

Psychiatric facilities in Nova Scotia are required to post copies of the legislation relating to patients' rights "in a place within the hospital where they can be seen".[77] The province's facilities are required to provide advice, in written form, regarding patients' rights in relation to correspondence, telephone calls, visiting rights, "the right to counsel" and the right to have a "file reviewed by a review board or a court".[78]

In Quebec, a regulation under the *Mental Patients Protection Act*[79] requires that an involuntary patient must be given a form entitled "Rights and Recourses of Persons Admitted for Close Treatment". This form sets out in detail the legal rights and remedies available to a patient who wishes to contest his or her involuntary detention. In Saskatchewan, the *Mental Health Services Act* provides that an involuntary patient:

> (a) shall be informed promptly of the reasons for his apprehension or detention, as the case may be; and
> (b) is entitled on his own request to receive a copy of the certificate, warrant or order pursuant to which he has been apprehended or is detained, as the case may be, as soon as is reasonably practicable.[80]

The Saskatchewan legislation does not require, however, that the patient be provided with a *written* explanation of the rights and remedies available to contest his or her involuntary status.

In the Yukon, the mental health legislation stipulates that no person shall be deprived of any right or privilege by reason of having received mental health services or by reason of being named in any form or certificate under the statute.[81] The Act lists a number of rights of mental health patients, including the right to receive communications in the language with which the patient is most familiar, unrestricted access to visitors, legal representation, telephones and the mails, the right to wear clothing or apparel of the patient's choice unless doing so would constitute a danger or offend others, and the right to be informed about the legal process that has led to the patient's involuntary detention and the patient's right to challenge the involuntary status.[82]

The legislation of a particular province or territory may not address the subject of patient rights in the detail that one finds in some statutes. In any jurisdiction, however, a denial or restriction of basic rights simply

---

77 *Ibid*, s. 70(7).

78 *Ibid*, s. 70(8).

79 *Regulation respecting the application of s. 27 of The Mental Patients Protection Act*, R.R.Q. 1977, c. P-41, r. 1.

80 S.S. 1984-85-86, c. M-13.1, s. 16(1).

81 *Mental Health Act*, S.Y. 1989-90, c. 28, s. 40(1).

82 *Ibid.*, ss. 40(1.2)-41.

because a patient suffers from a psychiatric illness, and not for a clinical or therapeutic reason authorized by law, may amount to a denial of the patient's common-law rights or the patient's rights under the *Charter*.

Patients' Advocates

A number of jurisdictions have enacted legislation authorizing the representation of psychiatric patients by the patient advocate. In Alberta, the patient advocate is appointed by the provincial cabinet and is charged with investigating complaints from, or relating to, formal patients.[83] The patient advocate is authorized to engage the services of lawyers, psychiatrists or other persons having special knowledge[84] and is required to prepare an annual report summarizing his or her activities in the year. Where the patient advocate investigates a complaint, he or she is required to:

- notify the board of the facility in which the formal patient is detained of the nature of the complaint,
- notify the formal patient in writing that the complaint has been received and is under investigation,
- notify the other person named in the complaint of the investigation,
- contact the formal patient and conduct any necessary investigation.[85]

The patient advocate may request, in writing, a copy of a policy or directive of the facility, and medical records or documents relating to the patient who is the subject of the complaint. The board of the facility must "within a reasonable time after [receiving] the request, provide access to the materials requested".[86]

In New Brunswick, the government "may designate persons, services or organizations as patient advocate services".[87] It is the duty of patient advocate services to offer advice and assistance to persons who are detained in a psychiatric facility or who have been certified as involuntary patients.[88] The administrator of a psychiatric facility must ensure that the appropriate patient advocate service is given notice of such persons and of any other orders made which relate to the continued detainment of the patient in a

---

[83] *Mental Health Act*, S.A. 1988, c. M-13.1, s. 45.

[84] *Ibid.*, s. 46(2).

[85] Alta. Reg. 310/89, s. 3.

[86] *Ibid.*, s. 5(5).

[87] *Mental Health Act*, R.S.N.B. 1973, c. M-10, s. 7.6(1).

[88] *Ibid.*, s. 7.6(2).

psychiatric facility or the authorization of medical or psychiatric treatment without the consent of an involuntary patient.[89] A patient advocate has the right at all reasonable times to meet with the patient, to attend hearings and to have access to books, records and other documents relating to the patient who is the subject of advocacy.

Psychiatric Records

Access to psychiatric records in Canada may differ from access to non-psychiatric records. Generally, it is the practice for a health-care facility to release records to a patient upon receipt of an authorization signed by the patient. In the case of psychiatric records, however, the psychiatric facility may have some concern that release of records to the patient may be harmful to the patient or to others. In some instances, there may be justification for concluding that a psychiatric patient will misinterpret or distort the contents of the psychiatric record in a way that may be harmful to the patient's own health. Release of the record may divulge to the patient the names of individuals (*i.e.*, family or friends) who have been in communication with the caregivers and who may have been responsible for the patient's admission to the psychiatric facility in the first place. There may be a legitimate fear that divulging the names and participation of those individuals may put them at risk. In those circumstances, psychiatric facilities must consider carefully the advisability of releasing records to a patient simply on the basis of a signed authorization.

At the same time, there must be a legitimate concern that release of the record may lead to harm to the patient or to others before a psychiatric patient's access is restricted. If access is refused simply because the request has been made by a psychiatric patient, a court will likely interpret the refusal as discriminatory and unacceptable. In addition, the facility will have to consider carefully whether release of some part of the record may be permissible, as opposed to a complete refusal.

Several jurisdictions in Canada have provisions in their mental health legislation that restrict access to psychiatric records. In Manitoba, for example, the *Mental Health Act* contains a statutory mechanism for the review of requests for release of psychiatric records. The legislation provides that no person shall "disclose, transmit or examine a clinical record" unless certain conditions set out in the legislation are met. A review board may choose not to release the clinical record to a psychiatric patient in circumstances where disclosure of the record is likely to result in harm to

---

[89] *Ibid.*, s. 7.6(3).

the treatment or recovery of the patient, or is likely to result in serious physical or serious emotional harm to another person.[90]

In Quebec, the restricted access provisions in the *Health Services and Social Services Act*[91] refer generally to the "user's record" and do not appear to be exclusive to the patient's psychiatric record. In that province, the access to some or all of the record may be denied if it is likely to be "seriously prejudicial to the user's health".[92] In the absence of an agreement in writing from a third person who is mentioned in the user's chart, a "user" is not entitled to information that would identify that third person or to any information that that third person may have communicated.[93] Ontario[94] and Manitoba[95] legislation also provides a right of correction to patients who have examined their psychiatric records and found the contents to be erroneous.

Notwithstanding the absence of specific legislation in some jurisdictions governing access to psychiatric records, administrators of facilities that treat psychiatric patients are well advised to consider whether a policy of restricted access, based upon the statutory provisions of Ontario and Manitoba, would be appropriate. The Supreme Court of Canada has indicated that patient records should not be released where to do so would be prejudicial to the patient or to others, subject to intervention by a court.[96] The release of records that would allow a patient to identify third parties, putting the third parties at risk, may have civil liability consequences for an institution lacking any policy for avoiding such a risk.

Relevant Legislation

Alberta

Mental Health Act, S.A. 1988, c. M-13.1

British Columbia

Mental Health Act, R.S.B.C. 1979, c. 256

---

90 *Mental Health Act*, R.S.M. 1987, c. M110, s. 26.9(2).

91 R.S.Q. 1977, c. S-4.2.

92 *Ibid.*, s. 17.

93 *Ibid.*, s. 18.

94 *Mental Health Act*, R.S.O. 1990, c. M.7, s. 36(13).

95 *Mental Health Act*, *supra* note 90, s. 26.9(9).

96 *McInerney v. MacDonald* (1992), 93 D.L.R. (4th) 415 (S.C.C.).

Manitoba

Mental Health Act, R.S.M. 1987, c. M110

New Brunswick

Mental Health Act, R.S.N.B. 1973, c. M-10

Newfoundland

Mental Health Act, R.S.N. 1990, c. M-9

Northwest Territories

Mental Health Act, R.S.N.W.T. 1988, c. M-10

Nova Scotia

Hospitals Act, R.S.N.S. 1989, c. 208. (*Note:* Nova Scotia does not have a separate statute dealing with mental health).

Ontario

Mental Health Act, R.S.O. 1990, c. M.7
Mental Hospitals Act, R.S.O. 1990, c. M.8

Prince Edward Island

Mental Health Act, R.S.P.E.I. 1988, c. M-6

Quebec

Mental Patients Protection Act, R.S.Q. 1977, c. P-41

SASKATCHEWAN

Mental Health Services Act, S.S. 1984-85-86, c. M-13.1

YUKON

Mental Health Act, S.Y. 1989-90, c. 28

CHAPTER 6

Consent to Treatment

Introduction

It has been long established that a patient must give a consent to treatment, and more recently, an informed consent. These principles are enshrined in the common law. In addition to the common law, a number of provinces have passed, or are in the process of passing, legislation that sets out very clear, and in some cases, strict requirements for obtaining consent to health care.[1]

An important role for the health administrator in modern health facilities is to ensure that health professionals comply with the law in this area. A signed consent may be of no legal consequence where material risks have not been explained to the patient, where the signature is the result of duress or undue influence or where the consent form is in a language the patient does not understand. Health administrators must ensure that caregivers in their facilities recognize the legal obligations owed to patients. A failure by health-care providers to comply with the law of consent can result in legal liability for the institution.

Consent to Physical Contact

As a general principle, no person may touch another person without the consent of the person being touched.[2] In some instances, consent can be

---

1 *Health Care (Consent) and Care Facility (Admission) Act*, S.B.C. 1993, c. 48 (passed, but not proclaimed as of January, 1996; expected proclamation spring, 1996); *Health Care Directives Act*, S.M. 1992, c. 33; *Health Care Consent Act, 1996*, S.O. 1996, c. 2; *Dependent Adults Act*, S.S. 1989-90, c. D-25.1; *Civil Code*, L.Q., c. 64, 1991, art. 1.10-25; *Dependent Adults Act*, R.S.A. 1980, c. D-32.

2 *Reibl v. Hughes*, [1980] 2 S.C.R. 880, 114 D.L.R. (3d) 1, 33 N.R. 361, 14 C.C.L.T. 1.

inferred. There may be no communication when a caregiver assists a patient in moving from a wheelchair to a bed, but the conduct of the patient in reaching out his or her arm for assistance is clear evidence that the patient consents to being touched for the purpose of that assistance. Similarly, where a patient holds out his or her arm to receive an injection or disrobes for a physical examination, there is an implied consent by the patient which makes it reasonable for the caregiver, even in the absence of verbal communication, to conclude that consent has been given.

There are, however, exceptions to the general principle. A police officer engaged in an arrest may be permitted to apprehend a suspect by physical coercion. Reasonable steps taken by health-care providers to restrain a patient who is an imminent danger to himself or herself or to others would not result in legal liability. A nurse who uses reasonable force for protection from a patient who is attempting to harm her or him is acting in self-defence and such conduct is not actionable. A physician who engages in cardiopulmonary resuscitation of a patient who is unconscious, and unable to provide any consent, oral or implied, does so in an emergency in which the patient's consent, assuming there is no evidence to the contrary, is inferred.

Battery

A caregiver who has physical contact with a patient, even if that physical contact is no more than a slight or superficial touching of the patient, commits a battery if there is no consent.[3] Hence, a health professional who pushes a patient into an examining room, who force-feeds an unwilling gerontological patient or who restrains a psychiatric patient who is not dangerous, but may be irascible, commits a battery for which civil damages can be awarded. A caregiver who obtains the consent of a patient to hold the patient's arm for the purpose of taking a blood pressure, but goes beyond that procedure and administers an inoculation, commits a battery. The consent must relate to the particular procedure that is going to be undertaken.[4] A physician who obtains a consent to operate on a patient's toe, but instead performs a spinal fusion, commits a battery.[5]

If a patient orally communicates his or her consent to a particular form of treatment, but that consent was obtained through intimidation or under duress, this is not a valid consent and a battery still occurs. It is possible to

---

3 *Beausoleil v. La Communauté des Soeurs de la Charité de la Providence* (1964), 53 D.L.R. (2d) 65 (Que. C.A.).

4 *Murray v. McMurchy*, [1949] 2 D.L.R. 442, [1949] 1 W.W.R. 989 (B.C.S.C.).

5 *Schwiezer v. Central Hospital et al.* (1974), 53 D.L.R. (3d) 494 (Ont. H.C.J.).

commit a battery through an intermediary. A patient who is subjected to x-rays, without having consented to the procedure, is the subject of a battery for which the caregiver who ordered the x-rays is liable. Where consent is obtained by deceit, the consent is vitiated.

In some cases, the damages occasioned by a battery will be minimal. For example, where a nurse takes a pulse against the patient's wishes, and no harm comes to the patient, damages will be nominal. If, however, a court considers that the conduct of a nurse was malicious or reckless, the possibility of punitive damages arises. Even if no civil remedy is sought, this does not preclude professional discipline proceedings against the offending health professional.

Informed Consent

A patient may consent to a particular kind of physical contact, but may do so on the basis of inaccurate or incomplete information. The inaccuracy or incompleteness of the information provided to the patient may be the result of carelessness on the part of the caregiver. In those circumstances, the courts have found that no battery occurs, but that there may be liability for the caregiver resulting from the negligent failure to obtain a consent from the patient which is truly informed.[6] A caregiver must disclose the material risks attendant upon a particular procedure. The risks that must be disclosed depend upon the nature of the procedure. Adverse consequences, which are highly unlikely or of a minor nature, are less likely to require disclosure. On the other hand, serious risks, which may lead to death or permanent injury, must be disclosed even though the chance they will occur is remote. Ultimately, a court will make its determination of liability based upon whether the disclosure that took place in a particular case was reasonable or not. The Supreme Court of Canada has held:

> In deciding whether a risk is material and therefore, one which should be explained to the patient, an objective approach should be taken. The crucial question in determining the issue is whether a reasonable person in the patient's position would want to know of the risk.[7]

The particular "position" of the patient is of special significance. The health professional obtaining the consent must consider not only what is "reasonable" from an objective point of view but also what is reasonable in

---

6 *Supra* note 2.

7 *Ciarlariello v. Schacter* (1993), 15 C.C.L.T. (2d) 209, at 222 (S.C.C.).

the circumstances of the particular patient. A patient who is self-confident and emotionally stable may wish to know more about a procedure than other patients. Some patients may express a "need *not* to know". It may be reasonable, where one is dealing with a patient who is highly emotional and where the treatment itself may be compromised by complete disclosure, to withhold or generalize information that the caregiver reasonably believes is likely to be harmful to the patient.

A negligent failure to disclose material risks will not result automatically in liability. Liability arises only where the negligent conduct has *caused* harm. Where a court concludes that the patient would have proceeded with the particular form of treatment, even if apprised of the material risks, there is no liability, as disclosure would not have prevented the harm from occurring. Conversely, where a court concludes it is likely that the patient would *not* have proceeded with the procedure if all material risks had been disclosed, liability will follow because the procedure, if properly explained to the patient, would not have been carried out.

In *Petty v. MacKay*,[8] an exotic dancer underwent cosmetic surgery to have tissue removed from an area of her abdomen so that she could continue her exotic dancing. The surgery was unsuccessful and the plaintiff sustained permanent disfigurement as a result. The trial judge concluded that a material risk of the surgery was not explained by the surgeon to his patient. Nonetheless, the judge dismissed the case. He found that even if the risk of disfigurement had been explained to the patient, she would have accepted the risk and gone ahead with the surgery. Consequently, the failure of the surgeon to disclose the material risk of abdominal disfigurement, though negligent, did not place the plaintiff in a worse position than she would have been in had the risk been disclosed.

In *Haughian v. Paine*,[9] a patient received a recommendation from a neurosurgeon for surgery to correct the herniation of a cervical disc. The surgery led to paralysis, which was later corrected, but nonetheless caused significant harm to the patient. The patient alleged a lack of informed consent. The Court held that the diagnosis of the neurosurgeon was correct and that his recommendation for surgery, as opposed to more conservative treatment, met a reasonable standard of care. The Court, however, also found that there had not been an adequate discussion of the risks involved in the surgery and that the patient, if informed of these risks and given the alternative of more conservative treatment, would not have consented to the surgery. The neurosurgeon was found liable for failing to obtain an informed consent, and damages were awarded.

Even where the communication of information may not have prevented the patient from undergoing the treatment, there may be liability for a

---

[8] (1979), 14 B.C.L.R. 382, 10 C.C.L.T. 85 (S.C.).

[9] [1987] 4 W.W.R. 97 (Sask. C.A.).

failure to communicate risks which would have resulted in less stress for the patient. In *Snider v. Henninger*,[10] the patient underwent an emergency hysterectomy after the surgeon had made several attempts to suture a uterine artery and had not succeeded. Although the Court found that the surgeon's care was not negligent and that the patient had no choice but to undergo the procedure, the physician was found negligent in that he had failed to forewarn her of the possibility of a total hysterectomy. That information would have enabled her to obtain a second opinion and to prepare for the loss of future child-bearing capacity. In effect, the patient was not informed of the risks in a *timely manner*, with the result that her stress was increased and her recovery compromised. She was awarded damages in the amount of $12,000.

Withdrawal of Consent

A situation may occur in which a patient has agreed to undergo a procedure, but changes his or her mind and withdraws consent. A consent may be expressed in clear and unequivocal terms in the physician's office, but the patient may refuse to sign a consent form in the hospital prior to surgery. In other cases, the communication of the withdrawal may be in less forceful terms — the patient expresses reservations to a family member or asks questions a nurse is unable to answer. The Supreme Court of Canada has held that if there is any question whether the patient is attempting to withdraw consent, it is incumbent upon the physician or other health practitioner administering the procedure to ascertain whether the consent has in fact been withdrawn. If, during the course of a procedure, a patient withdraws his or her consent, the procedure must be halted.[11]

In *Nightingale v. Kaplovitch*,[12] the patient was undergoing a sigmoidoscopic examination. The examination, at one point, became extremely painful and the patient screamed, "Stop, I can't take this any more." Nonetheless, the doctor proceeded with the examination. The patient made a sudden movement caused by pain and sustained a punctured bowel. The trial judge concluded that the perforation had occurred after the patient's consent had been withdrawn. He held that this was a battery, and furthermore, that the physician had been negligent in continuing the procedure when the patient had asked him to stop. Each case must be decided on its particular facts. In another case,[13] a patient suffering from

---

[10] (1992), 96 D.L.R. (4th) 367 (B.C.S.C.).

[11] *Ciarlariello v. Schacter*, *supra* note 7.

[12] Unreported, April 20, 1989 (Ont. H.C.J.).

[13] *Mitchell v. McDonald* (1987), 40 C.C.L.T. 266 (Alta. Q.B.).

acute muscular pain in her chest consented to receive a Cortisone injection into her chest muscle. At one point in the procedure, the patient cried out, "For God's sake, stop." In that case, however, the trial judge held that her exclamation did not constitute a withdrawal of consent, but rather, was an expression of pain and was not said for the purpose of having the procedure stopped.

Emergency Care

Where there is an urgent need for treatment and a valid consent is not possible, the caregiver may be exempt from obtaining the express and informed consent of the patient. A patient who has been rendered unconscious by an accident will be unable to consent to emergency treatment. It will be reasonable, however, for the caregiver, in the absence of evidence to the contrary, to infer that such a patient would want emergency treatment and would give the necessary consent if he or she were able to do so. An emergency does not exist, however, where the absence of intervention will not result in harm to the patient. If the patient's condition is not life-threatening and a delay in treatment will not harm the patient, the caregiver must wait until the patient is able to consent or until the appropriate substitute decision-maker is available to consent. Of course, if the condition of the patient begins to deteriorate, creating an urgent need for treatment, intervention without an express consent will be justified.

There may be situations in which the patient has given instructions, in advance, as to what treatment, if any, the patient should receive in an emergency. In *Malette v. Shulman*,[14] a physician was found to have committed a battery where a blood transfusion was given to an unconscious patient. The patient had been brought into the emergency department of a hospital following a car accident. She required an urgent blood transfusion. Her wallet contained a card identifying her as a Jehovah's Witness and stated that, for religious reasons, she did not want to receive a blood transfusion even in circumstances where her life was in danger. The physician, nonetheless, carried out a transfusion. The Court held that the card in the patient's wallet constituted clear evidence of the patient's desire to refuse life-sustaining treatment. The physician's conduct, though intended to save the life of the patient, was held to be unlawful. Damages were awarded.

The *Malette* case has implications for other areas of health care in which a patient withholds consent. It confirms that, as a matter of common law, a competent patient has an absolute right to refuse life-sustaining treatment.

---

[14] (1990), 72 O.R. (2d) 417 (C.A.).

The communication by the patient of a wish to forgo treatment may be in the form of a document executed by the patient prior to admission to hospital, in a power of attorney or similar authorization to a substitute decision maker or in a verbal agreement, between physician and patient, to a "do-not-resuscitate" order. The patient's right to refuse treatment, even where there is no specific statutory authority for doing so, was upheld by a Quebec court which authorized a hospital to discontinue life-sustaining treatment when requested to do so by a patient who was suffering from an incurable disease.[15]

Prerequisites of a Valid Consent

A thorough explanation of the material risks attached to a procedure is ineffective where the patient is incapable of understanding the nature of the procedure. A patient who has an emotional or intellectual disability may be incapable of understanding the nature or appreciating the consequences of the treatment proposed. One ought not to assume, however, that the patient who suffers from an emotional or mental disability is, by necessity, disqualified from consenting to a treatment or procedure. A patient who has a diminished level of intelligence or some other form of disability may be capable of understanding and appreciating a relatively simple medical procedure. On the other hand, if the particular treatment is quite complex, and the material risks inherent in the treatment are serious, but difficult to understand, one may then be compelled to obtain a consent through some form of substitute-consent mechanism.

From a practical point of view, routine, non-invasive procedures, to which no reasonable patient is likely to object, can be performed without concern that a patient's legal rights are being violated. If, however, the patient objects, or if the patient is incapable of objecting or consenting and the treatment or procedure is invasive or complex, it should not be undertaken. If the patient's well-being is threatened should the procedure not be undertaken, it may be necessary, in the absence of an emergency, to seek legal advice, obtain a substitute consent, or in extreme cases, a court order. Where an emergency arises and the patient is unable to consent, treatment can be administered. If, however, there is evidence that the competent patient does not wish to have emergency treatment, even in a life-threatening situation, the patient's wish must prevail.[16]

---

15 *Nancy B. v. Hôtel-Dieu de Québec,* [1992] R.J.Q. 361 (C.S.). See Chapter 12, Current Legal Issues in Health Care, the section on Termination of Treatment and The Right to Die.

16 *Supra* note 14.

Treatment of a minor may require the consent of a parent, guardian or next-of-kin. Some legal experts would argue that the performance of a procedure with parental consent, against the wishes of a minor, may be a violation of the minor patient's rights. Because a patient is youthful or elderly is not the governing criterion for consent. It has been held that where a minor is capable of understanding and appreciating the nature and consequences of a particular procedure or treatment, the minor is capable of giving a valid consent.[17] Where there is genuine conflict between the wishes of the minor patient and the wishes of a parent, guardian or next-of-kin, it may be necessary to seek legal advice.

In many cases the procedure for which consent is being sought will be viewed, from the caregiver's point of view, as beneficial to the patient. Recalcitrant patients may not consent readily and may be reluctant to consent without a full and thorough explanation. Caregivers, to whom the procedures are common, familiar and safe, may find this exasperating; however, the temptation to "pressure" patients to consent must be avoided. The consent must be voluntary. To extract a consent by devious or overly forceful means will vitiate the consent.

The British Columbia Ministry of Health and the Ministry Responsible for Seniors has recently passed consent legislation for that province in which the "elements" of consent are specifically catalogued. This catalogue is a useful guide for all health practitioners because it codifies the essential common-law elements of a proper consent. Under this legislation[18] an adult is deemed to consent to treatment if:

(a) the consent relates to the proposed health care;
(b) the consent is given voluntarily;
(c) the consent is not obtained by fraud or misrepresentation;
(d) the adult is capable of making a decision about whether to give or refuse consent to the proposed health care;
(e) the health care provider gives the adult the information a reasonable person would require to understand the proposed health care and to make a decision, including information about:
  (i) the condition for which the health care is proposed;
  (ii) the nature of the proposed health care;
  (iii) the risks and benefits of the proposed health care that a reasonable person would expect to be told about; and
  (iv) alternative courses of health care; and
(f) the adult has an opportunity to ask questions and receive answers about the proposed health care.

---

[17] *Johnston v. Wellesley Hospital* (1970), 17 D.L.R. (3d) 139 (Ont. H.C.J.).

[18] *Health Care (Consent) and Care Facility (Admission) Act*, s. 6.

Consent Forms

A document which constitutes evidence of the patient's consent may be a statutory requirement for some forms of health care. The public hospitals legislation of some jurisdictions requires the execution of a consent form which specifically authorizes some forms of treatment (*i.e.*, surgery and similar types of invasive procedures). In some cases, although not legally required, the execution of a consent form may be a valuable precaution to demonstrate the patient's willingness to undergo the treatment should a question be raised about it in the future.

The language of consent forms can vary widely. Imprecise language, or language that is too broad, may weaken the evidentiary consent of the executed form. For example, a form purporting to authorize a vast array of treatment or "all necessary treatments" while the patient is in the facility will carry little weight. Such a form will raise questions whether there was any meaningful explanation of the treatment to be afforded and of the material risks associated with it.[19] The identity of the person who requests that the patient sign the form may have an impact upon the weight the form will be given by a court. Where the procedure has been explained to the patient in the physician's office a week before the surgery, a form presented to the patient by a nurse shortly before surgery may carry little weight. The better course, by far, is to have the form signed by the patient in the physician's office at the time the risks and benefits of the surgery are explained. Alternatively (or, perhaps, in addition), the physician should meet with the patient personally, after admission, to confirm the patient's understanding of the procedure and to have the written consent executed or reviewed. Although physicians may argue that this is impractical, this practice has developed in some health facilities and is one which will reduce allegations that there was an absence of informed consent.

A consent form may speak of other necessary procedures that may become known only during the course of the surgery. For example, it is not unusual for a patient undergoing exploratory surgery to authorize, in advance, additional procedures (*i.e.*, removal of a tumour) where the need is recognized as the surgery develops. Any additional procedure, however, must be a necessary extension of the anticipated procedure.

In *Pridham v. Nash*,[20] a patient developed infection following abdominal surgery. At issue was whether the surgeon's "laparoscopic" examination went beyond the bounds of the patient's consent. The consent form signed by the patient included consent to "related procedures and to additional or alternative procedures as may be necessary or medically advisable during

---

[19] *Male v. Hopmans* (1965), 54 D.L.R. (2d) 592 (Ont. H.C.J.); affd (1967), 64 D.L.R. (2d) 105 (Ont. C.A.).

[20] (1986), 57 O.R. (2d) 347 (Ont. H.C.J.).

the course of such procedures". During the laparoscopic examination, the gynaecologist found two adhesions which he decided to "lyse" or cut. The patient later sued on the basis that there had been no consent to the lysing of the adhesions and this additional procedure had resulted in the infection. In finding that the additional procedures came within the language of the consent form, the trial judge commented:

> If the laparoscopic examination, an investigative procedure, had revealed a major problem requiring surgery then, in my view, the surgeon would not be entitled to rely on the original consent and the general words of the consent . . . to carry out the major surgery. The surgeon would have been required to consult further with the patient and obtain a further consent to the major operation. However, this case, in my view, is different. From a practical point of view it would have been foolish for Dr. Nash to wait for Mrs. Pridham to come out of the anesthetic and then seek her consent to go through the same incision again to cut the two adhesions. The additional curative surgery was of such a minor nature that it falls practically in the same category as taking a sample for biopsy.[21]

Where a patient underwent a hernia operation, and during the course of surgery a grossly diseased testicle was removed without the express consent of the patient, it was held that the act of removing the testicle was of an emergency nature, necessary to safeguard the patient's life, and, therefore, no expressed consent was necessary.[22] In *Murray v. McMurchy*,[23] however, a physician was found liable on the basis of a lack of consent where, in doing a routine Caesarian section, he tied off the patient's fallopian tubes to prevent further pregnancies. In *Brushett v. Cowan*,[24] an orthopaedic surgeon, while performing a muscle biopsy for suspected carcinoma, also carried out a bone biopsy. The consent form signed by the patient authorized the muscle biopsy, but not the bone biopsy. Subsequently, when the patient fractured her leg at the site of the bone biopsy, and discovered for the first time that the biopsy had been performed, she sued the surgeon in battery for performing the bone biopsy without her consent. While successful at trial, the patient was unsuccessful before the Newfoundland Court of Appeal. It found that the general words of the signed consent form were sufficient to authorize the bone biopsy without the express consent of the patient.

Who will perform the surgery or diagnostic procedure is an issue which may be of concern to patients, but may also be one which is rarely discussed. In some cases, the consent form will describe a particular physician, but it

---

21 *Ibid.*, at 352.

22 *Marshall v. Curry*, [1933] 3 D.L.R. 260 (N.S.S.C.).

23 *Supra* note 4.

24 (1990), 3 C.C.L.T. (2d) 195 (Nfld. C.A.).

may also allude to other health practitioners who may be required to assist in the procedure. In some teaching centres, junior physicians or residents may participate in the surgery and may carry out significant components of it. This is rarely discussed in express terms with the patient, though it seems obvious that there must be some training-ground for young doctors to obtain the necessary experience. Where something goes wrong during an operation, and legal proceedings result, who was holding the scalpel or other instrument at the material time may be of particular concern to the patient. Would the "necessary risk" have been reduced had the more experienced physician been carrying out the procedure? Does the relative inexperience of the resident augment what might otherwise be a risk which is not material? Should the patient be informed that a resident, however competent, is going to be carrying out a major part of the surgery? Should the patient be given the option of refusing surgery or seeking medical attention elsewhere if unwilling to co-operate?

COMPETENCY

Whether the patient is competent to give consent to the proposed treatment has become a significant issue in the law relating to consent to treatment. The recent evolution of legal principles in this area prohibits the over-simplification of information provided to patients by health-care providers. As the explanation necessary to obtain an informed consent has become more specific and complex, the question naturally raised is whether the patient receiving such an explanation is equipped to receive it. Where patients are very young or very old, or where the nature of the disease may contribute to confusion or impaired cognition, the ability of the patient to consent may be reduced or non-existent. The fact that some provinces have passed mental health legislation specifically distinguishing involuntary patients from competent patients demonstrates a recognition that the two conditions cannot be equated. In Ontario, the government has established several bodies to inquire into competency-relative issues.[25] Most importantly, there is growing recognition that a determination of competency must be related to the particular transaction under review and that it is inappropriate to presuppose that incompetence in one area is indicative of "global incompetence". Hence, a patient who is incompetent to make decisions

---

[25] Ontario, Advisory Committee on Mental Competency, *Enquiry on Mental Competency* (Toronto: Queen's Printer for Ontario, 1990); Ontario, Advisory Committee on Substitute Decision Making for Mentally Incapable Persons, *Final Report of the Advisory Committee on Substitute Decision Making for Mentally Incapable Persons* (Toronto: Guardianship and Advocacy Review Committee, 1988).

about his or her psychiatric treatment may be quite competent to make a decision whether an appendix should be removed or not or about the management of his or her own finances. A determination that an individual is mentally incompetent on a global basis without relating that incompetence to a particular subject-matter or area of decision-making may constitute an overly broad determination of incompetency, and hence, a denial of individual rights.

Courts are increasingly cognisant of the difficulty some patients may have in giving an informed consent, even where the explanation for the procedure is detailed and complete.[26] Some provincial governments have moved to enact legislation imposing statutory obligations on health-care providers to ensure that a patient is competent to give an informed consent. The most pronounced of these statutory initiatives occurred in Ontario where the government enacted a package of legislation relating to consent to treatment: the *Health Care Consent Act, 1996*[27] and the *Substitute Decisions Act, 1992.*[28]

The *Health Care Consent Act, 1996*[29] presumes that all patients are capable of making their own decisions unless there are reasonable grounds to believe that a person may be incapable of making a decision. The patient is capable of making the particular decision if he or she is able to understand the information required to make the decision and is able to appreciate the consequences of the decision.[30] The Act outlines three activities in the health-care setting that require the patient's consent. These are: treatment, admission to a care facility and "personal assistance services". When a health practitioner wishes to treat, admit or perform a personal assistance service and there are reasonable grounds to believe that the patient may be incapable, the health practitioner must first assess capacity to determine if the patient is able to give or to refuse consent. If the health practitioner determines that the patient is incapable with respect to the decision, the decision must be made by a substitute decision maker on the patient's behalf. There are procedures in the Act for the patient to challenge the determination of incapacity before the Ontario Consent and Capacity Board.

---

26 *Petty v. MacKay, supra* note 8; although the patient's action was dismissed, the Court held that there was an obligation on the plastic surgeon to assess the patient's emotional stability when obtaining a consent to elective breast surgery. In *Hess v. Bissell* (1988), 48 A.R. 81, 45 D.L.R. (4th) 621 (Q.B.), the Court held that a patient with a compulsive personality disorder had consented, nonetheless, to the surgery and that there had been a sufficient assessment of the patient's psychological state by the physician carrying out the surgery.

27 S.O. 1996, c. 2.

28 S.O. 1992, c. 30 [am. S.O. 1996, c. 2].

29 S.O. 1996, c. 2.

30 *Ibid.*, s. 4.

The *Health Care Consent Act, 1996*, replaces complex, highly criticized consent to treatment legislation and has received a measure of support from the Ontario Medical Association.

> It is hoped that the new health care consent law will enhance physicians' understanding of their obligation to provide adequate information to patients in order to obtain informed consent, remind physicians that they must respect the right of capable individuals to make unwise or risky treatment decisions, and provide information to patients deemed incapable about their rights and options under the law.[31]

From the health-care administrator's point of view, legislation of this nature — whether justifiable and progressive or obstructive and unnecessary — will impose another level of legal process on the facility. Steps must be taken to ensure that health-care providers are attuned to their legal obligations and the corresponding rights of the patients; where treatment decisions result in the intervention of third parties — government agents and tribunals — care must be exercised to ensure that the correct procedures are followed, and, where applicable, that the facility and its health-care providers receive appropriate advice and legal representation.

Substitute Decision-Making

A number of provinces have passed, or are in the process of passing, legislation which provides a mechanism for obtaining patient consent in circumstances where the patient is incapacitated.[32] In some provinces, regulations passed pursuant to public hospitals legislation contain provisions authorizing family members to give a substitute decision where the patient is below the legal age of consent or is incapacitated.[33] The legal validity of such provisions was called into question by the Supreme Court of Canada

---

[31] Barb LeBlanc, "Physicians' Guide to the New Health Care Consent Act" (April, 1996) Ont. Med. Rev. 35.

[32] *Supra* note 1.

[33] For example, s. 37 of the Administration Regulation N.B. Reg. 91-32 under the New Brunswick *Public Hospitals Act*, provides:

> (1) Subject to subsection (2), no surgical operation shall be performed on a patient unless a consent in writing for the performance of the operation has been signed by
> (a) the patient,
> (b) the spouse or one of the next of kin or parents of the patient, if the patient is unable to sign by reason of mental or physical disability, or
> (c) the parent or guardian of an unmarried minor who has not, according to the terms of the *Medical Consent of Minors Act*, attained majority.

in *Re Eve.*[34] In that case, the parents of a girl with Downs Syndrome sought authorization of a sterilization procedure for their daughter who had reached puberty. In concluding that the procedure was unnecessary and not in the best interests of the child, the Court also ruled that the regulation under which the authorization was sought to be exercised was no more than a procedural guide for obtaining written consent and would give no more substantive authority to the parents than they would have under common law or through some other statutory authority.

In *Ney v. Canada (Attorney General),*[35] a group of parents brought an application to set aside legislation that gave children under the age of legal majority the right to consent, in certain circumstances, to their own care and treatment. They argued that the legislation[36] infringed the rights of children and parents and was contrary to the *Charter of Rights and Freedoms.* In rejecting their application, the judge held that the legislation created no new rights or obligations and was perfectly consistent with the common law in this area. Relying upon British authorities, he adopted the principle that

> an infant who is capable of appreciating fully the nature and consequences of a particular operation or of particular treatment can give an effective consent thereto, and in such cases the consent of the guardian is unnecessary; but . . . where the infant is without that capacity, any apparent consent by him or her will be a nullity, the sole right to consent being vested in the guardian.[37]

In effect, where a child has sufficient intelligence and maturity to understand and appreciate the nature and consequences of the proposed treatment, he or she is capable at common law of consenting to such treatment. If a child does not meet this test, and as a result is incapable of consenting, the consent of a parent or guardian will be required.[38]

In *Walker (Litigation Guardian of) v. Region 2 Hospital Corp.,*[39] a 15-year-old child was diagnosed as suffering from acute myeloid leukaemia. Although a treatment consisting of a blood or blood products transfusion was recommended, the child, who was a Jehovah's Witness, refused this treatment. The hospital applied for an order that the child be declared a "mature minor" capable of giving or withholding his own consent to having any transfusion of blood or blood products form part of his treatment. At

---

[34] [1986] 2 S.C.R. 388.
[35] (1993), 102 D.L.R. (4th) 136 (B.C. S.C.).
[36] *Infants Act,* R.S.B.C. 1979, c. 196, s. 16.
[37] *Supra* note 35, at 140 (quoted from Nathan, *Medical Negligence* (1957), p. 176).
[38] *Ibid.*
[39] (1994), 4 R.F.L. (4th) 321 (N.B.C.A.).

first instance the Court rejected the application and issued an order that the child be given blood transfusions if, in the opinion of his doctors, it was likely that he would die if he did not receive them. This decision, however, was overturned by the New Brunswick Court of Appeal. The New Brunswick *Medical Consent of Minors Act* provided that if two medical practitioners were satisfied that a minor was mature and able to consent to medical treatment, that the proposed treatment was in the best interests of the minor and his continuing health and well-being, and the minor consented, then the consent process was legally acceptable. The Court of Appeal voted that, because all of these prerequisites were satisfied, there was no need for a court to intervene. In effect, it held that the "mature" minor had a right to refuse treatment and that the child's wish not to receive blood or blood product transfusions should be respected.

In Manitoba, where a comprehensive legislative regime has been introduced for substitute decision-making, patients are permitted to make advance decisions in relation to treatment or non-treatment[40] and to appoint proxies who will make treatment decisions on the patient's behalf when the patient is no longer able to do so: "[e]very person who has the capacity to make health care decisions may make a health care directive".[41] Although there is a presumption that a patient under the age of 16 does not have the capacity to make decisions about treatment, the presumption of incapacity is rebuttable.[42] That is, if the child or adolescent can demonstrate that he or she is capable of making the treatment decision, the decision will be allowed to stand. "Capacity" is defined as the ability "to understand the information that is relevant to making a decision and . . . to appreciate the reasonably foreseeable consequences of a decision or lack of decision".[43] The legislation also points out that a "person may have capacity respecting some treatments and not others and respecting a treatment at one time and not at another".[44] For example, an adolescent may have the capacity to make a decision about minor, elective surgery, but not serious, invasive treatment that may be life-saving. In either case, the treatment-giver will be required to consider the "capacity" of the patient in relation to the particular treatment. If the competent decision of the patient is to refuse treatment, no matter what the consequences, the treatment cannot be given. Likewise, if a valid advance directive is given by

---

40 "Treatment" is defined as "anything that is done for a therapeutic, preventive, palliative, diagnostic, cosmetic or other health-related purpose, and includes a course of treatment": *Health Care Directives Act*, S.M. 1992, c. 33, s. 1.

41 *Ibid.*, s. 4(1).

42 *Walker (Litigation Guardian of) v. Region 2 Hospital Corp.*, *supra* note 39.

43 *Supra* note 40, s. 2.

44 *Ibid.*, s. 6(2).

the patient, it must be followed, even where to do so means death for the patient.[45] A proxy, however, is not authorized to consent to treatment that is primarily for the purpose of research or not for the protection of the patient's health unless the directive expressly says so.[46] Although no action lies against a proxy who acts "in good faith" and fails to make treatment decisions on behalf of a patient, nor against a person who administers, or refrains from administering, treatment "in good faith" or without knowledge of a directive or its contents, anyone who "willfully conceals, cancels, obliterates, damages, alters, falsifies or forges a directive or a revocation of a directive" may be punished by a fine of not more than $2,000, up to six months in prison, or both.[47]

In Ontario, the *Health Care Consent Act, 1996* divides substitute decision makers into five categories:

- court-appointed guardian;
- attorney with power of attorney for personal care;
- representative appointed by the Consent and Capacity Board;
- family members given authority by the *Health Care Consent Act, 1996*; and
- Public Guardian and Trustee.[48]

This is a hierarchial list. The highest ranking person, who meets all of the requirements in the legislation, becomes the substitute decision maker. To qualify, the substitute decision maker must:

- be capable of making decisions regarding treatment;
- be at least 16 years old, unless the substitute decision maker is the incapable patient's parent;
- not be prohibited by a court order from contacting the incapable patient;
- be available to advise the health practitioner if the patient consents; and
- be willing to become the substitute decision maker.[49]

---

45 Of course, the activity of the health-care provider is limited to the withdrawal or withholding of treatment; the directive cannot authorize proactive measures which harm the patient or accelerate death; *Rodriguez v. British Columbia (Attorney General)*, [1993] 3 S.C.R. 19, 82 B.C.L.R. (2d) 273, 107 D.L.R. (4th) 342, [1993] 7 W.W.R. 641, 85 C.C.C. (3d) 15.

46 *Supra* note 40, s. 14.

47 *Ibid.*, s. 27.

48 *Health Care Consent Act, 1996*, S.O. 1996, c. 2, s. 20.

49 *Ibid.*, s. 20(2).

The family members given statutory authority to become the substitute decision maker without prior authorization are also listed in hierarchal order in the Act as follows:

- spouse or partner;[50]
- child or parent;
- non-custodial parent with rights of access only;
- brother or sister; or
- any other relative.[51]

All substitute decision makers must be guided by the following principles when making decisions on behalf of the incapable patient.

(1) Decisions must be based on wishes the substitute decision maker knows about, which were made when the patient was over 16 and was still capable; and
(2) If a wish is not known, or it is impossible to comply with the wish, the decision must be made in the incapable patient's best interests.

Best interests includes consideration of:

(1) the values and beliefs that the patient held when capable;
(2) any prior wishes of the patient; and
(3) the effects of the treatment including whether:
   (i) the treatment is likely to improve the condition, prevent the condition from worsening, reduce the rate at which the condition worsens,
   (ii) the expected benefit outweighs the risk, and
   (iii) this is the least intrusive course of effective treatment.[52]

Not all provinces have enacted this form of comprehensive legislation. Nonetheless, in the absence of such legislation, the courts are likely to apply many of the principles embodied in it. It is also likely that in provinces and territories in which there is no similar comprehensive regime, such legislation will be enacted in the future.

For health-care administrators, this growing area of the law provides a significant challenge. A considerable degree of education will be required

---

[50] Spouse includes persons of the opposite sex who have cohabited for one year, or are the parents of a child or have a cohabitation agreement. Partner includes persons who have been living together for one year, who share a relationship of primary importance.

[51] *Supra* note 48, s. 20(1).

[52] *Ibid.*, s. 21(1).

to alert health-care providers to their new obligations and the concurrent rights of patients. Systems that operate only on the basis of traditional common-law principles or under out-dated legislation will have to be brought up to date; where patients are not afforded the legal right to make their own treatment decisions, in advance, by written directive or proxy, the institution risks legal liability.

CHAPTER 7

Malpractice and Institutional Liability

INTRODUCTION

Patients expect that treatment by health professionals will improve or remedy their disease or condition. They tend not to think that their condition will worsen, even if treated appropriately, or that an attempted cure may not be effective. Patients and their families are often unaware of the risks associated with complex medical procedures. They tend to consider modern health professionals as technological wizards who will diagnose their condition, prescribe the correct form of surgery or treatment, and then, while alleviating their symptoms, restore them to good health.[1] Where the result is unexpected — to the patients and family at any rate — there may be recourse to the courts.

Frequently, patient dissatisfaction and court proceedings arise from poor communication. The limitations inherent in the treatment plan were poorly explained, poorly understood or both. There may have been a failure to follow up with the patient and family where results of treatment were not as good as anticipated. In some instances the patient may have complaints that are legitimate, but not a sufficient basis for a lawsuit. All claims, whether successful or not, are a burden to the health facility. There are legal and administrative costs in defending any legal claim, even if it is without merit.

In some cases, the legal proceeding will be justified. Errors, though inadvertent, will occur. An award of damages may be appropriate. Where there is a finding of malpractice, the reputation of the facility and its health professionals may be tarnished. The majority of claims will relate to patient care; the minority will be the type of claims associated with any institution: occupiers' liability, commercial disputes and allegations of liability in relation to the operation of vehicles and equipment.

Health administrators frequently will have a role in attempting to avoid legal proceedings, or where they cannot be avoided, in providing assistance

[1] Contrast this with Voltaire's adage that "the art of medicine consists of amusing the patient while nature cures the disease".

to legal counsel and support to health professionals where the conduct of the latter is the subject of the lawsuit. Administrators have responsibility for ensuring that a quality assurance/risk management programme is in effect, which will reduce the likelihood of negligence. Where an unfavourable or unanticipated outcome gives rise to a patient complaint, a prompt response from administration may avoid a lawsuit. Where a lawsuit is commenced, or is likely to be commenced, health administrators will participate in the necessary investigation. They should have an understanding of the legal consequences and limitations on confidentiality for such investigations. They may be required to swear an affidavit of documents on behalf of the health facility, represent the facility at the examinations for discovery, and possibly, testify at trial. Where civil actions are ongoing, requests may be made by auditors, insurers, board members and others for information about the status and likely outcome of the litigation.

Intentionally Tortious Conduct

A tort is a civil wrong compensable by an award of damages. Conduct is *intentionally* tortious when a person deliberately engages in a wrongful act that results in damage to other persons or property. Although most civil actions involving health facilities are based upon allegations of negligence, some cases allege that the defendant committed an intentional tort. At common law, a nurse who restrains a competent patient against the patient's wish, a physician who transfuses blood contrary to the instructions contained in an advanced directive or a security officer who confines an unruly patient to a room without lawful right, all commit intentional torts.

There are numerous varieties of intentional torts in the health care context. Touching of any sort, without the patient's consent, is a battery. It may not be a battery if the patient is incompetent. It is not a battery if there is an emergency and an unconscious patient's consent cannot be obtained. When a physician injected an anesthetic into a patient's arm, thinking it was in the patient's best interest, but against the patient's express instructions, this was held to be a battery.[2]

Where a surgeon, having received consent to carry out one procedure, carries out another one at the same time, without obtaining consent to that particular procedure, this may constitute a battery. On the other hand, where a surgeon notices, while performing kidney surgery, that the patient has acute appendicitis, it is likely that a court would conclude that

---

2 *Allan et al. v. New Mount Sinai Hospital* (1980), 28 O.R. (2d) 356, 109 D.L.R. (3d) 634 (H.C.J.).

there was an implied consent by the patient, who was under anesthesia at the time, to the removal of the appendix.[3]

The intentional tort of false imprisonment may arise in the health-care context. If a patient is detained in an area, contrary to his or her will, and there is no legal basis for the detention, this constitutes false imprisonment. To detain or restrain a patient for discourteous conduct, or because a doctor insists on speaking to the patient before discharge or because the patient wishes to leave the facility against medical advice, also constitutes false imprisonment. It may, however, be acceptable to detain a patient where there is a risk that the patient will harm others or where a patient is engaged in conduct that gives rise to reasonable grounds for arrest and detention.

Libel and slander are intentional torts. Should a health professional express, orally or in writing, information that is untrue and defames the patient's reputation, liability may be found. Release of confidential information by a health facility may constitute an invasion of privacy and result in liability for an intentional tort.[4]

Negligence

Negligence in the course of administering care and treatment to a patient constitutes malpractice. In order to succeed in a malpractice claim, or in any other claim involving allegations of negligence, the claimant must demonstrate the four essential components discussed below.

1. Duty of Care

The patient must demonstrate that there was a relationship that gave rise to a duty of care. Ordinarily, in a malpractice case, the direct relationship is with a health-care professional for whose conduct the facility may, or may not, have a direct legal responsibility.[5] A nurse who took no part in the care of a patient or who was not working at the time the patient came to harm, will have had no obligation at the material time to care for the patient. An attending physician who admits the patient to the hospital will be responsible for the patient's treatment throughout the admission. The physician is obliged to take reasonable steps to ensure that the patient

---

3 See Chapter 6, Consent to Treatment, for further discussion of the concept of battery.

4 *Roth v. Roth* (1991), 9 C.C.L.T. (2d) 141 (Ont. Gen. Div.).

5 See the section on "Vicarious Liability", at page 144.

receives the appropriate treatment, if not from the physician directly, from qualified health personnel. The health professional's duty is restricted to his or her area of expertise, unless the health professional undertakes to administer treatment for which he or she is not qualified. A patient cannot expect a nurse to provide health-care services that are in the professional domain of a physician. It is not expected that a nurse will provide telephone advice to a prospective patient as to the best method for being transported to hospital or that a hospital has a duty to call in a cardiologist for a patient with chest pain where the emergency department is staffed with qualified nurses and an emergency physician.[6]

A duty of care arises only in circumstances in which the event giving rise to the duty is reasonably foreseeable. In *University Hospital Board v. Lepine*,[7] the patient was an epileptic who was admitted to hospital. He was put into a room on the fourth floor of the hospital. Suddenly, and without warning, and in the presence of members of the hospital staff, he jumped onto a chair, leaped through the window, fell to the ground and sustained serious injuries. It was found at trial, and again in the Alberta Court of Appeal, that the hospital was negligent because it had failed to provide constant supervision by keeping the patient "under the care of a competent orderly or nurse at all times". The decision was overturned, however, by the Supreme Court of Canada which found that the conduct of the patient was not reasonably foreseeable by the hospital or its staff. Speaking for the Court, Justice Hall stated:

> I am impelled to the conclusion that Lepine's sudden leap through the window was not an event which a reasonable man would have foreseen and have been required to take more precautions than were available in this case. Short of having put Lepine in some restraining device or of keeping him at ground level, both of which were rejected by the appellate division as being necessary or required, the injuries sustained by Lepine were the result of an impulse on his part which could not reasonably have been foreseen. To hold otherwise would, in my judgment, make doctors and hospitals insurers against all such hazards which they are not.[8]

---

6 *Bateman v. Doiron* (1991), 8 C.C.L.T. (2d) 284 at 288-91 (N.B.Q.B.); affd (1993), 18 C.C.L.T. (2d) 1 (N.B.C.A).

7 (1966), 57 W.W.R. 5 (S.C.C.).

8 *Ibid.*, at 26. However, the hospital was held liable in *De Jong (Litigation Guardian of) v. Owen Sound General and Marine Hospital*, [1996] O.J. No. 809 (Gen. Div.). In that case, a psychiatric patient threw himself through a window, staggered onto a nearby highway and was killed. The hospital was negligent for putting the plaintiff in a room where the glass was easily breakable, failing to provide adequate observation of the potentially suicidal plaintiff and failing to hold an intake conference within the time specified by the hospital guide-lines. The attending physician was negligent for either misdiagnosing or misprescribing medication to the plaintiff and for failing to adequately assess the risk that he

In contrast, in *Dowey v. Rothwell*,[9] the patient advised a nurse that she felt she was about to experience a seizure. The nurse failed to put up the guardrails on the bed. The patient experienced a *grand mal* seizure and fell to the floor, breaking her arm. The Court held that the possibility of the patient falling off the examining table was reasonably foreseeable and the nurse was found negligent.

2. Breach of Duty of Care

Once a patient in a malpractice action has demonstrated that a duty of care existed, the patient must prove that there was a breach of that duty of care. The patient may come to harm in a manner that is unanticipated. Upon analysis, one may suggest modes of treatment or practice that may have prevented the harm. The fact that one can suggest improvements or modifications in the care of a patient, in retrospect, however, is not a sufficient ground upon which to advance an action for malpractice. Likewise, where the harm results from a material risk that is known to be associated with the procedure, this will not be a cause for complaint if the patient has been informed appropriately and in advance about the risk.

The conduct of the institution and its health professionals will be judged on whether the care provided met a reasonable standard in the particular circumstances of the case. In order to demonstrate malpractice, the patient must lead evidence at trial which demonstrates that the conduct of the defendant has fallen below reasonable or acceptable standards.

Health professionals are required to exercise that degree of care and skill reasonably expected of a normal, prudent practitioner of the same experience and standing.[10] A hospital or health facility has an obligation to meet standards reasonably expected by the community it serves in the provision of competent personnel and adequate facilities and equipment and also with respect to the competence of physicians to whom it grants privileges to provide medical treatment. A hospital may not be directly responsible for the negligence of physicians who practise in it, but it is responsible to ensure that doctors on staff are reasonably qualified to do the work expected of them.[11]

---

posed. The Chief of Psychiatry was negligent for inadequately informing himself about the glass in the patient's room and for failing to take steps to ensure that the glass was strong enough to protect against the risk of flight.

9 (1974), 49 D.L.R. (3d) 82, [1974] 5 W.W.R. 311 (Alta. S.C.).

10 *Crits v. Sylvester*, [1956] O.R. 132, 1 D.L.R. (2d) 502 (C.A.); affd [1956] S.C.R. 991, 5 D.L.R. (2d) 601.

11 *Yepremian v. Scarborough General Hospital* (1980), 28 O.R. (2d) 494, 13 C.C.L.T. 105 (C.A.).

In *Cavan v. Wilcox*,[12] a registered nurse practising in New Brunswick was sued by a patient who had a part of his left hand amputated. Gangrene had developed following an injection given by the nurse. The New Brunswick Court of Appeal overturned the trial judge's dismissal of the patient's action and found the nurse negligent for having improperly injected bicillin into the circumflex artery of the patient's left arm.

The Supreme Court of Canada, however, on reviewing the trial evidence, highlighted the evidence of nursing and medical experts who testified that nothing was taught to nurses, at that time, in regard to the presence of the circumflex artery in the deltoid muscle and the possibility of an injection going into that artery. The Supreme Court concluded that there was ample evidence to support a finding that the injection was given "without any fault" on the part of the nurse. Because there was no evidence of a nursing standard having been breached (in fact, the evidence was the opposite) the Supreme Court held that there was no evidence of "negligence" on the part of the nurse, even though it was clear that the patient had come to harm as a result of the injection.

A health professional may commit an error in judgment, but this does not lead to the conclusion that he or she has breached a duty of care by providing substandard care.[13] In short, in order to prove malpractice, it is not sufficient for a court to find that the facility or its health professionals might have done better or that another facility and its health professionals might have done better. The court must find that there has been a breach of the *reasonable* standard of health care.

Occasionally, the burden of proof will shift to the health facility and its caregivers to demonstrate that a reasonable standard was met. The principle of *res ipsa loquitur* may lead to a finding of liability where a court concludes that it is unlikely for the injury or harm to have occurred without negligence. In such cases it may be said that the result "speaks for itself" in demonstrating negligence. The patient may have no inkling as to how, or why, the harm has occurred. If the plaintiff proves that he or she was injured while in the complete control of the defendant, and that ordinarily, in such circumstances, injuries do not occur without negligence, it is then incumbent upon the defendant to demonstrate that there is an explanation equally consistent with negligence or no negligence. Unless the defence can do so, a finding of liability will be made.

In *Cosgrove v. Gaudreau*,[14] it was admitted that during surgery a sponge had been left undetected in the abdominal cavity of a patient. It was not

---

[12] [1975] 2 S.C.R. 663, 9 N.B.R. (2d) 140, 50 D.L.R. (3d) 687 (*sub nom. Wilcox v. Cavan*), 2 N.R. 618; revg (1973), 7 N.B.R. (2d) 192, 44 D.L.R. (3d) 42 (N.B.C.A.).

[13] *Elverson v. Doctors Hospital* (1974), 4 O.R. (2d) 748, 49 D.L.R. (3d) 196 (C.A.); affd (1976), 65 D.L.R. (3d) 382n, 17 N.R. 157 (S.C.C.).

[14] (1981), 33 N.B.R. (2d) 523 (Q.B.).

discovered until one year after the surgery when the patient began to experience abdominal pain. The trial judge stated that he could come to no other conclusion but that in the ordinary course of events a sponge is not left behind in the abdominal cavity. The explanation that the scrub nurse reported a correct sponge count and that the physician relied upon it was not considered to be an explanation that was equally consistent with negligence or no negligence. Rather, the trial judge concluded that the mishap could not occur without negligence, despite a record by the nurses of an accurate sponge count. Obviously, the count recorded was incorrect. Damages were awarded in favour of the plaintiff.

In *Ferguson v. Hamilton Civic Hospitals*,[15] an allegation that negligence should be found on the principle of *res ipsa loquitur* was rejected by the Court. In that case, a plaintiff had become quadriplegic following a bilateral carotid arteriography. The evidence disclosed that paralysis was a remote risk of the procedure. It could occur without negligence. There was no evidence that the arteriography had been performed negligently or that there had been negligent follow-up treatment. In those circumstances, the trial judge found that there was ample evidence that the paralysis could occur despite reasonable care on the part of the defendants. The principle of *res ipsa loquitur* was found to have no application and the action was dismissed.

3. The Breach of Duty Must Result in Damages

The purpose of a civil action is to request from the court an award of monetary compensation for injury or harm. Unless a breach of the duty of care has resulted in injury or harm, there can be no basis for a civil suit. It has been held that a foetus is not a person,[16] and consequently, that no action for damages can be advanced on behalf of a still-born foetus, even though the stillbirth is the result of negligence. Similarly, no damages can be recovered for sorrow, grief, embarrassment or hurt feelings. Hence, if the loss can be expressed only in those terms, there being no physical or economic impact from the malpractice, no malpractice proceedings can be brought.[17]

Where a patient is unable to demonstrate an entitlement to damages, and consequently has no basis for a civil action for damages, the patient may be entitled, nevertheless, to initiate discipline proceedings against the health professionals who may be guilty of professional misconduct or

---

[15] (1983), 40 O.R. (2d) 577 (H.C.J.); affd (1985), 50 O.R. (2d) 754 (C.A.).

[16] *Mathison v. Hofer* (1984), 27 Man. R. (2d) 41, [1984] 3 W.W.R. 343, 6 C.C.L.I. 58, 28 C.C.L.T. 196 (Q.B.).

[17] *Montgomery v. Murphy* (1982), 37 O.R. (2d) 631 (H.C.J.).

incompetence. Without a claim for monetary damages, however, no civil action can be pursued.

4. Causation

It is possible to have a case in which a duty of care arises, the duty is breached, damages are sustained, but the particular breach did not *cause* the injury.[18] In *MacDonald v. York County Hospital Corp.*,[19] a patient had been treated in hospital for a fractured dislocation of the ankle. The general surgeon had applied an unpadded cast over only two layers of cloth and did not carefully supervise the condition of the patient or issue special instructions concerning the supervision of the patient. Subsequently, the patient developed gangrene and had to undergo an amputation of his leg below the knee. The trial judge found that the nurses had been aware of the patient's deteriorating condition for an 18-hour period, but had done nothing more than record the apparent changes in the patient's condition and had failed to advise the physician of the drastic increase in the classic signs of circulatory impairment. The trial judge found the hospital and its nursing staff partially responsible for the injuries sustained by the patient.

The hospital appealed the decision of the trial judge to the Ontario Court of Appeal. The Court of Appeal observed:

> . . . the symptoms observed that evening were those of change, indeed, serious change; but Doctor Vail was closely cross-examined by counsel for the respondent as to his probable course of conduct had he been notified of the changes which had occurred and, while he said that he would have attended at the hospital and examined the respondent's condition, he was very doubtful that he would have taken any action at that time. While it may be that the nurses were remiss in not calling the doctor and therefore negligent, there is, in view of the doctor's evidence, no reason to believe that the negligence was a contributory cause of the respondent's loss.[20]

In other words, though there was conclusive evidence that the nurses had failed to meet the appropriate standard of care, the evidence of the physician was that he would not have acted even if the appropriate standard had been met by the nurses reporting the serious changes to him. Consequently, the nurses' negligence did not *cause* any harm to the plaintiff.

---

18 *Barnett v. Chelsea and Kensington Hospital Management Committee*, [1969] 1 Q.B. 428.

19 [1972] 3 O.R. 469, 28 D.L.R. (3d) 521; varied (1973), 1 O.R. (2d) 653, 41 D.L.R. (3d) 321 (C.A.); affd [1976] 2 S.C.R. 825, 66 D.L.R. (3d) 530, 18 N.R. 155.

20 *Ibid.*, at 679 (1 O.R. (2d)).

Similarly, in *Lawson v. Laferrière*,[21] it was held that a physician's negligent failure to diagnose breast cancer in a patient did not incur liability as it could not be demonstrated, on a balance of probabilities, that if the patient had been informed earlier of her condition, her life would have been prolonged.

There is some support for the proposition that negligence, which is a *possible* cause of a patient's poor outcome, is actionable. For example, where a physician negligently continued to perform eye surgery, despite observation of a haemorrhage in the patient's eye, it was held that the physician's negligence was a possible cause of the patient's blindness and damages were awarded.[22]

Contributory Negligence

It is possible to have more than one breach of duty which causes the injury. Where the injury arises as a result of multiple breaches, this is referred to as contributory negligence. Each province and territory has legislation permitting a court to allocate responsibility among the parties who have breached their duty and contributed to the injury for which compensation is sought in the civil proceeding.[23]

In *Bergen v. Sturgeon General Hospital*,[24] a 25-year-old woman was admitted to hospital complaining of abdominal pains. The general practitioner saw her in the emergency department and then admitted her to hospital with a diagnosis of acute gastroenteritis. Subsequently, a general surgeon made a tentative diagnosis of pelvic inflammatory disease and suggested a gynaecological consultation. A gynaecologist also believed that the condition was pelvic inflammatory disease and prescribed antibiotics. Although appendicitis was considered at various times, it was never ruled out. The patient died as a result of acute appendicitis five days after being admitted to hospital. The trial judge found a number of the defendants liable including the patient's attending physician who had not attended promptly at the hospital when the patient's condition deteriorated suddenly, the general surgeon and the gynaecologist for failing to rule out appendicitis, and several nurses for their failure to inform other nurses of the patient's condition and to call promptly for the assistance of a physician.

---

21 [1991] 1 S.C.R. 541, 6 C.C.L.T. (2d) 119.

22 *Farrell v. Snell*, [1990] 2 S.C.R. 311, 72 D.L.R. (4th) 289. This is a somewhat controversial area in the law of medical negligence and, more generally, tort law; for further discussion see Salvatore Mirandola, "Lost Chances, Cause-in-Fact and Rationality in Medical Negligence" (1992), 50 U. of T. Fac. L. Rev. 258.

23 *E.g.*, *Negligence Act*, R.S.O. 1990, c. N.1.

24 (1984), 28 C.C.L.T. 155 (Alta. Q.B.)

Vicarious Liability

At common law the principle of *respondeat superior* — let superiors be responsible for the negligence of agents and employees under their control or supervision — means that health facilities will have *vicarious* liability for their employees. In some instances, the relationship between the health facility and the health professional makes it clear that the facility will be vicariously liable for the conduct of the health professional. Nurses, for example, are usually employees of the facility in that they are supervised and paid directly by the hospital or health facility. The situation is less clear in the case of nurses who may be hired to work in the facility through an outside agency.[25] Similarly, such personnel as technicians, orderlies, psychologists, physiotherapists and others working within the hospital or health-care facility are likely, on the basis of their employment relationship, to be persons to whom the principle of vicarious liability will apply. Even when there is no direct employment relationship, circumstances may dictate that there are sufficient control factors to lead to a finding of vicarious liability. It has been suggested that medical residents are employees of the hospital, for whom hospitals would be vicariously liable, where the hospital has the right to engage and discharge residents and direct the manner in which residents provide services to patients.[26]

Physicians who are credentialed and granted annual privileges by hospitals in Canada are generally considered independent practitioners for whom hospitals are not liable vicariously. In the leading case of *Yepremian v. Scarborough General Hospital*,[27] a patient suffered a cardiac arrest with resulting brain damage following commencement of treatment for a diagnosed diabetic condition. The diagnosis of diabetes had been missed initially by a family physician and another general practitioner working in

---

[25] The principle of "ostensible agency" may mean that the health facility will be responsible for a nurse, even if there is no direct employment relationship, if it is reasonable for the patient to conclude, based upon the surrounding circumstances, that the nurse is an employee of the hospital or health facility.

[26] *Ferguson v. Hamilton Civic Hospitals*, *supra* note 15, at 614 (40 O.R.). In *Edwards v. Valtchev* (1984), 45 C.P.C. 310 (Ont. Co. Ct.), it was held that a hospital was obliged to make enquiries of a hospital resident for the purpose of informing itself for discovery. The Court held that members of the hospital's "house staff", by virtue of being regulated under an agreement between the hospital and university, which included the hospital's commitment to provide medical insurance to interns, were subject to a "degree of control" exercised by the hospital. It was suggested that the interns were "agents" of the hospital and that the hospital could be vicariously liable for their conduct.

[27] *Supra* note 11.

the emergency department. Once the patient's condition was diagnosed, he received treatment by the internist on call who started the patient on insulin. The internist also prescribed sodium bicarbonate, but in an excessive dosage, and failed to administer potassium to counteract an insulin side-effect. It was found that the internist was negligent and that his negligence was the effective cause of the patient's brain damage.

The patient and his family, however, had not sued the internist. At trial, it was argued by counsel for the plaintiffs that the hospital ought to be liable for the conduct of the internist and that such liability was based upon the hospital's "non-delegable duty of care to the patient". The trial judge adopted this argument and awarded damages against the hospital. This decision was overturned by the Ontario Court of Appeal. In a split decision by a five-member panel, the three-judge majority emphasized the fact that the internist was a fully qualified medical specialist with expertise in endocrinology. He had applied for admission to the medical staff of the hospital and had been appointed by the Board of Governors on an annual basis. He was not an employee of the hospital. He received no remuneration from the hospital, though he was given a right to practise there and make use of the hospital facilities. He had responsibilities in the emergency department. He billed the Ontario Health Insurance Plan for service rendered to patients. Patients made no direct payment to the hospital.

Mr. Justice Arnup, speaking for the majority, emphasized the fact that no court in Canada had ever found that there was a non-delegable duty of care on the part of a hospital before and that, though patients coming into the emergency department had a right to expect good quality medical treatment, it was not reasonable to expect that a hospital, by virtue of having granted privileges to a physician, would compensate the patient for a mistake made by that physician. In rejecting the principle of the hospital having a "non-delegable duty of care" Arnup J. commented:

> The Government exercises a substantial degree of control over public hospitals, through Regulations and especially through the hospitals' finances. If liability is to be imposed upon hospitals for the negligence of its medical staff, including specialists, not employed by the hospitals, whether directly or by imposing a statutory duty to provide such services, it should be the function of the Legislature, as a policy question, to decide whether and under what conditions such liability is to attach.[28]

To date, no government in Canada has enacted legislation imposing such a duty on hospitals.

---

[28] *Ibid.*, at 527.

The decision in *Yepremian* is controversial, but it has been followed by other Canadian courts.[29] In *Robertshaw Estate v. Grimshaw*,[30] it was argued that the hospital should be liable for the conduct of staff physicians who, it was alleged, had failed to diagnose the deceased patient's burst aneurysm. The Manitoba Court of Appeal rejected this argument, though it acknowledged the possibility that

> . . . a hospital might assume a wider responsibility if it volunteers to be responsible for non-employees. In this case, however, there is not a scintilla of evidence that either of the defendant hospitals gave undertakings or encouraged the belief that the hospitals would accept responsibility for the provision of care within the premises.[31]

In *Papp v. North York Branson Hospital*,[32] a motor vehicle accident victim was rushed to the emergency department of the hospital. Initially, he complained of headache, but had normal vital signs and no obvious injuries. Three hours later he was transferred to another hospital, at which time he was unconscious with fixed pupils that did not react to light. A large intercranial blood clot was diagnosed and removed, but the patient suffered permanent brain damage. It was alleged that the hospital was responsible for the negligent conduct of physicians who had not diagnosed the condition and had failed to intervene properly. Aside from rejecting the allega-

---

[29] The only reported case which has presented a significant challenge to the reasoning in *Yepremian* is *Lapointe v. Hopital Le Gardeur* (1989), 2 C.C.L.T. (2d) 97 (Que. C.A.). A majority of the Quebec Court of Appeal held that the defendant hospital should be liable in conjunction with an emergency physician for failing to secure the safe transfer of a young patient with a laceration of the humeral artery to an appropriate hospital. The Court found a contractual relationship between the hospital and the patient. In doing so, it relied upon certain differences in the *Civil Code* (as opposed to the common-law foundation for *Yepremian*), and it cited certain differences in the health-care system in Quebec. The dissenting judgment followed closely the reasoning of the majority in *Yepremian*. On an appeal to the Supreme Court of Canada, however, the Supreme Court found that it was not necessary to deal with the issue of the hospital's responsibility for the emergency physician as it found that there was no fault on the part of the physician and, on that basis, dismissed the plaintiff's action. Hinting at the controversy of the law in this area, Madam Justice L'Heureux-Dube stated that "however tempting it might be, it would be neither wise nor appropriate to undertake a review of such important matters in this context": (1992), 10 C.C.L.T. (2d) 153, at 155.

[30] (1989), 57 Man. R. (2d) 140 (C.A.).

[31] *Ibid.*, at 144.

[32] Unreported, April 4, 1995 (Ont. Gen. Div.).

tions of negligence, the trial judge reaffirmed the law in *Yepremian*: a hospital is not liable for the conduct of independent physicians and the fact that there was a system of "teamwork" in the emergency department comprised of physicians and nurses (the hospital being vicariously liable for the conduct of the latter) did not change the hospital's relationship with the physicians as independent practitioners.

Whether physicians who are granted privileges at hospitals in Canada will continue to be considered independent practitioners for whom the hospital is not, in law, responsible remains an unanswered question. In the United States, the concept of physicians in hospitals being "independent practitioners" is being eroded.[33] It has been suggested by one American author that the concept of the physician as an independent medical practitioner is no longer appropriate.

> Since the public views the hospital as one entity, the hospital should be liable regardless of whether the physician is considered an independent contractor. Even if the distinction is retained generally in tort law, it is no longer a viable distinction in the field of hospital liability . . . a private fee-for-service doctor should be considered an agent of the hospital for the purposes of tort liability since the hospital creates the medical staff, approves its by-laws, reviews its work and holds the staff accountable for the quality of clinical practice.[34]

---

[33] See *Grewe v. Mt. Clemens General Hospital*, 404 Mich. 240, 273 N.W.2d 429 (1979), in which it was held that it is not sufficient to put an emergency patient on notice that the treating physician is an independent contractor. The Court concluded that the physician was an ostensible agent for whom the hospital was estopped from denying liability. In *Capan v. Divine Providence Hospital*, 410 A.2d 1282 (Pa. Super. Ct. 1979); 287 Pa. Super. 364, 430 A.2d 647 (1980), the Supreme Court of Pennsylvania found a hospital liable for the conduct of a physician, even though the physician was not an employee. In so finding, the Court stated:

> The changing role of the hospital and society creates a likelihood that patients will look to the institution rather than the individual physician for care . . . . Thus, a patient today frequently enters the hospital seeking a wide range of hospital services rather than personal treatment by a particular physician. It would be absurd to require such a patient to be familiar with the law of respondeat superior, and so to inquire of each person who treated (the plaintiff) whether he is an employee of the hospital or an independent contractor . . . . Similarly, it would be unfair to allow the "secret limitations" of liability contained in a doctor's contract with the hospital to bind the unknowing patient. (430 A.2d, at 649)

[34] Arthur F. Southwick, *The Law of Hospital and Health Care Administration*, 2nd ed. (Ann Arbour, Mich.: Health Administration Press, 1988), p. 581.

INSTITUTIONAL LIABILITY

Aside from a finding that a health facility is vicariously liable for its agents and employees (but not for its independent practitioners) a court may conclude that a facility has direct liability for breach of its duty to administer or manage the facility according to a reasonable standard. In *Yepremian*, Mr. Justice Arnup, for the majority, differentiated between an undertaking to provide medical care and an undertaking "to select competent doctors". He found that a patient did not have a right to expect that a hospital would undertake medical care, but did have the right to expect that it would exercise care in choosing members of its medical staff.

> . . . a member of the public who knows the facts is entitled to expect that the hospital has picked its medical staff with great care, has checked out the credentials of every applicant, has caused the existing staff to make a recommendation in every individual case, makes no appointment for longer than one year at a time, and reviews the performance of its staff at regular intervals.[35]

In effect, while hospital health facilities may not be responsible for the conduct of independent practitioners or contractors, they do, nonetheless, have responsibility for taking reasonable precautions to ensure that those persons chosen to carry on activities in the facility, whether for medical, maintenance or security purposes, are competent and qualified to do so. Failure to exercise care in the selection of personnel working within the facility, to evaluate their activities from time to time or to follow-up where there are complaints or concerns expressed, may result in direct liability for the institution.

It has been held that hospitals have an obligation to provide safe places with safe systems for those patients they accept for care; they have a duty to provide proper facilities and protocols along with competent, adequate supervision.[36] A plaintiff was denied judgment against a hospital where the Court found that the system of coverage for the cardiovascular intensive

---

[35] *Yepremian v. Scarborough General Hospital* (1980), 28 O.R. (2d) 494, at 514, 13 C.C.L.T. 105 (C.A.).

[36] *Kielley v. General Hospital Corp.* (1994), 125 Nfld. & P.E.I.R. 236 (Nfld. T.D.). In *H.(M.) v. Bederman* (1995), 27 C.C.L.T. (2d) 152 (Ont. Ct. (Gen. Div.)), additional reasons as to costs Dec. 27, 1995, Doc. Cobourg 2581/91,2581A/91 (Ont. Ct. (Gen. Div.)), a woman was awarded $6,000 in damages when a male patient at a cosmetic surgery clinic sexually assaulted her when the two were left momentarily alone in the post-surgery room. The judge decided that the physician running the clinic was obligated to take reasonable care to ensure that the patient was safe while on the premises.

care unit by residents was "adequate in conception and in actual practice", that the hospital's "call system in use was adequate" and that the hospital, contrary to the plaintiff's allegations, did not fail to enforce its own rules.[37] In a case in which a 33-year-old patient's heart condition was not diagnosed, the emergency physicians were found liable, but the hospital was exonerated on the ground that the hospital,

> provided proper and functioning equipment and facilities; that it had in place adequate systems to properly assess and tend to the needs of patients and staff and that it employed qualified and competent staff to provide an acceptable level of hospital care.[38]

In *McLean v. Carr Estate et al.*,[39] a patient who had fallen from an all-terrain vehicle died after being admitted to the emergency department of a hospital. Although judgment was given against the emergency physician, the action was dismissed as against the hospital on the ground that there had been no breach by the hospital of its duty to "maintain and communicate proper information to caregivers". It was also held that there was no evidence that the hospital failed to adequately maintain its CAT scanner. In another case, an action was dismissed against a hospital where a patient treated for a dog bite developed a rare bacterial infection and died. It was held that there was "no evidence to indicate the system in place for the training and update of the Hospital Medical Staff was below any required standard", and that on the contrary,

> . . . the evidence clearly establishes ongoing medical and support staff meetings, discussions and lectures to constantly monitor and apprise staff of events surrounding the workings of the Emergency Department at the Victoria General Hospital and of development in emergency medicine in general.[40]

It was also found that the hospital was not negligent for not having a written protocol or checklist for the emergency treatment of bite wounds on the basis that none of the experts who testified at the trial had testified that "such protocols were the norm".

In *Pittman Estate v. Bain*,[41] however, a hospital was found negligent in the implementation and design of its blood transfusion look-back programme. In that case, the plaintiff's husband had been transfused with

---

37 *Thompson Estate v. Byrne et al.* (1992), 114 N.S.R. (2d) 395 (T.D.).

38 *Briffett v. Gander & District Hospital Board et al.* (1992), 103 Nfld. & P.E.I.R. 271, at 282 (Nfld. T.D.).

39 (1994), 116 Nfld. & P.E.I.R. 271 (Nfld. T.D.).

40 *Grant Estate v. Mathers et al.* (1991), 100 N.S.R. (2d) 363, at 382 (T.D.).

41 (1994), 112 D.L.R. (4th) 257 (Ont. Gen. Div.).

contaminated blood and contracted an HIV infection. This information was discovered subsequently as a result of the hospital's look-back programme and the information was passed on to the patient's physician. The physician, however, did not pass the information on to the patient who continued to have sexual relations with his wife. The husband died and shortly thereafter the wife learned that she too had been infected with the HIV virus. It was found that the hospital should have developed alternative notification measures when it was learned that it would take an unreasonably long period of time to achieve a need that was urgent, and further, that in notifying the patient's family physician of the patient's HIV status, the hospital, along with Canadian Red Cross Society, had not ensured that sufficient information was available to the family physician to prompt him to provide an adequate warning to the patient.

THE LITIGATION PROCESS

1. STATEMENT OF CLAIM

A civil suit is commenced by the issuance of an originating document setting out the substance of the claim. This document, which in most provinces is referred to as a "statement of claim", may name as plaintiffs not only the patient who complains of the treatment which was given but also family members who may have incurred damages as a result of the harm to the family member. Where the patient has died, the administrator or executor of the estate will be made a party. The statement of claim may name as defendants any facility or any person who provided care to the patient. The named defendants will often include the hospital or health facility where the patient's treatment was administered and some, or all, of the health professionals involved in the patient's care.

As noted, health facilities are responsible for the conduct of health professionals who are considered to be their employees or agents. Where there is vicarious liability, it is not necessary that the health professional who is negligent be named as a party to the lawsuit for liability to be found against the institution. Consequently, the fact that someone involved in the treatment of a patient is not named as a defendant in the lawsuit does not mean that his or her conduct will not be the subject of scrutiny or criticism.

The statement of claim, in addition to naming parties to the lawsuit, will set out the factual background giving rise to the lawsuit, the monetary sum being claimed in damages and will describe the allegations of negligence being made against the defendants. Often, the allegations advanced in the statement of claim are broad and far-reaching. A plaintiff is required to plead all grounds upon which an eventual finding of liability may be made. Statements of claim are drafted and issued by lawyers early in the proceedings, often before the issues in the lawsuit have been well-defined. It is not unusual to find in a statement of claim very broad allegations that, ultimately, cannot be supported. It is not necessary for a plaintiff to prove every allegation contained in the statement of claim. Consequently, most statements of claim contain a large catalogue of allegations, many of which will not be relevant to the ultimate decision at trial.

The statement of claim (or similar originating document), once issued by the court, must be served *personally* upon the defendants to the lawsuit. Often, service of the statement of claim upon the hospital or health facility will be made through the office of the administrator. Service upon the administrator is effective service upon the hospital or facility. It is not, however, effective service upon other defendants who are named in the statement of claim, whether they are employees or agents. In some situations, an agreement may be made between counsel acting for the facility to accept service on behalf of those defendants who will be represented by counsel for the facility, but who have not yet been served personally. This arrangement is not made in every case, however, and the administrator ought not to indicate, as a matter of course, that service upon the institution is effective service upon its agents and employees named as defendants in the lawsuit. Rather, the administrator should communicate with those individuals named to ascertain if they have, as yet, been served. If they have not, it may be appropriate to apprise them that they have been named as defendants in a lawsuit and can expect to be served personally with the statement of claim. In advising counsel for the health facility that there has been service of the statement of claim upon the facility, information should also be provided about whether service has been effected personally upon agents or employees of the hospital who are named as defendants. Counsel may wish to have it confirmed that the agent or employee is content to be represented by counsel for the facility before accepting service on their behalf or delivering a statement of defence.

2. Limitation Periods

In order to advance a civil claim, the court proceedings must be commenced within a stipulated time period. This is to prevent claimants from coming forward many years after the events complained of when records, witnesses and other evidence may no longer be available. Generally, in Canada the limitation period for claims in contract and negligence is six years. Some jurisdictions, however, have a statutory limitation period that applies to hospitals or health facilities. Ontario, New Brunswick and

Newfoundland have a statutory limitation period that prevents an action being commenced by a patient more than two years after the date of discharge or the date upon which the patient ceased to receive treatment at a hospital.[42] Prince Edward Island's hospital legislation contains a provision with similar language, but for one year.[43] In Saskatchewan, actions will not be brought against any "person, partnership or corporation owning or operating a hospital, nursing home or other institution or the board of governors or board of management of any such institution, or any officer or employee thereof acting within the scope of his employment, . . . after the expiration of three months" unless, within a year, an application is made to a judge to extend the limitation period.[44] It should be noted that in the case of patients who are minors or mental incompetents, the limitation period generally runs until the patient reaches the age of majority or becomes competent.[45]

Special limitation periods may apply to health professionals. In Ontario, the *Health Professions Procedural Code* [46]states that:

> No person who is or was a member is liable to any action arising out of negligence or malpractice in respect of professional services requested of or rendered by the person unless the action is commenced within one year after the date when the person commencing the action knew or ought to have known the fact or facts upon which the negligence or malpractice is alleged.[47]

In British Columbia, actions against health professionals based in tort, negligence, malpractice, battery or assault must be commenced within two years of the date the cause of action arose.[48] In New Brunswick, that province's *Medical Act* requires any action against a physician for "negligence or malpractice" to be commenced within two years after the professional services terminated or one year after the person knew, or ought to have known, the facts upon which the claim is based.[49] Again, as in the case of limitation periods concerning institutional defendants, limitation periods applicable to health professionals will not run against minors or incompetents who are deemed not to be in a position to exercise their rights until they have achieved majority age or have become competent.

---

[42] *Public Hospitals Act,* R.S.O. 1990, c. P.40, s. 31; *Public Hospitals Act,* R.S.N.B. 1973, c. P-23, s. 17; *Hospitals Act,* R.S.N. 1990, c. H-9, s. 36.

[43] *Hospitals Act,* R.S.P.E.I. 1988, c. H-10, s. 13.

[44] *Hospital Standards Act,* R.S.S. 1978, c. H-10, s. 15.

[45] *Swain Estate v. Lake of the Woods District Hospital* (1992), 90 O.R. (3d) 74, 93 D.L.R. (4th) 440 (C.A.); *Lawson v. Hospital for Sick Children* (1990), 74 O.R. (2d) 11, 71 D.L.R. (4th) 557 (Div. Ct.)

[46] *Regulated Health Professions Act, 1991,* S.O. 1991, c. 18, Sch. 2.

[47] *Ibid.,* s. 89(1).

[48] *Limitations Act,* R.S.B.C. 1979, c. 236.

[49] S.N.B. 1981, c. 87, s. 67.

In Canada, questions about what limitation period will apply, whether there is a specific limitation period applicable to a specialized health facility such as a hospital or nursing home, whether there are special limitation periods applicable to health professionals who participated in the events giving rise to the claim and whether there are relieving provisions or circumstances which may extend the limitation period for an indeterminate time are not easily answered and may be the subject of intense legal scrutiny should litigation be commenced. The legal complexity of this area underscores the need for health facilities to recognize that claims may be advanced on behalf of patients many years after the events giving rise to the complaint. In many cases, a witness's memory of the patient, if there ever was a memory, may have faded. The availability of records, and the accuracy and completeness of the records, will be critical to the defence. Where there is an untoward or unanticipated event at a health facility that seems likely to give rise to litigation in the future, health administrators are well advised to consult their insurers or legal counsel to ensure that important evidence is collected and retained.

3. Statement of Defence

All provinces and territories require that a defendant who is served with the statement of claim in an action deliver a statement of defence to the allegations contained in the statement of claim if the lawsuit is going to be defended. Often, the rules of court provide for a stipulated time period during which the statement of defence must be delivered. In practice, however, especially in more complicated malpractice proceedings, the lawyers for the various parties will be instructed to agree to extensions of time so that a proper investigation can be conducted and arrangements can be made for legal representation.

Where there are multiple defendants, more than one statement of defence may be delivered. If a lawsuit is commenced against a doctor, a nurse and a hospital, each may retain separate counsel and each may deliver a separate statement of defence. In practice, counsel retained by the hospital or health facility will represent nurses as well as the hospital since nurses are, in most cases, employees for whom the hospital or health facility is vicariously liable. Physicians, if independent practitioners, will retain separate counsel and deliver a separate statement of defence.

4. Production of Documents

Once the statement of claim has been issued and served and a statement of defence delivered, the rules of court of each province require that the parties disclose and produce to one another any documents relevant to the civil proceedings. In a malpractice proceeding, the most important document is likely to be the health record. Parties may also have in their possession, and be required to produce, documents such as incident reports, emergency room manuals, hospital policies and procedures, quality control records, employment records, privileging documentation and internal memoranda. These documents, however, must be produced only if relevant to the particular proceedings. Likewise, a plaintiff may be required to produce medical reports in relation to the plaintiff's current health and condition, health records in relation to treatment that preceded or followed the treatment complained of, any business or employment records that may substantiate the claim for damages and any notes or records compiled by the plaintiff or others in relation to the allegations made in the statement of claim.

In addition to documentation that parties are required to disclose and produce to other parties in the lawsuit, there may be documentation that the parties are required to disclose, but not to produce. Inevitably, documentation will be created by the parties and their lawyers relating to the actual conduct of the lawsuit. For example, when a hospital administrator is aware that a lawsuit has been commenced, or is likely to be commenced, he or she may call in a lawyer or insurer to conduct an investigation. Statements may be taken from health personnel to assist the lawyer in the defence of the lawsuit. Correspondence may be exchanged among legal counsel, the hospital and individual defendants named in the lawsuit. Experts may be consulted to provide written opinions on the standard of care to be expected of the various defendants.

Although the parties may be required to disclose the existence of documents created in relation to the actual conduct of the lawsuit, they may not be required to produce such documentation to the other parties. Such documentation is considered "privileged". The privilege exists so that lawyers and their clients will be able to conduct their case in a confidential manner without having to disclose to an adverse party in the civil suit the entire basis for the defence or prosecution of the case.

There are two main grounds upon which privilege may attach to documents in a civil litigation. The first is "solicitor-client privilege". Documents that are exchanged between the party and his or her counsel, letters of opinion, reports on the status of the case, written statements or memoranda prepared by the client for the lawyer, are not subject to disclosure. Second, documents that are prepared in anticipation of, or for the primary purpose of, litigation may not be disclosed to the other parties in the lawsuit. For example, a report prepared by an investigator who has been asked to conduct an investigation into an event that is likely to give rise to a lawsuit need not be disclosed to another party, though it may be necessary to disclose any relevant facts which have become known as a result of the investigation. Both of these grounds of privilege allow the parties and their counsel to engage in frank and open discussions about legal matters and to have investigations conducted where litigation is anticipated.

There is also a third possible ground for privilege which is less frequently advanced. There are cases to suggest that certain documents may be privileged because it is in the interest of the public that they remain privileged. For example, in *Smith v. Royal Columbian Hospital*,[50] the Court held that certain documents produced in a peer review process by physicians in the hospital need not be disclosed in a lawsuit. The rationale is that the disclosure of such documents would prevent physicians from engaging in open communication, and possibly criticism, of their peers under a peer review system designed to ameliorate services.

The concept of privilege is important for health administrators. Often, investigation of an event giving rise to a lawsuit will take place long before the statement of claim has been issued and served. In some instances, the health administrator may initiate an investigation for quality assurance/risk management purposes. As part of the investigation, hospital personnel may be requested to prepare memoranda outlining their own involvement in the incident. Such memoranda may contain unsolicited opinions as to what went wrong, who was at fault, and how similar incidents can be avoided in the future. Sometimes, such opinions are sincere, accurate and helpful. On other occasions, such opinions may be defensive, inaccurate and misleading. Caution should be exercised in carrying out broad investigations where there has been an incident or event resulting in injury or harm to a patient. While the authors of these memoranda may believe that their comments are confidential, this is unlikely to be the case. Where it seems likely that an incident will lead to litigation, the health administrator should consider direct contact, immediately, with the health facility's insurer or legal counsel for advice on how the investigation should be conducted before embarking upon it. Generally, if an investigation is conducted under the direction of, and for the benefit of, legal counsel because litigation is anticipated, the product of that investigation will be privileged.

All provinces and territories require parties to lawsuits to provide affidavits of documents in which the parties swear that they have disclosed all documentation relevant to the lawsuit. The health administrator who is responsible for legal affairs within the facility may be required to swear such an affidavit. Generally, the affidavit will list those documents that the party has in his or her possession and does not object to producing, and also, those documents that the party has in his or her possession, but objects to producing on the ground of privilege.

---

50 (1981), 29 B.C.L.R. 99, 123 D.L.R. (3d) 723 (S.C.).

5. Examinations for Discovery

Once pleadings have been exchanged and relevant documentation disclosed and produced, counsel for the various parties will make arrangements to conduct examinations for discovery. This process, as the name implies, is to permit each party to "discover" the merits and weaknesses of the opponent's case. It allows a party to obtain, if possible, admissions that will assist in narrowing the issues for trial or that will assist the party in advancing his or her position at trial.

At an examination for discovery a party's lawyer conducts an oral examination of any other party who is adverse in interest in the proceedings. Consequently, the plaintiff's lawyer will be permitted to examine any physician, nurse or other health professional who is named as a party to the action, and as well, a representative of the health facility if the facility has been named as a party. In some jurisdictions it is possible to conduct an oral examination for discovery of a witness to the proceedings who is not a party. In other jurisdictions, witnesses are examined for discovery relatively infrequently and only by court order.

Although an examination for discovery is a part of the court process and is authorized by the rules of court, it is not conducted in court. It is conducted in private offices, outside of court, with only the parties, their lawyers and a reporter present. Usually, each party will be examined separately with only the lawyers for the various parties present in the examination room. The testimony of the party being examined will be recorded and a transcript will be made of the examination. The party is required to answer all proper questions relating to the matters in issue in the proceeding. If there is disagreement among the lawyers as to what constitutes a proper question, it may be necessary to have the matter decided by the court at a later date.

An examination for discovery can be a time-consuming and daunting procedure for the party being examined. Since the purpose of the examination is to "discover" the opposing party's case, the questioning is likely to be wide-ranging and detailed as counsel attempt to bring to the surface any facts or information which may be of assistance to their own client's case. Health facility representatives who are examined for discovery may be asked very detailed questions about their own background, the general operation of the hospital, the practices and policies within the hospital, the background and qualifications of the personnel who treated the patient, the equipment and facilities available within the institution, the training, orientation and continuing education programmes for health personnel and whatever other information may be available to the representative. The representative is required to inform himself or herself about the circumstances of the case in order to testify on behalf of the institution. In many instances, the representative will not be in a position to answer the question immediately and may be required, on the advice of counsel, to give an "undertaking" to make an inquiry or search for the information being requested. For example, a representative testifying on behalf of a hospital may be required to obtain a copy of a particular medication policy, to make inquiries about the number and identity of nurses working on a particular ward when an event occurred, to review personnel records for evidence of prior misconduct, to obtain and produce maintenance records for a certain piece of equipment or to ask employees of the hospital, who are not named in the lawsuit, for their best recollections of the event. Ordinarily, the answers to these undertakings will be supplied by written correspondence to counsel. At trial, however, the answers will be treated as sworn evidence of the representative and therefore must be accurate.

It is difficult to overstate the impact that examinations for discovery can have upon the ultimate disposition of the civil action or to over-emphasize the necessity of being well prepared for discovery. A witness who testifies at an examination for discovery does so under oath and is sworn to tell the truth. Because the evidence of each party is recorded and transcribed, the answers given to questions at the examination for discovery will be available at trial. They will be relied upon by the various parties to form conclusions about the evidence that will be heard at trial and about the likely success or failure of the case. Portions of the discovery transcript of one party, which assist another party, can be read into the record at trial and will constitute evidence against the party whose transcript is read.

Should the testimony of the witness at trial deviate from the witness's testimony at the examination for discovery, a transcript of the discovery evidence can be used, in open court, to demonstrate the inconsistency in the witness's testimony and to persuade the court that the witness's evidence at trial is inaccurate. In effect, the evidence given at examination for discovery will set the tone for the entire lawsuit; any attempt to modify, at a subsequent date, evidence given at the examination for discovery is likely to be challenged.

6. Pre-Trial

The litigation process may include a pre-trial. In some jurisdictions, and at some levels of court, a pre-trial is mandatory. Alternatively, a pre-trial may be requested by the parties or the court may direct that one be held in appropriate cases. As malpractice litigation often involves complicated medical issues and the testimony of numerous experts, a pre-trial is very common in those proceedings.

A pre-trial usually occurs after discoveries and before trial. It is presided over by a pre-trial judge, who will not be the trial judge, and is attended by counsel for the various parties. Ordinarily, no parties or witnesses attend. The format is more like a meeting than a court proceeding. Memoranda may be filed by the various counsel outlining the evidence given at the examinations for discovery. Counsel may have statements from witnesses and may advise the pre-trial judge what evidence a witness is likely to give at trial. Transcripts from the examinations for discovery will be available. Often, reports will have been prepared by expert witnesses and these will be used at the pre-trial to demonstrate what the evidence of the experts will be concerning the relevant medical, nursing or other standards that will be under consideration at trial.

The main purpose of the pre-trial is to determine, with the assistance of a pre-trial judge, whether the action is capable of resolution through settlement. As the pre-trial judge will not be the judge who hears the case at trial, counsel for the various parties may feel free to disclose information at the pre-trial in a less adversarial manner than may occur at the actual trial. The pre-trial judge may provide the parties with the benefit of his or her views on liability and damages. The pre-trial judge may suggest that certain facts are likely or unlikely to be proved at trial. There may be discussion of the legal issues to be decided at trial. The pre-trial judge may suggest possible compromises that may form the basis for a settlement.

Where a pre-trial settlement is not possible, the pre-trial judge may attempt to reach agreement on minor issues. For example, the parties may agree to certain facts at the pre-trial, which can then be communicated to the judge presiding at trial, so that the trial can be shortened. In some cases, it may be possible to formulate an agreement in relation to the damages that will be awarded if liability is found.

7. Alternative Dispute Resolution

In recent years there has been a movement away from the traditional litigation process to a process involving "alternative dispute resolution" (ADR). The traditional litigation process is expensive, time-consuming, and where the matter proceeds to trial, a "gamble" for all those involved. The legal formality associated with traditional litigation is often alienating to the parties. Litigation based upon an adversarial system of justice, complex rules of evidence, and in some unfortunate cases, posturing by parties or their counsel, will mean no resolution of the civil dispute for years. The sheer expense of the litigation process may defeat a valid claim. Financial stress on governments responsible for the administration of the civil litigation system has resulted in a shortage of courtrooms, fewer judges and lengthy waits for trial. It is not uncommon for a civil lawsuit, once declared ready for trial, to wait months, or even years, for the commencement of trial. Even where a matter does proceed to trial, a trial judge, after weeks of hearing evidence, may produce a result which surprises all of the parties and satisfies no one.

In this context, some parties to civil proceedings have begun to use ADR methods for resolving disputes. There are a number of methods. One is mediation, which may be as simple as a meeting among counsel and parties, moderated by a mediator who will attempt to assist the parties in achieving a resolution of their dispute. The mediator may be a retired judge or some other individual whose experience and opinion is highly respected by the parties. That individual may be able to facilitate a resolution. Where, as in a malpractice case, the central issue in the case is the quality of care provided, it may be appropriate to invite experts having relevant expertise to comment upon the standard of care exercised by the health professional whose conduct is under scrutiny. A face-to-face meeting of experts, who may have opposing views, early on in the proceedings and long before trial, may correct misunderstandings and enlighten adversaries to the justice of the other side's position.

In some cases, the parties may choose to engage in binding or non-binding arbitration. An arbitrator, or arbitration panel, may be appointed to consider the evidence and arrive at a decision. There may be an agreement to "informalize" the process to reduce the expense and accelerate a resolution.

8. Settlement

The vast majority of civil actions are settled prior to trial. Settlement may occur at any stage in the proceedings, though settlement is most likely to occur following the examinations for discovery or following pre-trial. Most settlements take place without any admission of liability. A settlement may consist of the plaintiff withdrawing the claim prior to trial with no payment by the defendant. Where a plaintiff receives settlement proceeds, as a condition of settlement, the plaintiff may be required to execute a release containing a formal acknowledgment that the defendant or defendants, in settling the case, do not make any admission of liability, and furthermore, that in accepting the settlement proceeds, the plaintiff surrenders the right to bring any other proceeding in regard to the subject-matter of the lawsuit.

In some instances, a significant component of the decision to settle a civil action will arise from economic considerations. The likelihood of a successful defence to a claim must be balanced against the risks of an unsuccessful defence and the significant legal costs generated by such proceedings. To a certain extent, allegations of professional negligence against health professionals will be viewed as an attack on their reputation and prestige. In those circumstances, the defence may take a "harder line" and refuse to settle a case unless there is concrete evidence, by a qualified professional, that a reasonable standard of care has been breached.[51]

In a complex malpractice proceeding where there are numerous issues and where there will be testimony from a number of experts, it is not unusual for a single party to incur costs in excess of $100,000 to prosecute or defend the matter through trial. Almost invariably, where a health facility or professional is sued, any award of damages will be paid by an insurer or professional association. Depending upon the amount of the settlement proposal, an insurer may be persuaded, from a strictly economic point of view, that settlement is advisable, even where there is a strong likelihood that the case can be defended successfully.

For example, if a plaintiff is prepared to accept the sum of $25,000 as a settlement and to execute a release acknowledging that there has been no admission of liability and renouncing any claim to future proceedings, such a settlement may be attractive to an insurer where the cost of defending the proceeding is likely to exceed $25,000. Moreover, an inherent risk in any litigation lies in the impossibility of predicting, with certainty, the ultimate outcome. The uncertainty of the outcome often engenders in parties a willingness to accept or to pay a sum in settlement that represents only a fraction of the damages that would have been recovered if the action were successful at trial.

9. Trial

If an action is not settled or resolved by some ADR mechanism, it will be placed on a list of cases and ultimately called to trial. Malpractice trials, because of their complex nature, tend to be lengthy. A malpractice trial is unlikely to take less than a week, and, in most cases, will take several weeks to try.

Because of the technical complexity of the issues arising in malpractice cases, they are most often tried by a judge alone. A malpractice trial may proceed with a jury, however, where the issues of liability are not overly intricate or complex.[52]

---

[51] For example, most physicians in Canada are members of the Canadian Medical Protective Association. Membership qualifies them for defence and financial protection should they be named as defendants in a lawsuit. Generally, it is the policy of the Canadian Medical Protective Association to defend actions against physicians through to the end of trial in the absence of convincing evidence of malpractice, even where financial considerations might dictate otherwise.

[52] *Soldwisch v. Toronto Western Hospital* (1982), 39 O.R. (2d) 705, 139 D.L.R. (3d) 642, 30 C.P.C. 274 (H.C.J.); *DeBoer v. Bosweld* (1991), 5 O.R. (3d) 413 (Gen. Div.).

10. Appeal

Generally, it is possible to appeal a civil verdict where it is a legal issue being appealed. The appeal is decided on the basis of the evidence that was heard at trial, and there is no rehearing of the evidence by the appellate court. Findings of credibility made by a trial judge will not be overturned on appeal unless the trial judge has made a palpable and overriding error.[53] Although it is possible to introduce new evidence on appeal, the right to do so is very restricted as the law requires that all necessary and available evidence be led at trial. Failure to do so will not be a viable ground of appeal.[54] In effect, the chance of having a verdict overturned on appeal is limited; this accentuates the importance of preparation and expending a maximum of effort at trial.

Areas of Liability for Hospitals and Other Health Facilities

In Canada, the reported cases involving hospitals and other health facilities are too numerous to summarize or categorize in any comprehensive way. There are, however, areas giving rise, on a more frequent basis than others, to legal proceedings against health facilities. There are also cases that do not arise frequently, but when they do, the health facility will bear a significant portion (if not all) of the burden of defending the claim. It is these types of cases to which health administrators should direct particular attention in anticipating litigation where untoward events have occurred.

1. Emergency Cases

Health facilities that treat emergency cases — usually hospitals — are likely to attract cases in which it is alleged that the treatment and care offered gives rise to civil liability. The nature of emergency health care dictates the treatment of patients in high-risk situations who require, in some cases, immediate and intensive treatment. Frequently, patients brought to emergency departments have a poor outcome. Seriously ill patients and their families tend to be intolerant of even slight delays in treatment. Large numbers of users who access emergency departments for minor complaints make it difficult to prioritize treatment. A patient may be seen by a large number of practitioners — a triage nurse, an assessment

---

[53] *Lensen v. Lensen*, [1987] 2 S.C.R. 672, 44 D.L.R. (4th) 1.

[54] *Whitehall Development Corp. v. Walker* (1977), 17 O.R. (2d) 241 (C.A.).

nurse, an emergentologist and specialists. What is, in fact, a highly organized system of emergency medicine may appear chaotic to the uninformed layperson. The intense pressure to treat the illness or injury to the exclusion of other considerations may leave family members, and even the patient, resentful of the sometimes brusque demeanour of busy health practitioners. These factors may augment the perception that the health care afforded to the emergency patient was unsatisfactory or substandard. A significant component of civil suits brought against hospitals by patients involve allegations of negligence in the provision of emergency health care.

In *Bateman v. Doiron*,[55] a patient who previously had been diagnosed with angina, died of cardiac arrest in the emergency department of a hospital. Prior to the cardiac arrest, the patient had been admitted twice to the hospital. On the first occasion, he complained of chest pain, but did not present in immediate distress. The patient was discharged from the hospital by the consulting cardiologist. The patient returned to the emergency department a short time later when the pains persisted and his condition worsened. The patient was attended by nurses and the general practitioner on staff at the hospital. Once the general practitioner recognized that the patient was having a heart attack, he called in the consulting cardiologist. He also attempted on numerous occasions, unsuccessfully, to intubate the patient. It was alleged that the emergency nursing staff was negligent in its response to information that the patient was returning to the hospital with more severe symptoms and that they ought to have recommended a better system of transportation and dealt with the patient more quickly upon his arrival. It was alleged that the hospital failed to ensure that the physician on staff in the emergency department was competent. The Court concluded, however, that the nurses did meet an acceptable level of practice and that at all times they "showed skill and judgment in the decisions made within their area of responsibility". The Court recognized the practice of granting privileges to general practitioners who would work in the emergency department and found that the hospital should be judged by "standards reasonably expected by the community it serves" and not by the standard of emergency service one might expect at "large teaching facilities". It was held that although the emergency physician had not diagnosed a cardiological problem as promptly as one might have wished, this did not constitute negligence and that his inability to intubate the patient did not indicate the absence of the skill normally to be expected of family practitioners staffing emergency departments in similar hospitals.

Although the action did not succeed, the intense and comprehensive allegations made against the hospital and its staff in *Bateman* are typical of

---

55 (1991), 8 C.C.L.T. (2d) 284 (N.B.Q.B.).

civil proceedings that arise out of emergency cases in which the diagnosis is difficult, the most highly trained specialists are not immediately available, there are a number of health practitioners involved in the treatment of the patient and the outcome is poor.

Even though many of the reported cases involving allegations of negligence in emergency care have not been successful, they nonetheless represent an area with a significant amount of litigation and thereby constitute a considerable strain on hospital resources and the expenditure of significant legal costs. Emergency services, therefore, should be given considerable attention by health administrators charged with reducing the risk of legal exposure to the hospital or health facility.

2. Medical Devices, Products and Equipment

Another area of potential liability, of particular application to health-care facilities, is where it is alleged that a device, product or piece of equipment resulted in harm to a patient. Generally, the health facility will be responsible for supplying medical devices and products to be used in the facility. It will have control over the purchase and maintenance of equipment used for treating patients. The health facility may have programmes for orienting and training health-care providers in the use and operation of the equipment. As with standard treatment, health facilities will be expected, as a matter of law, to provide up-to-date supplies and equipment consistent with the supplies and equipment being employed by health facilities in similar circumstances. While fiscal restraints may make it difficult for a health facility to purchase and maintain state-of-the-art supplies and equipment, legal liability will not be avoided if the supplies and equipment being used in the facility are substandard, poorly maintained or operated by inadequately trained personnel.

Hospitals are often involved in treatment procedures in which a product or device is implanted or introduced into the patient's body. Recent litigation has involved breast implants, heart valves and blood products. Where a device is experimental, of questionable quality or subject to recall, health administrators should ensure that continued use of such products does not expose the hospital to legal liability. In the recent case of *Pittman Estate v. Bain*,[56] the trial judge concluded, after a detailed analysis of the legal principles, that a hospital may be bound by ordinary commercial obligations in relation to equipment and supplies used in the care of patients. In that case the trial judge found that the supply of blood products to the patient was from a voluntary system and was not a commercial transaction; therefore, the ordinary warranty of implied fitness for purpose

[56] *Supra*, note 41.

did not bind the hospital. The case, however, suggests an area of increased exposure for hospitals and health facilities where patients sustain injuries as a result of defective equipment or products.

Health facilities have a legal obligation to participate and assist in "look-back" or "recall" programmes to identify defective products that may constitute a risk of harm to the patient or to others. Similarly, facilities should ensure that equipment and supplies used for the treatment of patients are free from defect and fit for the purpose for which they are used.

3. Obstetrical Cases

For hospitals that provide labour and delivery facilities to patients, this is an area of significant risk. There are two important reasons to highlight this area. First, in an era when health-care consumers have come to expect miracles from health practitioners, a poor outcome for a newborn, though medically explainable, may be incomprehensible to the layperson. Second, where childbirth results in a poor outcome, the consequences may be catastrophic and may result in a multi-million dollar damage award should liability be found.

Consequently, for health administrators of hospitals with obstetrical departments, this area merits intense scrutiny. Special care should be taken to ensure that health professionals working in the obstetrical area are highly trained and extremely competent. Inevitably, despite the best of care, a birth will occur in which the child's health is significantly compromised. The hospital should have a counselling system in place to provide support to parents in this difficult situation. Often, a civil claim constitutes a last resort by mystified parents who want an understandable explanation for the cause of their injured child. Ensuring that there is a system in place to provide this explanation in a way which is sensitive and comprehensible to a layperson may reduce the risk of a lawsuit. As with most malpractice cases, the adequacy and accuracy of the labour and delivery record will be critical. Ambiguities and inaccuracies, even where the care has been exemplary, may cause a court to conclude, especially in a tragic case, such as one involving a severely damaged infant, that the treatment was substandard.

In *Granger (Litigation Guardian of) v. Ottawa General Hospital* [56a] the attending nurse and nurse supervisor, and, thus, the hospital, were negligent for failing to notify the obstetrician of decelerations in the fetal heartbeat of an infant who was then born with very severe disabilities. Although several physicians, including the patient's obstetrician, were parties to the action, they were exonerated on the basis that their treatment

[56a] [1996] O.J. No. 2129 (Gen. Div.).

did not fall below the standard expected of normal, prudent practitioners with the same training. The staff obstetrician was entitled to rely on the information given to him by the nurse because nurses are professionals who possess special skills and knowledge and they have a duty to communicate their assessments to the physician. The judge stated "it seems to me that one of the hallmarks of the Canadian health system in a tertiary care hospital such as the Ottawa General with all of its attendant teaching responsibilities, is that those involved in obstetrics work as a team and that the interaction between members of that team is vitally important particularly in terms of reliance on one another for the provision of accurate information".

4. Operative and Post-Operative Care

Surgery, an invasive procedure, gives rise to a number of risks and is an area in which claims for civil compensation frequently arise. Even the most routine surgery has risks in relation to unexpected bleeding, anaesthesia and infection. Patients understand, intuitively, that surgery is more "radical" than other forms of non-invasive treatment. Nonetheless, where the outcome is poor or unanticipated, patients with the assistance of their counsel and other experts will scrutinize the health record and history of events to determine whether the cure or treatment has been substandard.

In *Krujelis v. Esdale*,[57] a ten-year-old patient had been admitted to hospital for elective surgery to correct overprominent ears. The surgery was performed without complication, but in the post-anaesthesia recovery room of the hospital the boy sustained a cardiac arrest causing severe and permanent brain damage. The trial judge found that there was a period of 20 to 28 minutes when no observations were made of the unconscious patient. He concluded:

> . . . the tragic events which occurred during the critical 20-28 minutes were the result of there being inadequate observation of the patient, and that that inadequacy arose from the absence of three of the five nurses on duty, on coffee break during what is ordinarily the busiest time of the day for the [post-anaesthetic recovery room].

Administrators should confirm that there are systems in place to identify and monitor "high-risk" surgical cases and to ensure that the surgical performance and subsequent monitoring of surgical patients is of a consistent and high quality. Moreover, patients undergoing high-risk procedures should be monitored to ensure that if, unavoidably, there is a poor

---

[57] (1972), 25 D.L.R. (3d) 557 (B.C.S.C.).

or less-than-optimum outcome, steps can be taken to explain to the patient and family what has occurred and why.

5. Informed Consent

The subject of informed consent has been dealt with in a preceding chapter.[58] This area, however, is worthy of mention in the context of malpractice and institutional liability as it is an area generating a significant number of claims. The responsibility for obtaining an informed consent from a patient for a particular procedure rests with the practitioner carrying out the procedure. Frequently, this will be the physician, but in many institutions there is a practice of delegating the function of having a consent form signed by the patient to another practitioner, frequently a nurse.

An adequate system for ensuring that the material risks of a procedure are explained to the patient, and that this procedure is documented, will reduce the likelihood of legal proceedings in this area. Moreover, a system requiring the practitioner who obtains the informed consent to have the consent form signed as a part of the same transaction is likely to reduce litigation.

6. Medication or Injection Errors

This is another area giving rise to a significant number of claims in which allegations are made against health facilities, and, frequently, the health practitioners whom they employ. In some cases, the adverse consequences of an injection or medication error may be minimal or inconsequential. In other cases, the results may be catastrophic. Systems to ensure that medications are properly prescribed, dispensed and administered to patients in health facilities will reduce litigation and should have the particular attention of the health administrator.

7. Non-Treatment-Related Patient Injuries

The monitoring and management of patients who are at risk of falling or wandering or similar non-treatment-related incidents is an area meriting the attention of health facility administrators. A considerable number of claims are advanced as a result of injuries to patients that do not arise from treatment, but from activities or events that might occur in any setting. Elderly patients and patients in chronic-care facilities, nursing

---

[58] See Chapter 6, Consent to Treatment.

homes and psychiatric facilities, are particularly prone to injury as a result of falls. In *Jinks v. Abraham and Welland County General Hospital*,[59] a patient suffering from schizophrenia was admitted to hospital and was prescribed a course of treatment involving the administration of the drugs of choice for this type of illness. The patient showed signs of weakness and disorientation. He suffered several fainting spells that appeared to result from postural hypotension. After he had a restless evening, the nurses on the morning shift could not locate him. Noise was detected from a bathroom near the patient's room. The bathroom door was locked from the inside and it was necessary to obtain a key to open it. The patient was found lying on his side in a bathtub with the water running. He could not be revived. His left upper arm, left forehead and the left side of his nose were scalded by the hot water. The trial judge found that the most likely cause of death was accidental drowning due to a hypotensive reaction to the drugs he was receiving. It was found that certain safety features in the bathroom were missing or not working, that no one could tell from the nursing station when someone was in the bathroom and that the only key was in an inner office in the nursing station and took some time to retrieve. The hospital was found liable in negligence.

On appeal, the hospital relied upon a rule forbidding patients to use the bathtubs at the early hour in which the accident took place. The Court of Appeal rejected this argument, however, and upheld the trial judge's decision.

> The hospital cannot insulate itself from liability by means of a rule, which to its knowledge had been breached on other occasions, forbidding patients the use of the bathtubs at the early hour in which this accident took place. The deceased could have been denied access to the tubroom by the simple expedient of having the tubroom door locked. By allowing him access to the tubroom and thereby enabling him to lock himself into the room and isolate himself at a point in time when it could reasonably be foreseen that he might suffer a hypotensive reaction to the drugs he had ingested that morning, the hospital was in breach of its duty to protect this patient against the risk of physical injury that he might sustain if, due to his condition, he were to faint while in the process of taking or preparing for a bath. While, as counsel for the hospital contends, there may have been no causal connection between the deficiencies found by the trial judge in certain of the hospital's safety features in the tubroom and the patient's death, we are satisfied that on the whole of the evidence in this case the hospital did not meet the requisite standard of care called for in the circumstances.[59a]

---

[59] [1989] O.J. No. 1492 (Ont. C.A.).

[59a] *Ibid.*, at 2.

For health practitioners who have been trained to focus on the diagnosis and treatment of disease, and not on the general management of patients who may have difficulty walking, using the bathroom, and getting in and out of bed, this aspect of care and treatment is a significant challenge. In some cases, encouraging the patient to get back on his or her feet, though risky, may be necessary to the patient's eventual recovery. Reduced resources make it difficult to monitor and control patients who ignore directions and advice. Practitioners are not legally authorized to restrain a competent, but non-compliant, patient who engages in behaviour or activities that put him or her at risk. Practitioners must carefully chart their efforts to persuade these patients to refrain from such conduct or activities in order to defend a claim should such an untoward event occur.

CHAPTER 8

Inquests and Inquiries

Introduction

Legal proceedings such as criminal prosecutions, malpractice actions and disciplinary hearings are said to be "adversarial" in nature. The parties to these proceedings are adverse in interest. Ordinarily, one party will be called upon to prove that there has been a breach of law or of a professional standard. The health-care practitioner and institution will be called upon to defend their conduct, and, if not successful, damages will be awarded or a penalty assessed.

The inquest is a class of legal proceeding not designed to be adversarial in nature. It is said to be "inquisitorial".[1] It involves the investigation, traditionally by a coroner, of an unexplained or suspicious death.[2] Inquests may involve investigating the conduct of health-care professionals, the management of health-care facilities and the treatment and care of patients. Inquests are not intended to adjudicate criminal or civil liability, or to exercise a disciplinary function; in fact, the tribunal conducting the inquest may be barred from making any finding of fault.[3]

It is not unusual for deaths that have occurred in health-care facilities to be investigated by a coroner, or in some Canadian jurisdictions, a medical examiner. The Chief Coroner of Ontario has reported:

> Deaths following treatment in hospital where the family alleges malpractice are an increasing problem in Ontario . . . probably the most volatile and potentially hazardous area of a hospital is the Emergency Department. Emergency Departments are generally overcrowded and require decisions as to whether or not hospital admission is necessary. The most common complaints regarding emergencies are that the diagnosis was missed, that patients were required to spend long periods of time in Emergency waiting for

---

1 R.C. Bennett, "The Ontario Coroners' System" (1986-87), 7 Advocates Quarterly 53, at 62.

2 C. Granger, *Canadian Coroner Law* (Toronto: Carswell, 1984), p. 64.

3 For a brief history of the role of coroners, see T.D. Marshall, *Canadian Law of Inquests* (Toronto: Carswell, 1991), Chapter 2.

> a bed in hospital and did not receive adequate care, or cases such as overdoses that are diagnosed late and treated too lightly. Nursing home deaths are commonly disputed by the family, and the major issue usually centres on the level of treatment that is received. In addition, coroners hear from families dissatisfied with psychiatric care, whether it is a wrong diagnosis resulting in the release of the patient prior to his suicide, or placement in housing that leads to problems and ultimately death.[4]

Provincial Legislation

All provinces and territories have passed legislation codifying the common-law office of the coroner and giving those empowered by law the capacity to investigate unexplained or suspicious deaths, and, where appropriate, to conduct inquests.

The nature and number of inquests have changed dramatically in recent years. At one time, inquests were more frequent, but they were relatively short hearings in which the inquiry focused on the particular questions formulated by the relevant legislation. It was unusual for an inquest to take more than one or two days.

In more recent years, inquests have become lengthy proceedings that have more in common with wide-ranging public inquiries than with the traditional inquest. Inquests have also become increasingly adversarial. Whereas at one time inquests were called only when there was a "mysterious death", inquests involving health facilities rarely involve a mystery. It is relatively clear from the health record who the patient was and "how, when, where and by what means" the death occurred. An inquest is more likely to occur where there is criticism by family or friends or where the coroner or medical examiner, in the course of the investigation, has uncovered an area of concern or criticism and has concluded that it ought to be dealt with in the context of a public hearing.

Numerous parties may seek standing. Some will be represented by counsel. Procedural wrangling may take place. Tactical manoeuvring for the purpose of future civil proceedings has become commonplace. Challenges may be made to the authority and jurisdiction of the coroner to conduct the inquest. All this may attract considerable publicity. Where there is criticism of the health-care facility or the health professionals — which is often the case when an inquest has been called to investigate a patient's death — much of the publicity may be adverse. The jury may make far-

[4] J. Young, "An Overview of the Ontario Coroners' System" in *Inside Inquests* (Toronto: Law Society of Upper Canada, Department of Continuing Legal Education, 1993), p. A-1. Reproduced with the permission of Dr. James G. Young.

reaching recommendations on how the health facility should be operated or how patients should be treated. Although these recommendations may not have the force of law, in most cases they will be circulated following the inquest and the party to whom the recommendations apply will be expected to follow up. Failure to comply with the recommendations of the jury may lead to civil liability in a future case. A response, after the fact, that the recommendations are inappropriate or impractical will carry little weight.

The changing nature of inquests was confirmed recently by the Ontario Divisional Court in a case involving an inquest called to investigate the circumstances surrounding the deaths of disabled patients at two residential health facilities.[5] The inquest related to the deaths of four young adults at one institution and 17 children at the other. Applications for judicial review were brought during the course of the inquest to determine certain jurisdictional and procedural issues that had arisen. In the course of its reasons, the Court stated:

> The public interest in Ontario inquests has become more and more important in recent years. The traditional investigative function of the inquest to determine how, when, where, and by what means the deceased came to her death, is no longer the predominant feature of every inquest. That narrow investigative function, to lay out the essential facts surrounding an individual death, is still vital to the families of the deceased and to those who are directly involved in the death.
>
> A separate and wider function is becoming increasingly significant; the vindication of the public interest in the prevention of death by the public exposure of conditions that threaten life. The separate role of the jury in recommending systemic changes to prevent death has become more and more important. The social and preventive function of the inquest which focuses on the public interest has become, in some cases, just as important as the distinctly separate function of investigating the individual facts of individual deaths and the personal roles of individuals involved in the death.[6]

Another less frequent, though not unusual, form of inquisitorial proceeding is that of the public inquiry. In contrast to inquests, inquiries do not necessarily involve death and may involve a broad range of issues from specific occurrences to government policy. Again, all provinces in Canada have passed legislation providing for the appointment of individuals by government to carry out investigations and to inquire, sometimes by way of hearing, into certain issues or events. One of the most well-known, and

---

5 *People First of Ontario v. Porter, Regional Coroner, Niagara* (1991), 5 O.R. (3d) 609, 50 O.A.C. 90, 85 D.L.R. (4th) 174 (Div. Ct.); revd (1992), 6 O.R. (3d) 289 (C.A.).

6 *Ibid.*, at 619 (O.R.).

perhaps notorious, examples was the inquiry following the death of a number of infant patients at the Hospital for Sick Children in Toronto.[7]

THE CORONER SYSTEM VERSUS THE MEDICAL EXAMINER SYSTEM

The majority of provinces in Canada have passed legislation that calls for the investigation of violent or unnatural deaths by a coroner.[8] Three provinces — Alberta, Manitoba and Nova Scotia — have passed legislation establishing the office of "medical examiner".[9] In Newfoundland, there is no specific statute; rather, inquiries into violent or unnatural deaths are conducted by judges under the Newfoundland *Summary Proceedings Act.*[10]

In the coroner system, which is most closely aligned to the traditional common-law institution, the coroner is empowered to investigate, and, where appropriate, hold inquests into violent or unnatural deaths. In most cases, the coroner will be a medical doctor, though the specific provincial legislation may not require this. There may be a chief coroner who is responsible for regional coroners acting under his supervision.[11] Often, the regional coroners will carry out their duties on a part-time basis. In Ontario, in 1993, the Chief Coroner was assisted by the Deputy Chief Coroner and eight full-time Regional Coroners. Initial investigations were carried out by one of approximately 400 "investigating coroners", most of whom were experienced family physicians.[12] Under the system, the coroner will not only investigate a death but also, where it is deemed necessary to conduct an inquest, a coroner (not necessarily the same coroner who conducted the investigation) will preside over the inquest.

Where the legislation establishes the role of a "medical examiner", the medical examiner will conduct the initial investigation in much the same manner as will a coroner. The medical examiner will interview witnesses, police, forensic experts and others. The medical examiner ordinarily will

---

7 Ontario, *Report of the Royal Commission of Inquiry into Certain Deaths at the Hospital for Sick Children and Related Matters* (Toronto: Ministry of the Attorney General, 1984) (Commissioner: Mr. Samuel Grange).

8 British Columbia: *Coroners Act*, R.S.B.C. 1979, c. 68; New Brunswick: *Coroners Act*, R.S.N.B. 1973, c. C-23; Ontario: *Coroners Act*, R.S.O. 1990, C.37; Prince Edward Island: *Coroners Act*, R.S.P.E.I. 1988, c. C-25; Quebec: *Causes and Circumstances of Death Act*, R.S.Q. 1977, c. R-0.2; and Saskatchewan: *Coroners Act*, R.S.S. 1978, c. C-38.

9 *Fatality Inquiries Act*, R.S.A. 1980, c. F-6; *Fatality Inquiries Act*, S.M. 1989-90, c. 30; *Fatality Inquiries Act*, R.S.N.S. 1989, c. 164.

10 R.S.N. 1990, c. S-30.

11 For example, Ontario *Coroners Act*, *supra* note 8, s. 3.

12 Young, *supra* note 4, at A-5.

carry out an autopsy and will prepare an autopsy report and a record of the investigation.

The decision whether or not an inquest will be held, however, is not within the domain of the medical examiner. In the medical examiner system, a board or agency is appointed under the governing legislation to review the findings and the report of the medical examiner in order to determine whether or not a public inquiry, similar to the traditional inquest, will be held. Where a determination is made to hold a public inquiry, it will ordinarily be conducted by a judge, and, depending upon the particular legislation, either with or without a jury.

Initial Investigation

Generally, the provincial legislation provides for the mandatory reporting of unusual or unexplained deaths to the local coroner or medical examiner. A number of provincial statutes set out in detail the type of death considered to be reportable. A number of these deaths will have occurred in a health-care context. For example, under the Alberta *Fatality Inquiries Act* "any person having knowledge" is required to report

(a) deaths that occur unexplainedly;
(b) deaths that occur unexpectedly when the deceased was in apparent good health;
(c) deaths that occur as the result of violence, accident or suicide;
(d) maternal deaths that occur during or following pregnancy and that might reasonably be related to pregnancy;
(e) deaths that may have occurred as the result of improper or negligent treatment by any person;
(f) deaths that occur:
  (i) during an operative procedure,
  (ii) within 10 days of an operative procedure,
  (iii) while under anaesthesia, or
  (iv) [repealed by S.A. 1991, c. 21, s. 9(3)] or
  (v) any time after anaesthesia and that may reasonably be attributed to that anaesthesia;
(g) deaths that are the result of poisoning;
(h) deaths that occur while the deceased person was not under the care of a physician;
(i) deaths that occur while the deceased person was in the custody of a peace officer;
(j) deaths that are due to:
  (i) any disease or ill-health contracted or incurred by the deceased,
  (ii) any injury sustained by the deceased, or
  (iii) any toxic substance introduced into the deceased

> as a direct result of the deceased's employment or occupation or in the course of one or more of his former employments or occupations.[13]

In addition, the legislation may require that the coroner or medical examiner be notified where the deceased was a prisoner, a patient of a psychiatric facility, or where the deceased was an infant or child.

Where a coroner or medical examiner is notified of a reportable death, he or she will carry out investigations to establish such things as the identity of the deceased, the date, time and place of death, the circumstances under which the death occurred, the cause of death and the manner of death. The coroner or medical examiner is empowered to take possession of the body of the deceased, as well as other items or things that may be pertinent to the investigation, such as clothing, weapons, medication, documents, etc. It may be an offence in some jurisdictions to interfere with the body or physical evidence pertinent to the investigation.

The coroner or medical examiner will examine the body of the deceased and may conduct an autopsy. In some instances, the autopsy may be conducted by a trained pathologist under the supervision of the coroner or medical examiner. The autopsy will include, ordinarily, external examination of the body as well as the possibility of

> dissection, removal and gross examination of the internal organs, weighing and measuring, study and testing of tissue samples, recovery of bullets and other foreign objects, photographing and x-raying, and study of the surrounding physical context. These may lead into further scientific procedures such as ballistic tests, fingerprint tests and so forth.[14]

In addition to examining the physical scene of the death and conducting an autopsy, some provinces provide that the medical examiner or coroner will have "specific statutory powers of entry, inspection, search and seizure . . . to facilitate effective investigation".[15] Often, a coroner or medical examiner will require the assistance of other physicians, experts or police in order to carry out the investigation.

Upon completion of the investigation into a death, the coroner or medical examiner will prepare a report for review by the appropriate authorities and may take further steps to investigate the death, depending on his or her findings. In some instances, there may be disclosure of the findings, and, possibly, of the report or parts of the report, to the press,

---

[13] *Supra* note 9, s. 10(2).

[14] Granger, *supra* note 2, p. 158.

[15] *Ibid.*, p. 170.

family members and other members of the public. The Ontario *Coroners Act* provides:

> Every coroner shall keep a record of the cases reported in which an inquest has been determined to be unnecessary, showing for each case the identity of the deceased and the coroner's findings of the facts as to how, when, where and by what means the deceased came by his or her death, including the relevant findings of the *post mortem* examination and of any other examinations or analyses of the body carried out, and such information shall be available to the spouse, parents, children, brothers and sisters of the deceased and to his or her personal representative, upon request.[16]

Even where an inquest is not held, the coroner's investigation often leads to recommendations in a less formal setting than is usually the case with an inquest. For example, where the death has occurred in a "hospital, nursing home or psychiatric facility" a request for an inquest or further investigation can result in intense scrutiny of the institution. Co-operation may avoid the expense and publicity of an inquest.

> Often the coroner or Regional Coroner will ask the complainant to detail his/her concerns in writing. The investigating coroner reviews the complaint along with the written record from the institution and any other available information, such as a police report. Detailed reviews are often necessary in medical cases involving operative procedures, children's deaths and institutional care in settings, such as nursing homes, homes-for-the-aged and rest homes. For this reason specific standing committees of experts have been established and sit regularly, such as the Anaesthesia Review Committee, Long Term Care Review Committee and the Paediatric Review Committee. These medical experts are from both academic and non-academic medical settings and review cases at the request of the Chief Coroner. The full medical chart, along with the autopsy results and the coroner's investigation to date, are supplied to the committee. Generally the committee assigns a particular member to conduct the initial review. That physician then discusses the case following review with the committee at large and a preliminary opinion and set of concerns is formulated. These are passed on to the Regional Coroner and investigation coroner. This information often forms a useful basis to decide the next course of action. Commonly the Regional Coroner and the local coroner will organize a meeting with the affected institution and medical staff. This Regional Coroner's review will discuss the case in detail in an informal way and hopefully result in a set of recommendations to help prevent similar deaths in the future. The family are then informed of the results of this review.[17]

---

[16] *Supra* note 8, s. 18(2).

[17] Young, *supra* note 4, pp. A-11–A-13.

Inquests and Public Inquiries into Deaths

At common law, where a coroner's investigation was not conclusive in establishing a satisfactory explanation for a violent or unexplained death, an inquest was held. In the coroner system, that decision is usually made by the investigating coroner. In the medical examiner system, as noted above, that decision will be made by some other person or agency based upon the findings of the medical examiner. Although there may be a great many investigations conducted by coroners or medical examiners, very few of these result in an inquest or inquiry. Ontario's Chief Coroner has reported that the number of inquests held annually in Ontario has dropped significantly. Twenty years ago there were 1,200 inquests annually. That figure is now approximately 150.

> At present, most of the 150 inquests per year are selected because there is an obvious need for the public to understand the circumstances and there are recommendations that will protect the public in future. This decreased number of inquests is by design. The office of the Chief Coroner feels that it is a better use of limited resources to do fewer inquests but cover topics in more detail. Such inquests receive more coverage and seem to result in more implementation of recommendations.[18]

The criteria for holding an inquest or inquiry into a death ordinarily are set out in the governing legislation. An inquest or inquiry may be necessary in order to complete an investigation. It may also be necessary in order to "satisfy curiosity or suspicion, to eliminate speculation, or to publicize a hazard or a danger and obtain recommendations or measures to avoid such deaths in the future".[19] The Ontario *Coroners Act* provides:

> When making a determination whether an inquest is necessary or unnecessary, the coroner shall have regard to whether the holding of an inquest would serve the public interest and, without restricting the generality of the foregoing, shall consider,
>
> (a) whether the matters described in clauses 31(1)(a) to (e) are known;[20]
> (b) the desirability of the public being fully informed of the circumstances of the death through an inquest; and
> (c) the likelihood that the jury on an inquest might make useful recommendations directed to the avoidance of death in similar circumstances.[21]

---

[18] *Ibid.*, p. A-13.

[19] Granger, *supra* note 2, p. 195.

[20] For example, who the deceased was; how the deceased came to his or her death; when the deceased came to his or her death; where the deceased came to his or her death; and by what means the deceased came to his or her death.

[21] *Supra* note 8, s. 20.

In most provinces, the legislation gives the coroner or agency responsible for deciding whether to hold an inquest a great deal of discretion in making that decision. In some cases, the decision to hold an inquest or inquiry may be the result of considerable pressure from family, friends or interest groups. In fact, the Chief Coroner of Ontario has made it clear that input from these parties can have a considerable influence.

> On occasion, special interest groups, the press or a ministry of government may call for an inquest. The true facts of the investigation must then be compared with the claims that are being made to see whether an inquest would be useful. If the facts being written or discussed publicly vary too much from the facts the investigation is revealing, then it may be necessary to hold the inquest simply to set the record straight and correctly inform the public.[22]

The possibility of an inquest or inquiry being held as a result of such influence is an indication of the measure of co-operation which ought to be forthcoming from a health-care facility where a coroner is involved. A lack of co-operation may lead to a distortion or misunderstanding of what has occurred, and consequently, to an inquest.

An inquest or public inquiry into a death generally will take the form of a hearing. In most instances, the hearing will be open to the public.[23] The legislation, however, may state that an inquest can be held in private.[24]

The coroner, or the tribunal conducting the public inquiry, has broad powers to regulate the proceedings:

> He can administer oaths and affirmations for all purposes of the inquiry. He may adjourn the proceedings when and for how long he thinks is proper. He can prevent irrelevant or unreasonable cross-examination of witnesses

---

22 Young, *supra* note 4, p. A-13.

23 For example, the British Columbia *Coroners Act, supra* note 8, s. 29, provides:

> An inquest shall be open to the public except that the coroner may hold all or part of the hearing closed to the public
>
> (a) where the coroner is of the opinion the national security might be endangered; or
>
> (b) where a person is charged with an indictable offence under the *Criminal Code*, and relevant evidence with respect to that person's conduct may be given at the inquest.

24 Arguably, such a broad privacy provision contravenes the *Charter of Rights and Freedoms*. In *Edmonton Journal v. Canada (Attorney General) et al.* (1984), 37 Alta. L.R. (2d) 287, 13 D.L.R. (4th) 479 (*sub nom. Re Edmonton Journal and Alberta (A.G.) et al.*), [1985] 4 W.W.R. 575, 17 C.R.R. 100 (C.A.); leave to appeal to S.C.C. refused (1984), 17 C.R.R. 100n, the Alberta Court of Appeal upheld the reasoning of the lower court judge, who concluded that a coroner's inquest or a fatality inquiry was not a court proceeding to which the *Charter* applied.

> and improper arguments. He determines what is admissible in evidence. He can make such rulings and give such directions as may be necessary to preserve order and prevent abuse of process. He can call for the assistance of police officers to enforce his directives and either punish those who contravene them for contempt or, if he himself does not have the power to do this, apply to other authorities to impose such penalties.[25]

An inquest or public hearing into a violent or unnatural death will proceed in a manner similar to a court proceeding. Initially, witnesses will be called by a Crown Attorney who will conduct an examination-in-chief to elicit their testimony. Following the examination-in-chief, those parties with standing, or their counsel, will have an opportunity to cross-examine the witness. The coroner or judge will exercise a judicial function to oversee the general management of the inquest, determine what evidence will be admissible or relevant,[26] place restraints upon cross-examination, if necessary, and make determinations as to standing.

In Ontario, the coroner must give standing to any person who "is substantially and directly interested in the inquest".[27] In British Columbia, standing is given to a person who "may be affected by evidence likely to be adduced at an inquest".[28] Generally, those who are given standing will be entitled to appear personally, to be represented by counsel at an inquest, and to call evidence and cross-examine witnesses. Subject to the evidence being relevant, a party who has standing will be able to issue a summons to have any person testify whose testimony may bear upon the issues being considered at an inquest.

---

[25] C. Granger, *Canadian Coroner Law* (Toronto: Carswell, 1984), pp. 243-44.

[26] J. Young, "An Overview of the Ontario Coroners' System" in *Inside Inquests* (Toronto: Law Society of Upper Canada, Department of Continuing Legal Education, 1993), at p. A-14, states:

> The measure of what is relevant to the inquest should be that there is good evidence that the events in question do bear a direct relationship to this death. Nursing home deaths often create this situation since the various parties, such as family, special interest groups, the nursing home, the doctors and the Ministry of Health, all have different views as to what is relevant. The family may be interested in looking at all aspects of care given their relative (including medical, nursing, dietary and recreation) for the entire time the deceased lived in the home. This would lead to a far-ranging, long and expensive inquiry. The argument could be made that besides abusing the rights of the other participants in the inquest, an inquiry that wanders outside the circumstances of death also is less effective overall. The coroner must carefully consider the submissions of all parties concerning scope and allow only relevant testimony.

[27] *Coroner's Act, supra* note 8, s. 41. See also *Re Brown and Patterson* (1974), 6 O.R. (2d) 441, 53 D.L.R. (3d) 64, 21 C.C.C. (2d) 373 (Div. Ct.).

[28] *Coroners Act, supra* note 8, s. 37.

Where a death occurs in a health-care setting, doctors, nurses and other health practitioners who cared for the patient may be called upon to testify. These witnesses will be examined and cross-examined. It is not unusual for a Crown Attorney, or possibly other parties, to call expert evidence to assist the jury in understanding the health-care issues involved and to comment upon the performance of the health-care practitioners involved. The jury, upon hearing the evidence, may make recommendations that imply weakness or fault, despite no specific finding of fault being made.[29]

A witness who testifies at an inquest or public inquiry may be protected from the use of her or his testimony in subsequent civil or criminal proceedings to which she or he is a party. For example, under the *Fatality Inquiries Act* of Alberta, "no answer given by a witness at a public inquiry shall be used or be receivable in evidence against him in any trial or other proceeding . . . other than a prosecution for perjury".[30] It is not clear, however, that the testimony of a witness at an inquest, who is *not* a *party* to the subsequent proceeding, cannot be used in evidence. For example, if a nurse testified at an inquest, and then was called on a subsequent occasion to testify in the course of a civil proceeding to which the nurse was not a party, it is arguable that the earlier testimony can be used to cross-examine the nurse in the course of her evidence in the civil proceeding. A witness may be entitled to retain and have counsel present at an inquest or inquiry, though the right of counsel to participate may be severely limited.[31]

The governing provincial legislation may require the coroner to hold an inquest even where a decision has been made not to hold one. In *Re Gregoire and Thompson et al.*,[32] a decision was made not to hold an inquest after a patient had died in hospital, though a physician had questioned whether the patient's care, or lack thereof, contributed to the death. On application to the court, an inquest was ordered as there was uncertainty about the cause of death.

In *Lawson v. British Columbia (Solicitor General)*,[33] the British Columbia Court of Appeal upheld an order of the Solicitor General that an inquest

---

[29] It should be noted that a relatively large percentage of inquests or public hearings arise in the health-care context. For example, in 1987, there were 210 inquests held in Ontario. Of these, 22 concerned deaths in hospitals. Source: Ontario Coroner's Office.

[30] R.S.A. 1980, c. F-6, s. 42(1).

[31] See *Coroners Act*, R.S.O. 1990, c. C.37, s. 43: "A witness at an inquest is entitled to be advised by his or her counsel or agent as to his or her rights but such counsel or agent may take no other part in the inquest without leave of the coroner."

[32] (1988), 51 D.L.R. (4th) 131 (N.B. Q.B.).

[33] (1992), 63 B.C.L.R. (2d) 334 (C.A.).

be held about the circumstances in which a patient had died after refusing blood transfusions following a Caesarian section. Questions had been raised about the possible influence of co-religionists, posing as family members, in the patient's refusal.

In *Saxell v. Campbell*,[34] it was held that the coroner had no jurisdiction to order that an inquest be held where an "inquiry" under the British Columbia *Coroners Act* had already been held. In that case there had been a stillbirth at a delivery attended by a midwife. There was a suggestion of "cover-up" at the hospital to which the mother had been taken when fetal distress developed. The inquiry had already concluded that the midwife had "assisted in [the mother's] rapid expedient admission to hospital when she recognized fetal distress", and, therefore, no formal inquest was required. This case highlights the benefit derived by a health facility from co-operating with the coroner or medical examiner.

JURIES

Traditionally, juries are employed as fact-finders in coroner's inquests.[35] In some jurisdictions, this is still the practice, though in others it is not. In a number of jurisdictions the employment of a jury at an inquest or public inquiry is optional.

Once the hearing of evidence has been concluded, the coroner or officer conducting the inquest or inquiry may permit those parties who have standing, either themselves or through their counsel, to make arguments and submissions to the coroner or officer and to the jury if there is one. The arguments and submissions may suggest what findings should be made in relation to the circumstances of death and also what recommendations the coroner, officer or jury may choose to make. The coroner or officer conducting the hearing may also sum up the evidence and issue a charge to the jury regarding the findings it must make.

The role of the jury is to make findings in regard to the circumstances of death. Traditionally, juries were empowered to name individuals responsible for the death if they came to the conclusion that the death occurred as a result of a criminal act. Currently, under the legislation of some provinces, the jury is prohibited from making a finding of legal responsibility, and where the jury comments in its verdict in a manner that offends this principle, the verdict may be set aside.

In *MacKenzie v. MacArthur*,[36] the deceased had been brought to the

---

34 (1987), 21 B.C.L.R. (2d) 44 (S.C.).

35 Granger, *supra* note 25, p. 230.

36 (1980), 25 B.C.L.R. 303, 119 D.L.R. (3d) 529, 57 C.C.C. (2d) 130 (S.C.).

Vancouver General Hospital. The examining physician concluded that the patient was suffering from a personality disorder. The patient was taken from the hospital to jail where he was again examined by a physician. Thereafter, the patient was sent to another hospital where he was refused admission when it was learned that he already had been at Vancouver General Hospital. He was returned to Vancouver General Hospital where the previous diagnosis of a personality disorder was reconfirmed. Plans were made for further tests. Before further testing occurred, however, the patient died.

An inquest was held. The evidence of the health-care participants was heard. The jury was instructed by the coroner that it could not make any finding of legal responsibility or reach any conclusion of law. In reviewing the evidence, however, the coroner suggested to the jury that it should consider that one of the attending physicians had treated the deceased in a careless fashion. The coroner supplied the jury with a typewritten sheet containing possible findings, including the suggestion in regard to the treating physician. Subsequently, the jury returned a verdict that concluded that the physician had treated the deceased in a careless fashion, had failed to conduct an adequate examination and did not keep adequate records of the examination that he did perform.

It was held by the British Columbia Supreme Court that the verdict reached by the jury was a finding of legal responsibility, which was improper and contrary to the provisions of the *Coroners Act*. The decision of the court in this case is consistent with the general principles that coroners' inquests or public inquiries into death are to be "inquiries" rather than proceedings to determine civil or criminal liability.

The coroner, in the course of instructing the jury, may express a view on matters of evidence in order to assist the jury in arriving at a verdict. Generally, coroners have considerable leeway in charging a jury and their comments can have a significant impact upon the jury's verdict, as well as any recommendations the jury might make. Where the coroner's instruction involves a forceful statement of opinion that may amount to a direction to the jury, however, the verdict will be set aside.[37]

Recommendations

One of the major functions of the inquest or public inquiry is to present recommendations to the proper authorities that might avoid or reduce the risk of a death occurring in similar circumstances in the future. It has

---

[37] *Re Beckon* (1992), 9 O.R. (3d) 256, 57 O.A.C. 21 (*sub nom. Beckon v. Deputy Chief Coroner (Ont.)*, 93 D.L.R. (4th) 161 (C.A.).

been suggested by the Chief Coroner of Ontario that "approximately 75% of recommendations from inquests result in changes and implementation by the affected agencies, ministries and persons".[38] It is the practice of the Ontario Coroner's Office to send verdicts and recommendations to appropriate groups who may be affected by verdicts and recommendations.

In Canada, there have been numerous inquests or inquiries arising out of deaths in hospitals and other health facilities. Juries commonly make broad and detailed recommendations that can have a significant impact on health care practices, for example:

- where a patient had died during the night following admission to the Emergency Department, the jury recommended that the hospital policy requiring admitting physicians to see their patients within four hours of admission should be strictly enforced and that where the admitting physician is not available within that time frame, the nursing staff should call another physician to examine the patient.[39]
- where an elderly gentleman had died following an unwitnessed confrontation with another resident at a nursing home, the jury's recommendations included recommendations in relation to the security and supervision of residents who have an aggressive or violent nature and for which earlier medical records be made available to facilitate the assessment and placement process of residents in nursing homes or long-term care facilities.[40]
- where a patient died as a result of massive blood loss after admission to the Emergency Department following a motor vehicle accident, the jury made broad recommendations in relation to the operation of trauma units and the training and qualifications of trauma staff and the management and organization of the hospital's trauma programme.[41]
- in an inquest which examined a number of deaths at a home for young or infant patients who were severely and chronically ill, the jury made broad recommendations in relation to the administration of medical care to children, the administration of morphine to children with complex medical needs and the interaction between caregivers and parents in relation to expectations for medical care, do-not-resuscitate orders, palliation and death processes.[42]

---

[38] Young, *supra* note 26, p. A-22.

[39] Alberta, Office of the Medical Examiner, *Annual Review, 1989*, p. 17.

[40] *Ibid.*, p. 20.

[41] *Re Richard Youngman*, verdict of Coroner's Jury of Ontario, dated February 18, 1992.

[42] *Re Elizabeth Davis et al.*, verdict of Coroner's Jury of Ontario, dated April 16, 1992.

- where a resident died following a fall from a broken sling attached to a mechanical lifting device, the jury made recommendations in relation to adequacy of staffing to maintain residents' safety, the mandatory inspection of equipment, and the number of health-care personnel required to perform a transfer operation on a lifting device.[43]
- where a patient had consumed methyl hydrate and was released from the Emergency Department in the mistaken belief that he had consumed rum, the jury made recommendations in relation to the role of nurses in confirming the consumption of poison, the amendment of hospital poison protocol policies in the province and record keeping by hospital emergency departments in cases where there are reports of poison consumption.[44]
- where a patient died in hospital following the administration of numerous medications and infrequent monitoring by the medical and nursing staff, recommendations were made in relation to the monitoring of patients following the administration of strong medications, the frequency of taking vital signs and training in relation to the use of a gasgow, Scale S.[45]
- where the coroner found that morphine in the deceased patient's blood exceeded the therapeutic range and that lack of charted documentation coupled with the behaviour of medical and nursing personnel created the perception that something covert was being done, the coroner recommended that the hospital develop guidelines and procedures defining "comfort measures", the circumstances for their use, the sequence for application in relation to the withdrawal of life support and the charting of such procedures.[46]
- where a 12-year-old patient died as a result of pericardial tamponade following surgery, recommendations were made to the hospital in relation to the written policy for the placement of central venous catheters and continuing education to all nursing personnel who care for patients with central venous catheters, including the recognition of and treatment for cardiac tamponade.[47]
- where a patient died of hypothermia following admission to hospital and transfer by ambulance, it was recommended that medical and

---

43 *Re Grace Patterson,* verdict of Coroner's Jury of Ontario, dated June 26, 1991.

44 *Re Ricky Snider,* verdict of Coroner's Jury of Ontario, dated May 25, 1992.

45 *Rapport D'Enquete Concernant Le Déces De Madame Laurette Gagnon,* April 17, 1989 (Quebec).

46 *Re Rebecca Klooster,* verdict of Coroner's Inquest of British Columbia, dated December 10, 1992.

47 *Re Christina N. Fraser,* verdict of Coroner's Inquest of British Columbia, dated March 22, 1993.

> nursing staff be given an "in service" on hypothermia, its complications and hospital protocol for treatment, that there be a comprehensive assessment of the emergency department and that all physicians working in the emergency department have advanced A Trauma Life Support Certification.[48]

Ostensibly, inquests and public inquiries into deaths are divorced from civil proceedings, and, as noted, in many jurisdictions the jury or officer hearing the evidence is barred from making findings on legal responsibility or fault. Although the main purpose of an inquest or a public inquiry is to make findings and recommendations that will avoid or reduce the risk of a death occurring in similar circumstances in the future, the participants at an inquest or public inquiry may have a somewhat different agenda. One lawyer has suggested that the primary rule of counsel for the family of the deceased at an inquest may involve "the assembling of evidence for anticipated litigation", and that in those situations, "the verdict of the jury is of secondary importance".[49] In a similar vein, and probably in response to activities by prospective plaintiffs at inquests and public inquiries, "individuals and entities whose conduct may be perceived as having caused or contributed to the death have increasingly found it necessary to retain counsel to represent their interests at the inquest".[50]

Consequently, inquests and public inquiries into deaths frequently involve proceedings that appear more adversarial than inquisitorial and at which the management of health facilities and the conduct of health-care practitioners may be closely scrutinized. There may be an underlying intention in the minds of some parties to build a case for future civil proceedings and an award of compensation. Health administrators whose institutions become involved in inquests should consider seeking legal advice and, possibly, obtaining representation at the inquest or public inquiry. In some instances, nurses, physicians and the health-care facility will be entitled to, or seek to retain, separate counsel. It may be tactically advisable for counsel representing health-care participants to consult and co-operate with one another in preparing to examine and cross-examine witnesses and in formulating arguments and submissions.

---

48 *Re James Astin*, verdict of Coroner's Inquest of British Columbia, dated January 27, 1993.

49 David W. Scott, "Representing The Family At The Hearing", in *Inquests and the General Practitioner* (Toronto: Law Society of Upper Canada, Department of Education, 1987), E-1.

50 Michael E. Royce, "Tactical and Practical Considerations for Counsel Acting For a Potential Defendant in Civil Proceedings" in *Inquests and the General Practitioner* (Toronto: Law Society of Upper Canada, Department of Education, 1987), I-2.

Retaining Counsel for Representation at Inquests

In some instances, the involvement of a health-care facility in an inquest will be peripheral. For example, if the deceased patient was injured on the work site, but died later in hospital, the main area of inquiry will relate to occupational health and safety issues in the deceased's workplace. A representative of the Medical Records Department may be subpoenaed so the deceased patient's medical records can be entered into evidence. The record will provide a detailed description of information which will assist in arriving at a verdict; for example, "where" the deceased died. In such a case, however, it is unlikely that the hospital will be the subject of any criticism at the inquest or that it will be affected to any significant degree by any of the recommendations that may arise from the inquest.

On the other hand, if a worker received what appeared to be relatively insignificant injuries on the work site, and later died in hospital, the focus of the inquest, and its impact upon the hospital, may be significant. In that case, the main area of inquiry may involve the hospital's emergency system, the level of nursing and medical care available to patients, the quality of care that was administered, the type of equipment available, the policies and procedures within the institution and a multitude of other issues directly involving the hospital. The inquest may give rise to numerous recommendations that will affect the hospital, and in some cases other hospitals. Findings or recommendations that suggest that the system can be improved may receive wide publicity. Recommendations may compel a hospital to alter the way in which its emergency department operates. There may be civil, and in rare cases criminal, implications. In such a case the hospital administrator will be well-advised to retain legal counsel well in advance of the inquest and to ensure that the institution and its health professionals are represented at the inquest itself.

Whether a health-care facility and its staff are represented by counsel at an inquest will involve weighing the following factors:

- Will the family of the deceased patient be represented by counsel, and, if so, what is the reputation of that lawyer? Is it someone who has been involved in other inquests? If so, has he or she attempted to use the inquest to build evidence or to attract publicity?
- Is the matter one that is likely to result in a civil action, and, if so, will the damages in issue be significant?
- Is it likely that health professionals for whom the health facility is responsible in law will be called to give evidence? If so, will their evidence touch upon areas of concern or criticism which may have given rise to the inquest?
- Is any health professional who will testify at the inquest likely to express criticism of the health facility or its staff, *i.e.*, allege inadequate staffing, inadequate equipment, deficient policies or procedures?

- Is the inquest likely to attract considerable publicity?
- Is there scope for far-reaching recommendations that will apply to the health facility?
- Has standing been granted to a public advocacy or interest group that is likely to result in an inquiry that goes beyond the facts directly connected to the death of the patient?

JUDICIAL REVIEW

Generally, there can be no appeal of the verdict of the coroner, the jury or the officer conducting the public inquiry into the death. Where the inquest or public inquiry is conducted in a manner outside its jurisdiction or in breach of the governing legislation, however, a party or person affected by the verdict may apply to a court to have the verdict set aside. Applications for judicial review have been entertained by the court in circumstances where the coroner refused standing to someone at an inquest,[51] where it was alleged that there was bias or a reasonable apprehension of bias on the part of the coroner,[52] where the inquest verdict involved a finding of legal responsibility,[53] where it was alleged that an inquest could not be held in the circumstances of a stillbirth,[54] where it was alleged that the coroner lacked jurisdiction to seize privileged documents,[55] where it was alleged that summonses to witnesses who were judicial officers should be quashed[56] and where it was alleged that the public was improperly excluded from an inquest.[57]

---

[51] *Re Brown and Patterson* (1974), 6 O.R. (2d) 441, 53 D.L.R. (3d) 64, 21 C.C.C. (2d) 373 (Div. Ct.).

[52] *Evans v. Milton* (1979), 24 O.R. (2d) 181, 97 D.L.R. (3d) 687, 46 C.C.C. (2d) 129, 9 C.P.C. 83 (C.A.); leave to appeal to S.C.C. refused (1979), 24 O.R. (2d) 181n; also *Re Reid and Wigle* (1980), 29 O.R. (2d) 633, 114 D.L.R. (3d) 669 (H.C.J.).

[53] *MacKenzie v. MacArthur, supra* note 36.

[54] *Bassett v. Saskatchewan (A.G.)* (1983), 23 Sask. R. 11, 149 D.L.R. (3d) 721, 5 C.C.C. (3d) 518 (C.A.).

[55] *Re Scottish & York Ins. Co. and Harpur* (1981), 42 O.R. (2d) 201 (H.C.J.); *Mrazek v. Rolf* (1983), 27 Alta. L.R. (2d) 91 (Q.B.).

[56] *Re Reinking* (1984), 3 O.A.C. 137 (Div. Ct.); *Re Allan and Ontario (A.G.)* (1984), 47 O.R. (2d) 164, 11 D.L.R. (4th) 537, 14 C.C.C. (3d) 178 (Div. Ct.).

[57] *Edmonton Journal v. Canada (Attorney General) et al.*, (1984), 37 Alta. L.R. (2d) 287, 13 D.L.R. (4th) 479 (*sub nom. Re Edmonton Journal and Alberta (A.G.) et al.*), [1985] 4 W.W.R. 575, 17 C.R.R. 100 (C.A.); leave to appeal to S.C.C. refused (1984), 17 C.R.R. 100n.

Generally speaking, however, the court before whom an application for judicial review has been brought will exercise considerable deference and may be reluctant to overturn a determination made by the coroner or officer presiding over the hearing unless the determination is clearly wrong. In fact, the court's power to intervene has been characterized by one court as "a very scrawny power", unlikely to be exercised unless there has been a clear breach of substantive rights by an excess of statutory jurisdiction or failure to adhere to the principles of natural justice.[58]

A court will interfere only in cases of jurisdictional error. It will be only in rare cases that an inquest will be interrupted for the purpose of seeking a review by the court.

> The public interest requires that the coroner be able to go about his/her job without intermittent interference by the courts, particularly on issues within the specialized medical and curial expertise of the coroner.
>
> If inquests were conducted by judges or lawyers or royal commissioners, they would have a more legalistic or policy focus. One unique value of an inquest is that it is conducted by men and women with a medical orientation who bring to their task their medical experience and their situation-sense of patients, families, illnesses, medical record confidentiality, medical institutions, and medical care.[59]

In particular, courts will exercise "curial defence" where the issues in the case involve issues of health care in which it is perceived that a medically trained coroner will have great expertise.

Opinion evidence offered by an unqualified witness, advocacy of a particular theory for the manner of death, or failure to investigate persons who may have knowledge concerning the death of the deceased are grounds upon which the verdict of the jury may be set aside by a court.[60]

Public Inquiries

In addition to an inquest, there is another legal procedure designed to be inquisitorial in nature, as opposed to adversarial, which may, on occasion, be employed to conduct an investigation in the field of health care. The federal government and each province have enacted legislation allowing the Lieutenant-Governor-in-Council to authorize the appointment of a

---

58 *Re Reid and Wigle, supra* note 52, at 637 (O.R.).

59 *People First of Ontario v. Porter, Regional Coroner, Niagara* (1991), 5 O.R. (3d) 609, at 645-46, 50 O.A.C. 90, 85 D.L.R. (4th) 174 (Div. Ct.); revd (1992), 6 O.R. (3d) 289 (C.A.).

60 *New Brunswick (Chief Coroner) v. Coyle Estate* (1991), 120 N.B.R. (2d) 228 (Q.B.).

commissioner (or commissioners) to conduct a public inquiry concerning any matter connected with the good government of the country or province.[61] Once appointed, a commissioner has many of the powers held by a coroner or judge presiding over an inquest; he or she may hold hearings, summon witnesses, grant standing, control cross-examination and make recommendations. Commissioners may be ordered by the government to conduct inquiries in a wide spectrum of areas. On a number of occasions federal and provincial inquiries have been given terms of reference that related directly to health care.[62]

RELEVANT LEGISLATION

ALBERTA

Fatality Inquiries Act, R.S.A. 1980, c. F-6
Public Inquiries Act, R.S.A. 1980, c. P-29

BRITISH COLUMBIA

Coroners Act, R.S.B.C. 1979, c. 68
Inquiry Act, R.S.B.C. 1979, c. 198

---

[61] See the pertinent legislation, listed at the end of the chapter, for the precise wording employed in each statute.

[62] For example: Canada, *Royal Commission on Health Services* (Ottawa: Queen's Printer, 1964-1965) (Commissioner: E.M. Hall) (under R.S.C. 1952, c. 154); Canada, *Commission of Inquiry into the Non-Medical Use of Drugs* (Ottawa: Information Canada, 1970) (Commissioner: Gerald LeDain) (under R.S.C. 1970, c. I-13); Canada, *Commission of Inquiry on the Pharmaceutical Industry* (Ottawa: Supply and Services Canada, 1985) (Commissioner: Harry C. Eastman) (under R.S.C. 1985, c. I-13); Ontario, *Commission of Inquiry into the Confidentiality of Health Information* (Toronto: Queen's Printer, 1980) (Commissioner: Horace Krever) (under R.S.O. 1971, c. 49); Ontario, *Royal Commission of Inquiry into Certain Deaths at the Hospital for Sick Children and Related Matters* (Toronto: Ontario Ministry of the Attorney General, 1984) (Commissioner: Samuel Grange) (under R.S.O. 1980, c. 411); Canada, *Royal Commission on New Reproductive Technologies* (Ottawa: Canada Communications Group, 1993) (Commissioner: Patricia A. Baird) (under R.S.C. 1985, c. I-13); Canada, *Commission of Inquiry on the Blood System in Canada: Interim Report* (Ottawa: Canada Communication Group, 1995) (under P.C. 1993-1879).

Canada

Inquiries Act, R.S.C. 1985, c. I-11

Manitoba

Fatality Inquiries Act, S.M. 1989-90, c. 30

New Brunswick

Coroners Act, R.S.N.B. 1973, c. C-23
Inquiries Act, R.S.N.B. 1973, c. I-11

Newfoundland

Public Inquiries Act, R.S.N. 1990, c. P-38
Summary Proceedings Act, R.S.N. 1990, c. S-30

Northwest Territories

Coroners Act, R.S.N.W.T. 1988, c. C-20
Public Inquiries Act, R.S.N.W.T. 1988, c. P-14

Nova Scotia

Fatality Inquiries Act, R.S.N.S. 1989, c. 164
Public Inquiries Act, R.S.N.S. 1989, c. 372

Ontario

Coroners Act, R.S.O. 1990, c. C.37
Public Inquiries Act, R.S.O. 1990, c. P.41

Prince Edward Island

Coroners Act, R.S.P.E.I. 1988, c. C-25
Public Inquiries Act, R.S.P.E.I. 1988, c. P-31

Quebec

Causes and Circumstances of Death Act, R.S.Q. 1977, c. R-0.2
Public Inquiry Commissions Act, R.S.Q. 1977, c. C-37

Saskatchewan

Coroners Act, R.S.S. 1978, c. C-38
Public Inquiries Act, R.S.S. 1978, c. P-38

Yukon

Coroners Act, R.S.Y. 1986, c. 35
Public Inquiries Act, R.S.Y. 1986, c. 137

CHAPTER 9

Employment and Labour Relations Law

INTRODUCTION

A large component of the legal portfolio for a health facility will involve the legal relationship of employer and employee. Health administrators, in managing the workplace, will be involved in interviewing, hiring, supervising, disciplining, and in some cases, terminating employees. In some instances, these activities will take place in the context of the traditional common-law employment contract; in others, employees will be unionized and the employment relationship will be in the context of a collective bargaining agreement. Health administrators must be familiar with the basic legal regime in Canada if they are to avoid unnecessary conflict or controversy. Knowledge of fundamental principles will assist health administrators in avoiding pitfalls leading to litigation, and where, unavoidably, litigation arises, in supporting and instructing legal counsel for the health facility.

MINIMUM EMPLOYMENT STANDARDS

Federal and provincial governments in Canada have passed legislation which ensures minimum employment standards to employees in their respective jurisdictions.[1] There are minimum age requirements for full-time employment. Those who have not reached a certain age (14[2] to 17[3]) are prohibited from engaging in full-time employment, or employment that would interfere with school work, that is considered to be unwholesome or harmful[4] or that would require them to work at certain hours

---

1 See the list of relevant legislation at end of this chapter.

2 *Labour Standards Code*, R.S.N.S. 1989, c. 246, s. 68.

3 *Canada Labour Code*, R.S.C. 1985, c. L-2, s. 179.

4 *Employment Standards Act*, S.N.B. 1982, c. E-7.2, s. 39 [am. 1984, c. 42, s. 22 (French version)].

(*i.e.*, 10:00 p.m. to 7:00 a.m.).[5] Employers are required to keep basic personnel records, including such information as the name, age and address of the employee as well as the employee's wage rate, hours of work, vacation periods and pay, leaves of absence, date of lay-off or discharge and corresponding notices. Full-time employment, in most jurisdictions, is limited to an eight-hour day and 40 hours of work per week.

The first minimum wage legislation, passed in Ontario in 1920, was for the purpose of providing a "living wage" to women who were drastically underpaid — often much less than men for the same work.[6] Employment standards legislation in each jurisdiction contains a minimum pay rate for employees which is increased by government from time to time. Minimum employment standards also regulate the amount of overtime that an employee may work and the obligation of the employer to pay extra for overtime work. It is mandatory that employers allow employees to take a vacation every year and that employers pay the employee during the vacation period. Employees are entitled to take time off on statutory holidays, or, in the alternative, to receive additional compensation when they are required to work on a statutory holiday.

Employees may be entitled to take a leave of absence for such events as pregnancy or adoption. All Canadian jurisdictions provide for unpaid maternity leave of 17 to 18 weeks, depending upon the jurisdiction. Employment continues throughout the period of leave and the employer is required to reinstate the employee to the position she held prior to the leave, or to another position of a similar nature. In some jurisdictions, there is an additional "parental leave" allowing either or both parents to take an unpaid leave upon the birth of a child or where a child has been adopted.[7]

In the absence of a collective agreement providing otherwise, an employer is not required to continue the employment of an employee, no matter how satisfactory the employee's services may be. At common law, an employer may dismiss an employee, even where there has been no disobedience, misconduct or neglect of duties by the employee; however, the employer is required by law to compensate the employee for the employer's failure to give reasonable notice. The principle of reasonable notice is an implied term of the employment contract. It presupposes that

5 *Labour Standards Act*, S.N. 1977, c. 52, s. 44 [am. 1987, c. 41, s. 11].

6 *Canadian Master Labour Guide*, 5th ed. (Don Mills: CCH Canadian Ltd., 1990), p. 73.

7 *Viz. Canada Labour Code*, *supra* note 3, s. 206.1; Manitoba: *Employment Standards Act*, R.S.M. 1987, c. E110, s. 37; New Brunswick: *Employment Standards Act*, *supra* note 4, ss. 43-44.02 [am. S.N.B. 1984, c. 42, s. 24; 1988, c. 59, ss. 17 and 18]; Quebec: *An act respecting labour standards*, R.S.Q. 1977, c. N-1.1, s. 81; Saskatchewan: *Labour Standards Act*, R.S.S. 1978, c. L-1, s. 29.1.

at the time of hiring it was understood by the parties that the employer would give reasonable notice to the employee of an intention to terminate to enable the employee to make alternative employment arrangements. Of course, the employee will not be entitled to reasonable notice where the employee has conducted himself or herself in a manner that justifies immediate termination of the employment contract.

Minimum employment standards in Canada require the employer to give a stipulated period of notice to the employee unless there is just cause for immediate dismissal. The notice period ranges from one week to eight weeks, depending upon the length of employment. A shorter period of employment will merit a shorter period of notice; a longer period of employment merits longer notice. The employee may or may not be required by the employer to continue to work during the notice. If an employer wrongfully terminates an employee and asks the employee to leave his or her employment immediately, this does not affect the employer's obligation to continue to pay the employee throughout the notice period. On the other hand, if an employee is given working notice and does not continue to work during the notice period, though expected to do so by the employer, the right to be paid throughout the notice period is forfeited.

Wrongful Dismissal

Legislation guaranteeing minimum employment standards does not prevent an employer and an employee from entering into employment contracts that provide benefits exceeding the minimum standards. In some cases, the employment contract will be in writing and contain provisions expressly agreed upon by the parties. Absent any formal agreement, oral or in writing, certain common-law terms will be implied automatically by the employment relationship. Employment contracts are considered to be contracts of "personal service" and, as such, courts will not require either party to honour the contract by specifically performing it. The only remedy available to the employee is monetary damages for the employer's failure to give reasonable notice. A contract of service between an employer and employee entitles the employee to seek compensation for wrongful dismissal.[8]

The amount of compensation for wrongful dismissal is based upon the court's assessment of what constitutes a reasonable period of notice to an employee that he or she will be required to seek alternative employment.

---

8 *Barton v. Agincourt Football Enterprises Ltd.*, [1982] 1 S.C.R. 666, 134 D.L.R. (3d) 1, 42 N.R. 97, 18 B.L.R. 27.

The award of damages will be based upon the amount that the employee would have earned during such notice period. Where the employer gives a period of notice that is judged, subsequently, to be too short, the employee will be entitled to the amount of wages he or she would have earned during the additional period which the court deems to be reasonable. Also, if the employee is able to mitigate and find new employment, the income earned from the new employment will be subtracted from the award. In calculating the period of reasonable notice, the court will look at factors such as the age and educational background of the employee, the length of service, the level of seniority and, to a certain extent, the availability of alternative employment.

Assessing the appropriate notice period is, to some extent, an art. There is no scientific formula to be followed. On the other hand, the range for the appropriate notice period is fairly narrow; it rarely exceeds two years. Health administrators are well-advised, at the time of dismissal, to consider payment to the employee of an amount consistent with what is a reasonable, perhaps even generous, notice period. The alternative may be lengthy and expensive legal proceedings in which the cost of the legal services may exceed the saving, if any, on the notice period.

In *Ellis v. Burnaby Hospital Society*,[9] the Court held that a 22-month notice period was appropriate for a 49-year-old nurse-manager who had been employed at the hospital for almost 25 years and who was dismissed following a structural reorganization of the nursing administration at the hospital. In *Edwards v. Royal Alexandra Hospital*,[10] a 56-year-old nurse who occupied a mid-management position was dismissed when her position was eliminated due to economic reasons. She had been employed at the hospital for 36 years, with the exception of a four-year period spent elsewhere. The trial judge found that the appropriate notice period was 21 months.

In *Gagne v. Smooth Rock Falls Hospital*,[11] a hospital's business manager was dismissed after 19 years of service. The Court noted that she had been employed in a specialized field in a remote community in northern Ontario. She had to move in order to find new employment, which she obtained nine months after termination. The Court found that there was no basis for the employee having been terminated without notice — the termination having occurred shortly after the conclusion of a sexual relationship between the business manager and a more senior employee. A 12-month notice period was deemed appropriate. In *Anderson v. Peel Memorial Hospital Association*,[12] the director of a pharmacy had been employed at

---

[9] (1992), 42 C.C.E.L. 239 (B.C.S.C.).

[10] (1994), 5 C.C.E.L. (2d) 196 (Alta. Q.B.).

[11] (1991), 39 C.C.E.L. 281 (Ont. Gen. Div.).

[12] (1992), 40 C.C.E.L. 203 (Ont. Gen. Div.).

the hospital for a period of seven years. Although the stated reason for her dismissal was incompetence, this position was abandoned at trial and the only issue was the appropriate length of notice. The Court awarded a notice period of 12 months. In *Peitich v. Clark Institute of Psychiatry*,[13] a senior psychologist was dismissed after 23 years of employment. At the time of dismissal, he was 53 years old. The Court found that there was "limited employment opportunity" in his field, which was forensic psychology. The judge held that a notice period of two years was appropriate.

As stated, an employee will not be entitled to reasonable notice of termination in circumstances where the employer is justified in treating the employment contract as at an end. Termination in these circumstances generally is referred to as "termination for just cause". Minor acts not consistent with an employee's duties will not be considered sufficient to warrant immediate dismissal; however, serious breaches of duty in direct violation of the employer's interests will be sufficient. Each case must be decided upon its own facts. Where an employer has countenanced earlier breaches without a warning or indication of disapproval, a court may conclude that the employer condoned the employee's misconduct, and this may disentitle the employer from terminating the employment contract without notice.

The burden of proof that termination without notice was justified rests with the employer. That this proof can be very difficult to demonstrate is confirmed by numerous reported cases in which courts have rejected the employer's position that termination without notice was justified. Although an employee's conduct may be unsatisfactory, blameworthy and deserving of censure or discipline, that does not mean that an immediate termination of employment without notice can be justified.

Conduct clearly unamicable to the continued employment relationship, assuming that it has not been condoned earlier by the employer, will constitute grounds for immediate dismissal. Where a hospital's director of nursing lost his professional status as a registered nurse following disciplinary proceedings, it was held that his loss of professional qualification rendered impossible the performance of the vast majority of his duties under the employment contract; therefore, his dismissal was justified.[14] An executive director of a mental health association who, contrary to the express instructions of her immediate supervisor, publicized a private letter and sought the support of the press in protecting her own position, was found to have been justly dismissed without notice because "she was guilty of misconduct and had in effect destroyed her own effectiveness as executive director" of the organization.[15] A nursing home's summary

---

[13] (1988), 19 C.C.E.L. 105 (Ont. H.C.J.).

[14] *Thomas v. Lafleche Union Hospital Board* (1991), 36 C.C.E.L. 251 (Sask. C.A.).

[15] *Williston v. C.M.H.A.-Moncton* (1993), 46 C.C.E.L. 251 (Man. Q.B.).

dismissal of a nurse who had left medications with residents, administered incorrect doses, and who had in one instance given the wrong medication, was justified as the nurse had been seriously incompetent in the performance of her duties.[16]

Damages for Mental Distress and Punitive and Aggravated Damages

Termination, whether for just cause or not, is likely to be a traumatic experience for the employee. In recent years, employees have recovered damages not only for the failure of the employer to give reasonable notice of termination but also for damages where the circumstances of the dismissal have resulted in significant mental suffering to the employee or where a court considered that the conduct of the employer in terminating employment was deserving of censure.

In *Speck v. Greater Niagara General Hospital*,[17] a senior nurse commenced an action for wrongful dismissal against her employer after being dismissed on the ground that she was unable to perform her managerial duties satisfactorily. In addition to advancing a claim for damages resulting from the employer's alleged failure to give reasonable notice, the nurse claimed damages for mental suffering caused by the dismissal.

The plaintiff, who had been employed by the hospital for 13 years (and employed at other hospitals for 20 years before that), testified at trial that she was "stunned by her sudden dismissal".[18] She became "distraught and full of anxiety". She suffered from sleeplessness and loss of appetite. She lost 15 pounds. She returned to the care of her psychiatrist who increased her medication. She testified that the firing "wiped her out". At the time of trial, her depression had continued and she was bitter about the destruction of her nursing career and felt hopeless about her professional future and financial position.

The trial judge commented that although all of the individual defendants who gave evidence on behalf of the hospital had not intended to cause suffering to the plaintiff, they acted, nonetheless, without any thought to the consequences of the termination to the plaintiff, and, in doing so, they engaged in a "reckless breach" of the hospital's employment contract

---

16 *Meaney v. Anges Pratte Home* (1989), 74 Nfld. & P.E.I.R. 18, 231 A.P.R. 18 (Nfld. T.D.).

17 (1983), 43 O.R. (2d) 611, 2 D.L.R. (4th) 84, 2 C.C.E.L. 21 (H.C.J.).

18 *Ibid.*, at 619 (O.R.).

with the plaintiff. The Court concluded that at the time the nurse was dismissed,

> The defendant hospital had virtually no complaint about her clinical nursing skills, and it is clear from the evidence that her skills of this type were good. The dissatisfaction of the hospital was entirely with her performance as a supervisor, that is, in her ability to direct junior nurses and other staff in an effective and harmonious way. If the hospital had given her reasonable notice, and permitted or encouraged her to carry on in a face-saving way while she tried to find employment in another hospital as a staff nurse (*i.e.*, not as a supervisor), I think the plaintiff probably would have found work in another hospital that would have been acceptable to her.
>
> By dismissing her for cause, the hospital crushed the plaintiff and led her to fear that she could never get employment in another hospital because of the unfavourable references that would be given by the hospital . . .
>
> I have decided on the balance of probabilities that virtually all of the mental suffering experience by the plaintiff was caused by the defendant's breach of contract, that is, by the way in which she was terminated: without notice because of cause, rather than by the termination itself.[19]

The judge concluded that the plaintiff should have been given nine months' notice of termination. In addition, the judge awarded the plaintiff the cost of drugs and transportation in connection with medical treatment for her depression caused by the wrongful dismissal and the sum of $15,000 to compensate her for the suffering and loss of enjoyment of life which she sustained as a result of the mental distress negligently inflicted by the hospital.

A court may also award punitive damages to punish or deter an employer from engaging in egregious or malicious conduct, or aggravated damages to appease a plaintiff for the employer's misbehaviour. Where, in dismissing an employee, a hospital employer engaged in conduct that had the effect, though unintended, of "demeaning" the employee, aggravated damages of $25,000 were awarded.[20] Where members of a hospital's administration, in dismissing an employee for incompetence, did not have an honest belief that the allegations of incompetence were true, the plaintiff was awarded $5,000 in punitive damages.[21] A court may also decide to award punitive court costs against an employer where termination of an employee was carried out in a "callous" manner and where the severance notice contained "mistruth and fabrication".[22]

---

19 *Ibid.*, at 620-21.

20 *Rock v. Canadian Red Cross Society* (1994), 5 C.C.E.L. (2d) 231 (Ont. Gen. Div.).

21 *Anderson v. Peel Memorial Hospital Association, supra* note 12.

22 *MacAlpine v. Stratford General Hospital*, unreported, May 12, 1995 (Ont. Gen. Div.) (Kennedy J.).

Labour Relations and Collective Bargaining

Health professionals comprise a substantial percentage of unionized workers in Canada. Many employer-employee relationships in health facilities are governed by collective agreements. The employment relationships may be with nurses, nursing assistants, therapists, dieticians, ward clerks, technicians, maintenance staff and a variety of other workers within the facility. Collective agreements are negotiated between an employer and a union representing the interests of a particular group of employees. These agreements are designed to cover the most important, and sometimes the most controversial, aspects of the employment relationship. Collective bargaining is regulated in each province and territory of Canada by labour relations statutes. These statutes contain codes of procedure for collective bargaining. The statutes deal with issues such as certification of trade unions, contents of collective agreements, guide-lines for negotiations and procedures for arbitration where differences arise. The statutes establish labour relations boards to exercise regulatory authority over the collective bargaining process and to act as mechanisms for solving disputes between the employer and the employee, the employer and the union, and in some cases, the union and the employee.

Labour arbitration is a procedure used to interpret and to enforce the collective agreement. The power to arbitrate is limited to those disputes arising out of disagreements concerning interpretation of the collective agreement. Aspects of employment that do not touch upon provisions of the collective agreement are not arbitrable. For example, where a collective agreement did not provide a right to grieve an unfavourable evaluation, it was held that a nurse had no right to an arbitration of a grievance in relation to her evaluation.[23] Where an ambulance driver grieved a requirement that he perform tasks he considered to be those of an orderly and not authorized by the *Ambulance Act*, it was held that the matter was properly within the jurisdiction of the provincial Health Facilities Appeal Board, and was not a matter for arbitration as it did not involve the interpretation, application, administration or alleged violation of the collective agreement.[24]

---

[23] *Re New Orchard Lodge/Extendicare Ltd., Ottawa and Ontario Nurses' Association* (1983), 12 L.A.C. (3d) 221 (Ont.-Swinton).

[24] *Re Kirkland & District Hospital and Service Employees Union, Local 478* (1988), 34 L.A.C. (3d) 385 (Ont.-Weatherhill).

Management Rules and Decisions

Collective agreements usually contain provisions supporting the right of the employer to manage the workplace. Management rights may include responsibility for maintaining order, discipline and efficiency; hiring, assigning, classifying, and discharging staff; determining hours of work and methods of working; and identifying services to be performed and the equipment to be used. Although broad, the exercise of management rights must be consistent with the terms of the collective agreement. A management rule or policy must be reasonable, and it must be considerate of special circumstances that may arise in an individual case. Where there is a dispute whether management is acting within the scope of the collective agreement, or in a manner that conflicts with the terms of the agreement, a party to the collective agreement may resort to arbitration. Generally, an employee is required to comply with a management rule, even where there is disagreement, until the dispute has been resolved by arbitration. This principle has given rise to the colloquialism: "obey now, grieve later".

Reasonableness

Whether a management rule or policy is reasonable will be evaluated in the context of the collective agreement and the "business purpose" of the enterprise. The main business purpose of a health facility is the care and treatment of patients.

Where a new no-smoking policy was implemented at a facility that provided care for cancer out-patients, an arbitrator ruled that the ban was consistent with the health facility's desire to show leadership in cancer prevention, and therefore it was reasonable.[25] The same decision sets out general principles to be followed where management decides to initiate new rules or policies in the workplace. The rule or policy must be consistent with the collective agreement, be clear and unequivocal and be enforced consistently, and the consequences of non-compliance must be brought to the attention of employees before any disciplinary action is taken.

In *Re Greater Niagara General Hospital and Ontario Nurses' Association*,[26] a part-time nurse applied for a full-time position, but was denied the position because she failed a physical examination. She grieved on the basis that her hypertension would not affect her ability to do the job. She also

---

[25] *Re Thameswood Lodge and London and District Service Workers' Union, Local 220* (1984), 15 L.A.C. (3d) 228 (Ont.-Verity).

[26] (1987), 32 L.A.C. (3d) 140 (Ont.-Brown).

grieved on the basis that other job transfers had not required a physical examination. The grievance was denied. The board of arbitration held that the physical examination was a condition of employment that arose in the hiring process and was not a term of the collective agreement that could be grieved. It confirmed that the hospital had a legitimate business purpose in ensuring that its employees were fit to perform the work required without undue risk to the employee, the hospital or its patients.

A decision adversely affecting an employee without achieving a legitimate business purpose is not reasonable. Where a hospital established an anti-nepotism rule, management claimed that the rule was consistent with its authority to hire under the collective agreement, and therefore it was not subject to arbitration. The board of arbitration disagreed, stating:

> if it [the employer] chooses to maintain a policy on nepotism, [it must] make it apparent on the face of the document that it will only be invoked consistently with the terms of the agreement *and then only when real and substantial business considerations require it to do so.*[27]
>
> [Emphasis added]

In that case, the arbitration board said that the hospital could refuse a position to a prospective employee only if the presence of a family member would affect his or her ability to perform the duties of the vacant position, or if it would create a perception of favouritism or cause employee malaise.

Even where management is able to demonstrate a business purpose for its decision, there must be a reasonable relationship between the intended objective and the means chosen to attain it. Where surgical nurses who were called in to assist in off-hours were required to "scrub stretchers" as part of their duties, it was held that the hospital's interest in the "efficient deployment of nursing personnel during a time period to justify the costs incurred by the call-in" was not sufficient to justify the assignment of non-nursing tasks. The board of arbitration ruled that in the absence of evidence that scrubbing stretchers was an urgent requirement, which could not be handled in some other way, it was unreasonable to require nurses to engage in duties they did not perform ordinarily.[28]

Even where there is no express stipulation for "reasonableness" in a collective agreement, fairness and common sense dictate that management should conduct itself in a manner that is reasonable. Nonetheless, where a hospital attempted to lay off 55 nurses' aides, and it was argued by

---

[27] *Re McKellar General Hospital and Ontario Nurses' Association* (1984), 15 L.A.C. (3d) 353, at 365 (Ont.-Beatty).

[28] *Re Lennox and Addington County General Hospital and Ontario Nurses' Association* (1986), 25 L.A.C. (3d) 97 (Ont.-Emrich).

the union that there was an obligation on the hospital to establish the "reasonableness of its action", the arbitration board held that it could not import a specific general requirement of reasonableness and fairness into the agreement. However, the language of the management right clause, when read in the labour relations context and in the context of the collective agreement as a whole, supported an implied requirement to act in a *'bona fide'* fashion. It was held that the decision to lay off employees must result from a consideration of "prevailing economic and business conditions" and would be reasonable only if there is "an honesty of purpose" in the decision.[29] For hospitals and other health facilities, a "legitimate business purpose" may involve patient care and related concerns, such as safety, sanitation or institutional security.[30] A management rule may be considered unreasonable, even where the collective agreement authorizes a particular management rule, if it is inconsistent with other provisions in the collective agreement.

A management decision that does not take into account the circumstances of an individual case may be judged arbitrary, and, consequently, unreasonable. In *Re Sherbrooke Community Society and Saskatchewan Union of Nurses, Local 22*,[31] a nurse asked for an eight-day leave of absence during July and August. The hospital refused because of its rule that no leaves would be granted during those two months. The nurse filed a grievance through her union, stating that she had made the request four months ahead of time and that the administration could easily have found someone to replace her in that time. She also stated that the hospital had refused to listen to, or to consider, the reasons why a leave of absence was necessary. The board of arbitration ruled that the hospital had acted unreasonably because it gave no consideration to the nurse's specific request: "Discretion cannot properly be reduced to a mechanical exercise by the administrator of any legal regime."[32] Where a hospital refused to allow empty boardrooms to be used for its staff's union meetings, it was held that the hospital's decision was arbitrary.

> [T]he test is not the reasonableness of the employer's decision but rather whether the employer has in fact exercised its discretion, that the discretion has been exercised by the proper authority, on the particular facts of the case and is not tainted by capriciousness, bad faith or discrimination.[33]

---

29 *Re Toronto East General Hospital and Service Employees' Union, Local 204* (1984), 13 L.A.C. (3d) 400, at 408 (Ont.-Burkett).

30 *Re University of British Columbia Health Sciences Centre Hospital Society and Hospital Employees' Union, Local 180* (1985), 21 L.A.C. (3d) 132, at 134 (Ont.-Munroe).

31 (1981), 2 L.A.C. (3d) 97 (Sask.-Norman).

32 *Ibid.*, at 102.

33 *Re Trenton Memorial Hospital and Ontario Nurses' Association* (1984), 15 L.A.C. (3d) 440, at 446 (Ont.-Emrich).

"Obey Now; Grieve Later"

An employee's refusal to carry out an order or direction from a supervisor may be detrimental to patient care. Where an employee has refused to comply with a direction or request of management, the employee may be subject to discipline, even in circumstances where management's conduct was unjustified. This principle has particular application to the health-care setting in which a worker's refusal to carry out a direction or order may be detrimental to patients.

In *Re Abbie J. Lane Memorial Hospital and Nova Scotia Nurses' Union,*[34] a nurse was hired on condition that she would not be posted to a particular floor where her husband worked. On being requested to "float" to that floor, the nurse objected. She was then sent home for the day without pay. She grieved the suspension. The arbitrator ruled that even if she did consider an assignment on the particular floor a breach of her employment contract, she was not entitled to disobey a direct order — she should have carried out her assignment as requested and grieved later.

It is possible for an employee to file a grievance where he or she questions the legitimacy of a management rule before it has been applied.[35] The employee can thereby avoid the prospect of being put in the position of having to follow a rule that may be unjust, or in the alternative, of disobeying the rule and facing discipline. The hearing of a grievance is permitted even though no employee's rights have been adversely affected. In *Re Religious Hospitallers of Hotel-Dieu of St. Joseph of the Diocese of London and Service Employees' Union, Local 210,*[36] the hospital instituted a rule that required employees to remain on hospital premises during their lunch hour to be available in an emergency. A grievance was filed by the union representing medical records personnel. Hospital management took the position that the employees were required to follow the rule and grieve later and that the rule was not arbitrable in the absence of a grievance by a specific employee. The arbitration board allowed the pre-emptive grievance, however, deciding to assess the legitimacy of the management rule rather than exposing an employee to the threat of discipline for testing what might not be a legitimate management rule. The arbitration board ruled that if management wished to exercise control and authority over employees during the lunch break, the employees would have to be paid; otherwise, the rule was invalid.

Although the general rule is that an employee must obey management pending resolution of a dispute through the grievance process, there are

---

34 (1981), 2 L.A.C. (3d) 126 (N.S.-Christie).

35 *Re McKellar General Hospital and Ontario Nurses' Association, supra* note 27.

36 (1983), 11 L.A.C. (3d) 151 (Ont.-Saltman).

exceptions to the rule. Employees are entitled to disobey management where obedience would result in

(1) the performance of an illegal act;
(2) harm to the health or safety of the employee or others; and
(3) a situation in which a successful grievance of an unjustified order would not give adequate redress to the employee.[37]

DISCIPLINE

While health-care management has the authority to evaluate, critique and oversee unionized employees, it can discipline or dismiss employees only where there is "just cause". A grievance may arise when an employee disputes a decision by management to reprimand, demote, suspend or dismiss the employee.

A threshold issue is whether management's conduct constitutes "discipline". Negative comments, warnings or unfavourable evaluations may not constitute disciplinary conduct.

> Common sense dictates . . . that there should be some latitude in an employer to make negative comments respecting an employee's performance without necessarily incurring the risk of a grievance with the full panoply of procedures that might ensue.[38]

Employer conduct amounting to discipline must "involve or result in a change in status or monetary loss to the employee".[39] Consequently, a poor reference letter may not be considered a matter of discipline where the letter is written "in good faith and without malice" and its purpose is not to "punish or penalize", but only to evaluate for future employers.[40] Similarly, routine performance evaluations that contain negative comments are not a matter of discipline if no practical result follows. A form setting out a negative evaluation may allow the employee to make his or her own written comments and this information may be considered in the future by an arbitrator should the unfavourable evaluation become a matter of

---

[37] See *Re Riverdale Hospital and Canadian Union of Public Employees, Local 79* (1985), 19 L.A.C. (3d) 396, at 403 (Ont.-Burkett).

[38] *Re City of Toronto and Canadian Union of Public Employees, Local 79* (1984), 16 L.A.C. (3d) 384, at 391 (Ont.-Picher).

[39] *Edmonton & Rural Auxiliary Hospital & Nursing Home, District 24 and Alberta Association of Registered Nurses,* [1981] 3 W.L.A.C. 301, at 304 (Alta.-Laux).

[40] *Re New Orchard Lodge/Extendicare Ltd., Ottawa and Ontario Nurses' Association, supra* note 23, at 228.

discipline. An employer will not be answerable to the grievance process for "every utterance which expresses less than complete approval of an employee's job performance and which might at some point be taken into account in a way that affects the employee's career".[41]

A performance evaluation may be an act of discipline, however, if it is accompanied by a warning that continued poor performance could result in suspension or discharge and if the evaluation will be used to demonstrate a pattern of poor performance that may culminate in suspension or discharge. Factors determining whether an evaluation constitutes a matter of discipline include whether it was in writing and forms part of the employee record, whether it was communicated to the employee and the union, whether it refers to specific incidents related to poor job performance, whether it contains some sanction (such as a warning or caution), whether it was reviewable through the grievance procedure and whether it would be relevant in showing a pattern of conduct in a future disciplinary proceeding.[42]

Progressive Discipline

Generally, before disciplinary action can be taken, an employee must be made aware of the employer's dissatisfaction and must be given an opportunity to remedy substandard performance. A series of informal meetings, imprecise performance evaluations and verbal reprimands will make it difficult to demonstrate that the employee has been the subject of "progressive discipline". An employee must be told, in specific terms, that job performance has not been satisfactory and must be improved, and that, if it is not, it will lead to demotion, suspension or termination. In *Re Extendicare Ltd. (St. Catharines) and Ontario Nurses' Association,*[43] a nurse was discharged after a series of verbal warnings, meetings and critical evaluations. She grieved the discharge and was successful on the ground that the employer had failed to communicate clearly its dissatisfaction with her job performance. Although she was aware that her employer was not satisfied with her job performance, it was not made clear to her that this could result in her discharge. She was awarded one year's salary in lieu of reinstatement.

In *Re Edith Cavell Private Hospital and Hospital Employees' Union, Local 180,*[44] the chief cook of a private hospital was asked to resign; when he

---

41 *Re Children's Hospital of Eastern Ontario and Ontario Nurses' Association* (1987), 30 L.A.C. (3d) 238, at 245 (Ont.-Adell).

42 *Re Calgary General Hospital and Canadian Union of Public Employees, Local 8* (1986), 23 L.A.C. (3d) 25 (Alta.-Beattie).

43 (1981), 3 L.A.C. (3d) 243 (Ont.-Adams).

44 (1982), 6 L.A.C. (3d) 229 (B.C.-Hope).

refused to do so, he was discharged. The alleged ground for discharge was incompetence. At arbitration it was ruled that the discharge was unjust. The arbitration board held that in discharging an employee for "non-culpable deficiency in job performance", the hospital was required to

(1) define the standard of job performance required;
(2) establish that the standard was communicated to the employee;
(3) give reasonable supervision and instruction to the employee to assist in achieving the standard;
(4) establish the employee's inability to meet the standard to the extent that it renders her or him incapable of doing the job; and
(5) give reasonable warnings to the employee that a failure to meet the standard would result in discharge.

Right to Union Representation

Most collective agreements contain provisions requiring that employees be afforded protection or representation where disciplinary action is taken. Consequently, where an employee is the subject of some form of discipline, a union representative may be invited to a meeting between the employer and the employee, or the union may receive a copy of a negative evaluation.[45] A kitchen worker discharged by a hospital without being afforded union representation was ordered reinstated with full compensation for lost wages and benefits. The arbitration board made it clear that

> [A]bsent a provision to the contrary, the right to retain union representation at the point of discipline, and any corollary right to be so advised, is a fundamental and substantive right, the failure of which will void the discipline in question.[46]

In *Re St. Joseph's Hospital (Brantford) and Ontario Nurses' Association,*[47] a collective agreement in force between the nursing staff and the hospital entitled a nurse to be represented by a union representative whenever steps were taken to impose discipline. A nurse involved in a medication error was suspended by the hospital without a union representative being notified or present. An arbitration board held that the suspension was

---

45 *Re Calgary General Hospital and Canadian Union of Public Employees, Local 8, supra* note 42.

46 *Re Toronto Western Hospital and Canadian Union of Public Employees, Local 1744* (1985), 19 L.A.C. (3d) 191, at 201 (Ont.-Picher).

47 (1987), 28 L.A.C. (3d) 408 (Ont.-Picher).

improper; if the employee had been represented, the hospital might have been persuaded to modify the form of discipline it proposed to take or to make some other arrangements that would ensure patient safety.

Even where there is no obligation on the part of the employer to allow union representation or to communicate with the union, unnecessary and expensive arbitration proceedings may be avoided where the union is kept fully informed. If the union is persuaded that appropriate steps have been taken to warn the employee of impending discipline, that there are substantive reasons for the discipline and that the particular form of discipline is appropriate in the circumstances, it is less likely to oppose the employer's action.

Dismissal

Arbitrators have considerable scope in deciding what penalties are appropriate. Unless the parties specify in the collective agreement that a particular penalty will be imposed summarily for a particular offence, all aggrieved dismissals are open to review to see whether the disciplinary measure "seems just and reasonable in all the circumstances".[48] The board will want to know if the disciplinary standard was applied discriminatorily, if there were mitigating circumstances and if the employee is capable of rehabilitation.[49] Where a decision to dismiss is overturned, the employer may be required to pay a sizeable compensation package or to reinstate the employee.

Some arbitrators have cautioned against substituting disciplinary discharges with lesser penalties in the health-care field. It has been said that such substitution creates the danger of arbitral "second-guessing" of patient-care standards fixed by the expert body, namely, the health facility's administration. It may be that a certain amount of deference should be paid to a health facility administration's judgment, particularly where the employee's misconduct may affect the safety of patients or the reputation of the hospital.[50] Other arbitrators, however, maintain that a certain area of arbitral expertise remains in assessing whether the dismissal was unjust where the interpretation of the collective agreement, possible discrimination or mitigating circumstances are involved.[51]

---

48 *Re Belleville General Hospital and Service Employees' Union, Local 183* (1985), 18 L.A.C. (3d) 161, at 163 (Ont.-England).

49 *Ibid.*

50 *Re Government of Province of British Columbia and British Columbia Government Employees' Union* (1980), 26 L.A.C. (2d) 71 (B.C.-Hope).

51 *Re Belleville General Hospital and Service Employees' Union, Local 183, supra* note 48.

The employer bears the onus of demonstrating that there was just cause for dismissal.[52] The employer must show that the employee committed a serious infraction, which he or she knew, or should have known, would lead to serious disciplinary measures, including dismissal, or in the alternative, must show that there is a well-documented record of progressive discipline in the case of non-culpable deficiency in work performance.

Arbitration boards have acknowledged that health facilities have a significant business interest in maintaining public confidence.[53] For example, a health professional's off-duty conduct, though not directly related to professional life, may be damaging to the health facility if the conduct has attracted much public attention. There must, however, be a factual basis to the assertion that the employee has forfeited public trust.[54] In *Oshawa General Hospital and Ontario Nurses' Association*,[55] a nurse was convicted of possession of marijuana and given a suspended sentence by the Court. She was discharged by the hospital on the ground that the presence of marijuana in her home reflected poor judgment and that knowledge of her conviction could have a negative impact upon the hospital's image in the community. At arbitration, the nurse testified that she did not use the substance, that her child was kept away from it, that it was her husband who had been growing it and that there was nothing she could do about it. She claimed that her husband's activity had been the source of serious and frequent quarrels. It was argued on her behalf that her off-duty conduct was immaterial if it did not reflect upon her nursing abilities. In ruling in favour of the nurse, the arbitrator held that there was no basis to conclude that the nurse's poor judgment in her personal situation would carry over into her professional activities; her work record and history were good. The hospital was unable to demonstrate that a continuation of the nurse's employment would cause the hospital to lose public confidence.

A refusal by an employee to perform essential aspects of the employment position is likely to constitute just cause for dismissal. One exception to this general rule is where performance of the job would result in violation of the non-discrimination clause found in most collective agreements. In *Re Peterborough Civic Hospital and Ontario Nurses' Association*,[56] an ICU nurse, because of her religious beliefs, refused to commence blood transfusions and was dismissed as a result. The arbitration board held that the

---

52 *Re Oshawa General Hospital and Ontario Nurses' Association* (1981), 2 L.A.C. (3d) 201 (Ont.-Betcherman); *Re Belleville General Hospital and Service Employees' Union, Local 183, supra* note 48.

53 *Ibid.*

54 *Ibid.*

55 *Ibid.*

56 (1981), 3 L.A.C. (3d) 21 (Ont.-Ellis).

hospital had violated the non-discrimination clause of the collective agreement. Although the board agreed that it was an essential duty for a nurse in ICU to "hang blood", it was not an essential duty for a nurse on a regular floor. The nurse's religious beliefs could have been accommodated by transferring her to a different floor. On the issue of accommodation of religious beliefs, the board stated (at p. 34):

> An employer who can accommodate without significant cost to itself or to its other employees the inability for serious reasons of an individual employee to comply with one of its rules but chooses instead to terminate that employee cannot in our view be said to have terminated for just cause.

The arbitration board ordered that the nurse be reinstated without loss of seniority or benefits on the condition that she accept work in another hospital unit.

An employer must consider other forms of discipline as alternatives to dismissal. Where an employee of a hospital housekeeping department was suspended indefinitely pending the verdict of an assault charge, the arbitrator ruled that although the hospital had legitimate safety interests in keeping the griever away from other employees, it should have given him an alternative work assignment that required less contact with the other employees or should have provided him with closer supervision.[57]

Equal Treatment

Employers may trigger a grievance under the collective agreement, a complaint pursuant to relevant human rights legislation or other legal remedies where they discriminate on the basis of a specified ground, such as a person's race, colour, sex, religion, physical or mental disability or place of origin.[58] An employer is prohibited from discriminating in the recruitment process, in employment application forms or in remuneration to employees. It is also not permissible to engage employment agencies that discriminate. Legislation in Ontario, the Yukon and the Northwest Territories include provisions prohibiting discrimination in *any* aspect of employment.[59] Manitoba's human rights legislation contains provisions which

---

[57] *Re Humber Memorial Hospital and Canadian Union of Public Employees, Local 1080* (1982), 6 L.A.C. (3d) 97 (Ont.-Davis).

[58] All provinces share these grounds of discrimination. Some provinces have additional grounds.

[59] Ontario: *Human Rights Code*, R.S.O. 1990, c. H.19, s. 4; Yukon: *Human Rights Act*, R.S.Y. 1987, c. 3, s. 8(b); Northwest Territories: *Fair Practices Act*, R.S.N.W.T. 1988, c. F-3, s. 2.

include a detailed enumeration of protected aspects of employment, such as "opportunity to participate in the employment", "customs and practices", "training and advancement", "seniority" and "remuneration".[60]

A rule or policy purporting to treat everyone equally may be ruled, nonetheless, discriminatory. Discrimination can occur where there is no intent to discriminate on the part of the employer. A rule which requires part-time employees to work on Saturdays, even though applied uniformly, is discriminatory if it causes undue hardship to an employee who is precluded from working on Saturdays because of a genuine religious belief.[61] A rule or standard adopted for sound business or economic reasons and applied equally may still be discriminatory. Employers must make an effort to avoid undue hardship by providing modified duties to those employees who are affected by the rule where it is reasonable to do so.

If an employee requests that he or she not be given Friday evening or Saturday shifts because of a genuine religious belief, the health facility cannot arbitrarily dismiss the request. An effort should be made to identify alternatives, such as adjusting the schedule or transferring the employee to another area, department or service. If, in the end, there is no feasible alternative, the facility may be justified in refusing the request. Similarly, if a nurse is physically incapacitated and cannot perform all of the duties in her field, the health facility should attempt to accommodate him or her by assigning some of the duties to others or by transferring the nurse to another position.

An employer may be entitled to "discriminate" where the rule or policy is a *bona fide* occupational requirement. The rule or policy must be imposed honestly, in good faith, and in the sincerely-held belief that it is necessary for the adequate performance of the work. It must be reasonably necessary to ensure the efficient and economical performance of the job without endangering the employee, his or her fellow employees or the general public.[62]

Whether a person's gender can be a valid consideration in formulating management policies has arisen in the health-care context. In *Sunnyside Home for the Aged v. London And District Service Workers' Union*,[63] a nursing home had a policy prohibiting male nursing attendants from caring for female residents. Female attendants, however, were permitted to care for male residents unless the resident objected. Although the arbitrator found that the policy in the nursing home was motivated by "morality and decency", he nonetheless held that the policy was discriminatory as it treated

---

60 *Human Rights Code*, S.M. 1987-88, c. 45, s. 14(2).

61 *Ontario Human Rights Commn. v. Simpsons-Sears Ltd.* (1985), 23 D.L.R. (4th) 321 (S.C.C.).

62 *Ontario Human Rights Commn. v. Borough of Etobicoke* (1982), 132 D.L.R. (3d) 14, at 19-20 (S.C.C.).

63 (1985), 21 L.A.C. (3d) 85 (Ont.-Picher).

male attendants differently from female attendants. It was held that there was no legitimate business or professional justification for the distinction.[64]

Consequently, a health facility that prefers to have a male, rather than a female, nursing assistant for a particular position may not be guilty of discrimination if it can be shown that the facility introduced the policy in the sincerely-held belief that it was in the interests of the hospital and patients, and more objectively, if it were proven that being male was a genuine occupational requirement in a job that required male catheterizations.[65] If, however, there were reasonable alternatives (such as assigning male staff to catheterize those patients who requested a male nurse), the requirement would not pass the objective branch of the test and would therefore not be deemed *bona fide*.[66]

Workers' Compensation

All provinces and territories have enacted workers' compensation legislation to provide compensation, on a no-fault basis, to employees who are injured on the job. The administrative agency that deals with workers' compensation is generally called the Workers' Compensation Board. In Quebec, the agency is known as the Commission de la Sante et de la Securite du Travail. In Newfoundland, it is called the Workers' Compensation Commission. These agencies/or boards are statutory corporations having responsibility for the administration of the legislation and the adjudication of claims.

Workers' compensation is an industrial insurance system based upon the principle of collective liability for employee injuries. Health facilities, such as hospitals and nursing homes, are collectively responsible for the costs of work-related accidents involving their employees. Employers pay a rate or premium based upon total employee remuneration.[67] Rates are

---

64 *Ibid.*, at 104; but see *McKale v. Lamont Auxiliary Hospital* (1986), 8 C.H.R.R. D/3659 (Alta. Bd. of Enquiry); affd [1987] 3 W.W.R. 748 (Q.B.) and *Huronia District Hospital v. Service Employees' Union* (1980), 25 L.A.C. (2d) 183 (Ont.-Schiff).

65 *Huronia District Hospital v. Service Employees' Union, supra* note 64.

66 "If a reasonable alternative exists to burdening members of a group with a given rule, that rule will not be *bona fide*": I. Christie, G. England, B. Cotter, *Employment Law in Canada*, 2nd ed. (Toronto: Butterworths, 1992), p. 437.

67 As of August 1994, the rate payable to the workers' compensation accident fund by Ontario's hospital employers was $1.87 per $100 of payroll. Telephone interview, Ontario Workers' Compensation Board, Assessments Division, August 3, 1994.

adjusted according to an employer's accident record. A health facility that objects to a worker's claim, on the ground that it is not a compensable claim, may appear before the board to advocate its position. Either party may appeal.

Eligibility for Benefits

In Canada, compensation coverage is generally compulsory. Only a few excluded industries or workers remain. Doctors, for example, are likely to be ineligible for compensation as they are not "employees" of the hospital. They may sue a hospital in tort for injuries that result from an accident in the hospital if the hospital is at fault. Other health-care workers are likely to be protected by workers' compensation legislation, regardless of status (*i.e.*, whether they are full-time, part-time or casual employees) and regardless of fault. Compensation is generally payable where:

(1) A worker has coverage under the provincial or territorial workers' compensation legislation.
(2) The worker probably has a disablement or condition that is compensable under the legislation.
(3) The disablement, condition, loss or death probably resulted from the employment.

To qualify for benefits, an employee must demonstrate that a "personal injury by accident arising out of and in the course of employment [was] caused to the worker".[68] If a hospital worker falls on the slippery floor of a ward, the injury can be described as arising out of employment. The employer's premises include the parking lot, cafeteria, outdoor eating areas and any other area over which the employer has some measure of control. A frequent condition for which compensation is sought in the health-care field is repetitive strain injury arising over a prolonged period of time due to the nature of the work, such as repeated lifting of patients.

As a rule, a worker is "in the course of employment" from the time of reporting to work until the end of the shift. This generally includes accidents in the parking lot or while travelling, if the travel is work-related. Although ordinary commuting to and from work is not usually compensable,

---

[68] See *Workers' Compensation Acts*: R.S.B.C. 1979, c. 437, s. 5(4); S.A. 1981, c. W-16, s. 19(4); S.S. 1979, c. W-17, s. 31(1); R.S.M. 1987, c. W200, s. 4(5); R.S.O. 1990, c. W.11, s. 4(1); R.S.N.B. 1973, c. W-13, s. 7(2); R.S.N.S. 1989, c. 508, s. 9(1); S.P.E.I. 1994, c. 67, s. 6(1); R.S.N. 1990, c. W-11, s. 43; R.S.N.W.T. 1988, c. W-6, s. 14; R.S.Y. 1986, c. 180, s. 7(4).

if an employee, such as an on-call radiology technician, is telephoned by the employer and told to come in, he or she would be eligible for compensation if injured in transit.[69] Some activities, like eating lunch, may be considered incidental to work though other, exclusively personal activities, will not be deemed to occur "in the course of employment".

A claim may be denied if the employee does not promptly report the injury or condition or does not obtain immediate medical attention. A claim is not barred if it is the result of multiple causes, some of which are not related to the employment; the test is: "would the worker be suffering from the disability but for the employment event, exposure or circumstance?"[70]

Compensation and Employers' Duties

Injured workers receive compensation for the period of time in which they are unable to work due to their workplace injury or disability. Payments are made from the collective accident fund to which employers contribute. Employers have obligations in addition to maintaining contributions to the fund.

Most provinces legislate that an injured worker is to be given full wages by his or her employer for the day of the injury or disablement itself.[71] Where the worker requires first aid and is later determined to have sustained a compensable injury, the employer is responsible for first aid and for any initial transportation (such as ambulances to another hospital) that may be required.[72] Employers are often called upon to collaborate with the compensation board in retraining or re-employing an injured employee.[73]

In cases where an employee is *temporarily* disabled, the employment relationship is neither terminated nor suspended; in some jurisdictions, a *permanent* disability does not terminate employment but may qualify as just cause for dismissal if the disability cannot be accommodated or if an equivalent job cannot be found.

In Ontario, New Brunswick and Quebec, employers have significant obligations to rehabilitated employees injured in the workplace. In On-

---

69 *Office of the Worker Adviser Guide* (Ministry of Labour, January 1994).

70 T.G. Ison, *Workers' Compensation in Canada,* 2nd ed. (Toronto: Butterworths, 1989), p. 58.

71 *Workers' Compensation Acts*: S.A. 1981, c. W-16, s. 20(1); R.S.O. 1990, c. W.11, s. 4(2); R.S.N. 1990, c. W-11, s. 47; R.S.Q. 1977, c. A-3.001, s. 59.

72 For example, *Workers' Compensation Act,* R.S.B.C. 1979, c. 437, s. 70.

73 Ison, *supra* note 70, p. 145.

tario, where an enterprise employs more than 20 people and where the injured worker was employed there for at least one year prior to the injury, the employer must offer re-employment in one of two ways: if the board determines that an injured worker is able to perform the essential duties of the job, the employer must offer to reinstate the worker to his or her pre-injury position or to a position of a comparable nature and rate of pay;[74] alternatively, if the board concludes that the employee is unable to perform the essential duties of the pre-injury position, the employer must offer the worker "the first opportunity to accept suitable employment that may become available with the employer".[75] This duty of re-employment lasts for either two years from the date of the injury or one year after the board has notified the employer of the worker's medical ability to perform the pre-injury duties of employment, whichever comes first.[76] Quebec's legislation also dictates that employees receiving compensation are not to lose seniority or drop in level of pay.[77]

Claims by Health-Care Workers

In recent years, claims for worker compensation in the health-care field have grown significantly.[78] Some of this increase is attributable to claims being advanced for conditions or diseases that do not arise from an accident or a similar traumatic event. Health-care workers may be exposed to chemicals, drugs, contagious bacteria and viruses. Researchers have found that hospital pharmacists and nurses are exposed to levels of antineoplastic agents in certain drugs that are potentially carcinogenic and hazardous to women's reproductive systems.[79]

The coverage of disease in workers' compensation is generally more restrictive than the coverage of injuries. Diseases are more difficult to trace back to a single source. There may be multiple causes. It is harder to distinguish between industrial diseases and illnesses for which the general sick pay scheme and, not workers' compensation, is appropriate. Several

---

74 *Workers' Compensation Act*, R.S.O. 1990, c. W.11, s. 54(4).

75 *Ibid.*, s. 54(5).

76 *Ibid.*, s. 54(8).

77 *Industrial Accidents and Occupational Diseases Act*, R.S.Q. 1977, c. A-3.001, s. 180 (benefits and pay) and s. 235 (seniority).

78 In the ten-year period between 1982 and 1992, workers' compensation claims by Ontario health-care employees rose by 40 per cent, *Workers' Compensation Annual Report* (Ont. W.C.B., 1993), p. 18.

79 James J. McDervitt, et al., "Exposure of Hospital Pharmacists and Nurses to Antineoplastic Agents" (1993), 35 J. of Occupational Medicine 57.

provincial statutes contain lists of diseases that will be considered for compensation: infections, hearing loss due to exposure to noise over time, osteoarthritis, contagious diseases, allergic reactions and disabilities caused by the gradual absorption of a chemical through the skin or by inhalation are all examples of compensable diseases. Generally, a disease is compensable if it can be shown that the disease resulted from "exposure to a substance relating to a particular process, a trade or occupation in an industry" or if it is a "disease peculiar to or characteristic of a particular . . . occupation".[80]

Examples of disorders that have been classified as injuries include wounds, fractures, sprains, strains, dislocations, burns and any other disorder caused by trauma. Although controversial, stress has also been considered a compensable injury.[81] "Injury" can include a disability resulting from activity over time or from a specific incident. Mental disorders with an undiagnosed organic cause are also compensable. Degenerative disc disease has been recognized as a compensable occupational disease. The disease may be caused by substantial periods of heavy lifting, and thereby directly affects nurses, nurses' aides and orderlies who lift and handle patients on a daily basis. In British Columbia, claims for compensation based on back over-exertions account for well over half of all claims by nurses, nursing aides and orderlies.[82]

Stress has also been considered an occupational disease. This is a particularly contentious claim, perhaps because it is often impossible to distinguish between personal and occupational stress, both of which lead to stress-related disorders, such as heart attack, exhaustion or nervous breakdown. Workplace stress has gained more attention in the last few years, as public hearings by the Ontario Workers' Compensation Board into the issue in early 1992 demonstrate.[83] Boards are still undecided on the issue, but some decisions have been made that at least partially recognize that workplace stress is as much a disabling disease as any other.[84] "Burn-out", however, has been determined not to be an acceptable psychiatric diagnosis for the purposes of compensation.[85]

---

80 *Workers' Compensation Act*, R.S.O. 1990, c. W.11, s. 1.

81 See *Decision* 1030/89, 20 W.C.A.T.R 46 and *WCAT Decision* 397/92, two recent cases in which the Ontario Workers' Compensation Appeals Tribunal granted compensation to police officers for job-related stress.

82 *Trend in Types of Accident by Occupation, 1988-1992,* British Columbia, Workers' Compensation Board of British Columbia, Statistical Services Department (July 1993), Table 4.

83 *The Dispatch* (Ont. Hospital Association, Jan. 1992).

84 *WCAT Decision* 1030/89 and *WCAT Decision* 397/92, *supra* note 81.

85 Ont. WCB Decision #809/92 (May 4, 1994).

Injuries

Among the most prominent injuries afflicting hospital workers are herniated discs,[86] strained muscles[87] and "overuse syndrome".[88] As with diseases, it is sometimes difficult to determine the significant factors among multiple causes for injuries; an employee need only prove that, medically, the tasks involved with the position or the specific event on the day of the injury contributed significantly to the disablement.

Some employers and boards have been successful in their objections to a worker's claim on the ground that the worker's misconduct was so serious and wilful that the claim should not be allowed. A claim is barred if the injury:

(a) resulted from serious/wilful misconduct;
(b) resulted *solely* from that cause and was not partly caused or aggravated by the premises, equipment or other aspect of the workplace;
(c) did not result in death or serious and/or permanent disability.

Examples of wilful misconduct are horseplay and fighting among employees. Although a claim is not barred because one employee was injured by another's horseplay, the injury may be found not to have arisen out of the course of employment if the injured worker was the one to initiate the horseplay and if the activity can be shown to have been a substantial deviation from the course of employment.[89]

Violence in the Workplace

Violence toward health-care workers is becoming a significant occupational hazard.[90] According to the British Columbia Workers' Compensation Board, acts of violence and force were the second-highest cause of injuries to nurses, orderlies and nursing assistants in that province for the

---

86 See, for example, Ont. WCB Decision #360/88 (October 7, 1988), involving a nursing staff member who was awarded compensation for a pre-existing back problem that was aggravated by lifting/moving patients.

87 Ont. WCB Decision #1133/87 (April 14, 1988), involving a nursing assistant.

88 Ont. WCB Decision #423/89 (May 26, 1989), a Registered Nursing Assistant was awarded compensation for lumbar strain due to repeated lifting of patients.

89 Ison, *supra* note 70, p. 65.

90 Health and Safety Commission, *Violence to Staff in the Health Services* (London: HMSO, 1987); G.M. Liss, *Examination of Workers' Compensation Claims Among Nurses in Ontario for Injuries Due to Violence* (Ont. Ministry of Labour, March 1993).

five-year period ending in 1992.[91] According to the same survey, occupational violence accounts for more compensation claims for health-care workers than for all other occupations combined. Violence in the workplace accounts for 12.7 per cent of claims by nurses and 13.3 per cent of claims by nursing aides and orderlies. Violent acts against nurses doubled between 1984 and 1988. Acts range from kicks and punches, to rape, severe beatings and assault with weapons or sharp objects.[92] In 1989 the Manitoba Association of Registered Nurses made a study on occupational violence and discovered that half of Manitoba's nurses are physically attacked by patients at some point during their careers. In Ontario, almost six out of ten nurses say they have been physically assaulted during their nursing careers,[93] and 17 per cent have been sexually assaulted at work.[94]

In Ontario between 1987 and 1989, for the small number of claims successfully filed by nurses for injuries due to violence, the associated costs were over $850,000; these costs do not include the associated financial burden of staff turnover, modified duty, overtime associated with replacement staff and the general effect on staff productivity.[95] Workers' Compensation Boards have awarded compensation for physical injuries resulting from workplace violence and have recognized post-traumatic stress disorder as a compensable injury that is causally related to a particularly serious act of violence.

British Columbia has implemented workers' compensation regulations regarding workplace violence. According to the British Columbia regulations, violence means "the attempted or actual exercise by a person, other than a worker, of any physical force so as to cause injury to a worker, and includes any threatening statement or behaviour".[96] The regulations direct employers to perform a risk assessment of the workplace[97] and where a risk of injury is identified, the employer shall,

> (a) establish procedures, policies and work environment arrangements to eliminate the risk to workers from violence,
> (b) where elimination of the risk to workers is not possible, establish procedures, policies and work environment arrangements to minimize the risk to workers, and

---

91 *Trend in Types of Accident by Occupation, supra* note 82, Table 4.

92 As documented in *Violence in the Workplace* (Toronto: Ontario Nurses' Association, October 1991), p. 7.

93 *Ibid.*

94 *Supra* note 90, p. 1.

95 *Ibid.*, pp. 7-8.

96 Workers' Compensation Regulations B.C. Reg. 269/93, s. 8.88.

97 *Ibid.*, s. 8.90

(c) establish procedures for reporting, investigating and documenting incidents of violence in accordance with the requirements of section 6.[98]

In addition, employers have a duty to inform employees of the risk of violence from persons (patients, for instance) who have a history of violent behaviour,[99] and a duty to train staff members to recognize the potential for violence and how to respond appropriately.[100]

Occupational Health and Safety

Until recently, the regulation of occupational health and safety was through the workers' compensation legislation of most provinces. Only British Columbia and Quebec retain the amalgamation of these two regimes; the other provinces have enacted separate health and safety legislation. Although some provinces have different names for their health and safety legal regimes,[101] the legislation is most commonly known as "occupational health and safety" legislation.

The regulatory schemes provide for the imposition of rights, duties and obligations on workers, employers and supervisors. Duties that are not fulfilled may lead to substantial penalties. Health-care administrators, like other employers, have the onerous obligation of taking "every precaution reasonable in the circumstances for the protection of a worker".[102]

The workplace should be self-regulated; employers and supervisors should hold the greatest responsibilities. In addition, government inspectors may enter the workplace to conduct inspections, order compliance, carry out investigations and lay charges.

Employers, supervisors and workers who fail to comply with the legislation face stiff penalties. In Manitoba, the maximum fine for an individual's first offence is $15,000 and $2,500 a day for continuing the offence. A repeat offender may be fined $30,000 for a second or subsequent offence

---

[98] *Ibid.*, s. 8.92.

[99] *Ibid.*, s. 8.94.

[100] *Ibid.*, s. 8.95.

[101] In Manitoba, it is the *Workplace Safety and Health Act*, R.S.M. 1987, c. W210; in British Columbia, the legislation is contained within the *Workers' Compensation Act*, R.S.B.C. 1979, c. 437, and in all other provinces under their respective *Occupational Health and Safety Acts.*

[102] See for example, Ontario: *Occupational Health and Safety Act*, R.S.O. 1990, c. O.1, s. 25(2)(h); Nova Scotia: *Occupational Health and Safety Act*, R.S.N.S. 1989, c. 320, s. 9; and Manitoba: *Workplace Safety and Health Act*, R.S.M. 1987, c. W210, s. 4(1).

and $5,000 for each day of non-compliance.[103] In Ontario, a non-corporate employer may be fined up to $25,000 and/or 12 months in jail; the penalty for a corporation could be as high as $500,000. Although the maximum penalty is imposed only in the most egregious of cases, the elevated ceiling for penalties has sent a signal to the courts that the legislatures intend much heavier penalties to be meted out as a specific and general deterrent. The amount of any fine imposed will depend upon a variety of factors:

- the extent of the actual or potential harm to the public and to employees;
- the size of the hospital or health facility and the perceived ability to pay;
- the maximum penalty prescribed by statute; and
- the need to enforce regulatory standards by general deterrence.[104]

In general, "[w]ithout being harsh, the fine must be substantial enough to warn others that the offence will not be tolerated. It must not appear to be a mere licence fee for illegal activity".[105]

EMPLOYERS' DUTIES

Employers' general duties are enumerated in the governing statutes, with more detailed measures specific to a particular industry outlined in health and safety regulations.[106] General duties include:

- providing and maintaining a workplace, equipment, tools and systems that are safe;
- training, instructing and supervising workers to ensure their safety;
- notifying workers of potential hazards;

---

103 *Ibid.*, Man. s. 55(1).

104 *R. v. Cotton Felts Ltd.* (1982), 2 C.C.C. (3d) 287 (Ont.C.A.).

105 *Ibid.*, at 295.

106 Although a number of industries are covered by specific safety regulations, such as mining and construction, in most provinces hospitals are not and are ordinarily expected to conform to the standards set out in the O. Reg. for Industrial Establishments and any other regulations that can reasonably be applied to their operations as guides to safe work practices. Ontario, however, passed O. Reg. 67/93, "Health Care and Residential Facilities", under the *Occupational Health and Safety Act,* addressing such issues as the disposal of syringes and hazardous liquids, the handling of antineoplastic drugs and protective clothing

- ensuring that all employees are familiar with the proper use of all devices and equipment; and
- providing all prescribed protective equipment, devices and materials.[107]

Health-care workers may be exposed to chemicals and drugs that may cause serious illnesses and injuries if handled or administered improperly. Housekeeping staff must handle soaps, detergents and disinfectants. Laboratory technicians work with alkalis that have been held responsible for various illnesses, including haemorrhagic cystitis and bladder tumours.[108] Pathologists and technologists working in the autopsy room are exposed to formalin, and its resulting irritation of the mucous membranes, especially of the nose and respiratory tract. Formaldehyde is also considered a suspect human carcinogen. Nurses and doctors are at risk of inhaling fumes and gases in many different contexts; for instance, it has been reported that female health-care workers exposed to waste anaesthetic gases may have a greater risk of spontaneous abortion.[109] Less extreme side-effects of exposure to anaesthetic gases are also common, including headache, fatigue, irritability and sleep disturbances.[110]

Many jurisdictions have detailed provisions regarding the use and identification of hazardous materials incorporated into their respective occupational health and safety legislation. An employer is required to keep inventories of hazardous chemicals, their ingredients, methods of proper use, dangers and location in the workplace.[111] Employers may be obligated to post data sheets with this safety information in a conspicuous place and must provide instruction to workers exposed or likely to be exposed to a hazardous material.

At least one province has also responded to the particular dangers associated with drugs. Ontario's Health Care and Residential Facilities

---

of x-ray technicians. The Yukon is currently contemplating regulations or a code of conduct to deal with ergonomics and the health-care professional: Telephone interview, Yukon Occupational Health and Safety Branch, August 24, 1994.

107 See for example Ontario: *Occupational Health and Safety Act,* s. 25; Nova Scotia: *Occupational Health and Safety Act,* s. 9; and Manitoba: *Workplace Safety and Health Act,* s. 4(2).

108 Russell Frith and Albert Strickler, "Occupational Health Hazards in Hospitals: An Overview" (1991), 12 Occupational Health in Ontario 89, at 93.

109 *Ibid.*, at 94.

110 It is interesting to note that Ontario's Health Care and Residential Facilities O. Reg. 67/93 has a specific provision (s. 96) on anaesthetic gases. This provision requires that hospitals install "effective scavenging systems to collect, remove and dispose of waste gases" and to perform a regular monthly inspection for leakage.

111 See for example Ontario's *Occupational Health and Safety Act,* Part IV.

Regulation under the *Occupational Health and Safety Act* addresses the hazards associated with antineoplastic drugs most often used in cancer treatment.[112] The regulation states that hospitals "shall, in consultation with the joint health and safety committee . . . develop, establish and put into effect written measures and procedures to protect workers who may be exposed to antineoplastic agents or to material or equipment contaminated with antineoplastic agents".[113] There follows a more detailed list of measures to be addressed by the committee and administration, as well as a requirement that the administration provide training and instruction to workers. The explicit mention of the need for management to consult with the joint health and safety committee points to the need for a flexible, progressive policy-making regime that will respond to the dangers associated with these drugs.[114]

Defence of Due Diligence

A breach of occupational health and safety legislation by an employer, supervisor or worker will not result in a conviction if the defendant can demonstrate that it exercised "due diligence" in its health and safety activities. In essence, where the court finds on the evidence that a defendant has established a "proper system to prevent the commission of the offence" and that "reasonable steps have been taken to ensure the effective operation of the system",[115] no conviction will follow. A "proper system" will follow the guide-lines established in the governing legislation; particularly important are proper training and monitoring systems that function well.

In *R. v. Stratford General Hospital*,[116] a hospital was charged under Ontario's occupational health and safety legislation in regard to an exposure of asbestos in the workplace. Ministry of Labour inspectors had concluded that there was loose asbestos insulation in the basement area of the hospital and that the hospital had not complied with earlier inspection orders requiring it to institute and maintain a programme of training and instruction for workers in proximity to the material and to maintain and repair the exposed material. At trial, however, the charges were dismissed on the ground that the hospital had retained the services of a consultant

---

[112] O. Reg. 67/93, s. 97.

[113] *Ibid.*, s. 97(1).

[114] For example, a recent study has found that the common use of biological safety cabinets in hospitals may not be enough to control inhalation exposures: James J. McDevitt et al., "Exposure of Hospital Pharmacists and Nurses to Antineoplastic Agents" (1993), 1 J. of Occupational Medicine 57.

[115] *R. v. Sault Ste. Marie*, [1978] 2 S.C.R. 1299.

[116] (1992), 7 C.O.H.S.C. 188 (Ont. Ct. Prov. Div.).

who was viewed as an expert in the field of asbestos and who had concluded, on the basis of his own inspections, that the insulation was intact, well-protected and did not pose an immediate inhalation hazard to workers. It was found that hospital management had concluded that it did not have immediate problems as a result of the consultant's report and had concluded that there was no hazardous asbestos in the hospital. The trial judge also found that the hospital acted without unreasonable delay to repair areas that were discovered during a subsequent inspection by the ministry.

Refusal to Work

Generally, occupational health and safety legislation gives workers a right to refuse to work where continuing to work poses a danger to themselves or to others. In some provinces, special provisions apply to health-care workers. In Ontario, for example, a right to refuse or stop work is not extended to health-care workers where a perceived danger or hazard is "inherent" or a "normal condition" of the worker's employment. Further, a health-care worker cannot refuse to work where to do so would "directly endanger the life, health or safety of another person".[117] Arguably, the restricted right of health-care workers to refuse to work in conditions that may be potentially unsafe or hazardous places an extra burden on the employer to ensure that all reasonable precautions are taken to protect workers from harm.

Nonetheless, a worker's inappropriate refusal to work cannot be tolerated where that refusal may endanger patients. In *Re Mount Sinai Hospital and Ontario Nurses' Association*,[118] three nurses were suspended without pay when they refused to provide nursing care to a patient who was ordered to be admitted to the intensive care unit of the hospital. They refused to work on the basis that the ICU was already filled to capacity and that, in their professional judgment, an additional patient could not be safely accommodated. Their job action was ruled to be insubordinate, as it jeopardized the care of patients in the unit. They received a three-day suspension.

In *Brown v. Dr. Everett Chalmers Hospital*,[119] a dietary worker, who was pregnant, refused to carry out her normal duties of pushing carts because her doctor had advised her not to push or pull heavy carts. A board of arbitration ruled, however, that the right to refuse to work could not apply to "personal reasons" unrelated to an unsafe job task under the

117 *Occupational Health and Safety Act*, R.S.O. 1990, c. O.1, s. 43(1)(b).

118 (1978), 17 L.A.C. (2d) 242 (Ont.).

119 (1990), 2 C.O.H.S.C. 117 (N.B. Arb. Bd.).

circumstances complained of by the worker. It was held not to be a sufficient basis upon which to refuse to work.

Relevant Legislation

Canada

Canada Labour Code, R.S.C. 1985, c. L-2

Alberta

Employment Standards Code, S.A. 1988, c. E-10.2
Labour Relations Code, S.A. 1988, c. L-1.2

British Columbia

Employment Standards Act, S.B.C. 1980, c. 10
Industrial Relations Act, R.S.B.C. 1979, c. 212, ss. 128-137

Manitoba

Employment Standards Act, R.S.M. 1987, c. E110
Labour Relations Act, R.S.M. 1987, c. L10

New Brunswick

Employment Standards Act, S.N.B. 1982, c. E-7.2
Industrial Relations Act, R.S.N.B. 1973, c. I-4

Newfoundland

Labour Relations Act, S.N. 1977, c. 64
Labour Standards Act, S.N. 1977, c. 52

Nova Scotia

Labour Standards Code, R.S.N.S. 1989, c. 246
Trade Union Act, R.S.N.S. 1989, c. 475

Ontario

Employment Standards Act, R.S.O. 1990, c. E.14
Labour Relations Act, 1995, S.O. 1995, c. 1

Prince Edward Island

Labour Act, R.S.P.E.I. 1988, c. L-1
Minimum Age of Employment Act, R.S.P.E.I. 1988, c. M-8

Quebec

An act respecting labour standards, R.S.Q. 1977, c. N-1.1
Labour Code, R.S.Q. 1977, c. C-27

Saskatchewan

Labour Standards Act, R.S.S. 1978, c. L-1
Trade Union Act, R.S.S. 1978, c. T-17

CHAPTER 10

Hospital Privileges

INTRODUCTION

The evaluation of applicants, the delineation of their privileges and the appointment and reappointment of physicians to the medical staff represent areas of significant responsibility for health-care administrators and board members of public hospitals.[1]

In Canada, the majority of health professionals working in hospitals are employees. They include nurses, physiotherapists, respiratory technologists, psychologists, and other non-medical health professionals. Physicians, traditionally, are "independent practitioners" to whom the "privilege" of using the hospital facility is afforded, and thus the relationship is not one of employment.[2] An increasing number of health officials have attained a degree of autonomy and professional status more traditionally associated with physicians.[3] Some hospitals are discussing bylaw amendments that would allow health professionals, other than physicians, to be granted privileges in hospitals so they might admit and treat their patients there. In Ontario, a Task Committee reviewing the *Public Hospitals Act*[4] has recommended that all regulated health professions be permitted to apply for appointment in hospitals and that those health professionals have the

---

1 For the most part, this chapter is applicable to the relationship between public hospitals and those health professionals to whom "privileges" are granted by the institution. Traditionally, this has involved physicians and dentists, but few other health professionals. In recent years, the range of health professionals to whom privileges are being granted has expanded. In Ontario, mid-wives are being granted privileges and the Hospital Management Regulation under the *Ontario Public Hospitals Act* has been amended to reflect this (see R.R.O. 1990, Reg. 965 [am. O. Reg. 761/93]). In Saskatchewan chiropractors are entitled to be granted privileges (*Hospital Standards Act*, R.S.S. 1978, c. H-10.).

2 *Yepremian v. Scarborough General Hospital* (1980), 28 O.R. (2d) 494, 110 D.L.R. (3d) 513, 13 C.C.L.T. 105, 3 L. Med. Q. 278 (C.A.): revg (1978), 20 O.R. (2d) 510, 88 D.L.R. (3d) 161, 6 C.C.L.T. 81, 2 L. Med. Q. 216 (H.C.J.).

3 See Chapter 3, Canadian Health Professions — Status and Discipline.

4 R.S.O. 1990, c. P.40.

same procedural rights in relation to their hospital appointments as do physicians.[5]

Although physicians may carry on a major part of their medical practice in the hospital, they will often have outside offices. A physician on staff at a university-affiliated teaching hospital will have a university appointment. The independent practitioner is not paid by the hospital (except nominally, for example, for acting as chairperson of a department or in some other official capacity), but bills the provincial health insurance plan, on a fee-for-service basis, for the treatment of patients in the hospital.

For many physicians, an appointment to the medical staff of a public hospital is a demonstration of a high level of professional standing to patients and peers. As important, perhaps, is the financial opportunity associated with an appointment to a public hospital. Failure to obtain an appointment, or its loss, can be a considerable detriment to a physician's professional standing and pocketbook.

Economic constraints in the Canadian health-care system have made a staff appointment to a public hospital a valuable, and sometimes coveted, commodity. At one time, for a young doctor setting up practice in a community, an appointment to the medical staff of the local hospital was little more than a formality. This is no longer the case. Current fiscal restraints render an expansion of the medical staff of a hospital a less frequent and a costly occurrence. Moreover, physicians on staff, who are already chasing relatively fewer health-care dollars, may not be enthusiastic to take on a new colleague. Currently, there are more hospitals looking for ways to reduce staff appointments than there are hospitals seeking to expand — a phenomenon for which there may be significant legal consequences. A physician who is not appointed to the staff of a hospital, or is not reappointed, no longer has the luxury of simply turning his or her sights elsewhere as opportunities are few. Even if the hospital is justified in not appointing or reappointing a physician, a perception of injustice by the physician may still provoke expensive litigation.

Government regulation of the appointment process has produced a maze of statutory provisions in some jurisdictions. A health-care administrator or board member in a public hospital must acquire, at the very least, a working knowledge of the statute governing the appointment process in his or her institution. He or she must develop an awareness of the pitfalls to be avoided and when to obtain timely and expert legal advice. A single "privileges battle" can result in enormous legal expense.[6] A finding

---

5 *Into the 21st Century — Ontario Public Hospitals: Report of the Steering Committee, Public Hospitals Act Review* (Toronto: Ontario Ministry of Health (1992), Chapter 7.

6 The Canadian Medical Protective Association, which provides legal counsel to physicians involved in malpractice and professional discipline proceedings, now provides legal counsel to physicians involved in privileges disputes.

by a tribunal or a court that a physician's rights have been violated may result in an award or settlement of several hundred thousand dollars or more. Preventing a battle from starting is a result of good management by the hospital and co-operation by the medical staff.

Reasonable Care in the Appointment Process

The hospital, through its board, must exercise due care in the appointment and reappointment of its medical staff. There must be an effective method of peer review. Failure to have applicants properly evaluated by such bodies as the Credentials Committee or the Medical Advisory Committee may result in direct liability for a hospital where the health professional fails to meet a reasonable standard of care.

It is now common in medical malpractice actions for the plaintiff to allege that the hospital failed to exercise care in the evaluation and appointment of the physician. Ongoing monitoring of physicians is an obligation of the hospital. Where a lawsuit is commenced by a patient against a physician and the hospital, the hospital may be compelled to produce the documents that formed part of the appointment or reappointment process. The documents may include the application of the physician, letters of reference, complaints and minutes of the evaluating committees and of the hospital board.

A superficial evaluation will expose the hospital to the risk of legal liability. Where the hospital was in possession of information that demonstrated a risk to patients at the time of appointment or reappointment, the hospital may be found liable for failing to take reasonable precautions to discipline or supervise the physician. For example, reservations expressed by a referee about a physician's ability to provide qualified emergency care may return to haunt the hospital should an emergency patient allege substandard emergency treatment by the physician, or criticism, during the reappointment process, of a physician's declining surgical skills may eventually result in liability for a hospital that takes no preventative measures to protect the public.

Authority of the Board of Governors or Trustees

In all jurisdictions in Canada, the board of the hospital (or other health facility where there are medical staff appointments)[7] is the entity with

---

[7] Generally, the legal concepts discussed in this chapter apply to public hospitals

ultimate responsibility for the appointment, suspension or termination of an appointment. Most public hospitals legislation deems this a statutory obligation of the board. Although other individuals or committees within the hospital may be involved in evaluating applications, checking credentials, interviewing applicants and making recommendations for appointment, only the board is authorized to make the appointment. And, though a board may accord considerable deference to the recommendation of a Medical Advisory Committee, or others within the hospital, it must make its own, independent decision about the particular appointment.

> The Board of Governors of a public hospital is entrusted by its community with the responsibility of providing a program of health care tailored to the particular needs of that community. The Board must establish objectives that are within the capacity of its plant and resources. It must create a balance within its medical staff to ensure a broad base of expertise, and select a staff capable of developing excellence in health care while attaining the most efficient utilization of the facilities and resources of its hospital.
>
> The public is entitled to expect that every hospital will justify its enormous expenditures of public funds by providing the best health care of which that hospital is capable. Careful choice of personnel is an important aspect of efficient management.[8]

Principles of Administrative Law

Administrative law governs the decision-making powers and procedures of tribunals, including any executive or quasi-judicial body whose authority is assigned directly or indirectly by statute.[9] The authority of a hospital board and the procedures it follows when making decisions are associated with

---

as these are the health facilities for which there are statutory provisions governing the appointment, suspension and termination of privileges. Legislation governing the activities of other health facilities, such as nursing homes and chronic-care facilities, do not have similar legislation. However, similar principles may apply where it is the practice of the health facility to "appoint" a physician or physicians to treat patients in the health facility. The absence of statutory provisions does not mean that the health facility, where the legal relationship arises in the form of an "appointment" or similar relationship, can ignore the common-law principles of natural justice and fairness which are discussed in this chapter.

8 *Re Sheriton and North York General Hospital*, a decision of the Ontario Hospital Appeal Board, December 6, 1973, approved in *Re Board of Governors of the Scarborough General Hospital and Schiller* (1974), 4 O.R. (2d) 201, at 224-25 (Div. Ct.).

9 S. Blake, *Administrative Law in Canada* (Toronto: Butterworths, 1992), p. 1.

this area of the law. Generally, the allocation of privileges must comply with certain principles of administrative law. In practice, compliance with these principles can be a challenge. Not only are these principles loosely defined but also they have undergone significant change in the last 20 years. Decisions, at one time straightforward, are now complex and multi-faceted.

In the early 1970s, the Saskatchewan Court of Appeal upheld the decision of a hospital board to dismiss a physician from its medical staff where it considered this to be in the best interest of the hospital.[10] The Court held that the board had

> an absolute discretion and is not answerable for its decisions when it acts within its powers and prescribed procedural requirements.[11]
>
> The Court reasoned that the hospital board, in dismissing the physician, had performed "an administrative act, and not a judicial one", and in doing so, that the board had "absolute discretion" and was not answerable for decisions that were within the powers prescribed by its own bylaws.[12]

A converse ruling was made in *Re Crux and Leoville Union Hospital Board.*[13] In that case, a physician was notified by a hospital board that his privileges would cease and would not be renewed. He was given no notice prior to the decision being made, and he sought judicial review to have the decision of the board overturned. The Court reviewed the bylaws of the hospital in detail. The bylaws provided that before final action was taken by a hospital board to reduce, suspend or terminate a physician's privileges, the member of the medical staff affected was to be afforded a "hearing" before the hospital board. The Court held that the hospital had not acted in accordance with its own bylaws, and, therefore, quashed the resolution of the board withdrawing the admitting privileges of the physician. Further, the Court held that an amendment to the Saskatchewan *Hospital Standards Act* providing an opportunity for a physician suspended or dismissed from the medical staff to complain to the Minister of Public Health did not prejudice the right of the physician to bring an action in a court of competent jurisdiction.

The decision in *Re Crux,* which required that the physician be given a hearing, is consistent with current administrative law principles, statutory procedural requirements and most hospital bylaws. Today, it is unlikely that a Canadian court would countenance a unilateral dismissal of a physician based upon the "absolute discretion" of the hospital.

---

10 *R. v. Board of Governors of the University Hospital et al., ex p. Marian* (1970), 15 D.L.R. (3d) 767, [1971] 1 W.W.R. 58 (Sask. C.A.).

11 *Ibid.*, at 770 (D.L.R.).

12 *Ibid.*

13 (1972), 29 D.L.R. (3d) 601 (Sask. Q.B.).

An important principle of administrative law is that the body empowered to make a decision must be the one that makes it. Generally, it is not proper to delegate the decision to another body in place of the one with the statutory authority.[14] Nor is it proper to "adopt" what is, in reality, the decision of some other tribunal or body without considering the matter on its merits.[15] The statutory authority for granting, renewing, suspending or revoking privileges rests with the hospital board. While other bodies may be involved — the Credentials Committee, or the Medical Advisory Committee — these bodies do not have the power to make a decision that the board is authorized to make.

In *Helson and Fong v. The Board of Governors of the Oshawa General Hospital*,[16] the board had delegated the authority to maintain and revoke privileges to the head of the radiology department. The Hospital Appeal Board held that this delegation of authority by the hospital board was unlawful and ordered that the matter be referred back to the hospital board so that it could investigate and deliberate the matter in its own right. In *Re Braun and Surrey Memorial Hospital*,[17] a physician's application for associate staff privileges was considered by a Search and Selection Committee. There was no provision in the hospital bylaws for such a committee. It was concluded that the Committee had "performed the function of the Board of Trustees" and, in doing so, intruded upon the clear-cut procedure provided for in the Regulations to the British Columbia *Hospital Act*.[18]

A number of provincial statutes specifically state that the Medical Advisory Committee (or its equivalent) may *recommend* an appointment or reappointment, but that the ultimate decision rests with the board. For example, in Quebec, a council of physicians, dentists and pharmacists makes a recommendation to the board of directors of an "institution" with respect to an application for appointment before privileges are granted. The board of directors then reaches a decision based on several factors including the organization plan of the institution, the resources available, the specific requirements of the institution and the "supra-regional vocation of the institution".[19]

---

14 *Re Bimini Neighbourhood Pub Ltd. and Gould* (1984), 7 D.L.R. (4th) 556, at 559 (B.C.S.C.).

15 R.W. Macaulay, *Practice and Procedure before Administrative Tribunals* (Toronto: Carswell, 1988), Vol. 2, pp. 22-10.9–10; H.W.R. Wade, *Administrative Law*, 6th ed. (Oxford: Clarendon Press, 1988).

16 August 12, 1982, Ontario Hospital Appeal Board.

17 January 23, 1989, British Columbia Medical Appeal Board.

18 R.S.B.C. 1979, c. 176.

19 *An Act respecting health services and social services*, R.S.Q. 1977, c. S-4.2, s. 237. See also *Public Hospitals Act*, R.S.O. 1990, c. P.40, ss. 36 and 37; *Hospitals Act*, R.S.A. 1980, c. H-11, s. 27. In some other provinces, the issue is addressed in the

Natural Justice

Natural justice is an important concept in administrative law. It embodies two fundamental procedural requirements for judicial and quasi-judicial proceedings. First, the adjudicator or tribunal must be neither interested in the matter being decided nor biased toward one of the parties involved. Second, before a decision is made, the party affected must receive appropriate notice of the case against him or her and have the opportunity to respond.[20] Natural justice is applied on a sliding scale. Its stringency will depend upon the provisions of the body's enabling legislation, the nature of the matter being decided and the circumstances of the case.[21] Procedural defects in a proceeding may amount to a denial of natural justice. Natural justice requires that sufficient notice be given and that there be some form of "hearing". At times, an oral hearing is required, rather than an exchange of written documents. Natural justice may require the tribunal to allow the cross-examination of witnesses, to grant an adjournment of proceedings to permit one party to prepare his or her case, or to refrain from consulting or communicating with one party in the absence of others. Natural justice may be presumed to apply unless specifically overridden by statute.[22] A denial of natural justice in proceedings related to physicians' privileges may lead to a judicial review of the proceedings or an appeal to an appeal tribunal or court.

It has been held that the refusal of a hospital board to grant an adjournment to allow a physician to prepare for a hearing, and its subsequent termination of privileges in the absence of the physician and his counsel, constituted a denial of natural justice and the hospital board's decision was set aside.[23]

---

statute's regulations: B.C. Reg. 289/73, s. 15(4); N.B. Reg. 92-84, s. 26; Hospital Management Regulations, EC574/76, s. 6.

20 The rules of natural justice are often referred to in their latin terms: *nemo judex in sua causa debet esse* ("no man can be a judge in his own cause") and *audi alteram partem* ("hear the other side").

21 *Syndicat des employés de production du Québec et de l'Acadie v. Canadian Human Rights Commission; Canadian Broadcasting Corp. et al., Mis en cause* (1989), 62 D.L.R. (4th) 385, at 425 (S.C.C.).

22 *Québec (Commission des Relations Ouvrières) v. Alliance des Professeurs Catholiques de Montréal,* [1953] 2 S.C.R. 140, at 154.

23 *Sreedhar v. Outlook Union Hospital Board,* [1973] 2 W.W.R. 120; also see *Basu v. Bettschen et al.*, [1975] 6 W.W.R. 421 (Sask. C.A.), in which it was held that failure by the board to give any reasons for not reviewing an applicant's appointment prior to the hearing, and then refusing to allow the applicant to call witnesses, constituted a breach of natural justice and its decision was set aside. In *Re Cockings and University Hospital Board* (1975), 54 D.L.R. (3d) 581 (Sask. Q.B.), the Court intervened where the board of the hospital refused to allow

Fairness

The concept of fairness is linked closely to the concept of natural justice and may only be a term describing a less formal application of the same concept. When making administrative decisions, public boards and tribunals have a duty to adopt a fair process. The doctrine of fairness requires that, before a decision is made, the person against whom a decision may be made must be informed of the reasons for the authority's intended decision and must be given the opportunity to respond to the case against him or her.[24] According to the Supreme Court of Canada, such a duty falls on "every public authority making an administrative decision which is not of a legislative nature and which affects the rights, privileges or interests of an individual" and which has a serious effect on the individual.[25] Consequently, in *every* situation in which a hospital is called upon to exercise its power in relation to the granting, suspension or revocation of privileges, measures must be taken to ensure that a fair process is adopted. The absence of a stipulated process in the governing statute does not mean that no process was intended.

As with natural justice, the procedures required by the duty of fairness will depend on the particular case. For example, in a case where a family's troublesome conduct caused them to be evicted from public housing, it was held that letters from the property manager warning the mother were sufficient notice, and that the opportunity to discuss her situation with a community worker was a fair opportunity to respond.[26] In the case of immigrants applying for refugee status, however, it has been held that the opportunity to submit documents and to respond in writing was not sufficient. The applicants were entitled to a full oral hearing.[27]

The process for imposing a one-week suspension on a physician may differ greatly from the process required for imposing a permanent revocation. The operative prerequisite is fairness.[28] If an appeal tribunal or court

---

the physician a right to be heard, either through himself or through witnesses, and restricted the physician, in stating his case, to having his counsel make representations to the board.

24 *Re Nicholson and Haldimand-Norfolk (Regional Municipality) Commissioners of Police* (1978), 88 D.L.R. (3d) 671, at 682 (S.C.C.).

25 *Cardinal and Oswald v. Director of Kent Institution* (1985), 24 D.L.R. (4th) 44, at 51-52 and 56 (S.C.C.).

26 *Re Webb and Ontario Housing Corp.* (1978), 93 D.L.R. (3d) 187, at 197 (Ont. C.A.).

27 *Singh et al. v. Canada (Minister of Employment and Immigration)* (1985), 17 D.L.R. (4th) 422 (S.C.C.).

28 In *Zahab v. Salvation Army Grace General Hospital Ottawa* (1991), 3 Admin. L.R. (2d) 307 (Ont. Gen. Div.); leave to appeal to Court of Appeal granted September 3, 1991, Chadwick J., in considering whether the Court ought to intervene

is satisfied that the process adopted by the hospital was fair, it is unlikely to set aside or modify the hospital's decision. For example, it has been held that a hospital Selection Committee empowered to advertise vacancies, interview candidates and make recommendations to the board of a hospital is bound to observe a general duty of fairness or the rudiments of natural justice.[29]

In *Zahab v. Salvation Army Grace General Hospital*,[30] the Court concluded that a physician whose privileges had been revoked by the hospital had not been treated fairly. A physician from an outside hospital had been invited to conduct an independent review and had prepared a report that was unfavourable to the physician whose privileges were under scrutiny. Although the Medical Advisory Committee met and considered the matter, they did not receive a copy of the report of the independent reviewer. A vote was conducted by telephone subsequent to the meeting and the members of the Medical Advisory Committee voted to support revocation. In reinstating the physician pending his appeal of the Ontario Hospital Appeal Board decision, the Court held that he had not been "treated fairly" in that:

> The procedure before the medical advisory committee did not give him an opportunity to be heard or even to attend.
>
> The medical advisory committee had limited and selective information on which to base their recommendations.
>
> The committee did not have the benefit of discussion with each other.
>
> Members of the committee were involved in the initial investigation, therefore should not have been involved in the decision-making process.
>
> The hearing before the hospital board was not a hearing. It was one-sided and arbitrary in nature.[31]

---

where a physician's privileges had been revoked by a hospital, stated "it is really the consequences of the decision that must be looked at to determine if the applicant has been treated 'fairly'".

29 *Re Peterson and Atkinson* (1978), 23 O.R. (2d) 266 (Div. Ct.).

30 *Supra* note 28.

31 *Ibid.*, at 323. In *Roper v. Executive Committee of the Medical Board of the Royal Victoria Hospital* (1974), 50 D.L.R. (3d) 725 (S.C.C.), however, the Supreme Court of Canada held that there was no right to be heard, or to call witnesses, in support of an application for privileges where there was no such requirement in the statutory regulations governing the management of hospitals. Furthermore, the Court held that an administrative body cannot transform itself into a quasi-judicial body by extending a limited opportunity to the applicant to present his or her case. *Quaere* whether this case still constitutes the law in Canada: see *Sierra Club of Western Canada et al. v. The Province of British Columbia* (1984), 11 Admin. L.R. 276 (B.C.S.C.), which held that, in that context at least, "the Roper case is probably no longer good law" (at 278).

The denial of a right to a fair hearing will render a decision invalid.[32]

In *Re Braun and Surrey Memorial Hospital*,[33] the Medical Appeal Board of British Columbia held that "great mistakes" had been made in rejecting a physician's application for associate staff privileges. These mistakes included giving considerable weight to what was plainly hearsay evidence and not disclosing the contents of an unfavourable letter of reference to the physician so that he could "fully and fairly understand the accusations and reply accordingly". The board concluded that the physician "was not treated fairly" and ordered that he be appointed to the associate staff of the hospital.

It may not be acceptable for the board of a hospital to revoke or not to renew a physician's privileges where there is no previous history of documenting complaints and attempting to effect more moderate forms of disciplinary action. In *Re Board of Management of Grace General Hospital of Ottawa and Burgess*,[34] the Divisional Court of Ontario, in reaching its decision to reinstate a physician's privileges following suspension by a hospital, relied upon the reasons of the Hospital Appeal Board stating that:

> The response of the hospital in the past to a deteriorating situation between [the physician] and the staff has been totally inadequate with an almost complete lack of documentation or previous disciplinary action.[35]

Ontario and Alberta have statutes imposing minimum standards of procedure to be used by public boards and tribunals.[36] In other jurisdictions, hospital boards may be subject to the provisions of their province's *Public Enquiries Act* or to procedures imposed upon them by their enabling statute. Even where there are no statutory provisions in place setting out procedural guide-lines, a decision, which may impact materially upon a physician's privileges, must be accompanied by a process that provides an appropriate measure of natural justice and fairness. Where there is doubt about the process, the hospital should seek legal advice.

Reasons

At one time, it was thought that there could be no relief for an applicant whose application was rejected, even though no reasons were given by the

---

32 *Cardinal, supra* note 25, at 57.

33 January 23, 1989, British Columbia Medical Appeal Board.

34 (1985), 51 O.R. (2d) 435 (Div. Ct.).

35 *Ibid.*, at 437.

36 *Administrative Procedures Act,* R.S.A. 1980, c. A-2; *Statutory Powers Procedure Act,* R.S.O. 1990, c. S.22.

hospital board for the rejection.[37] The current law, however, is that administrative tribunals — and this would include a hospital board — are required to give reasons for significant decisions. A few provincial statutes state this requirement specifically.[38] Even in the absence of a statutory provision, however, natural justice and fairness may require reasons to be given. Generally, it is good practice to give reasons for any decision that may have a significant impact upon an individual or group. Reasons are best formulated at the time the decision is made. It is not satisfactory, and may be a ground upon which the reasons can be attacked, if they are created retrospectively in order to "fit" a particular decision. Moreover, the exercise of formulating clear and concise reasons is likely to assist in the decision-making process and to result in a decision that is just and capable of being sustained if contested before another tribunal.

In *Desai v. Brantford General Hospital*; *Desai v. St. Joseph's Hospital*,[39] two physicians were restricted by the hospital from carrying out certain anesthetic procedures. An external review had been conducted and a written report had been prepared. When being informed of the hospital's decision, the physicians were advised of the report and of the hospital's willingness to provide a copy to them. The Hospital Appeal Board of Ontario held that although there were no express reasons set out in the hospital's decision, it incorporated, by reference, the contents of the external reviewer's report. The report made it clear that each physician's competence to perform certain anesthetic procedures was being challenged and listed the nature of the complaints. It was held that although the hospital had "met the test for the giving of written reasons", it did not "get high marks for its method" of so doing.[40] The Hospital Appeal Board suggested that it would have been preferable for the hospital board to have formulated in its letter a summary setting out its reasons. On appeal to the Court, it was held that the hospital's reasoning was deficient, and the matter was remitted to the board of the hospital so it could give appropriate reasons.

In *Hutfield v. Fort Saskatchewan General Hospital*,[41] the decision of a hospital board not to grant privileges to an applicant was overturned. There had been no opportunity for the applicant to make representations to the board and no reasons were given for the board's refusal. The Court commented:

---

[37] *Andreas v. Edmonton Hospital Board*, [1944] 4 D.L.R. 747 (Alta. C.A.).

[38] *Public Hospitals Act*, R.S.O. 1990, c. P.40, s. 35(7): the applicant is entitled to written reasons if he or she so requests; *An Act respecting health services and social services*, R.S.Q. 1977, c. S-4.2, s. 241.

[39] (1991), 87 D.L.R. (4th) 140 (Ont. Ct. Gen. Div.).

[40] *Ibid.*, at 145.

[41] (1986), 24 Admin. L.R. 250, 49 Alta. L.R. (2d) 256, 74 A.R. 180 (Q.B.); affd (1988), 60 Alta. L.R. (2d) 165, 89 A.R. 274, 52 D.L.R. (4th) 562, 31 Admin. L.R. 311 (C.A.).

> . . . the Sphinx-like inscrutability of the recommendation of the medical staff and of the decision of the Board opens the door to suspicions, however unfounded they might be if the reasons were given, that the reasons are based on irrelevant considerations, bad faith, misconceived policy considerations, or errors of fact. Sunlight can dispel such suspicions. An open window is a guarantee that the person whose interests are affected by the decision has been dealt with fairly and in accordance with law.[42]

In describing what reasons would be appropriate, the Court stated:

> . . . nor can the Board possibly "consider" the application "carefully" if the written report merely states baldly such things as "the credentials of the applicant are inadequate" or "the applicant is unsuitable". Sufficient details must be given in the written report to enable the board to reach a rational decision as to the credentials, training, suitability, experience and references of the applicant, taking into account both the recommendation received and the reasons given.[43]

Bias

The issue of bias arises frequently in administrative law. A party who appears before a tribunal for adjudication is entitled to be heard by a tribunal that is unbiased and that raises no reasonable apprehension of bias. In *Grenier v. Region 1 Hospital Corp. (Southeast)*,[44] while an associate staff member of a hospital was away for certain studies, he received notice that his privileges would not be renewed. He was told he could reapply upon his return to Moncton. On an application by the physician, the hospital board's decision was set aside. The Court found that there had been a failure to disclose information to the physician, and further, that two non-board members had addressed the hospital board in the absence of the physician. It was held that this constituted unfair treatment and raised a suspicion of bias on the part of the board.

In *Tam v. St. Joseph's Health Centre and Hynes*,[45] a hospital decision, which deprived a physician of his full privileges, was sent back to the hospital by the Court for reconsideration. In so doing, the Court pointed out the necessity for the hospital board to remain impartial and objective in its consideration of the matter.

---

[42] *Ibid.*, at 271 (Admin. L.R.).

[43] *Ibid.*, at 275.

[44] (1993), 133 N.B.R. (2d) 232, 341 A.P.R. 232 (Q.B.).

[45] (1985), 10 O.A.C. 286 (Div. Ct.).

> The Board's function is not to "stick by" its staff. The Medical Advisory Committee are not "running the hospital". The Board is, or should be.
>
> When the Board reconvenes it must deliberate the issue without any feeling of regimental loyalty for its staff or anyone else in a spirit of calmness and impartiality that, unfortunately, does not appear to be entirely true of the partial hearing it held. The acrimony displayed on that occasion was entirely out of place. Nothing less than complete objectivity will suffice. The Board should, of course, avoid acting as a cat's paw for any side in a private dispute but its governing concern must be the good of the Health Centre.[46]

On the other hand, it is not unusual and is clearly permissible for a board to place significant reliance upon its administration and medical staff in making decisions about appointments. Whether there is a need for a particular brand of expertise, whether the impact of a new appointment will be positive or negative, or whether a particular physician is performing appropriately under a current appointment are all matters about which the board must be informed in order to make its decision. Reasons setting out an analysis of the information or evidence provided to the board and demonstrating a convincing basis for the decision will indicate that the board has properly considered information and evidence, but that it made its own decision. A decision and reasons that are short and non-explanatory may give the impression that the board has simply adopted, without analysis, the recommendations of others.

Prior consideration of the matter by members of a hospital board, or some of its members, may constitute grounds that create bias or a reasonable apprehension of bias. It may be appropriate for members who have been involved in an investigation, or earlier proceedings, to withdraw. Where there is a concern that the whole board has been "tainted" by previous consideration of the matter, it may be necessary, on consent of the parties, to request that the matter be dealt with by the provincial appeal board or the court.

Provincial appeal boards (where they exist) may not be enthusiastic about conducting hearings or other procedures intended to be conducted at the hospital level. Nonetheless, where the hospital board is not in a position to conduct a hearing because of its prior involvement, this is one option that may be considered. Other options include agreement by the parties to a reduced quorum of the board or some form of arbitration. If raised, the issue of bias should be dealt with early and openly. Counsel for the physician and the hospital may be able to reach an agreement on how to accommodate any concern of bias. If the issue is raised during the course of a hearing, it may be too late to deal with it. This is a difficult issue and, where it arises, the hospital will wish to have legal advice.

---

[46] *Ibid.*, at 290.

Bias is not always present in cases in which the hospital board has previously dealt with the matter. In *Stewart v. Board of Governors of the Wadena Union Hospital*,[47] the hospital suspended a physician's privileges for seven days. When the physician began court proceedings to overturn the decision, the hospital rescinded its earlier decision and commenced an inquiry in accordance with its bylaws. The physician sought a court order to prevent the inquiry from proceeding on the ground that there was a real likelihood of bias. The Court found, however, that the temporary suspension order did not result in a likelihood of bias, which would prevent the board from "disposing of the charges on their merits".

In *LeBaud v. Chaleur Regional Hospital*,[48] the Medical Advisory Committee of the hospital had recommended the suspension of a physician as a result of several complaints related to his conduct. The doctor, with his counsel, had attended the meeting of the Medical Advisory Committee at which the recommendation had been made. Before the board of the hospital could meet to consider the recommendation, the physician applied to the Court for judicial review. The Court held, however, that its intervention was inappropriate. The board had made no "decision on the merits" that the court could review and there was no reasonable apprehension of bias. In *Re Jow and Board of Governors of Regina General Hospital*,[49] it was held that a failure to give a physician the particulars of the grounds for her suspension could have been remedied if the physician had applied for a hearing of the hospital board. The physician had been suspended after an investigation by a Special Committee.

Where the reasons furnished by the Medical Advisory Committee are given to the board of a hospital prior to a hearing, but the reasons do not give any detail, or detailed account, of the evidence, this does not amount to previous investigation or consideration by the board.[50] To avoid any apprehension of bias, however, it may be preferable not to deliver the Medical Advisory Committee's reasons to the board prior to the board's hearing.

In some jurisdictions, the administrative law requirement that the board of the hospital be unbiased has been codified in the governing statute. For example, in Ontario, the *Public Hospitals Act*[51] prevents a board from hearing a matter it has already considered. It requires:

---

47 [1979] 1 W.W.R. 671 (Sask. C.A.); see also *Re Cockings and University Hospital Board* (1975), 54 D.L.R. (3d) 581 (Sask. Q.B.).

48 (1987), 83 N.B.R. (2d) 280 (C.A.).

49 (1978), 86 D.L.R. (3d) 93 (Sask. Q.B.); affd (1979), 100 D.L.R. (3d) 98 (C.A.).

50 *Re Sutherland and Board of Governors of Pembroke General Hospital* (1973), 1 O.R. (2d) 438 (H.C.J.).

51 *Supra* note 38, s. 39(4).

> Members of the board holding a hearing shall not have taken part in any investigation or consideration of the subject-matter of the hearing before the hearing and shall not communicate directly or indirectly in relation to the subject-matter of the hearing with any person or with any party or representative of a party except upon notice to and opportunity for all parties to participate, but the board may seek legal advice from an adviser independent from the parties and in such case the nature of the advice should be made known to the parties in order that they may make submissions as to the law.

Other provinces, including New Brunswick and Newfoundland, prevent board members from voting on matters in which they have a pecuniary or other interest.[52] New Brunswick regulations also stipulate that relatives of employees of the hospital, members of the board and members of the medical staff may not be appointed to the board.[53]

Court Intervention

Generally, court intervention by way of judicial review will not be available to a physician whose privileges have been affected where he or she has an appeal mechanism available for appealing the decision, but has not used it.[54] A court will interfere where the physician has an alternative remedy or a right of appeal only if there are exceptional circumstances.[55] Similarly, where a physician fails to exercise a right to appear before the hospital board to contest a finding of a Special Committee appointed by the board, which resulted in the physician's dismissal, the Court has held that it would not interfere with the decision of the hospital.[56] Also, the Court will not intervene where an applicant doctor has the right of appeal to a provincial medical appeal board.[57]

In *Ojo v. Willett Hospital*,[58] a doctor's application for judicial review was dismissed where the doctor had a convenient alternative remedy in the

---

52 *Hospitals Act*, R.S.N. 1990, c. H-9, s. 7(5); N.B. Reg. 92-84, s. 10.

53 N.B. Reg. 92-84, s. 6.

54 *Chakravorty v. Attorney General for Alberta and Medical Executive Committee of Calgary General Hospital*, [1972] 4 W.W.R. 437 (Alta. S.C.). See also *Lawson v. Toronto Hospital Corp.* (1991), 46 O.A.C. 376 (Div. Ct.).

55 *Re Jow, supra* note 49, at 104 (86 D.L.R.). See also *Tobe v. North York Branson Hospital*, unreported, June 1, 1989 (Ont. H.C.J.). See also *Re Williams and Board of Directors of Kemptville District Hospital* (1986), 29 D.L.R. (4th) 629 (Ont. H.C.J.).

56 *Ibid.*

57 *Jain v. North and West Vancouver Hospital Society* (1974), 43 D.L.R. (3d) 291 (B.C.S.C.).

58 (1984), 6 O.A.C. 83 (Div. Ct.).

form of an appeal to the Ontario Hospital Appeal Board. A similar result was obtained in *The Board of Trustees of the Renfrew Victoria Hospital v. Diagnostic Imaging Consultants and Richmond Technology Services Ltd.*[59] The hospital terminated its contract with a corporation for the provision of diagnostic imaging services. The physicians affected alleged that there had been unlawful interference with their privileges, and they appealed to the Hospital Appeal Board. The hospital applied for a declaration by the Court that the decision to terminate the contract was a commercial matter and did not involve a revocation of privileges. It asked that the Court decide the narrow issue on the ground of expediency. The Court held that the Hospital Appeal Board was the "body with the appropriate blend of medical expertise, legal direction and public participation" to hear the matter and decide on the issue of privileges.

In addition, judicial review will not be available where an attack is made on the recommendation against appointment or reappointment by a Medical Advisory Committee. Rather, the appropriate forum in which the physician should challenge an unfavourable recommendation is the hearing before the hospital board.[60]

In the absence of an alternative statutory remedy, an application for judicial review may be appropriate. Judicial review is available to a first-time applicant for hospital privileges where the provincial statute provides an appeal remedy only to a "member or former member" of the medical staff of the hospital.[61] In *Zahab*,[62] a limited form of judicial review was sought. A physician, whose privileges had been revoked, applied to have them reinstated pending the outcome of his appeal to the Hospital Appeal Board. The Court ordered the privileges reinstated "based upon terms and conditions which will protect the public interest".[63]

Provincial Legislation Governing Privileges

A number of provinces and territories have enacted legislation regulating the procedure by which physicians apply for appointment and reappointment to the staff of public hospitals. Because the process is mandated by statute, failure to comply with the statute may lead to the process being set

---

59 Unreported, June 25, 1992, No. 4537/92 (Ont. Gen. Div.).

60 *Haber v. Wellesley Hospital* (1986), 16 O.A.C. 215 (Div. Ct.).

61 *Hutfield v. Fort Saskatchewan General Hospital, supra* note 41.

62 *Zahab v. Salvation Army Grace General Hospital Ottawa* (1991), 3 Admin. L.R. (2d) 307 (Ont. Gen. Div.); leave to appeal to Court of Appeal granted September 3, 1991.

63 *Ibid.*, at 323.

aside by an appeal tribunal or court, which can have serious consequences for the hospital. It is essential that those participating in the appointment and reappointment process — and this should include members of the Credentials Committee, the Medical Advisory Committee, department heads and board members and hospital administrators — have knowledge of the applicable statutory mechanisms. In some jurisdictions, the procedures to be followed are outlined in detail in the statute. The process may be labyrinthine. Without careful attention to the steps of the process, a hospital may find itself in breach of the applicable statute.

The process set out in the Regulations[64] passed pursuant to the British Columbia *Hospital Act*[65] is representative of the process in most other provinces. An application for a "permit" to practise medicine or dentistry in a hospital, or for the renewal of such a permit, must be made, in writing, to the administrator of the hospital. The Regulation requires the administrator to "forthwith refer the application to the credentials committee or some other appropriate body of the medical staff".[66] The Credentials Committee, or other appropriate body, must consider the application and report its recommendation in writing to the Medical Advisory Committee (or other executive body of the medical staff). That body must consider the report by the Credentials Committee and notify the board of the hospital, in writing, of its own recommendation. The board of the hospital must review the application, consider the recommendation of the Medical Advisory Committee, make a decision on the application and notify both the applicant and the medical staff of the hospital, in writing, within 120 days of receipt of the application. The Regulation further provides a physician whose application or reapplication has been refused, in whole or in part, with the opportunity, upon application in writing to the board, to appear in person to make representations to the board, which is required to "hear, consider, or reconsider the matter". The applicant may be represented by legal counsel if he or she desires and the board must advise the applicant in writing of its decision within 30 days.[67]

Where the applicant is dissatisfied with the decision of the board, or where the board fails to notify the applicant of its decision within the required period, the applicant may appeal to the British Columbia Medical Appeal Board.[68] Section 20 of the Regulation points out that the statutory provisions dealing with the appointment and reappointment of physicians and dentists to the medical staff

---

64 B.C. Reg. 289/73.

65 R.S.B.C. 1979, c. 176.

66 B.C. Reg. 289/73, s. 15(2).

67 *Ibid.*, s. 15(4), (5).

68 *Ibid.*, at s. 15(6).

> apply to every hospital under the Act notwithstanding the provisions of the bylaws, rules or regulations of the hospital and its medical staff, and the bylaws, rules and regulations of the hospital and its medical staff shall be deemed to be revised in accordance with, and to include, these regulations.[69]

With minor variations, the legislation in Ontario[70] and Quebec[71] is similar to that of British Columbia. For example, an applicant in British Columbia may make "representations" to the Board, and an Ontario applicant is entitled to a "hearing".[72] A dissatisfied applicant in Quebec may appeal to the *Commission des affaires sociales.*

In some jurisdictions, the process set out in the legislation is less specific and allows the hospital to develop its own procedure for appointments and reappointments to the medical staff. In Prince Edward Island, the board is required to pass bylaws providing for the "appointment and functioning of . . . a medical staff".[73] That province's legislation, however, does provide for the establishment of a Credentials Committee, a review of appointments by the Medical Advisory Committee of the hospital, and, ultimately, for the board of the hospital to make the decision that grants privileges to the applicant. The legislation also requires the board to pass bylaws providing the Medical Advisory Committee with authority to make recommendations to the hospital board regarding "the dismissal, suspension or restriction of hospital privileges of any member of the medical staff or the dental staff . . .".[74] The Prince Edward Island legislation has no stipulations for applications to be in writing, or for time frames within which the applications must be considered and upon which a decision

---

69 *Ibid.*

70 *Public Hospitals Act*, R.S.O. 1990, c. P.40. In late 1995, Bill 26, the *Savings and Restructuring Act, 1996* (S.O. 1996, c. 1) was tabled in Ontario. This is omnibus legislation affecting a large variety of statutes. It gives public hospitals in Ontario a broad new authority to revoke or transfer the privileges of a physician. Where a hospital board decides that a hospital will cease to operate, or the Ministry of Health directs a hospital to cease to operate, the board is able to refuse applications for appointment or reappointment, revoke existing appointments and substantially alter the privileges of any physician without the obligation to follow the process outlined under the *Public Hospitals Act.* Regulations proposed under the legislation further broaden the powers of public hospitals to restrict or terminate privileges.

71 *An Act respecting health services and social services*, R.S.Q. 1977, c. S-4.2 and *An Act respecting the Commission des affaires sociales*, R.S.Q. 1977, c. C-34.

72 *Public Hospitals Act, supra* note 70, s. 37(7).

73 *Hospital Management Regulations* EC574/76, s. 6(1)(a)(ii).

74 *Ibid.*, s. 6(6)(a)(vi).

must be made; nor are there any provisions that deal with the appearance of the applicant before the board to make representations. Nonetheless, this does not necessarily preclude the hospital's obligation to act in accordance with natural justice and fairness.

In Nova Scotia, the *Hospitals Act*[75] requires the board of the hospital to make bylaws, though there is no specific reference to applications for appointment or reappointment to the medical staff. Similarly, in Newfoundland, the *Hospitals Act*[76] provides the hospital with general bylaw-making authority, but it makes no particular reference to the appointment and reappointment of physicians. Hospital bylaws that conform to the detailed statutory provisions of some provinces (*i.e.*, British Columbia) are likely to withstand the review of an appeal tribunal or a court.

In New Brunswick, the Regulations[77] under the *Hospital Act*[78] state that a "medical practitioner" who wishes to be appointed to the medical staff of a hospital must apply directly to the board for appointment. Further, the board is required to "annually delineate, reduce, renew or extend the privileges" granted to each member of the medical staff "taking into consideration the needs and facilities of the hospital corporation and the training and abilities of the medical practitioners".[79] The board is required to "request advice from the medical advisory committee as to the appointments to be made and the privileges to be granted".[80] Section 26(5) of the Regulations states:

> a board . . . may at any time withdraw, reduce or alter the privileges it grants to any member of the medical staff.

Notwithstanding this provision, an arbitrary termination or a reduction of privileges without adherence to the principles of natural justice and fairness, if tested in court by an applicant for appointment or reappointment, will be set aside.[81]

In Saskatchewan, the board of every hospital must enact bylaws governing

> (a) the appointment, re-appointment, suspension, dismissal of, and other disciplinary action relating to a member of the medical staff.[82]

---

75 R.S.N.S. 1989, c. 208.

76 R.S.N. 1990, c. H-9.

77 N.B. Reg. 92-84, s. 26(1).

78 S.N.B. 1992, c. H-6.1.

79 *Supra* note 77, s. 26(3).

80 *Ibid.*

81 See *Michel v. Hôpital de Lamèque* (1989), 102 N.B.R. (2d) 350 (Q.B.).

82 Sask. Reg. 331/79, s. 3(2).

The regulation contemplates appointment of dentists and chiropractors to the hospital staff pursuant to an appointment and reappointment process. The *Hospital Standards Act*[83] allows a practitioner to complain, in writing, to the Minister of Health about a decision of a hospital board if the practitioner believes that his or her application was unfairly rejected. A failure by the board to notify the practitioner of its decision within the 30-day statutory period for such notice is also a ground for complaint. The minister has discretionary power to refer the complaint to an appeal board, constituted *ad hoc*, where the minister considers it is in the public interest that the complaint be heard by the tribunal. In the case of physicians, the minister is obliged to consult the College of Physicians and Surgeons and the Saskatchewan Health Care Association before making the decision whether to refer the complaint. The appeal board's hearing is *de novo* and the board may include reasons if it considers it advisable.[84]

In Manitoba, s. 29 of the *Hospitals Act*[85] permits the Lieutenant Governor-in-Council to make regulations with respect to "the method of appointing and terms of appointment of members of the medical staff of the hospital".[86] The current Regulations, however, do not stipulate an appointment process. Section 4 of the Regulation[87] does require each hospital serviced by an Area Standards Committee to forward a list of the surgical privileges of each physician on staff at that hospital, or of any changes, to the Committee's Chair. Although there is no mention in the Manitoba *Hospital Act* of a right to appeal, in 1973 a Medical Appointments Review Committee was established for the purpose of hearing

> appeals filed with it by an applicant whose application for medical staff privileges as defined by the hospital by-laws has been refused in whole or in part or whose staff privileges have been reduced or terminated by any hospital, or whose application has not been dealt with within a reasonable time, provided that the applicant has exhausted his rights of appeal at the hospital, including an appeal to the hospital board concerned.[88]

The Medical Appointment Review Committee is a private body governed by a constitution to which bodies responsible for the provision of health services in the province are parties. The agreement is careful to point out that

---

83 R.S.S. 1978, c. H-10, s. 24.

84 *Ibid.*, s. 26.

85 R.S.M. 1987, c. H120.

86 *Ibid.*, s. 29(o).

87 Man. Reg. 453/88 R.

88 *Medical Appointments Review Committee Agreement*, para. 10, as cited in a pamphlet published by the Manitoba Medical Appointments Review Committee, undated.

> the Committee does not have the power to compel a hospital to accept its recommendations, nor does the agreement under which it is constituted preclude or restrict the rights of any person to appeal directly by civil action to a court of proper jurisdiction with respect to his medical staff privileges at a hospital.[89]

In Alberta, the *Hospitals Act*[90] requires hospital boards to make bylaws for medical staff concerning the appointment, reappointment, termination or suspension of privileges. It further states that the bylaws must provide for "a procedure for the review of decisions made by the medical staff or the board pertaining to or affecting" privileges and must ensure that all applications reach the board within a prescribed period and that notice be given to an applicant for appointment within a reasonable time of the decision of the board. The statute also establishes the Hospital Privileges Appeal Board[91] to hear appeals of medical staff "aggrieved by a decision" of the hospital. Curiously, the jurisdiction of the Hospital Privileges Appeal Board is only for applications for reappointment, or for termination or suspension of physicians who already have privileges. It does not apply to *initial* applications for appointment. The only recourse for a physician who makes an initial application to a hospital, and whose application is rejected, may be to apply to a court for a judicial review of the decision.

A regulation passed pursuant to the *Territorial Hospital Insurance Services Act*[92] deals with the appointment of medical staff to hospitals in the Northwest Territories. It provides that the "hospital authority" shall appoint medical staff who shall "ordinarily hold their appointments for a period of one year". An application for appointment must be made "annually in writing". A hospital authority "may suspend or dismiss a member of the medical staff", and may "lay down limitations on surgical or other privileges of a member of the medical staff".[93] The Yukon Territory has a regulation almost identical to that of the Northwest Territories.[94]

Medical Staff Bylaws

In most hospitals, bylaws are created to deal specifically with the medical staff, usually called "Medical Staff Bylaws". These bylaws may include such

---

89 *Ibid.*, at para. 20.

90 R.S.A. 1980, c. H-11, s. 32.

91 *Ibid.*, s. 33.

92 R.S.N.W.T. 1988, c. T-3.

93 R.R.N.W.T. 1990, c. T-6, s. 68(1), (2) and (3).

94 Yukon O.I.C. 1977/130.

areas as categories of medical staff privileges (*i.e.*, active, associate, courtesy, etc.), standards for the completion of records, mandatory participation in the emergency department rotation, service on specified hospital committees, requirements for membership in the Canadian Medical Protective Association or other appropriate insurance, restrictions on certain types of procedures or activities, minimum standards for attendance at meetings or utilization and discharge requirements. Failure by a physician to comply with the hospital's medical staff bylaws may be grounds for disciplinary action.[94a]

As noted, a hospital bylaw may contain a specified procedure for taking disciplinary action against a physician. To be effective, the bylaw must comply with statutory framework as well as related principles of administrative law. A bylaw that does not conform to a province's public hospitals legislation, or that violates the principles of natural justice and fairness, may be invalid. An appeal tribunal or court may override such a bylaw in order to do justice. Hospital administrators should be alert to the fact that bylaws drafted as recently as five or six years ago may have been preempted by recent developments in the law. Automatic reliance upon a bylaw in carrying out a decision that affects a physician's privileges, without ensuring that the bylaw is in conformance with provincial or territorial legislation and relevant administrative law principles, may lead to legal proceedings, and ultimately, to a decision that restores the physician's privileges.

A physician, however, cannot take the position that his or her rights and obligations are governed exclusively by the public hospitals legislation, principles of administrative law and bylaws. A physician must comply with authorities within the hospital who are charged with the hospital's day-to-day operation. The exercise of "privileges" within the hospital encompasses co-operation by the physician with the board, management of the hospital, departmental heads and colleagues. Rules or guide-lines, necessary to the smooth operation of the hospital, may be established by the administration of the hospital. For example, in *Re Cockings and University Hospital Board et al.*,[95] it was held that additional rules and "directives" by depart-

---

[94a] In *Dr. Murray F. Matangi and Dr. Gerrald Adams v. The Board of Governors of Kingston General Hospital,* May 6, 1996, No. H.93/94 (Ont. Hosp. App. Bd.), a physician who resigned from his university appointment to avoid having to participate in the university department's financial pool argued that he was entitled, nonetheless, to maintain his staff appointment at the teaching hospital where he practised. The hospital's decision to terminate his privileges was upheld by the Ontario Hospital Appeal Board on the ground that the hospital's bylaws provided that a university appointment was a necessary prerequisite to his having been granted privileges in the first place.

[95] *Re Cockings and University Hospital Board* (1975), 54 D.L.R. (3d) 581 (Sask. Q.B.).

mental heads were contemplated by the hospital bylaws and were not something that a physician in a department could ignore with impunity.

Legal Conflicts Involving Hospital Privileges

1. New Applications

Most litigation involving hospital privileges arises out of the non-renewal, suspension or revocation of privileges. There are relatively few cases involving the initial application by a physician for privileges at the hospital. Nonetheless, the correct legal process for considering new applications must be followed. As obtaining privileges at a hospital in the community in which the physician has chosen to practise has significant implications for a physician's professional status and income, every application should be taken seriously. Guide-lines should be in place in the hospital to ensure that new applications are processed in a consistent manner and on a timely basis.

A hospital may wish to employ a selection process involving a form of advertisement to interested parties. The advertisement may generate numerous "applications". Does this mean that in every case where an application is received, a hospital must follow the procedure by which an "application" is put before the medical advisory committee, and the applicant must be given notice of the recommendation of the Medical Advisory Committee and a right to written reasons and a hearing before the hospital board? The process set out in most statutes was not designed to accommodate the numerous responses solicited by advertisement. To require that each response be fully processed would make the selection process expensive and unwieldy. The advertisement should be framed in such a way that it does not invite "applications", but rather, an opportunity for potential applicants to "express interest" in a particular position. The hospital may then send "applications" to those who qualify. In advertising a position on the medical staff, hospitals, with the assistance of legal counsel, should pay due regard to the governing legislation, the potential number of "applicants" and the particular terms contained in any advertisement, as an appeal board or a court may not view the selection process as acceptable.

In *Re Thompson and the Fraser-Burrard Hospital Society*,[96] a cardiac surgeon's application for privileges was refused by the hospital. Although the Appeal Board did not allow the appeal of the applicant, ruling instead

[96] March 27, 1992, British Columbia Medical Board.

that the physician's failure to accept limitations on his practice was a ground for refusing his application, it was critical of the appointment process.

> We consider that the Hospital erred in its relationship with this particular applicant in not giving him precise information regarding the appointment process and procedures to be followed. As well, when accepting Dr. Thompson's application, the Hospital should have presented Dr. Thompson with a clear description of the actual situation for which a surgeon was sought including the details of what we believe were completely justifiable limits. . . . As an Appeal Board which sits "*de novo*", it is not necessary that we hear details of what the Board did and did not do. Instead, it is important that we hear details of the process up to and including the advice given to the Board. In this instance we did hear that detail and consider that the process was flawed in that Dr. Thompson's application was never fairly considered, that recruitment into the position as second surgeon on the cardiac surgery team was not done in an objective manner and that the administration of the Hospital should have detailed the mechanism of appointments as well as the specific description of the position which was available.[97]

Where an applicant fails to make full disclosure to the hospital's credentials committee, this alone will justify the hospital in refusing an appointment.[98] It is a legitimate and reasonable exercise of the board's function in considering an application for privileges to require disclosure of the existence of liability insurance coverage as a condition of granting an appointment or reappointment to the medical staff.[99]

2. Collegiality

The personality traits of an applicant are relevant matters to be taken into account when deciding whether or not the applicant should be appointed to the medical staff.[100] A finding by the Hospital Appeal Board of Ontario that an applicant was a "difficult individual who might have caused friction or tension" was upheld as a relevant consideration by a hospital in determining whether to grant privileges to a physician.[101]

---

97 *Ibid.*, pp. 20-21.

98 *Re Tanhueco and Prince George Regional Hospital*, December 22, 1986, British Columbia Medical Appeal Board.

99 *Re Lewis and The Royal Inland Hospital*, 15 October 1986, British Columbia Medical Appeal Board.

100 *Re Schiller and Scarborough General Hospital* (1973), 2 O.R. (2d) 324 (Div. Ct.).

101 *Chin v. Salvation Army Scarborough Grace General Hospital* (1988), 28 O.A.C. 388 (Div. Ct.).

In *Re Hicks and West Coast General Hospital*,[102] an applicant for privileges was turned down "on the grounds of significant concerns regarding her interpersonal and clinical skills". Prior to her application, the physician had worked for a short period in the hospital as a *locum tenens*. One of the issues raised in the appeal was whether "interpersonal skills" constituted a proper ground for denial of hospital privileges. The Medical Appeal Board of British Columbia held:

> the Hospital's concern with the Appellant's lack of interpersonal skills was in itself a compelling reason for the refusal of privileges. We refer in particular to some, if not all, of the nurses' evidence, [the Appellant's] unjustified ignorance of the rules relating to discharge of patients, the unfortunate incident related to Dr. Fraser and the extraordinary memo she composed, which contained innuendo, glib comments and unprofessional statements. Despite her alleged frustration at the time — she said she felt a sense of hurt — it was tactless and ill-advised.[103]

In *Re Ledgerwood and Squamish General Hospital*,[104] the applicant's personality was considered, in combination with several other factors, in rejecting the physician's application for privileges. The Appeal Board heard evidence that another physician found the applicant to be "rude and arrogant". The hospital to which the physician had applied led a significant amount of evidence indicating a "long standing history of aggressiveness or perhaps inappropriate conduct" by the physician at other hospitals in Vancouver. Another physician described the applicant's personality as "prickly". The Appeal Board found that the applicant's personality constituted a factor in its decision not to overrule the decision of the hospital board.

> Without necessarily deciding whether [his] personality was such as to be disruptive or whether those complaints by the Hospital would be sufficient alone to deny privileges, it is clear to us that the cumulative effect of his lack of credibility, the geographic factor, his judgment and his personality is such that it would clearly be inappropriate to grant [the] appeal.[105]

In *Re Board of Management of Grace General Hospital of Ottawa and Burgess*,[106] a physician's privileges were not renewed where his conduct was "inconsistent with the spirit of collegiality that is imperative in a hospital environment" and where this contributed to "abrasive relationships". In *Rosenhek*,

---

[102] February 9, 1990, British Columbia Medical Appeal Board.
[103] *Ibid.*, at 36-37.
[104] April 5, 1990, British Columbia Medical Appeal Board.
[105] *Ibid.*, at 16.
[106] (1985), 51 O.R. (2d) 435, at 436 (Div. Ct.).

M.D. v. Metropolitan General Hospital, Windsor, Ontario,[106a] a physician had his privileges revoked on the grounds that he had a poor relationship with other health-care professionals in the hospital and that he suffered from extreme stress. Because of conflicts with other physicians he was not welcome to join a call group, requiring him to be on call seven days a week, 24 hours per day. The Hospital Appeal Board concluded that the physician should not have had his privileges revoked on the basis that he did not "fit in". The Board stated that "the hospital has an interest in ensuring appropriate coverage arrangements for physicians and that it has an obligation to interfere where such arrangements are not being made".

What defects in character or personality may constitute grounds for non-appointment will be difficult to specify in advance and will depend upon the facts of each case. For example, should the privileges of a physician be renewed where there have been allegations or findings of professional or criminal misconduct? Does it matter if the misconduct took place inside or outside the institution? What if the allegations or finding did not involve patients and were outside of the physician-patient relationship? In California, a court upheld the suspension of a physician's privileges where the physician had been convicted of participating in a conspiracy to murder his wife.[107]

3. Age

Hospital bylaws may contain provisions affecting a physician's privileges because of age. Physicians may be required to move from active staff to courtesy or consulting staff upon reaching a specified age. The board may wish to replace older physicians, whose skills and knowledge may be on the wane, with younger physicians who are more familiar with, and adept at, new techniques and procedures.

The issue of mandatory retirement of physicians was considered by the Supreme Court of Canada in *Stoffman v. Vancouver General Hospital.*[108] The board of a hospital approved a Medical Staff Regulation providing:

> Members of the Staff shall be expected to retire at the end of the appointment year in which they pass their 65th birthday. Members of the Staff who wish to defer their retirement may make special application to the board. The board shall request the Medical Advisory Committee for a recommendation in each such case. The Medical Advisory Committee shall, in making its recommendation, consider the report of a personal interview which shall

---

[106a] April 1, 1996 (Ont. Hosp. App. Bd.).

[107] *Miller v. National Medical Hospital of Monterey Park, Inc.,* 124 Cal. App. 3d 81 (1981).

[108] (1990), 76 D.L.R. (4th) 700 (S.C.C.).

> take place between the applicant and the Department Head concerned which shall include a review of the health and continuing performance of the applicant.[109]

Although the Supreme Court of Canada ruled that the *Charter of Rights and Freedoms* did not apply[110] to physicians working in a public hospital, in reaching its decision it examined the fundamental objective of the bylaw and whether there was a rational connection between it and the hospital's objective. The Court accepted as the fundamental objective of Regulation 5.04 the intention to

> . . . maintain and enhance the quality of medical care the Vancouver General is capable of providing. [The Regulation was] intended to promote excellence in the hospital's pursuit of its mandate as a centre of medical research and teaching and as the major acute care hospital in the province of British Columbia.[111]

In considering whether the means employed by the hospital to accomplish this objective were reasonable, the Court accepted that

> . . . those who are denied a renewal of their admitting privileges pursuant to Reg. 5.04 will be unable to continue their practices in the manner and to the extent that they have become accustomed. In some cases, failure to obtain a renewal will mean the complete cessation of long-standing practices and the end of professional careers. But the anguish and sense of loss this entails cannot be considered in isolation from the frustration and anger younger doctors would experience if they were prevented from entering into a full practice upon completion of long years of arduous study and preparation.[112]

It was suggested to the Court that an alternative means, involving a programme of skills-testing and performance evaluation, would be a fairer and more reasonable basis upon which to determine whether physicians who had reached the age of 65 should be permitted to continue. In rejecting this alternative, however, the Court stated:

> . . . such a programme would be costly both to implement and operate, a not unimportant consideration given the financially straitened circumstances in which most hospitals and the health care system generally must now operate. But more important is the invidious and disruptive effect such a programme would have on the environment in which all members of the hospital's

---

109 *Ibid.*, at 727.
110 *Ibid.*, at 741.
111 *Ibid.*, at 746.
112 *Ibid.*, at 751.

> medical staff must work . . . . skills testing and performance evaluation can be demeaning, especially when applied to highly trained and senior members of a professional community. As a trigger for the application of a rule of mandatory retirement, they would be the very antithesis of the kind of dignified departure that should be the crowning moment of a professional career. Just as detrimental is the added pressure which performance-based retirement would introduce into what must already be a very high pressure work environment. Nor is it difficult to imagine how such a scheme could sow suspicion and dissention among a hospital staff.[113]

In the *Vancouver General Hospital* decision, the mandatory retirement scheme did not involve an automatic non-renewal of a physician's privileges at age 65. Rather, the scheme provided a mechanism by which the physician, upon reaching age 65, could make a "special application" to the board of the hospital. The scheme also required the Medical Advisory Committee to make a recommendation to the board prior to the board's consideration of the special application. Whether such a mechanism *must* be part of a mandatory retirement scheme remains open to debate.

Where a regulation or bylaw permits a "special application", questions may be raised regarding the level of natural justice or fairness that will apply. For example, should a physician who wishes to make a "special application" to have his or her privileges extended beyond age 65 be permitted to make direct representations to the board? Can he or she be represented by counsel? Must there be a full-scale hearing? A process this extensive may place an unwarranted burden on the resources of the hospital. Nonetheless, where there is a hospital bylaw in place that provides for a non-renewal or modification of physician's privileges upon reaching age 65, attention should be paid to the concepts discussed in the *Vancouver General Hospital* case.

4. Staffing and Financial Considerations

Increasingly, as a result of financial considerations, hospitals are being called upon to limit the number of physicians on staff. A new physician in a department may have an impact upon the earnings of other members. This, itself, may not be a sufficient reason to limit staff members if an additional physician is required in order to provide good quality health care. On the other hand, an additional physician enjoying privileges at the hospital will utilize the hospital facility to treat patients, causing an increase in the hospital's operating costs. In granting privileges to physicians, the hospital is entitled to consider the financial impact upon the hospital and its ability to provide health care to the community. In diffi-

---

[113] *Ibid.*, at 752.

cult economic times, similar considerations may justify a reduction or non-renewal of physician privileges. A hospital board cannot adhere rigidly to its staffing requirements to the exclusion of other factors.[114] In imposing a moratorium on the expansion of a department or its medical staff, the hospital may be required to present evidence or statistics to justify the moratorium.[115] Similarly, in considering a new application, the board of a hospital may take into account the ratio of physicians to available beds and whether a particular department is adequately staffed or a speciality is filled.[116]

In *Chin v. Salvation Army Scarborough Grace General Hospital*,[117] it was held that the Board of Directors of a public hospital is legally entitled to determine the appropriate complement of doctors for its medical staff. The Court rejected as untenable the suggestion that a hospital is not legally entitled to limit the number of doctors on its medical staff. In *Re Powell River General Hospital and Dr. Hobson*,[118] a physician took a leave of absence from the staff of the hospital in July, 1989. In January, 1990, he applied for reappointment, which was refused by the board of the hospital. On appeal, the Medical Appeal Board of British Columbia ordered a reappointment with limited privileges. This reappointment allowed him to treat patients for conditions arising from diseases he had previously treated, but did not permit him to treat new patients in the hospital without the approval of the board. In so doing, the Appeal Board remarked:

> All parties concede that two general surgeons satisfy the needs of the community and the Hospital and that the community cannot support three general surgeons. Granting Dr. Hobson privileges will theoretically, if not practically, result in three general surgeons practicing in the community. Dr. Hobson admitted he will have to practice at a sufficient level to pay all of his costs, including malpractice insurance.
>
> It is often difficult to balance the determination of what is in the best interest of the Hospital or the public, which has been treated as synonymous, with the rights and individual aspirations of an individual physician . . . .
>
> On balance, there is insufficient evidence of any need or benefit to the Hospital in granting full privileges to Dr. Hobson and we are not convinced Dr. Hobson's livelihood or part-time practice would be materially affected if he did not have privileges. However, there may be a benefit to the community

---

114 *Re Aitken and Penticton Regional Hospital*, April 15, 1986, British Columbia Medical Appeal Board.

115 *Re Samson and St. Vincent's Hospital*, July 7, 1988, British Columbia Medical Appeal Board.

116 *Re Macdonald and North York General Hospital* (1975), 9 O.R. (2d) 143 (Div. Ct.).

117 *Chin*, *supra* note 101.

118 December 9, 1990, British Columbia Medical Appeal Board.

> if Dr. Hobson could continue to treat those patients that he had previously cared for and who may require his further assistance.[119]

In *Varcony v. Langley Memorial Hospital*,[120] the Medical Appeal Board was critical of the manner in which a hospital had dealt with a new application; nonetheless, the board supported the hospital's decision not to appoint a new staff member who "might increase costs of hospital operations". In so doing, the Appeal Board stated:

> There is no hospital in this province which can serve all the needs of the population which it serves. It is the responsibility of its Board of Management to determine which services are to be delivered to best answer the needs of the community and can be supplied by the hospital. The demands for any new service come from two sources: the community and the physicians practising in that community. In this case, no evidence has been submitted to suggest that the community itself felt the need for a plastic surgery service at the Hospital. Patients requiring this service have been looked after in nearby hospitals and in the referral centres in Vancouver. As well, the physicians practising in the Hospital gave no evidence that they felt that their patients were suffering from a lack of this service being immediately available in Langley. Although evidence was presented by the Hospital which revealed that the community was reaching a size where a plastic surgeon could be supported, the Manpower Committee of the Hospital has not yet recommended that the service be developed further than that which is currently available. Long-range plans obviously include this as an expansion service along with others, but no evidence was presented to suggest that plans have been developed to allow such an expansion in the near future.[121]

A hospital's right to limit or to restrict appointments to the medical staff for reasons of personnel and financial management may be limited by the relevant legislation or by the hospital's own bylaws. It should be ensured that the steps taken comply with any relevant legal authority. In *Lafrance v. St-Luc Hospital*,[122] the Board of Governors of the hospital adopted an organization plan setting up four services in the Department of General Surgery, and in effect, restricted the nature of the surgery carried out by one of its physicians. The relevant Quebec statute regulating the allocation of privileges to physicians permitted a restriction on privileges "on a lack of qualification, on scientific incompetence, negligence, misconduct or non-observance of the bylaws".[123] The Supreme Court of Canada ruled,

---

[119] *Ibid.*, at 4-5.

[120] January 16, 1992, British Columbia Medical Appeal Board.

[121] *Ibid.*, at 18-19.

[122] (1982), 42 N.R. 434 (S.C.C.).

[123] *An Act respecting health services and social services*, R.S.Q. 1977, c. S-5, s. 130, para. 6.

in support of the doctor, that the physician's privileges had been reduced on improper grounds, as the need for organizing the hospital was not a ground contained in the statute. The Court pointed out that "[i]t is hard to reconcile the dual objective apparently sought by the legislator, namely conferring wide administrative powers on the board of directors while at the same time providing protection for the privileges enjoyed by physicians".[124]

5. Competency

Non-renewal, suspension or revocation for alleged incompetency is one of the most difficult areas involving physician privileges. An allegation of incompetency against a physician is likely to have implications that go beyond the individual's privileges at the hospital. An allegation may result in a report to the appropriate regulatory body responsible for licensing physicians and thereby affect the physician's licence to practise. A physician who loses his or her privileges as a result of incompetency is likely to have great difficulty in obtaining privileges at another facility, even after undergoing remedial training. Allegations of incompetence against a physician, unless the allegations can be easily demonstrated, may result in complex and highly contentious litigation.

Because an allegation of incompetence can be so detrimental to the physician, natural justice and fairness take on increased importance. An appeal tribunal will not be sympathetic to a hospital that makes such allegations of incompetence in an unfair context. If the allegations of competence are not clear-cut or there is room for interpretation, an appeal tribunal or court will be inclined to give the benefit of the doubt to the physician where the process in which the physician's conduct was challenged is perceived to have been unfair. An appeal tribunal will also take into account the risk of harm to patients if physicians who are not fully competent are permitted to treat patients in a public hospital.

In *Re Hicks*,[125] a hospital considered such allegations as over-subscription for laboratory tests, improper choice of drugs, failure to obtain a consultation in the case of fetal distress, above-average length of stay for the physician's patients, failure to detect a pregnancy and failure to seek consultations from other physicians with greater expertise as possible grounds for incompetence. Although the Medical Appeal Board of British Columbia did not support all of the allegations of incompetence made against the physician, nonetheless, it upheld the decision of the hospital board not to grant privileges to the physician.

---

[124] *St-Luc, supra* note 122, at 441.

[125] *Supra* note 102.

> Every hospital has a duty imposed on it . . . to provide a high level of patient care. That duty is owed to the community which, in this country, supplies through taxes, the greater portion of the costs of operating the public hospitals. The onerous task faced by a hospital board is to ensure that the institution is run competently and efficiently. It is a delicate mechanism. If the total trust, co-operation and general team work of any of its constituent parts breaks down the result can be unfortunate for the hospital and community. This has been demonstrated in other appeals before this Board. There was no evidence before us that the Hospital Board acted capriciously or maliciously or that the medical staff, whose duty it was to make a recommendation to the Hospital Board exhibited bias . . . . Although we do not base our judgment alone on her patterns of practice, the concerns with her pharmacological knowledge, the Laboratory use or the Obstetrical and Dilantin audits, these factors, coupled with what, in our view, was a questionable inability to employ tact and a somewhat insensitive response to criticism is justification for a denial of privileges.[126]

In *Re Board of Governors of Northwestern General Hospital and Brown*,[127] a review of a physician's work was undertaken by the Medical Advisory Committee. The review was initiated as a result of the death of a baby born to a patient the physician was attending. As a result of that review, and of seven other incidents involving patient care, the physician's privileges were revoked. In revoking the privileges, the board of the hospital gave reasons including:

- failure to obtain obstetrical consultations for high risk cases and contravention of the Medical-Dental Rules and Regulations
- failure to order appropriate x-rays
- failure to provide adequate sedation
- allowing a patient to proceed in labour far beyond the acceptable length of safety
- failing to provide adequate personnel to assist with the resuscitation of a baby
- discharging a patient without adequate investigation of the patient's condition.[128]

On appeal by the physician, the Hospital Appeal Board found that his skill and judgment were deficient.

---

[126] *Ibid.*, at 37-39.

[127] (1985), 52 O.R. (2d) 591 (Div. Ct.).

[128] *Ibid.*, at 593.

In *Shephard v. Colchester Regional Hospital Commission*,[129] a physician's privileges were not renewed by the hospital. The hospital insisted that the physician undergo an assessment of competency prior to renewal. The physician took the position that the hospital had no legal authority to require such an assessment. Although the physician was successful at trial, the Nova Scotia Court of Appeal ruled against the physician.

> The legislation defining the powers of the Board is clear. The Board has the "control of the medical staff of the Hospital" and the power to make by-laws necessary for exercising that control. With these sweeping powers go a very grave responsibility — the charge of the welfare of those patients who entrust themselves to the hospital's care. In my opinion, the power of suspension given to the Board under [an article in its by-laws dealing] "with good cause" is a valid exercise of those delegated legislative powers.
>
> I cannot emphasize too strongly the heavy burden that falls upon a body entrusted with the responsibility of providing medical care to the public. True, the Board is composed almost wholly of lay persons. They must obviously rely on medical advice received through the credentials committee, the medical advisory committee and other staff physicians. However, the final responsibility is that of the Board members, and notwithstanding the professional advice given to them, the burden of decision is theirs. They must exercise a thoughtful, independent judgment and not act as a mere rubber stamp.
>
> In my opinion, control of the medical staff vests the Board with the power and imposes upon it the responsibility of taking all reasonable measures to ensure the competency of those working in the hospital under its control. This includes the power to evaluate the medical staff and insist that it meet all reasonable standards of competence that it may impose.[130]

6. Mid-Term Alteration, Suspension or Revocation

Generally, in Canada, the appointments of the medical staff in hospitals are renewed annually by the hospital board. Circumstances may arise, however, which require a response that cannot wait until the annual renewal process. An obvious example is a situation in which a patient, or patients, may be in danger. In those circumstances, the administration of the hospital has an obligation to respond quickly. Failure to do so may result in legal liability for the hospital. On the other hand, an arbitrary or unfair reaction may be judged harshly by an appeal tribunal or court. Finding a balance between a reasonable response and arbitrary intervention may be difficult. Even in an emergency, there is a duty to be fair. A

---

[129] (1991), 103 N.S.R. (2d) 361 (S.C. T.D.); revd (1995), 121 D.L.R. (4th) 451 (N.S.C.A.).

[130] *Ibid.*, at 472 (D.L.R.).

mid-term suspension or revocation can be devastating for the physician: it will undermine the physician in the eyes of his or her peers, affect the confidence of patients, and in most circumstances, bring the physician's practice to a halt. It may result in a loss of income. An alteration, suspension or revocation may have more significant consequences than a non-renewal. For example, in Ontario, a physician who appeals a mid-term suspension or revocation to the Hospital Appeal Board may not be permitted to practise while awaiting the outcome of the Hospital Appeal Board hearing or of any subsequent appeals. On the other hand, where there is a *non-renewal* of privileges, the statute provides specifically that the physician's privileges will continue intact until all appeal remedies are exhausted.[131]

In *Zahab*,[132] a physician's privileges were revoked mid-term by the hospital board following complaints about his surgical practice in the hospital and an unfavourable evaluation by an outside reviewer. The physician appealed to the provincial Hospital Appeal Board, but, in the meantime, he asked the Court to reinstate his privileges pending the outcome of the appeal. The hospital took the position that it had no obligation to provide the physician with a hearing as there was no provision in the *Public Hospitals Act* affording a hearing, and further, that the decision of the board revoking the privileges of the physician was an administrative act, and, therefore, the question of natural justice and a fair hearing did not apply.

Chadwick J. found that the board's decision was not an administrative one, but rather, that in deciding to suspend or revoke privileges, the board was acting in a "quasi-judicial role". Consequently, the physician was entitled to be treated, at the very least, "fairly". Chadwick J. did not conclude that the physician was entitled, on the facts of the case, to a "hearing", rather, the requirement of natural justice would depend upon the circumstances of each particular case and the subject-matter under consideration.

> The requirements of natural justice could be easily satisfied. The doctor could be provided with the nature of the complaint, in advance. The doctor could then have the report and opportunity to question the complainant regarding the allegations. The doctor could appear before the medical advisory committee and state his or her position. The medical advisory committee could make their recommendation based upon the evidence before them. As long as the committee members are not biased or have a conflict then they should be able to make reasoned recommendations to the hospital board. Due to the nature of the composition of hospital boards they

---

[131] *Public Hospitals Act*, R.S.O. 1990, c. P.40, s. 39(3).

[132] *Zahab v. Salvation Army Grace General Hospital Ottawa* (1991), 3 Admin. L.R. (2d) 307 (Ont. Gen. Div.); leave to appeal to Court of Appeal granted September 3, 1991.

> would probably follow the recommendations of their medical advisory committee, unless there is good reason not to follow the recommendation.[133]

There may be circumstances in which the administration of the hospital must intervene quickly, without first giving the physician an opportunity to respond to the allegation against him or her. The Nova Scotia Court of Appeal has held that a subsequent hearing by the board, where there has been a suspension of a member of the medical staff, can cure a defect in a prior suspension in which there has been no hearing.[134] In that case, the hospital administrator informed the physician by letter that his hospital privileges were suspended for an indefinite period. The grounds for the suspension related to an allegation that the physician had been under the influence of alcohol while performing medical treatments in the hospital. The administrator also relied upon the failure by the physician to maintain hospital records in accordance with hospitals bylaws and the provincial statute. The letter indicated that the matter would be referred to the board and that the physician would be given an opportunity to present his case to the board. A hearing date was set for one week following receipt of the letter of suspension by the physician. This date was rescheduled at the request of the physician. When the board did meet to consider the suspension, the physician was present and represented by his lawyer. Both the administrator and the physician gave evidence before the board. The administrator filed a number of documents and was cross-examined. The physician made a number of admissions substantiating the complaint. The board confirmed the suspension and revoked the physician's privileges for a 60-day period. Restoration of privileges was made conditional upon the physician continuing in an alcohol-rehabilitation programme and participating and co-operating in any quality assurance programme implemented by the hospital.

The physician sought judicial review of the hospital board's decision. Although he was initially successful,[135] on appeal to the Nova Scotia Court of Appeal the decision of the hospital board was upheld. The Court ruled that:

> Clearly under the bylaws the Board had the power to suspend any member of the medical staff. Its power was not dependent on the action of the administrator. It did so after giving the respondent a complete and fair hearing. With deference it cannot be said that the Board simply confirmed

133 *Ibid.*, at 322-23.

134 *Sacred Heart Hospital v. Aucoin*, unreported, September 10, 1991 (N.S.C.A.).

135 On the initial application for judicial review, the trial judge held that there had been no emergency warranting a suspension and that the physician had no notice of the suspension. He concluded that the suspension by the hospital administrator was illegal.

> the decision of the administrator. Even assuming an error on the part of the administrator the subsequent proceedings before the Board cured any defect.[136]

The Ontario Hospital Appeal Board has recommended strongly that hospitals in that province should have bylaws that would anticipate a situation in which an emergency arises or events are disclosed involving the conduct of a physician, and which require action to be taken immediately. In effect, even though there may be no specific provision in the provincial statute to deal with mid-term revocations or suspensions, that tribunal has urged that there be some mechanism in place to permit the hospital to immediately suspend privileges pending a formal hearing in which the elements of natural justice and fairness are preserved.[137]

In *Michel v. Hôpital de Lamèque*,[138] the board of a hospital suspended the privileges of a physician for one month on the basis of a recommendation by its Medical Advisory Committee. The doctor was not asked to appear before the board when it made its decision. The physician moved, in court, to have the suspension quashed. The Court held, citing an earlier decision, that the physician should have been given an opportunity to "confront his accusers and make answer to the complaints".[139]

Provincial Appeal Boards

Where an appeal body is established by the legislation, it may be empowered to conduct a hearing. The hearing is a hearing *de novo*; that is, the tribunal will hear and decide upon all the evidence and will not simply review the decision of the hospital board. The correct standard of proof

---

136 See, however, *Callaghan v. The Board of Trustees, St. Josephs General Hospital*, February 26, 1992, Ontario Hospital Appeal Board, in which the hospital had received a report from an outside evaluator indicating that the physician's "imaging studies demonstrate clinical incompetence that poses hazards to patients". An interim suspension issued by the Executive Committee of the hospital was set aside, even though the physician was invited to appear before the Medical Advisory Committee of the hospital to respond to the criticisms against him so that the Medical Advisory Committee could make a recommendation to the board whether the suspension should be continued.

137 *Nikore v. The Board of Governors, The Brantford General Hospital*, July 4, 1991, Ontario Hospital Appeal Board; *Miles v. The Board of Directors of the Humber Memorial Hospital*, July 26, 1991, Ontario Hospital Appeal Board.

138 (1989), 102 N.B.R. (2d) 350 (Q.B.).

139 *Ibid.*, at 356, citing *Lebaud v. Chaleur Regional Hospital* (1987), 83 N.B.R. (2d) 280, at 291 (C.A.).

for an appeal to the Appeal Board is the balance of probabilities.[140] Even where the statute does not provide for "new hearing" it has been held that the appeal board has the jurisdiction to "hear the case afresh".[141] On the other hand, a court, on appeal from a statutory appeal board, will give considerable weight to the decision of the statutory appeal board in areas that involve the appeal board's expertise and will not attempt to retry the case.[142] It has been held by the Divisional Court of Ontario that it will not interfere with the decision of the Ontario Hospital Appeal Board unless that decision is "manifestly wrong".[143]

Although the appeal process may result in a hearing *de novo*, this does not relieve the hospital of its obligation to treat the physician fairly. The hospital cannot act in an arbitrary manner and then justify its conduct by stating that the physician will have a full hearing at the appeal level. In *Nikore v. The Board of Governors, The Brantford General Hospital*,[144] the Ontario Hospital Appeal Board rejected the submission of hospital counsel that a mid-term revocation without a formal hearing was permitted by the statute and that the Hospital Appeal Board could cure any lack of fairness by replacing the hospital's decision with its own decision. In rejecting the submission, the Hospital Appeal Board stated:

> Too often the Hospitals are imposing upon this Appeal Board the duty of the Hospitals to provide the physicians with notice of the charges and to give him the opportunity to be heard. In fact, most cases which are now coming before this Board are mid-term revocation cases. This Board is being pushed therefore to hear cases, not of appeals *de novo*, but of hearings in the first instance, which of necessity take place several months after the physician has been removed from the Hospital.[145]

In Quebec, the decision of the *Commission des saffairs sociales* is final and there is no provision for appeal.[146] In jurisdictions where the statute does not provide for an appeal to a special tribunal or a court,[147] an application

---

140 *Brown, supra* note 127.

141 *Re Calgary General Hospital Board and Williams* (1982), 142 D.L.R. (3d) 736 (Alta. C.A.).

142 *Brown, supra* note 127, at 595.

143 *Re MacDonald and North York General Hospital* (1975), 9 O.R. (2d) 143, at 153 (Div. Ct.).

144 *Supra* note 137.

145 *Ibid.*, at 23-24.

146 *An Act respecting the Commission des affaires sociales*, R.S.Q. 1977, c. C-34, s. 23.

147 *Hospital Services Act*, R.S.N.B. 1973, c. H-9; *Hospitals Act*, R.S.N. 1990, c. H-9; *Territorial Hospital Insurance Services Act*, R.S.N.W.T. 1990, c. T-3; *Hospitals Act*, R.S.N.S. 1989, c. 208; *Hospitals Act*, R.S.P.E.I. 1988, c. H-10; *Hospital Insurance Services Act*, R.S.Y. 1986, c. 85.

may be brought for judicial review in which a court will review the actions of the board and will determine whether the procedures adopted by the hospital board conformed with the principles of natural justice and fairness.

Remedies of Appeal Boards and Courts

A broad range of remedies are available to appeal boards and courts. Some statutes contain specific provisions outlining the powers of the provincial appeal boards. For example, in Ontario, the Hospital Appeal Board may confirm the decision appealed from or direct a board or other person or body making the decision appealed from to take such action. The Ontario Hospital Appeal Board may even substitute its opinion for that of the hospital.[148]

An order for reinstatement of physicians by appeal tribunals or courts may be well-intentioned, but problematic. In *Bellechasse Hospital Corporation v. Pilotte*,[149] a physician's privileges were suspended and subsequently not renewed by the hospital. Although upholding an award of damages in favour of the physician, the Court refused to grant an order for reinstatement on the ground that reinstatement, on the facts of the case, "might lead to conflicts and difficulties, and the patient would be the first to suffer".[150]

In *Re Board of Governors of Northwestern Hospital and Brown*,[151] the Ontario Hospital Appeal Board ordered that a physician's obstetrical privileges be restored on condition that the hospital monitor and supervise his obstetrical activities in the hospital for one year and review his work at the end of the period. On appeal by the hospital to the Divisional Court, however, it was held that this condition was impractical given evidence before the Hospital Appeal Board by the Chief of Obstetrics in which he testified that in a community hospital members of the obstetrical department were busy practitioners, and having to supervise the physician whose competence was in issue would be "impossible".[152]

In *Callaghan v. The Board of Trustees, Saint Joseph's General Hospital*,[153] the Ontario Hospital Appeal Board set aside an interim suspension and ordered that a radiologist's full privileges be reinstated. Further, the board

---

[148] *Public Hospitals Act*, R.S.O. 1990, c. P.40, s. 41(5).

[149] [1975] 2 S.C.R. 454.

[150] *Ibid.*, at 463.

[151] (1985), 52 O.R. (2d) 591 (Div. Ct.).

[152] *Ibid.*, at 600-01.

[153] February 26, 1992, Ontario Hospital Appeal Board.

ordered that "to protect the public interest" the radiologist's work "shall be scrutinized in a manner to be determined by the Chief of the Department of Radiology". No evidence was heard by the Hospital Appeal Board on the practicality of such an order and, prior to the order being made, no notice was given to the parties that it was being contemplated. Consequently, the Hospital Appeal Board was not apprised, before it made its order, that the Chief of the department who would be responsible for supervising the radiologist's conduct was a defendant in a civil action commenced by the same radiologist in which several million dollars were claimed. The lawsuit alleged that the Chief of the department and other members of the medical staff had conspired against the radiologist to force him out of the hospital.

Civil Remedy for Procedural Breaches

In Canada, most of the "privileges litigation" to date has involved efforts by physicians to obtain new privileges or retain existing privileges at hospitals. This litigation can be time-consuming and expensive. Immediate access to an appeal tribunal or to a court may not be available, and, as a result, the final resolution of a hospital board's decision affecting a physician's privileges may not take place for months or even years. During that time — for example, where there has been a mid-term revocation based upon perceived danger to patients — the physician's practice may be curtailed and a significant income loss may result. An allegation of incompetence will harm the physician's reputation and he or she may incur very substantial legal costs.

Where an appeal tribunal or court finds that the hospital's decision is unwarranted or is deficient as a result of a failure to act fairly, a physician may seek civil redress from the hospital for any financial loss which has resulted. Where a physician is reinstated, there may still be a claim for lost income and legal costs incurred during the period in which his or her privileges were restricted or suspended. A claim may also include compensation for the long-term effect of the hospital's decision on the physician's practice. As noted above, reinstatement of the physician may not be a practical remedy where the battle over privileges has resulted in dissension and bad feelings among the medical staff. In that situation, the appeal board or court may resist reinstatement as a remedy, but leave open the possibility of substantial compensatory damages to the physician.

There have been several reported cases in Canada in which the physicians have received awards arising out of the improper suspension or revocation of their privileges. In *Bellechasse*,[154] the physician was awarded

[154] *Supra* note 149.

damages in the amount of $55,498 arising out of the improper suspension and non-renewal of his privileges. In *Schipper v. Lakeshore General Hospital*,[155] a hospital was found liable for damages as a result of breaching regulations under the *Quebec Hospitals Act*. The hospital's breaches included refusal of a hearing, immediate suspension (although the case was not "serious and urgent") and failure to give reasons for, and to inform the doctor of, recommendations affecting his status and privileges. The hospital was ordered to pay the doctor's lost income, as well as $35,000 for "besmirching of his professional reputation as a surgeon".

In *Abouna v. Foothills Provincial General Hospital Board (No. 2)*,[156] a physician's privileges were cancelled and revoked as a result of allegations of misconduct. On application to the Court it was held that although the allegations of misconduct against the physician were substantiated, the hospital had not implemented its revocation in accordance with the principles of natural justice. The physician was awarded $10,000 to compensate him for the period during which his privileges remained illegally revoked. In another case, however, a resident physician who had received an unsatisfactory evaluation by his university-appointed evaluators, resulting in the termination of his contract with the hospital, was not entitled to claim damages from the hospital.[157]

Hospital administrators and boards should recognize that civil actions by physicians seeking compensation for the improper suspension or termination of privileges represent an expanding field. Settlements of civil suits may be confidential or unreported. It is likely that hospitals will see more of these actions in the future as physicians compete for fewer positions and fewer health-care dollars.

---

[155] (1981), 7 A.C.W.S. (2d) 360 (Que. C.A.).

[156] (1978), 83 D.L.R. (3d) 333, [1978] 2 W.W.R. 130 (Alta. C.A.); also, see *McCaw v. United Church of Canada* (1991), 4 O.R. (3d) 481 (C.A.), in which the church's failure to follow its own manual of procedure in removing a minister's name from its rolls was found to have been made without legal authority and to warrant an award of damages to compensate the minister for the financial injury that resulted. This case provides a clear analogy to physician privileges.

[157] *Phillips v. Foothills Provincial General Hospital* (1989), 95 A.R. 268 (Q.B.).

CHAPTER 11

The Canadian Charter of Rights and Freedoms

INTRODUCTION

Since its passage into law in 1982, the *Canadian Charter of Rights and Freedoms*[1] has had an enormous impact on the Canadian legal system. While Canadian law, prior to passage of the Charter, had been interpreted by the courts to guarantee Canadian citizens certain rights and freedoms based upon common and natural law,[2] there was no clear codification of these rights and freedoms.

The *Canadian Bill of Rights*[3] was passed in 1960. It set out certain rights and freedoms similar in scope to those contained in the Charter. The *Bill of Rights,* however, was an ordinary statute passed by the federal Parliament. It was not a constitutional document. It applied only to federal legislation and not to the provinces. As an ordinary federal statute, it had no higher standing than other federal statutes, and, accordingly, courts interpreted restrictively its impact on legislation or activities of government. The *Canadian Bill of Rights* was replaced by the *Charter.* The *Charter* is a part of the Canadian Constitution and can be altered only by constitutional amendment. Because it is a part of the Constitution, the *Charter* supersedes any inconsistent statutes.

The *Charter* applies to both federal and provincial levels of government. It is designed to protect citizens from arbitrary or illegal acts of government. Government laws or activities that contravene the *Charter* are invalid.[4] It does not, however, apply to or invalidate the acts of private individuals or entities unless they have become, as a result of their conduct or activity, "agents" of the government. Therefore, the release of confidential

1 Part I of the *Constitution Act, 1982,* being Schedule B to the *Canada Act 1982* (U.K.), 1982, c. 11 ["the *Charter*"].

2 *Switzman v. Elbling and Quebec (A.G.),* [1957] S.C.R. 285, 7 D.L.R. (2d) 337, 117 C.C.C. 1 29; *Saumur v. Quebec (City),* [1953] 2 S.C.R. 299, [1953] 4 D.L.R. 641, 106 C.C.C. 289.

3 S.C. 1960, c. 44, reprinted in R.S.C. 1985, App. III.

4 *R. v. Big M Drug Mart Ltd.,* [1985] 1 S.C.R. 295, 37 Alta. L.R. (2d) 97, 60 A.R.

information by a physician, though perhaps in breach of the physician's common-law duty and professional code of conduct, is not a breach of the *Charter* where the physician is acting in the capacity of a private individual.[5] Similarly, it has been held that the actions of a public hospital, despite extensive public funding and regulation by government, are not the actions of a branch of the government subject to the *Charter.*[6]

The rights and freedoms entrenched in Canadian law by the *Charter* are not absolute. Section 1 of the *Charter* "guarantees" the rights and freedoms, subject only "to such reasonable limits prescribed by law as can be demonstrably justified in a free and democratic society". Thus, in interpreting the effect of the *Charter,* the courts must balance competing interests. Certain rights, by necessity, will be inhibited by others. The right to associate freely does not allow citizens to participate in a riot. The right to express oneself freely does not permit the making of obscene telephone communications to an unwilling recipient. Consequently, even though a particular right or freedom has been abridged, the court must then inquire under s. 1 of the *Charter* whether or not the abridgement is justified.

1. Fundamental Freedoms

Section 2 of the *Charter* lists certain "fundamental" freedoms. The first of these is "freedom of conscience and religion".[7] The Supreme Court of Canada has stated that this provision of the *Charter* protects "profoundly personal beliefs that govern one's perception of oneself, humankind, nature, and, in some cases, a higher or different order of being".[8] As such, protection goes beyond traditional religious denominations and may extend to less mainstream, even bizarre, religious practices if it can be demonstrated that a conduct or practice stems from strong moral or ethical convictions.[8a] Despite a reference in the preamble of the *Charter* to the

---

161, 18 D.L.R. (4th) 321, [1985] 3 W.W.R. 481, 58 N.R. 81, 18 C.C.C. (3d) 385, 85 C.L.L.C. 14,023, 12 C.R.R. 64.

5 *R. v. Dersch,* [1993] 3 S.C.R. 768.

6 *Stoffman v. Vancouver General Hospital,* [1990] 3 S.C.R. 483.

7 Section 2(a).

8 *R. v. Edwards Books and Art Ltd.,* [1986] 2 S.C.R. 713, at 759.

8a In *Hughes v. Children's Aid Society of Metropolitan Toronto* (1996), Court File No. RE1/95 (Ont. Ct. (Gen. Div.)), the patient, aged 13 1/2, was diagnosed with aplastic anaemia. She was a Jehovah's Witness and refused any treatment involving a transfusion of blood products. Without this treatment it was likely she would die. The oncologist and a consulting child psychologist determined that she was incapable of making a decision with respect to the treatment. There was an emergency child protection hearing at which the Children's Aid Society was granted wardship for a two-week period. The Children's Aid Society author-

"supremacy of God",[9] it is not necessary that the religious conviction be rooted in the belief in a supreme being. In fact, the *Charter's* guarantee of freedom of "conscience and religion" guarantees to Canadian citizens the right *not* to believe and to exercise atheistic or agnostic practices.[10]

Canadian courts have held the federal *Lord's Day Act* to be invalid as being too closely associated with certain religious sects and not with others,[11] declared certain employment practices under provincial human rights legislation to be discriminatory towards a Seventh Day Adventist employee who was unable to work on Saturdays,[12] and held legislation restricting Sunday shopping to be invalid.[13]

The second fundamental freedom listed in the *Charter* is "freedom of thought, belief, opinion and expression, including freedom of the press and other media of communication".[14] As with all other rights and freedoms contained in the *Charter*, freedom of expression is not absolute. Judicial consideration has involved the difficult balancing of that right with others.[14a] It has been held, for example, that freedom of expression is not infringed by s. 177 of the *Criminal Code*,[15] which prohibits wilful publication of false statements, tales or news;[16] that a professional code of ethics overrode the

---

ized the blood transfusions. The patient appealed the determination of incapacity and argued that her *Charter* right to exercise freedom of religion had been infringed. On appeal, the Court accepted that there was sufficient evidence to determine that the patient was incapable of making the treatment decision. The judge concluded that although the Court's intervention infringed the patient's right, the ability of the state to protect children requiring medical treatment who are not capable of making a treatment decision is a reasonable limit to their freedom of religion which is demonstrably justified in a free and democratic society.

9 "Whereas Canada is founded upon principles that recognize the supremacy of God and the rule of law:"

10 *Big M Drug Mart Ltd., supra* note 4.

11 *Ibid.*

12 *Ontario Human Rights Commission v. Simpsons-Sears Ltd.*, [1985] 2 S.C.R. 536.

13 *Peel (Regional Municipality) v. Great Atlantic & Pacific Co. of Canada Ltd.* (1990), 73 O.R. (2d) 289 (H.C.J.).

14 Section 2(b).

14a In *H.(M.) v. Bederman* (1995), 27 C.C.L.T. (2d) 152 (Ont. Ct. (Gen. Div.)), addition reasons to costs, Dec. 27, 1995, Doc. Cobourg 2581/91, 2581A/91 (Ont. Ct. (Gen. Div.)), a woman was awarded $6,000 in damages when a male patient at a cosmetic surgery clinic sexually assaulted her when the two were left momentarily alone in the post-surgery room. The judge found that the physician running the clinic was obligated to take reasonable care to ensure that the patient was safe while on the premises.

15 R.S.C. 1970, c. C-34 [now R.S.C. 1985, c. C-46, s. 181].

16 *R. v. Zundel* (1987), 58 O.R. (2d) 129, 18 O.A.C. 161, 35 D.L.R. (4th) 338, 31 C.C.C. (3d) 97, 56 C.R. (3d) 1, 29 C.R.R. 349 (C.A.); leave to appeal to S.C.C. refused (1987), 61 O.R. (2d) 588n, 23 O.A.C. 317n, 56 C.R. (3d) xxviii.

right of one teacher to express certain views about another teacher at a parents' meeting;[17] and that a prohibition against the publication of the names of juveniles involved in juvenile delinquency proceedings was a reasonable restriction on freedom of expression.[18] The obligation that prevents health practitioners from releasing information about the identity or treatment of patients, except in limited circumstances, is the result of similar constraints.

While recognizing an expanding role for freedom of expression in our society, the courts have held that freedom of expression must be balanced against the need for privacy in certain administrative proceedings. In *Re Hirt and College of Physicians & Surgeons of British Columbia,*[19] the Court held that the names and identities of complainants who gave evidence before a confidential inquiry could be kept secret when the proceedings were published. The Court concluded that although this constituted an infringement of freedom of expression in preventing access by the press for publication of the complainants' identities, it was nonetheless justified on the basis that an absence of confidentiality would deter patients from coming forward with complaints. Conversely, a court has refused to prohibit publication of the names of men charged with gross indecency on the ground that public access to information about criminal proceedings is a vital component of the process.[20]

In *Re College of Physicians and Surgeons of Ontario v. Larsen,*[21] a court ordered a podiatrist to refrain from using the prefix "Doctor" in his podiatric practice. The Court held that while the podiatrist's freedom of expression was infringed, that infringement was demonstrably justified under the *Charter* as there was wide-spread confusion among the public about whether podiatrists were medical doctors. In *R. v. Baig,*[22] the Court rejected an argument by the accused that British Columbia legislation, in prohibiting his use of the term "psychologist" to describe himself in the absence of being registered, was in violation of the *Charter.* While his right to free expression was restricted, this was demonstrably justifiable. Otherwise, it was held, the professional body's statutory authority to regulate its members would be meaningless and ineffective in protecting the public interest.

---

17 *Cromer v. British Columbia Teachers' Federation* (1986), 4 B.C.L.R. (2d) 273, 29 D.L.R. (4th) 641, [1986] 5 W.W.R. 638 (C.A.).

18 *Re Southam Inc. v. R.* (1986), 53 O.R. (2d) 663, 12 O.A.C. 394, 26 D.L.R. (4th) 479, 25 C.C.C. (3d) 119, 50 C.R. (3d) 241, 20 C.R.R. 7 (C.A.); leave to appeal to S.C.C. refused (1986), 26 D.L.R. (4th) 479n.

19 (1985), 60 B.C.L.R. 273, 17 D.L.R. (4th) 472, [1985] 3 W.W.R. 350 (C.A.).

20 *Re R. and Several Unnamed Persons* (1983), 44 O.R. (2d) 81 (H.C.J.).

21 (1987), 45 D.L.R. (4th) 700 (Ont. H.C.J.).

22 (1990), 9 W.C.B. (2d) 293 (B.C. Co. Ct.).

The last two fundamental freedoms protected by s. 2 of the *Charter* are freedom of peaceful assembly and freedom of association.[23] These two freedoms are most commonly associated with the right to engage in labour relations activities, such as forming a union or collective bargaining unit or engaging in a strike. Picketing is a common activity, engaged in by unions and others, for the purpose of communicating a particular message or position.

The right of anti-abortion activists to protest and picket is subject to reasonable limits and must be balanced against other fundamental rights. In *Ontario (Attorney-General) v. Dieleman*[24] the Attorney-General of Ontario sought to prohibit anti-abortion protest activity within 500 feet of locations that included the homes and offices of physicians who provided abortion services at hospitals and three clinics where abortion services were provided. The picketers were on public property and sometimes tried to speak to women entering a facility offering abortions. Sometimes, the posters identified the doctors by name. Some contained graphic statements and pictures protesting abortion. One protestor engaged in silent prayer vigils on public property near some of the locations, but did not carry signs or talk to patients. The application by the government alleged that the protest activities had a negative psychological impact upon patients seeking abortions. While concluding that the protestors' right to express their opinions was, for the most part, protected by the *Charter*, the court also recognized the physiological, psychological and privacy interests of women about to undergo an abortion as objectives of sufficient importance to warrant overriding a constitutionally protected right or freedom. The privacy interests of physicians and their families who were targeted by residential picketing were also seen as pressing and substantial considerations for the Court. A request for an injunction protecting the hospitals from picketing was refused as it was not demonstrated that the protest activities constituted an unreasonable interference with the operation of the hospitals or the appropriate interests of the patients and physicians, especially given the multiplicity of entrances and services at these locations. Limits, however, were placed upon the protesting activities at the office and residence locations of the physicians and at the abortion clinics. The limits placed were in relation to the location, size, nature and time of the protest activities. The picketers were barred from approaching within ten feet of a person who made it clear that he or she did not wish to receive communications from the protestors. The picketing of homes and families was barred in its entirety as the Court concluded that the repetitive presence of the picketers went beyond the purpose of communicating anti-abortion views and constituted an attempt to harass physicians,

---

23 Section 2(c) and (d).

24 (1994), 117 D.L.R. (4th) 449 (Ont. Ct. Gen. Div.).

their families and their neighbourhoods by impairing their ability to enjoy and occupy their homes and neighbourhoods.

2. Democratic Rights

The *Charter* contains provisions guaranteeing those rights one associates with a democracy: the right to vote, the right to stand for election and the right to an accountable government.[25] Under the *Charter*, every Canadian citizen is guaranteed the right to vote in federal and provincial elections. Every citizen has the right to be elected as a member of the federal Parliament or of a provincial legislative assembly. This right may be balanced, to some extent, by certain special requirements justified in a democratic society, *e.g.*, one must register to vote, or one may be required to make a modest deposit with the chief electoral officer in order to stand for election. The registration of voters is an acceptable qualification as it is designed to ensure that only qualified citizens vote and that each citizen has only one vote. The deposit of a sum of money by an electoral candidate ensures that candidates who run for election are serious-minded and that the process will not be trivialized. On the other hand, to establish an onerous registration procedure or to require a monetary deposit that could be afforded only by the rich would be considered an unjustified restriction on basic democratic rights, and, thereby, unconstitutional.

The *Charter* entrenches the concept of an accountable, duly elected government by requiring an election of the House of Commons or of any legislative assembly every five years, subject to an extension only in time of "real or apprehended war, invasion or insurrection".[26] The House of Commons and every legislature must sit at least once a year. Although nothing is said in the *Charter* about how long such a sitting must last, a court would probably rule that it must be sufficiently long to conduct the proceedings of a democratic government and not be of a token duration.

3. Mobility Rights

Section 6 of the *Charter* guarantees to every citizen of Canada the right to enter, remain in and leave Canada. Furthermore, it guarantees to every Canadian citizen and every person who has permanent residence in Canada the right to move and take up residence in any province and the right to pursue the gaining of a livelihood in any province. In effect, the *Charter* prevents the federal government, or any provincial or local government,

---

[25] Sections 3-5.

[26] Section 4(2).

from enacting legislation or engaging in practices having the effect of preventing individuals from travelling to and from, or working in, certain parts of Canada. Again, mobility rights are not absolute. They may be restricted by laws or practices that do not discriminate "on the basis of province of present or previous residence"[27] or by "reasonable residency requirements as a qualification for the receipt of publicly provided social services".[28] Mobility rights may also be restricted, justifiably, by programmes or activities aimed at amelioration of conditions of individuals in a province who are socially or economically disadvantaged where the employment rate in that province is below the employment rate in Canada.[29]

4. Legal Rights

Sections 7 to 14 of the *Charter* contain "legal rights". Section 7 guarantees the right to life, liberty and security of the person and the right not to be deprived of these rights except in accordance with the principles of fundamental justice. The meaning of the term "right to life" has been scrutinized closely by the Supreme Court of Canada in a series of cases involving abortion.[30] In those decisions, the Supreme Court refused to engage in a philosophical enquiry on when life begins or ends, but rather, restricted the application of the "right to life" to those individuals who traditionally have been interpreted to be "persons" by the courts.[31]

In *R. v. Morgentaler*, the Supreme Court of Canada held that liberty includes the right of an individual to a degree of autonomy in making decisions of fundamental personal importance.[32] The majority of the Court spoke of a woman's right of autonomy in terms that balanced the right of abortion, in certain circumstances, against protection of the foetus by the state. In that case, the Supreme Court of Canada held that the legal procedure by which the state afforded protection to the foetus was an unacceptable restriction on a woman's right to have access to abortion in certain situations.

It has been held that the right to "liberty" does not protect members of the medical profession from a mandatory retirement scheme established by a government-funded hospital.[33] It has been held, however, that denial

---

27 Section 6(3)(a).

28 Section 6(3)(b).

29 Section 6(4).

30 See Chapter 12, Current Legal Issues in Health Care, the Section entitled "Abortion".

31 *Tremblay v. Daigle*, [1989] 2 S.C.R. 530, 62 D.L.R. (4th) 634, 102 N.R. 81.

32 [1988] 1 S.C.R. 30, 44 D.L.R. (4th) 385, 37 C.C.C. (3d) 449, 62 C.R. (3d) 1.

33 *Stoffman v. Vancouver General Hospital* (1986), 30 D.L.R. (4th) 700, [1986] 6 W.W.R. 23, 25 C.R.R. 16, 14 C.C.E.L. 146, 87 C.L.L.C. 17,004; affd on other

to a qualified physician by a provincial statutory authority of a "billing number" under the provincial medicare scheme amounted to a denial of the physician's "right to liberty".[34] The concept of "security of the person" has been linked to an individual's right to "complete physical, mental, and social well-being".[35] It has been ruled that the transfer of an inmate with a heart condition to a location with restricted access to adequate medical services was a breach of the inmate's right to security of the person.[36] Although the decision was reversed on appeal[37] because there was no demonstrated jeopardy to the inmate, the Federal Court of Appeal left intact a suggestion by the trial court that restrictive access to medical services infringed an individual's right to security of the person.

A number of cases in the health-care context have raised questions about the right of patients to be protected from illegal search or seizure. In Saskatchewan, it has been ruled that "security of the person"

> includes a right to personal dignity and a right to an area of privacy or individual sovereignty into which the State must not make arbitrary or unjustified intrusions. These considerations also underlie the privilege against self-incrimination.[38]

The Supreme Court of Canada has stated that even if a sample has been obtained with the consent of the patient, use of the sample is restricted to medical purposes. The patient had a reasonable expectation that his privacy interests in the sample would continue into the future. In his reasons for judgment, Mr. Justice La Forest commented:

> The dignity of the human being is equally seriously violated when use is made of bodily substances taken by others for medical purposes in a manner that does not respect that limitation. In my view, the trust and confidence of the public in the administration of medical facilities would be seriously taxed if an easy and informal flow of information, and particularly of bodily substances from hospitals to the police, were allowed.[39]

---

grounds (1982), 21 B.C.L.R. (2d) 165, 49 D.L.R. (4th) 727, [1988] 2 W.W.R. 708 (C.A.); revd [1990] 3 S.C.R. 483, 76 D.L.R. (4th) 700.

34 *Mia v. Medical Services Comm. of B.C.* (1985), 61 B.C.L.R. 273, 17 D.L.R. (4th) 385, 15 Admin. L.R. 265, 16 C.R.R. 233 (S.C.).

35 See P. Garant, "Fundamental Rights and Fundamental Justice" in G.-A. Beaudoin and E. Ratushny, Eds., *The Canadian Charter of Rights and Freedoms,* 2nd ed. (Toronto: Carswell, 1989) p. 331, at 345.

36 *Collin v. Lussier,* [1983] 1 F.C. 218 (F.C.T.D.).

37 *Lussier v. Collin,* [1985] 1 F.C. 124 (C.A.).

38 *R.L. Crain Inc. v. Couture* (1983), 6 D.L.R. (4th) 478, at 502, 30 Sask. R. 191, 10 C.C.C. (3d) 119, 9 C.R.R. 287 (Q.B.).

39 *R. v. Dyment,* [1988] 2 S.C.R. 417, at 439, 73 Nfld. & P.E.I.R. 13, 229 A.P.R. 13,

It has been held that where a physician takes a blood sample illegally at the request of the police the physician is acting as an agent of the government, and, therefore, his or her actions are subject to the *Charter*.[40] In a more recent case[41] the Supreme Court of Canada confirmed that although misconduct by health practitioners in providing samples of bodily fluids to police without the consent of the patient does not, strictly speaking, violate the *Charter* where the health practitioners are not acting as agents of government, it is nonetheless clear that such conduct is wrong as it violates the practitioner's common-law duty of confidentiality to the patient. Where blood samples or records showing evidence of impairment are obtained as a result of lawfully authorized search warrants, however, the evidence will be admitted at trial.[42]

Health practitioners, especially those working in emergency departments, may frequently come into contact with law enforcement authorities. Patients may be brought to the hospital who have been involved in accidents or injured while engaged in criminal activity. Police officers who accompany the patient may be in the course of conducting a criminal investigation. They may seek the assistance and co-operation of nurses and doctors in the collection of evidence and the detention of the patient.

In *R. v. Dyment*,[43] the Supreme Court of Canada considered the conduct of a doctor who supplied a blood sample to a police officer who had brought a patient to the emergency department after the patient was involved in a car accident. The blood sample had been obtained by the physician for medical purposes. When the sample was turned over to the police officer at his request, it was analyzed and disclosed a blood-alcohol level exceeding the legal limit for driving under the *Criminal Code*.[44] The patient was not aware that the blood specimen had been obtained. The Court ruled that the taking of the specimen without the patient's consent, where not required by law and not part of a medical procedure, violates the right to security of the person under the *Charter*.

Hospital staff do not have any legal obligation to assist the police in the investigation of a crime. A test should not be carried out, without the patient's consent, simply because it will assist the police investigation. Where tests are carried out for a medical purpose, with the patient's consent, that consent is limited to use of the specimen or sample for the medical treatment and not to incriminate the patient in any criminal proceeding. If a

---

55 D.L.R. (4th) 503, 89 N.R. 249, 45 C.C.C. (3d) 244, 66 C.R. (3d) 348, 10 M.V.R. (2d) 1.

40 *R. v. Pohoretsky*, [1987] 1 S.C.R. 945.

41 *R. v. Dersch*, [1993] 3 S.C.R. 768.

42 *R. v. Erickson* (1992), 125 A.R. 68, 72 C.C.C. (3d) 75, 38 M.V.R. (2d) 260, 14 W.A.C. 68 (C.A.).

43 *Supra* note 39.

44 Now R.S.C. 1985, c. C-46, s. 253.

police officer obtains a warrant or subpoena, hospital staff will be obliged, as a matter of law, to provide to the police anything covered by the subpoena or search warrant.

There is, however, no legal requirement for a health practitioner to assist in investigative activity against his or her will. There is no requirement in the *Criminal Code* that a citizen actively assist in a criminal investigation. There is a provision in the *Criminal Code* authorizing health-care personnel to assist in an investigation in good faith, without fear of legal recourse by the patient.[45] As a practical matter, those involved in health care may wish to co-operate as a matter of civic duty, but this cannot be done in a manner that violates the patient's fundamental rights.

In *Reynen v. Antonenko*,[46] a case decided before the enactment of the *Charter*, a resident physician agreed, at the request of police, to carry out a sigmoidoscopy of a patient who was suspected of having secreted illegal narcotics in his rectum. The physician told the patient that he would have to perform a rectal examination and that it might be uncomfortable. The patient did not resist and positioned himself for the examination. Heroin was found. The patient sued the physician for assault and battery. The patient's claim was dismissed on the basis that the sigmoidoscopy could not have been conducted without the patient's full co-operation. The Court did not accept the patient's contention that he believed, at the time, that he had no other recourse but to submit to the procedure.

There may be some question with the advent of the *Charter* whether the physician's conduct in the *Reynen* case would sustain a challenge under the *Charter*. A patient who is under arrest and is brought to the hospital by police may be under considerable duress and the "consent" may be given in circumstances rendering the consent involuntary. If a health practitioner concludes that the test or examination requested as a part of the police investigation cannot be conducted without the free and voluntary consent of the patient, there should be no compliance with the police request.

It has been suggested that any procedure involving a significant risk to the health or physical integrity of the person, such as a surgical operation, would be unreasonable under the *Charter*, but that procedures such as enemas, intubations, rectal or vaginal searches would be acceptable if performed by medical personnel on reasonable grounds.[47] On the other hand, a court has refused to issue a search warrant to permit a doctor, at

---

45 R.S.C. 1985, c. C-46, s. 25(1).

46 (1975), 54 D.L.R. (3d) 124, [1975] 5 W.W.R. 10, 20 C.C.C. (2d) 342, 30 C.R.N.S. 135, (Alta. S.C.).

47 F. Chevrette, "Protection Upon Arrest or Detention and Against Retroactive Penal Law" in Beaudoin and Ratushny, *The Canadian Charter of Rights and Freedoms*, *supra* note 35, p. 387, at 406.

the request of the police, to remove a bullet from the shoulder of an accused.[48] Communications to police about the condition of the patient by hospital personnel may be a violation of the patient's right of privacy. Patient records and the information contained in them are confidential. Police officers have no right of access to a patient's chart in the absence of a subpoena or search warrant.

The activities of police officers in health-care facilities may also raise questions. Do police officers have any right to question patients who are ill and in need of emergency medical treatment? It would not seem that police officers have any higher right to "visit" patients than any other visitor. The overriding concern ought to be the welfare of the patient. Can a police officer attend in the operating room to observe an operation and apprehend the bullet removed from a patient for the purpose of maintaining "continuity" of evidence? Again, if the police officer's activity will in any way compromise patient care, *e.g.*, breaking the sterile seal or distracting operating room personnel, this may result in harm to the patient and is not authorized by law. In the absence of a court order, a police officer has no right to be in the operating room. A physician or nurse can testify in court that the particular bullet was removed from the particular patient.

The *Charter* has been a factor in numerous reported decisions concerning the rights of patients who have a mental handicap or are psychiatric patients. The British Columbia Court of Appeal has ruled that medical treatment without the consent of a mentally handicapped patient, where it is in the patient's best interest, is not an infringement of the right to life, liberty and security of the person. In such a case, a mentally disabled girl had a pronounced fear of the sight of blood. Her parents sought to give a substitute-consent for a hysterectomy. The Official Guardian objected on the ground that an elective treatment of this nature ought not to be carried out without the consent of the patient and that it violated s. 7. The Court held, however, that in all the circumstances it was in the best interests of the child to have the hysterectomy performed and that the treatment was not inconsistent with the *Charter*.[49]

---

48 *Laporte v. Langanière* (1972), 29 D.L.R. (3d) 651, 8 C.C.C. (2d) 343 (*sub nom. Re Laporte and R.*), 18 C.R.N.S. 357 (Que. Q.B.).

49 *Re K.* (1985), 63 B.C.L.R. 145, 19 D.L.R. (4th) 255 (*sub nom. K. v. Public Trustee*), [1985] 4 W.W.R. 724 (C.A.); leave to appeal to S.C.C. dismissed on jurisdictional grounds, [1985] 4 W.W.R. 757. But see *Re Eve*, [1986] 2 S.C.R. 388 (*sub nom. E. (Mrs.) v. Eve*), 61 Nfld. & P.E.I.R. 273, 185 A.P.R. 273, 71 N.R. 1, 13 C.P.C. (2d) 6, 31 D.L.R. (4th) 1, (*sub nom. E. (Mrs.) v. Eve*) 8 C.H.R.R. D/3773, where it was held that neither a disabled child's parents nor a court could authorize a hysterectomy for contraceptive as opposed to therapeutic purposes.

It has been held that provincial mental health legislation permitting the involuntary admission and detention of psychiatric patients is valid under the *Charter* as long as admission and detention occur in accordance with the principles of natural justice and in a way that strikes a balance between the rights of the individual and the general rights and obligations of society.[50] The continued detention of a patient diagnosed as a paedophile was not a violation of the patient's right to liberty where the evidence disclosed that his release into the community posed a serious risk of bodily harm to others.[51] A psychiatric facility is not required to prove beyond a reasonable doubt that a patient who has been found not guilty by reason of mental disorder is not a significant risk to society if released.[52] Nor is the admission of hearsay evidence at a review board hearing a violation of the *Charter*.[53] Government activity imposing care upon mentally ill, incompetent adults, is in violation of the *Charter* if it does so in a way that is "intrusive and devoid of . . . essential safeguards and procedures to ensure that the adult's rights to privacy and independent living are not violated".[54]

It has been suggested that access to medical care is a component of the right to "security of the person"[55] and that the "right to life" must be balanced against the right to a natural death.[56] The Law Reform Commission of Canada has suggested that in the absence of reasons to the contrary, medical authorities ought to assume that a patient would prefer life to death, even when the patient is not able to express a preference.[57] It has been held that a patient's right to refuse treatment, even where the refusal will result in death, is a fundamental right protected under Quebec's human rights legislation,[58] but that there is no right protected under the *Charter* that will allow a terminally ill patient to have others assist in his or her death.[59]

---

50 *McCorkell v. Riverview Hospital*, [1993] 8 W.W.R. 169 (B.C.S.C.).

51 *Penetanguishene Mental Health Centre v. Stock* (1994), 116 D.L.R. (4th) 550 (Ont. Gen. Div.).

52 *Davidson v. British Columbia (Attorney General)* (1993), 87 C.C.C. (3d) 269 (B.C. C.A.).

53 *Dayday v. MacEwan* (1987), 62 O.R. (2d) 588 (Dist. Ct.).

54 *Nova Scotia (Minister of Community Services) v. Keeble* (1991), 290 A.P.R. 377, 107 N.S.R. (2d) 377 (N.S. Fam. Ct.); additional reasons at (1992), 11 N.S.R. (2d) 36, 303 A.P.R. 36 (N.S. Fam. Ct.).

55 Garant, *supra* note 35, at 354.

56 B.M. Dickens, "The Right to Natural Death" (1981), 26 McGill L.J. 847.

57 Law Reform Commission of Canada, *Euthanasia, Aiding Suicide and Cessation of Treatment* (Report No. 20) (Ottawa: Supply and Services, 1983), p. 11.

58 *Nancy B v. Hôtel-Dieu de Québec*, [1992] R.J.Q. 361 (C.S.).

59 *Rodriguez v. British Columbia (Attorney General)*, [1993] 3 S.C.R. 519, 82 B.C.L.R. (2d) 273, 107 D.L.R. (4th) 342, [1993] 7 W.W.R. 641, 85 C.C.C. (3d) 15.

Section 8 of the *Charter* provides that everyone has the right to be secure against unreasonable search or seizure. The privacy right of a psychiatric patient, however, may be outweighed by the right of an accused to make a full answer and defence to a criminal charge.[60] The right of a psychiatric patient to send or receive mail privately may be subject, nonetheless, to a policy that requires mail to be opened under observation for security purposes.[61]

Section 9 provides that everyone has the right not to be arbitrarily detained or imprisoned. An individual cannot be detained under adult protection legislation simply because the individual engages in conduct that seems unusual or even risky. In *Ministry of Community Services v. Perry*,[62] an adult absconded from a psychiatric facility where she had been a patient for 16 years. An order was sought under Nova Scotia's adult protection legislation for a declaration that she was in need of protection and could be returned involuntarily to the facility. The evidence disclosed that she had been evicted from the hotel where she had been staying, lacked any plans for shelter or food and was at risk because of her history of failing to take medication. The application was refused on the ground that the evidence did not disclose a danger or risk significant enough to override the individual's right to make decisions about her own status and treatment.

Section 10 provides every individual with the right, on arrest or detention, to be informed promptly of the reasons for the arrest or detention, to be permitted to retain and instruct counsel without delay and to be informed of that right, to have the validity of any detention determined quickly, and to obtain a release if the detention is not lawful.

The right not to be arbitrarily detained or imprisoned may also have implications for health-care personnel. Generally, patients of health-care facilities such as hospitals, nursing homes and psychiatric facilities are free to come and go as they please. Patients who have been confined involuntarily to psychiatric facilities pursuant to a province's mental health legislation, however, must still be afforded certain procedural protections. In Prince Edward Island, the Court of Appeal has held that the *Charter* prohibits *unreasonable* detention and that the patient's rights under the *Charter* are in addition to any protection provided by the provincial mental health legislation.[63]

---

60 *R. v. Coon* (1991), 74 C.C.C. (3d) 146 (Ont. Gen. Div.).

61 *Everingham v. Ontario* (1993), 100 D.L.R. (4th) 199 (Ont. Gen. Div.).

62 (1990), 98 C.L.R. (2d) 263 (N.S. Prov. Ct.).

63 *Re Jenkins* (1984), 45 Nfld. & P.E.I.R. 131, 132 A.P.R. 131, (*sub nom. Reference re Procedures and the Mental Health Act*) 5 D.L.R. (4th) 577, 8 C.R.R. 142 (P.E.I. S.C.).

Section 11 of the *Charter* contains rights that are to be afforded to any person charged with a criminal offence. Such rights include the right to be informed without unreasonable delay of the specific offence, to be tried within a reasonable time, not to be required to testify against oneself, to be presumed innocent until proven guilty and not to be tried more than once for the same offence. Madam Justice Wilson of the Supreme Court of Canada specifically distinguished criminal offences from offences arising out of domestic or disciplinary matters, which are "regulatory, protective or corrective and which are primarily intended to maintain discipline, professional integrity and professional standards or to regulate conduct within a limited private sphere of activity".[64] Consequently, health practitioners charged with misconduct in professional disciplinary proceedings will not be afforded the same level of protection under the *Charter* as they will be afforded if they are charged with a criminal offence.

Sections 13 and 14 of the *Charter* provide witnesses certain rights in regard to self-incrimination and, to any party or witness, in regard to language interpretation. In *W. (C.) v. Manitoba (Mental Health Review Board)*,[65] a subpoena that would have required a psychiatric patient to testify against his will at his own review board hearing was quashed.

5. Cruel and Unusual Treatment or Punishment

Section 12 of the *Charter* provides that "[e]veryone has the right not to be subjected to any cruel and unusual treatment or punishment". The word "treatment" has obvious implications for health care. Certain types of treatment, such as lobotomies or castration, are by their very nature cruel and unusual.[66] For example, electric shock therapy, involuntary administration of hormonal medication to reduce sexual drive, confinement of patients in solitary settings and the use of physical restraints are all areas of treatment that, in certain circumstances, may raise *Charter* concerns.[67]

It has been questioned how the death penalty, if re-established by Parliament, can be said not to offend this provision by its very nature.[68] The

---

64 In *R. v. Wigglesworth*, [1987] 2 S.C.R. 541, 24 O.A.C. 321, 61 Sask. R. 105, 45 D.L.R. (4th) 235, [1988] W.W.R. 193, 81 N.R. 161, 28 Admin. L.R. 294, (*sub nom. Wigglesworth v. R.*) 37 C.C.C. (3d) 385, 60 C.R. (3d) 193, 32 C.R.R. 219.

65 (1992), 11 C.P.C. (3d) 11 (Man. Q.B.).

66 See the *Sexual Sterilization Act*, S.A. 1928, c. 37 (later R.S.A. 1970, c. 341; repealed S.A. 1972, c. 87).

67 See H. Savage and C. McKague, *Mental Health Law in Canada* (Toronto: Butterworths, 1987), pp. 127-28.

68 A. Morel, "Certain Guarantees of Criminal Procedure" in G.-A. Beaudoin and E. Ratushny, Eds. *The Canadian Charter of Rights and Freedoms*, 2nd ed. (Toronto: Butterworths, 1989), p. 497, at 550.

Saskatchewan Court of Appeal ruled recently, however, that a mandatory ten-year sentence for second degree murder, even where the killing was carried out as an act of mercy by the father of a severely disabled child, did not constitute cruel and unusual punishment.[69] Treatment may be cruel and unusual in so far as it is disproportionate to the anticipated benefit of the treatment.

6. Equality Rights

Section 15 of the *Charter* provides that "[e]very individual is equal before and under the law" and prohibits discrimination, including discrimination "based on race, national or ethnic origin, colour, religion, sex, age or mental or physical disability". It has been suggested that mental health legislation discriminates against psychiatric and non-psychiatric patients and between informal and involuntary patients.[70] The Alberta government has established the office of "Patient Advocate". The Alberta Patient Advocate, however, is empowered only to investigate complaints from or relating to "formal patients" and not "informal patients". One may question what rational basis there is for distinguishing between the two. Arguably, an informal patient who is threatened with involuntary confinement if he refuses to take prescribed medication is equally, if not more, entitled to advocacy assistance than a formal patient who is being compelled to take medication. Mandatory retirement rules are non-discriminatory where they do not establish an arbitrary and unfair system of retirement for physicians whose medical skills may be declining.[71]

It has been argued that every citizen in a province must have, within a reasonable distance from his or her residence, equal availability of medical services. In *Ponteix (Town) v. Saskatchewan*,[72] an application was brought for an interlocutory injunction to prevent what was perceived as reduced emergency nursing services at a local hospital. The Court found that changes had arisen as a result of the government's conclusion, in 1993, that significant alterations were necessary in the delivery of health services in Saskatchewan. The Court rejected the applicants' position that all people in Saskatchewan are entitled to the same standard of medical care regardless of where they choose to reside.

> This, of course, is a physical and economic impossibility for any government. It is surely incongruous in the extreme to expect that people who choose to

---

69 *R. v. Latimer*, [1995] 8 W.W.R. 609 (Sask. C.A.).

70 *Ibid.*

71 *Stoffman v. Vancouver General Hospital*, [1990] 3 S.C.R. 483.

72 Unreported, September 16, 1994 (Sask. Q.B.).

> reside, for example, on the north shore of Lake Athabaska, should be entitled to the same standard of health care on that north shore as is readily available to the people who live in Regina or Saskatoon. I cannot hold that the *Charter* requires the government to do that which is physically or economically impossible and patently unreasonable.[73]

In *Fernandes v. Director of Social Services (Winnipeg Central)*,[74] the Manitoba Court of Appeal was asked to rule whether a refusal to fund a hospital patient's request for a personal attendant infringed s. 15 of the *Charter*. The patient suffered from a muscular disease that caused progressive respiratory failure. He was mobile in an electric wheelchair and with appropriate care, which involved an attendant for 16 hours per day, would be able to live in his own apartment. The Court ruled that the patient was required to demonstrate that he had received unequal treatment before and under the law and that the treatment was discriminatory. The Court found that he was not receiving "unequal treatment under the law" and the fact that he was not being housed in a community-based residence, as opposed to a hospital, was not discriminatory.

> Fernandes remains as an in-patient for many reasons. He has a physical handicap which requires an attendant on hand 16 hours per day. He has no independent means to cover the costs of that attendant. He lost his primary caregiver in the fall of 1990 and has no family member or other person who can perform that function on his behalf. There are no other facilities with vacancies that can accommodate his needs. The hospital is available at no additional costs to the program under the Act. It was not his illness that led to his social admission to hospital. It was the loss of his caregiver coupled with the limited resources available in the community to provide the care he requires. The director's decision denying the request for an additional allowance did not amount to discrimination under the *Charter*.[75]

In *Ontario Nursing Home Assn. v. Ontario*,[76] a judge accepted that a difference in government funding between nursing homes and homes for the aged was "illogical and unfair", but nonetheless concluded that a patient receiving care at a lesser level of funding was not denied any equality right under the *Charter*. He held that any discrimination was based upon the type of residence occupied by the nursing-home patient and that this was not one of the enumerated grounds (*i.e.*, "race, national or ethnic origin,

---

[73] *Ibid.*, at para. 22.

[74] (1992), 7 Admin. L.R. (2d) 153 (Man. C.A.).

[75] *Ibid.*, at 167.

[76] (1990), 74 O.R. (2d) 365, 72 D.L.R. (4th) 166 (H.C.J.).

colour, religion, sex, age or mental or physical disability") in s. 15(1). In effect, the "place of residence is not a personal characteristic".

7. Minority Rights

The *Charter* also contains revisions that entrench certain linguistic and cultural rights in the Constitution. French and English are given constitutional status at certain levels of government, in the courts, in the receipt of government services and in language education. Section 25 of the *Charter* preserves existing aboriginal rights and freedoms. Section 27 provides that the *Charter* is to be "interpreted in a manner consistent with the preservation and enhancement of the multicultural heritage of Canadians".

8. Override Power

The *Charter* is a legal mechanism designed to prevent the enactment or operation of statutes that contradict basic human rights. Section 33 of the *Charter*, however, permits Parliament or any legislature to expressly declare one of its statutes to operate notwithstanding s. 2 or ss. 7 to 15 of the *Charter*. In one sense, s. 33 provides an escape hatch by which government can override the *Charter* in circumstances where it considers it to be expedient to do so. On the other hand, the very fact that such legislation would violate fundamental freedoms and legal rights should ensure that its use is very restrictive.

It has been suggested that the formal requirements of s. 33, which require an express declaration of the specific provision of the *Charter* that the legislation wishes to override, are designed to ensure that the decision to employ s. 33 is carried out with full knowledge of the facts and to encourage public discussion of the issues raised by its use.[77] Outside of Quebec, the power has been used on only one occasion.[78] In Quebec, the Parti Québécois enacted a statute in 1982 that purported to override the relevant provisions of the *Charter* in respect of *all* provincial legislation. The constitutionality of this statute itself was contested and ruled invalid by the Quebec Court of Appeal.[79] Section 33 provides, however, that any

---

[77] R. Tasse, "Application of the Canadian Charter of Rights and Freedoms" in Beaudoin and Ratushny, *The Canadian Charter of Rights and Freedoms, supra* note 68, p. 65, at 105.

[78] *The SGEU Dispute Settlement Act*, S.S. 1984-85-86, c. 111.

[79] *Alliance des professeurs de Montréal v. Quebec (A.G.)* (1985), 21 D.L.R. (4th) 354, 18 C.R.R. 195, [1985] R.D.J. 439, 21 C.C.C. (3d) 273 (Que. C.A.); leave to appeal to S.C.C. granted (1985), 21 C.C.C. (3d) 273n (settled out of court, January 16, 1990).

declaration that overrides the *Charter* ceases to have effect five years after it comes into force, though it may be re-enacted. In Quebec, there was no re-enactment in 1987 and the general override legislation, even if constitutional, expired. On three occasions, the Liberal government in Quebec has enacted specific legislation overriding the application of s. 15 of the *Charter.*[80]

PROVINCIAL HUMAN RIGHTS LEGISLATION

As noted above, the *Charter* applies to both federal and provincial levels of government but not to acts of private individuals or entities, unless they have become "agents" of the government. Although the *Charter* is often not applicable in a health-care setting, all jurisdictions in Canada have enacted some form of legislation in the area of human rights and, although the provisions vary from jurisdiction to jurisdiction, all jurisdictions have legislation that prohibits discrimination based on race, colour, religion, creed, marital status, physical disability, sex, or national, ethnic, or place of origin. Discrimination on the basis of mental disability is also prohibited in all jurisdictions.

For example, the Ontario *Human Rights Code*[81] accords individuals a right to equal treatment with respect to services, accommodation, contracts and in other areas.[81a] Provision of health-care services would thus be governed by the *Code.* Individuals are accorded equal treatment "without discrimination because of race, ancestry, place of origin, colour, ethnic origin, citizenship, creed, sex, sexual orientation, age, marital status, fam-

---

[80] *An Act to amend the Act to promote the development of agricultural operations,* S.Q. 1986, c. 54, s. 16; *Act to again amend the Education Act and the Act respecting the Conseil Supérieur de l'Éducation and to amend the Act respecting the Ministère de l' Éducation,* S.Q. 1986, c. 101, ss. 10, 11 and 12; *An Act to amend various legislation respecting the Pension Plans of the Public and Parapublic Sectors,* S.Q. 1987, c. 47, s. 157.

[81] R.S.O. 1990, c. H.19.

[81a] For example, a physician who owned the building in which his practice was based was ordered by the Ontario Human Rights Commission to provide wheelchair access by a ramp to the first floor, to make necessary renovations in the interior of the building to accommodate wheelchairs and to pay $500 in damages. This principle could be extended to hospitals to properly accommodate physically challenged people. J. Sack and V. Payne, "The Duty to Accommodate Disabled Patients" (1995), Vol. 62, No. 6, Ont. Med. Rev. 52.

ily status or handicap".[82] Note that even where the *Code* and not the *Charter* applies, the principles courts have used to apply the *Charter* are also useful to determine whether human rights violations under the *Code* have occurred.

---

[82] *Ibid.*, Part I, s. 1. In *Korn v. Potter* (1996), 134 D.L.R. (4th) 437 (B.C.S.C.), a decision by the British Columbia Council of Human Rights finding a physician guilty of discrimination for refusing to offer artificial insemination to a lesbian couple was upheld in the Supreme Court. He was ordered to pay damages to the couple and to stop discriminating against lesbians.

CHAPTER 12

Current Legal Issues in Health Care

TERMINATION OF TREATMENT AND THE RIGHT TO DIE

Death is a common event in hospitals and other health facilities. The best efforts of health-care providers will not always succeed. In most cases, death comes naturally and results in the termination of the patient's treatment. Death is pronounced by a physician, a death certificate is issued and arrangements are made for the disposition of the body.

In some instances, however, the occurrence of death and the termination of treatment is not so straightforward. Health professionals may be asked to terminate treatment while the patient is still alive.[1] This may accelerate, or even cause, the patient's death. Where the patient is unconscious, caregivers may be met with advance directives, signed by the patient or communicated by family members, that place limitations on treatment and compromise effective care. Where patients are in pain and death is inevitable, requests may be made for proactive steps to be taken that will accelerate or cause death. This type of activity may be more typical than society generally recognizes; many physicians privately admit to helping patients with incurable diseases to accelerate death or to commit suicide by medical means.[1a] The legal and medical issues are fraught with controversy, so much so that the concept of euthanasia has been called "the abortion debate of the next century".[2]

---

1 In an American survey of 852 nurses working in critical care units, 141 reported that they had received requests from patients or family members to perform euthanasia or to assist in suicide. One hundred and twenty-nine reported that they had engaged in such activity and an additional 35 reported that they had hastened death by pretending to provide life-sustaining treatment ordered by a physician. A. Asch, "The Role of Critical Care Nurses in Euthanasia and Assisted Suicide" (1996), vol. 334, No. 21, New England J. of Med. 1374.

1a Lawrence K. Altman, "More Physicians Broach Forbidden Subject of Euthanasia", *New York Times*, March 12, 1991, as cited in "Physician-Assisted Suicide and The Right to Die With Assistance" (1992), 105 Harv. L. Rev. 2021.

2 A. Solomon, "A Death of One's Own", *New Yorker*, May 22, 1995, p. 67.

In recent years there has been a small flood of Canadian legislation and judicial pronouncements affecting this area of the law. Although there is still significant confusion, these developments provide some guidance to health practitioners. And though it may not be possible (or even advisable) for health facilities to institute formal policies or protocols for assisted death, some understanding of the legal principles involved will permit health administrators to ensure that there is general compliance with the law in their own facilities and to identify specific situations for which legal advice should be sought.

1. The Criminal Code

In an environment in which do-not-resuscitate (DNR) orders and the withdrawal of life support systems are almost routine, the considerations of criminal liability seem counter-intuitive. Yet, recent court decisions in this area have focused on provisions of the *Criminal Code*[3] as the basic instrument of legal analysis. Where a patient sought an injunction to prevent the further administration of treatment without her consent and to compel the removal of a ventilator, the court considered whether the request would constitute a criminal act by those carrying out her request.[4] In another case, the court was asked to consider whether a woman suffering from amyotrophic lateral sclerosis had a right to assistance in bringing about her own death, despite a provision in the *Criminal Code* stating the opposite.[5]

The *Criminal Code* provides that "a person commits culpable homicide when he causes the death of a human being by means of an unlawful act".[6] It is also a crime to cause the death of another person by "criminal negligence".[7] Criminal negligence is defined as doing or omitting to do anything in wanton or reckless disregard for the lives or safety of others.[8] It is generally recognized that it is the duty of health professionals to preserve and protect the lives of their patients. The *International Code of Ethics* advises doctors to

> [b]ear in mind the importance of preserving human life from the time of conception until death.[9]

---

3 R.S.C. 1985, c. C-46.

4 *Nancy B. v. Hôtel-Dieu de Québec* (1992), 86 D.L.R. (4th) 385 (Que. S.C.).

5 *Rodriguez v. British Columbia (A.G.)*, [1993] 3 S.C.R. 519.

6 *Supra* note 3, s. 222(5)(a).

7 *Ibid.*, s. 222(5)(b).

8 *Ibid.*, s. 219.

9 *International Code of Ethics of the World Medical Association*, cited in David A. Frenkel, "Human Experimentation: Codes of Ethics" (1977), 1 Legal Med. Q. 7, at 13.

Guide-lines for ethical behaviour published by the College of Nurses of Ontario provide that a

> Sanctity of life . . . means that human life is precious, needs to be respected, protected, and treated with consideration . . . . Sanctity of life also includes considerations of the quality of life. It is difficult sometimes to identify what is human life and what society wants, values, and protects in relation to human life. It is even more difficult for health professionals, including nurses, to identify their own beliefs in relation to human life.
>
> Health professionals have made every reasonable effort to preserve human life. Technology now allows life to be preserved indefinitely. Many health professionals and clients believe that some treatments which preserve life at all costs are unacceptable when the quality of life is questionable.[10]

Activities of health professionals that result in the death of patients, by commission or omission, may constitute offences under the *Criminal Code*. Where an order is made not to resuscitate a patient in the event of further organic failure, does the order allow a death to occur that would not occur otherwise? When a dose of medication is given to a terminally ill patient in order to relieve pain, and it is known that the administration of the medication is also likely to cause or to accelerate the patient's death, does such "comfort care" constitute an offence?

One may argue that where such treatment is condoned, or indeed requested, by the patient or the patient's legal guardian, the treatment is carried out with the consent of the patient, and it is, therefore, acceptable. The *Criminal Code* provides, however, that anyone who counsels or procures a person to commit suicide, or who aids or abets a person to commit suicide, is guilty of an offence.[11] Moreover, s. 14 of the *Criminal Code* states that no "person is entitled to consent to have death inflicted on him". The term "suicide" is not defined in the *Criminal Code* but, generally, it means the willing cessation of one's own life. Consequently, even if the patient executes a written consent, specifically authorizing treatment which is likely to result in death, does this relieve the health professional of criminal liability?

One may argue that where death is imminent and measures are taken to alleviate pain — measures which, as a side effect, accelerate death — such measures are consistent with humane health care and offer dignity to the patient. The *Criminal Code* provides, however:

> Where a person causes to a human being a bodily injury that results in death, he causes the death of that human being notwithstanding that the

---

[10] College of Nurses of Ontario, *Guidelines for Professional Behaviour* (Toronto: The College, 1995), p. 10.

[11] R.S.C. 1985, c. C-46, s. 241. This was the provision that formed the main subject-matter of the *Rodriguez* case, *supra* note 5.

> effect of the bodily injury is only to accelerate his death from a disease or disorder arising from some other cause.[12]

Does treatment that alleviates pain, but impairs physiological functions and hastens death, constitute criminal conduct?

If an accused is able to demonstrate that his or her conduct did not *cause* the death of the patient, this may constitute a defence. In *R. v. Adams*,[13] a physician was accused of murdering a patient who had died of an overdose of morphine. He argued that his intention was to relieve the patient's pain and that the cause of death was the patient's illness and not the morphine. The trial judge instructed the jury that although the motive of relieving pain was not in itself a defence to the charge of murder, an acquittal should be registered if the jury found that the physician's conduct had not *caused* the death, and further, that a *marginal* shortening of life by administration of medication could not be described meaningfully as having *caused* the death.

It has been suggested that the defence of "necessity" may be available in certain situations.[14] The employment of prolonged resuscitative measures to restore a patient momentarily may constitute treatment which is cruel and ultimately useless. Health-care practitioners may feel justified in withholding treatment or in taking steps to hasten the inevitable. There is, at present, however, no legal precedent or statute to justify or support such conduct.

In fact, recent case law suggests that a defence of necessity is unlikely to be available in such circumstances. In *R. v. Latimer (R.W.)*,[15] the father of a 12-year-old girl suffering from severe cerebral palsy took his daughter's life by administering carbon monoxide. He and the rest of his family had actively and constantly cared for her at home throughout her life, but the father decided that, because of her suffering, the quality of his daughter's life had diminished to the point that it was no longer worth enduring. He was charged and convicted of second degree murder, and the conviction was upheld by the Saskatchewan Court of Appeal.

In ruling out a defence of necessity, the Court of Appeal held that the defence of necessity is available only in circumstances where the accused's illegal action or conduct is taken "in urgent situations of clear and imminent peril when compliance with the law is demonstrably impossible". It stated:

> This is not a case of withholding potentially life-prolonging treatment to a seriously disabled person. It deals with the deliberate decision to terminate

---

[12] *Ibid.*, s. 226.

[13] Unreported decision referred to in P. MacKinnon "Euthanasia and Homicide" (1984), 26 Crim. L. Q. 483, at 502.

[14] *Ibid.*, at 504.

[15] [1995] 8 W.W.R. 609 (Sask. C.A.).

> another's life rather than continue with the scheduled medical treatment and care. In such circumstances it is no defence for a parent to say because of a severe handicap, a child's life has such diminished value that the child should not live any longer. It does not advance the interest of the state or society to treat such a person as a person of lesser status or dignity than others.[16]

Latimer is distinguishable, perhaps, from the health-care context in that the death occurred outside of any health facility, death was not imminent, the cause of death was poisonous gas, which had no other purpose than to terminate the daughter's life (as opposed to medication which may relieve suffering, and, at the same time, cause death) and the person causing the death was a family member and not a health practitioner acting in a professional capacity. Nonetheless, it is doubtful that there are many "urgent situations of clear and imminent peril" that would authorize a physician or nurse to act in contravention of the *Criminal Code.* A court may not accept that there is a substantive difference between administering a noxious substance that causes death and administering a narcotic, which, in a high dosage, causes death. Health practitioners who administer medication or any other form of treatment for the purpose of accelerating or causing the death of a patient may be crossing the line and engaging in criminal conduct.

In several recent cases, health practitioners have pleaded guilty to a charge under the *Criminal Code* of administering a noxious substance (the Crown having withdrawn, at the same time, a charge in relation to murder). In *R. v. Mataya,*[17] a nurse was charged with first degree murder and, ultimately, convicted of administering a noxious substance when, during the withdrawal of life-support as requested by a patient's family, he administered a lethal dose of potassium chloride to the patient when complications developed. In that case, no prison term was imposed by the Court, though a conviction was registered and sentence suspended. Subsequently, the nurse's registration with the Ontario College of Nurses was revoked on the ground that his conduct would reasonably be regarded as disgraceful, dishonourable or unprofessional.[18]

In *R. v. De La Rocha,*[19] a physician was charged with second-degree murder and administering a noxious substance. He pleaded guilty to the second count and the murder count on the indictment was withdrawn. In that case, a patient who had tumours on her tongue and in her bronchial area had asked that she be extubated. Subsequently, large doses of

---

[16] *Ibid.*, at 642.

[17] Unreported, August 24, 1992 (Ont. Gen. Div.) (Weir J.).

[18] Discipline decision reported at (1993), 18:2 *College Communique* 26.

[19] Unreported, April 2, 1993 (Ont. Gen. Div.) (Loukidelis J.).

morphine were administered. At a point when the patient had stopped breathing and the heart rate had dropped to the low 50s, the physician asked a nurse to obtain potassium chloride for him. She refused. The doctor proceeded to obtain the potassium chloride and administer it himself. Once the potassium chloride was administered, the patient's death followed rapidly with an episode of ventricular fibrillation. In the circumstances, the conduct of the doctor was accepted by the Court, as well as by the family members of the patient, as being an act of compassion for the patient. The judge, in imposing sentence, reasoned that the heavy doses of morphine were not lethal, or intended to be lethal, to the patient. The judge concluded that the potassium chloride "was administered to a patient who had already stopped breathing". A conviction was entered, but sentence was suspended and the physician was put on probation for three years.

2. Withdrawal of Treatment Based Upon Patient Consent

The countervailing legal analysis to the *Criminal Code* is the law pertaining to informed consent. In *Nancy B.*[20] and *Latimer*[21] a significant consideration in the court's ultimate disposition was the presence or absence of consent. Where the *withdrawal* of treatment is in compliance with the express wish or directive of the patient, the likelihood of criminal or legal liability is reduced significantly.

Canadian law not only authorizes, but demands, the withdrawal of treatment where its continuation is inconsistent with the expressed wish of a competent patient. In *Malette v. Shulman,*[22] a patient was awarded damages against a physician, where the physician had administered treatment contrary to the patient's expressed wish. The patient was a Jehovah's Witness who had been seriously injured in a car accident. When brought to the Emergency Department of the hospital, she was unconscious, but her personal effects contained a card stating that she did not wish to receive any blood transfusion. Believing that in the absence of a blood transfusion, the patient was likely to die, the physician ignored the patient's wish and transfused blood. Although sympathetic to the physician and the altruistic principles that may have motivated his conduct, the Ontario Court of Appeal nonetheless upheld a trial judgment in which the physician was found to have committed a battery. The decision supports the principle that no treatment can be administered to any patient who refuses it, even if the decision is "foolhardy". Although the Court of Appeal relied upon

---

20 *Nancy B., supra* note 4.

21 *Latimer, supra* note 15.

22 (1990), 72 O.R. (2d) 417 (C.A.).

the rationale of individual religious freedom in supporting the patient's right to refuse treatment, the language in the decision means that there are few, if any, situations in which a health practitioner would be justified in administering treatment to a competent patient who is refusing it.[23]

In *Nancy B.*,[24] the Quebec Superior Court recognized the patient's right to refuse treatment even where the refusal is certain to result in death. Nancy was a 25-year-old woman suffering from an incurable neurological disorder who sought an injunction to have the use of a ventilator discontinued. Removal of the ventilator was likely to result in immediate death, but its removal was justified by the patient on the ground that her quality of life had so deteriorated that it was not worth living. Health personnel and the hospital did not directly oppose the patient's wish, but they were concerned that conduct compatible with the patient's wish might offend provisions in the *Criminal Code*. The physician who would be responsible for removing the respirator wished to be assured that she would not be engaged in a criminal act.

Issuing an order, which permitted the withdrawal of treatment pursuant to the patient's wish, the Court concluded that a physician who "interrupts the respiratory support of a patient, at the patient's informed request, in order to let nature take its course" would not be engaged in criminal activity. The respirator was removed pursuant to the patient's request and she died shortly thereafter. It is questionable whether an order is necessary, or even appropriate, in the circumstances. The health professionals involved were seeking a form of advance ruling that their conduct would not, at some future point in time, be judged criminal. Arguably, recent decisions in this area make it clear that a patient's right to refuse treatment *must* lead to the withdrawal of treatment. Failure to comply expeditiously with the patient's expressed direction may, according to *Malette*,[25] constitute a battery.[26]

---

[23] See, however, *Procureur General du Canada v. Hopital Notre Dame et E.T. Niemiec*, [1984] C.S. 426, in which the Quebec Superior Court authorized a hospital to force-feed, if necessary, and to treat surgically a *competent* adult detained pending deportation. The patient had swallowed a piece of wire and was refusing medical treatment on the rationale that he preferred death to a return to his own country. Whether *Niemiec* remains good law is questionable in the face of the subsequent decision in *Nancy B.* and its subsequent citation, with approval, by the Supreme Court of Canada in *Rodriguez*.

[24] *Nancy B., supra* note 4.

[25] *Supra* note 22.

[26] See also *Manoir de la Pointe Bleue (1978) Inc. v. Corbeil*, [1989] R.J.Q. 759, in which a Quebec Superior Court judge granted a declaration that a long-term care institution was not required to administer treatment nor to transfer a patient elsewhere without consent when the patient had executed a legal directive requesting that he be allowed to die by starvation.

Our courts have drawn the line, however, at conduct that goes beyond the withholding or withdrawal of treatment which permits death to occur by natural causes. Compliance with a patient's express wish to have "treatment" that will cause or accelerate death — even where continuation of the patient's life may seem cruel or useless — contravenes the *Criminal Code.*

In *Rodriguez,*[27] a 42-year-old woman suffering from amyotrophic lateral sclerosis sought to have s. 241(b) of the *Criminal Code*[28] declared invalid under the *Charter of Rights and Freedoms.*[29] Whereas there is no criminal prohibition against an individual taking his or her own life, Sue Rodriguez was concerned that her disease would leave her in such a disabled condition that she would not be able to terminate her own life without the assistance of others. Although a majority of the Supreme Court of Canada held that Rodriguez' rights to liberty and security of the person were violated by s. 241(b), it nonetheless held that this violation was consistent with principles of fundamental justice in a democratic society, and, therefore, justified. In examining the history of the common law in this area, as well as the law in other international jurisdictions, Mr. Justice Sopinka, speaking for the majority, held that the prohibition against assisted suicide was not "arbitrary or unfair". He held that there is a legal consensus that "human life must be respected and that we must be careful not to undermine the institutions that protect it". He found that the prohibition against assisted suicide served the purpose of discouraging

> [T]hose who consider that life is unbearable at a particular moment, or who perceive themselves to be a burden upon others, from committing suicide. To permit a physician to lawfully participate in taking life would send a signal that there are circumstances in which the state approves of suicide.[30]

The Supreme Court also referred to the difficulty of drawing a distinction between "active and passive forms of treatment" and whether the withdrawal of life support measures, knowing that death would result, is any different from taking steps in which death results directly from human intervention.

> The administration of drugs designed for pain control in dosages which the physician knows will hasten death constitutes active contribution to death by any standard. However, the distinction drawn here is one based upon

---

[27] *Rodriguez v. British Columbia (A.G.),* [1993] 3 S.C.R. 519.

[28] Section 241(b) of the *Criminal Code* prohibits anyone from aiding or abetting a person to commit suicide.

[29] Part I of the *Constitution Act, 1982,* being Schedule B to the *Canada Act, 1982* (U.K.), 1982, c. 11.

[30] *Rodriguez, supra* note 27, at 608.

> intention — in the case of palliative care the intention is to ease pain, which has the effect of hastening death, while in the case of assisted suicide, the intention is undeniably to cause death. The Law Reform Commission, although it recommended the continued criminal prohibition of both euthanasia and assisted suicide, stated, at p. 70 of the Working Paper, that a doctor should never refuse palliative care to a terminally ill patient only because it may hasten death. In my view, distinctions based upon intent are important, and in fact form the basis of our criminal law. While factually the distinction may, at times, be difficult to draw, legally it is clear. The fact that in some cases, the third party will, under the guise of palliative care, commit euthanasia or assist in suicide and go unsanctioned due to the difficulty of proof cannot be said to render the existence of the prohibition fundamentally unjust.[31]

In short, where a health practitioner engages in conduct which is *intended* to cause the death of a patient, such conduct, if this intention can be proved, will be judged criminal. On the other hand, where the intention is to administer treatment to relieve pain or in some other way assist the patient in coping with the disease, the conduct is not criminal.

3. Incompetent Patients

The legal analysis of informed consent is not available where the patient is not competent to give a consent, unless the patient has, by means of an advanced directive or the appointment of a substitute decision-maker, created a mechanism which allows a caregiver to obtain consent for the withdrawal of treatment. In *Malette*,[32] the patient was unconscious, but had completed a card that clearly directed that no blood transfusion be given. The current legal practice in Canada, which is supported by legislation in a number of provinces, allows patients to create advance directives that will be legally effective in circumstances in which the patient is not competent to communicate directly with caregivers. Similarly, Canadian law permits the patient to appoint a substitute decision-maker who can make decisions about the patient's care and treatment consistent with what he or she considers to be the wishes of the patient.

In many cases, an advance directive will not be available; nor will there be a substitute decision-maker to make decisions about the patient's treatment. The fact that family members or close friends may express views as to modes of treatment and whether treatment should continue may have some persuasive value to a caregiver, but that does not constitute a legal consent. The wishes of family and friends, in the absence of a

---

[31] *Ibid.*, at 607.

[32] *Supra* note 22.

formal appointment of a substitute decision-maker or an attorney for personal care, do not constitute legal authority which is binding upon the physician or other health professional.[32a] Moreover, where a physician is concerned that a substitute decision-maker or personal attorney is offering instructions for treatment that are inconsistent with the patient's best interests, this may be a basis upon which to question or challenge those instructions.

Generally, where a patient is not competent to direct his or her own treatment, and where there is no advance directive or authorized representative to direct treatment, it will be necessary to seek the approval of a court or appropriate administrative tribunal before withholding or withdrawing treatment that will result in the death of a patient. Although this issue has not come squarely before a court in Canada, it has been dealt with in other jurisdictions.

In *Cruzan v. Director, Missouri Department of Health,*[33] a patient had sustained brain damage that left her in a persistent vegetative state. There was no hope of recovery and she was not expected to live for more than several years. Her parents sought to have nutrition and hydration withdrawn, but the hospital refused to honour the request without a court order. The United States Supreme Court's analysis focused on whether there was clear and convincing evidence, in the absence of an advance directive, of what the incompetent patient's wishes would have been had she been in a position to make her own decisions about treatment. The Court upheld state legislation preventing the withdrawal of treatment in the absence of clear and compelling evidence of the patient's wishes. The result is anomalous in that the absence of such evidence seems to dictate that a patient must be kept alive artificially for an indefinite period unless he or she happened to have expressed a wish, in a way that constitutes "clear and compelling evidence", to the opposite effect.

In England, the House of Lords took a somewhat different, and perhaps more practical approach, in a similar case. In *Airedale N.H. Trust v. Bland,*[34] a 21-year-old patient had been in a persistent vegetative state for three and one-half years following an accident. He was being fed artificially and there was no hope of recovery or improvement in his condition. It was proposed that the artificial feeding be discontinued and that any antibiotic treatment not be offered if an infection appeared. The health authority

---

[32a] However, such legislation as the Ontario *Health Care Consent Act, 1996,* S.O. 1996, c. 2, authorizes the appointment of family members as substitute decision makers provided the incompetent patient does not have a court-appointed guardian or an attorney with power of attorney to fill this role. See Chapter 6, Consent to Treatment.

[33] 58 U.S.L.Week 4916 (U.S. 1990).

[34] [1993] 1 All E.R. 821.

for the patient's care applied to the Court for a declaration that it and the responsible physicians could discontinue lawfully all life-sustaining treatment and medical support. This action was supported by the parents and family of the patient. The House of Lords, in granting the request, focused its consideration on the patient's "best interest". Although deferential to what the patient might have wanted had he been able to express his wish, the Court concluded, in the absence of an advance directive, that it must consider what was best for the patient. Importantly, the Court expressed the opinion that the decision was not one that could be made by the doctors alone, and that in cases of such gravity it was necessary to apply to the Court for an order to discontinue treatment (although it was also suggested that as greater experience was gained in the area, the procedural requirements for obtaining Court authorization might be relaxed).

4. Brain Death and Patients in a Persistent Vegetative State

Cases in which the courts have authorized the withholding or withdrawal of treatment, assume, by definition, that the patient is *alive*. In *Nancy B.*, for example, there was no question that the patient was alive, competent, conscious and in full command of her faculties, despite severe and permanent physical incapacity. In *Airedale*, however, the patient was incompetent and judged to be in a "persistent vegetative state". In those circumstances, a threshold question arises whether the patient is already, for all intents and purposes, dead, so that the withholding or withdrawal of treatment does not accelerate or cause death. The task of pronouncing death is within the domain of the medical profession. There is, however, no simple medical definition. The Canadian Medical Association has employed the term "brain death" as a basis for defining death.[35] Manitoba has expressly recognized brain death as an acceptable criterion for determination of death.[36] In several reported decisions, Canadian judges have considered, in the criminal law context, whether someone is already dead where there has been "brain death" or where some or all of the body's vital functions have ceased to perform.[37] In *R. v. Malcherek*,[38] an English Court held that a physician's withdrawal of treatment did not cause the death of a patient who was already brain dead. One Canadian legal commentator has suggested:

---

[35] Canadian Medical Association, "A C.M.A. Position — Guidelines for the Diagnosis of Brain Death" (1987), 136 Can. Med. Assoc. J. 200A-B.

[36] *Vital Statistics Act*, R.S.M. 1987, c. V-60.

[37] See *R. v. Kitching and Adams*, [1976] 6 W.W.R. 697 (Man. C.A.), and *R. v. Green* (1988), 43 C.C.C. (3d) 413 (B.C.S.C.).

[38] [1981] 2 All E.R. 422.

> . . . the weight of legal and medical authority leads to no other sensible conclusion than that brain dead patients need not be maintained on life support mechanisms, and that no liability would attach as a result of a physician suspending life support from a patient determined to be brain dead in accordance with currently accepted medical practice.[39]

That commentator questions, however, whether a *persistent vegetative state* is sufficient for a court to conclude that life has ended. A cautious approach suggests that in the absence of direct legal authority in Canada, an application be made to the court of competent jurisdiction (or to the appropriate statutory tribunal) for a decision on whether a patient in a persistent vegetative state is an appropriate one for the cessation of treatment.

5. The Need for Legislation

The activities of Canadian lawmakers in this area have centred on legislation dealing with consent to treatment, advance directives and substitute decision-making. There has not been any significant reform of the criminal law to take into account recent developments in medical technology, the ability of health practitioners to extend life through artificial means and health-care practices that may permit, or even accelerate, death. Recently, considerable momentum has developed in support of legislation to modify *Criminal Code* provisions that do not seem to contemplate current attitudes and practices in relation to the withdrawal of treatment and assisted death.

The Canadian Senate released a report in 1995 on the subject of euthanasia and assisted suicide.[40] In its comprehensive *Report*, the Senate Committee addresses "a broad spectrum of end-of-life decisions that must be made every day by or on behalf of patients".[41] The recommendations of the Special Senate Committee include:

- the development and implementation of national guide-lines for *palliative care.*
- that the *Criminal Code* be amended the clarify the practice of providing treatment for the purpose of alleviating suffering that may shorten

[39] Joan Gilmour, "Withholding and Withdrawing Life Support from Adults at Common Law"(1993), 31 Osgoode Hall L. J. 473, at 503.

[40] *Of Life and Death — Report of the Special Senate Committee on Euthanasia and Assisted Suicide*, published under the authority of the Senate of Canada, May 1995. Material from the report of the Special Senate Committee is reproduced with permission.

[41] *Ibid.*, at 3.

life and the development of guide-lines and standards for the practice of *total sedation* of patients.

- that the *Criminal Code* be amended to explicitly recognize and clarify the circumstances in which the withholding and withdrawal of life-sustaining treatment is legally acceptable.
- that provinces and territories that do not have *advance directive* legislation adopt such legislation.
- that the *Criminal Code* provisions that relate to the offence of counselling suicide, aiding or assisting a suicide not be amended.[42]
- that non-voluntary euthanasia remain a criminal offence, but that the *Criminal Code* be amended to provide for a less severe penalty in cases where there is the essential element of compassion or mercy.[43]
- that voluntary euthanasia remain a criminal offence, but that similar to non-voluntary euthanasia, there be a less severe penalty for voluntary euthanasia where there is an essential element of compassion or mercy.
- that the prohibition against involuntary euthanasia continue under the present murder provisions in the *Criminal Code.*[44]

In some jurisdictions, practices (in some cases supported by legislation) have developed in which "end-of-life treatment" by physicians is tolerated and legally sanctioned.[44a] In the Netherlands, although assisted suicide remains punishable by up to 12 years in prison, guide-lines have been developed and approved by Parliament to allow euthanasia where:

---

42 This was a recommendation of the majority of the Special Senate Committee; a minority recommended that an exemption to s. 241(b) of the *Criminal Code* be added, under clearly defined safeguards, to protect individuals who assist in another person's suicide and that there be procedural guide-lines, both before and after the act of assisted suicide, to avoid abuse.

43 This suggested amendment would deal with a situation like that of *Latimer,* in which the mercy-killing of a daughter by her father drew, despite the compassionate circumstances recognized by all, a minimum ten-year sentence under the current provisions of the *Criminal Code.*

44 The Committee defined "involuntary" as an act *against* the wishes of a competent individual or a valid advanced directive; "non-voluntary" is defined as meaning *without the knowledge* of the wishes of a competent individual or of an incompetent individual.

44a For example, *The Rights of the Terminally Ill Act,* N. Terr. Austl. Laws, proclaimed in force July 1, 1996, was passed in the Northern Territory in Australia legalizing euthanasia in specified circumstances. The validity of this law was challenged in *Wake v. Northern Territory of Australia,* No. 112 of 1996, July 24, 1996 (S.C.N. Terr. Austl.). The appellants argued that the legislative assembly did not have the power to make a law of this nature. The majority decided that the legislature did have this power as it had the constitutional power to make laws for the "peace, order and good government of the Territory".

(1) the request for euthanasia must come from the patient and be voluntary, well-considered and persistent;
(2) the patient must have adequate information about his or her medical condition, the prognosis and alternative treatments;
(3) there must be intolerable suffering with no prospect of improvement, although the patient need not be terminally ill;
(4) other alternatives to the suffering must have been considered and found ineffective, unreasonable or not acceptable to the patient;
(5) euthanasia must be performed by a physician who has consulted an independent colleague;
(6) the physician must exercise due care, and there should be a written record for every case; and
(7) the death must not be reported to the medical examiner as a natural death.[45]

The approved procedure requires a physician to provide a full written report and complete a lengthy questionnaire under the jurisdiction's *Burial Act* for submission to the Municipal Coroner who forwards it to the local public prosecutor. Where the physician's conduct complies with the substantive and procedural guide-lines, a policy of non-prosecution is adopted. Nonetheless, concern has been expressed about whether the practice of euthanasia in the Netherlands is underreported and whether a large portion of euthanasia cases does not result from direct and persistent requests from patients.[46]

In Oregon, a legislative proposal for physician-assisted suicide was accepted recently by a 51 per cent majority of the State. Known as Ballot Measure 16, the law would allow physicians to prescribe pills that they knew would be used for a suicide by a terminally ill patient; it would allow physicians to be with the patients when they took the pills. The legislation is intended to apply only when physicians predict a patient's death as likely to occur within six months and requires that certain procedural safeguards be met.[47]

---

[45] See *Life and Death — Report, supra* note 40, at A-127–A-129.

[46] See H. Rigter et al., "Euthanasia in the Netherlands" (1989), 140 Can. Med. Assoc. J. 788. The Royal Dutch Medical Association has shifted its policy on euthanasia, indicating that it would be better if candidates ended their own lives rather than have the physician do it for them. This is tacit recognition that many physicians struggle with euthanasia as they feel their primary responsibility is to heal patients. An official with the Medical Association indicated that the new policy is meant to alleviate the emotional stress that doctors experience when performing euthanasia. "Dutch Doctors Revise Policy on Mercy Killing," *The [Toronto] Globe and Mail*, August 26, 1995, p. A2.

[47] Measure No. 16, *The Oregon Death with Dignity Act.* Implementation of the

End of life treatment remains a controversial and difficult area for health facilities and health practitioners in Canada. Of most concern is the fact that certain practices, including assisted suicide, are common in Canada despite clear criminal prohibitions and in the absence of any legal basis for a court relieving against the consequences of such criminal action. In his submission to the Senate Committee, Dr. Boadway, the Director of Health Policy for the Ontario Medical Association, advised the Committee that the practice of assisted suicide was "constant".[48] The Senate Committee, however, indicated that it was not possible for it to "gather accurate or complete information on the incidents of assisted suicide" and cited the submission of a chaplain from the New Brunswick health-care system who indicated that there was an absence of participation in the public hearings by those who were fearful of investigation and potential punitive action.[49] In effect, there appear to be health professionals who are engaged in what our legal system considers criminal conduct.

Health administrators and board members should monitor and discuss end-of-life practices carried out within their facilities and should obtain legal advice on how to best manage practices and educate health professionals in this difficult area. Decisions, either on an individual or a policy basis, ought not to be left in the hands of a single individual. Steps should be taken to structure the process in terms of what the decision is, who makes it, what factors are to be considered and whether the factors apply to a particular case. All hospitals and health facilities in which health practitioners may be engaged in treating dying patients ought to have ethics committees to review individual cases and proposals for treatment or non-treatment.

Experimental Care and Treatment

Innovation occurs through trial and error. Many health-care procedures are, in reality, experiments that have been demonstrated to work by repeated performance. Open heart surgery, although fraught with risk in its early development, has become almost routine with increased technology

---

legislation has been stalled by a constitutional challenge. Recently, the law was ruled unconstitutional by a U.S. Federal Court judge who held that it violated the "protection clause" of the U.S. Constitution's 14th Amendment; see *The Globe and Mail*, August 4, 1995, p. A9. It is not unlikely that new legislation in this area, perhaps as recommended by the Senate Committee, would receive a similar constitutional challenge under the *Canadian Charter of Rights.*

48 *Life and Death — Report, supra* note 40, at 54.

49 *Ibid.*

and expertise. Many treatments available to patients would not be available if they had not first been attempted in a more high-risk setting to "test" the result. Even the most common medical procedures are experimental: a "trial of labour" is little more than a controlled experiment to determine if a woman can deliver naturally or will be compelled to undergo a Caesarean section.

Many patients have benefited from modern, innovative medical techniques. The benefits obtained, however, raise questions about how innovative practices become routine and to what extent it is ethical to put patients at risk in order to achieve a benefit that may only accrue to other patients once experimental techniques have been perfected. There is an unavoidable tension between pioneering new techniques and the right of patients not to be used as subjects for scientific experiments. The obligation of a physician to obtain an informed consent places a high value on the patient's right to refuse treatment that may have risks that the patient is not prepared to accept.

Health administrators and boards of health facilities have a legal responsibility to ensure that experimental care and treatment carried out by health practitioners in their facilities conforms to ethical and legal principles. Although physicians and other health practitioners have international,[50] national[51] and professional[52] codes of ethics, there is a legal obligation on administrators of health facilities, in which experimental care and treatment may be ongoing, to ensure that ethical codes and legal principles are fairly applied.

In *Halushka v. University of Saskatchewan*,[53] a doctor involved a student in an experiment involving the introduction of a catheter under general anaesthetics. The doctor failed to disclose to the student, who was paid $50 to participate in the experiment, that the catheter would reach as far as his heart. The student suffered a heart attack during the experiment and later sued. Liability was found on the ground that a proper consent to an experimental procedure had not been obtained from the patient.

---

50 *Declaration of Helsinki, Recommendations Guiding Medical Doctors in Biomedical Research Involving Human Subjects*, adopted by the World Medical Assembly, Helsinki 1964, rev. Tokyo (1975), Venice (1983), Hong Kong (1989), reprinted at (1990), 41 I.D.H.L. 530; *Nuremburg Code of Ethics in Medical Research*, in *U.S. General Adjutant Department, trials of war criminals before the Nuremburg Military Tribunals Under Control Council Law No. 10 October 1946-April 1947*, v. 2: The medical case, Washington, DC: U.S. Government Printing Office, 1947, pp. 181-82.

51 Canadian Medical Association, *Code of Ethics* (Ottawa: Communications and Government Relations Dept., 1990).

52 *Professional Codes of Ethics: Ethics, Codes, Standards and Guidelines for Professionals Working in a Health Care Setting in Canada* (Toronto: The Hospital for Sick Children, 1992).

53 (1965), 53 D.L.R. (2d) 436, 52 W.W.R. 608 (Sask. C.A.).

In *Cryderman v. Ringrose*,[54] a physician performed a tubal sterilization in his office using the introduction of silver nitrate into the patient's fallopian tubes. The physician had learned about the technique from a medical article, which was termed a "preliminary report". The physician's sterilization of the patient was unsuccessful. The overwhelming weight of expert evidence at trial indicated that the technique employed by the physician was experimental. The Court found that the physician did not properly inform the patient about the procedure and the fact that it was of an experimental nature.

In *Coughlin v. Kuntz*,[55] an orthopaedic surgeon carried out an anterior cervical disectomy. This required the insertion of a plastic spacer in the narrowed disc space in the neck area. The procedure was developed by the physician and was in an "experimental stage". The procedure was in conflict with a recommendation of doctors from the Workers' Compensation Board who thought that shoulder surgery, instead of neck surgery, was appropriate. When complications ensued, the patient sued the physician. The Court found that the physician had failed to disclose to the patient the more conservative treatments that were available and that his use of an experimental surgical procedure unsupported by scientific clinical study, constituted negligence.

Failure of health practitioners to obtain an informed consent from the patient for experimental treatment may result in direct liability for the health facility. In *Weiss v. Solomon*,[56] a patient died after having submitted to a research programme in the defendant hospital. The programme involved the use of experimental optic drops in conjunction with the administration of an angiogram using a fluorene derivative. The patient died as a result of a rare, but known, reaction to the angiogram. It was alleged that the physicians responsible for the programme had failed to obtain an informed consent from the patient, and further, that the hospital in which the treatment was provided had failed to ensure that the research programme was carried out under its direction and control and that participants were provided with an appropriate level of information to permit them to give a free and informed consent.

The Court found that the research programme had been presented to, and approved by, the research committee of the hospital. The research protocol referred to the Helsinki Declaration and obliged the researchers to apprise the patient of all potential risks involved in the programme. The Court held that the research activity was clearly experimental and

---

[54] (1977), 6 A.R. 21, [1977] 3 W.W.R. 109 (Dist. Ct.); affd (1978), 89 D.L.R. (3d) 32, [1978] 3 W.W.R. 481 (C.A.).

[55] (1987), 17 B.C.L.R. (2d) 365, 42 C.C.L.T. 142 (S.C.); affd (1989), 42 B.C.L.R. (2d) 108, 2 C.C.L.T. (2d) 42 (C.A.).

[56] [1989] R.G.Q. 731, 48 C.C.L.T. 280 (C.S.).

could have no direct benefit to the patient, and, therefore, that the physician ought to have apprised the patient of all known risks, even those which were rare or remote, especially if the consequences could be serious. The evidence indicated that the risk of a cardiovascular accident had been minimized and had not been explained to the patient. It was also found that the research committee of the hospital had approved the consent form that was signed by the patient. The court held that the hospital had allowed the angiograms to be carried out without an appropriate pre-selection of patients and without an appropriate system for apprising patients of known risks. Both the physician and the hospital were found liable. In effect, the activities of a hospital's research or ethics committee may come under scrutiny in court proceedings, and if the conduct is inappropriate, these activities may result in legal liability for the institution.

The Law Reform Commission of Canada has made recommendations for the regulation of human experimental treatment in Canada.[57] The Commission has recommended that non-therapeutic biomedical experimentation should be considered legal where the subject's free and informed consent has been properly obtained and where there is an acceptable ratio between the risks incurred by the subject and the benefits expected to result from the experiment.

Procedures that are *purely* experimental are unlikely to have any direct benefit for the subject. Consequently, even the most minimal risk for the subject in a pure experiment may be difficult to justify. Most types of biomedical experimentation will be carried out in circumstances in which the patient stands to benefit if the innovative treatment being administered is successful. For example, patients who face certain death without organ replacement may volunteer to undergo risky surgery. Patients who are threatened with a terminal illness may be prepared to experiment with forms of treatment having severe side effects, but offering a chance of survival. In those instances, a greater risk may be justified by an anticipated benefit to the patient. In *Halushka*,[58] the experiment conducted by the physician was purely experimental; there was no anticipated benefit to the student. The student was only a means to test the form of catheterization which once clinically demonstrated, would be used on patients requiring treatment. In *Coughlin*,[59] the patient required treatment of the cervical spine and shoulder, but there were more conservative forms of treatment available. The patient was experiencing pain, but there was no urgency. The selection by the doctor of an experimental form of treatment, with a

---

[57] Law Reform Commission of Canada, *Biomedical Experimentation Involving Human Subjects*, Working Paper 61 (Canada, 1989).

[58] *Supra* note 53.

[59] *Supra* note 55.

significant risk of complications, was not justified when balanced against the likely benefit to the patient.

Some forms of scientific experimentation, in order to be clinically sound, involve deception of the subject. One group of subjects may be given the medication being tested and another group may be given a placebo. The experiment will not be valid if patients know which group they are in. Even the individual administering the experiment may not be aware of the purpose of the experiment or into which group the subjects fall. This is to ensure that the results are objective and not distorted, even inadvertently, by the participants. Such deception or non-disclosure may be necessary as a means of achieving research goals. The Law Reform Commission has recommended that in circumstances where participants must be kept in the dark, any deception or non-disclosure ought not to involve the non-disclosure of risk to the patient, the research must be of major scientific value, and subjects should be debriefed following the experimentation to inform them why deception was thought to be necessary.

The Law Reform Commission has recommended that non-therapeutic biomedical experimentation be considered legal where the subject's free and informed consent is obtained and the risks incurred are not disproportionate to expected benefits.[60] The term "risk" includes the nature of the risk, the potential gravity of the consequences and the likelihood that the risk will materialize. Even though the risk itself may not be serious in the potential harm to the patient if it occurs (*e.g.*, a skin rash from medication), the risk may, nonetheless, be disproportionate to the expected benefit of the innovative therapy if it is likely that all subjects will contract a rash. The experimentor must advise the subject, even though the side effect is minimal, that a rash is likely to occur and allow the patient to make a free and informed decision about whether or not he or she wishes to engage in the experiment.

The development of innovative therapies for children is highly problematic. It may not be possible to speak in terms of a free and informed consent when one is speaking of a child. The Law Reform Commission has recommended, however, that experimentation of a therapeutic nature, which offers a reasonable hope of benefiting the child, be considered legal where its ultimate aim is to provide an individual benefit for the child.[61] Therefore, the introduction of a new medication in the treatment of adolescent leukaemia, the use of innovative surgical techniques and the resort to organ transplantation may be justified if the risk involved in the procedure is proportionate to the anticipated benefit to the child. The Law Reform Commission has recommended that non-therapeutic

---

[60] *Biomedical Experimentation, supra* note 57, at 61.

[61] *Ibid.*, at 62.

experimentation should occur only when the research is of major scientific importance, where the research cannot proceed using competent adult subjects, or where the research is in relation to infant conditions and does not involve any serious risks for the child and a substitute consent is obtained from an independent third party.[62]

Non-therapeutic experimentation may be carried out upon tissue removed from patients during surgical procedures. Does the patient have any right to give or refuse consent to such activity? It has been suggested that where tissue or fluid has been removed from a patient, consent to its experimental use in the institution possessing it is not required.[63] In some circumstances, however, testing fluid or tissue may produce results having implications for the patient. If randomized testing of body fluid for the AIDS virus produces a positive result, should the patient from whom the body fluid was removed be informed? Should the local health authority be notified pursuant to provincial legislation requiring disclosure? If testing of tissue for a particular genetic strain reveals that offspring of the patient may be affected, should the patient be informed? Can failure to disclose result in liability should the patient bear a child who is disabled and whose birth or condition might have been prevented had the patient been aware of the genetic condition?

Canadian researchers have transplanted brain tissue from aborted fetuses to treat patients with Parkinson's disease.[64] The informed consent of the women having the abortions was obtained. The Law Reform Commission deals specifically with experimentation on embryos and fetuses. It recommends that any non-therapeutic biomedical experimentation on embryos and fetuses take place only after the experimentation has received a prior approval of a multidisciplinary ethics committee, only if the research is carried out in centres or hospitals recognized by public authorities and only where the consent of both parents of the embryo or fetus has been obtained.[65] The Commission has also recommended that the creation of embryos solely for the purpose of scientific research should be prohibited, that the reimplantation of embryos used for experimental purposes should be prohibited and that certain types of experimentation on embryos (such as cloning, ectogenesis, parthenogenesis and the crossing of human and animal gametes) should be prohibited.[66] The Commission has recommended

---

62 *Ibid.*

63 B.M. Dickens, "Information for Consent in Human Experimentation" (1974), 24 U. of T.L.J. 381, at 405.

64 "Canadians plan transplants of tissue from aborted fetuses", *The Globe and Mail*, July 14, 1988, A1.

65 *Biomedical Experimentation, supra* note 57, at 62.

66 *Ibid.*

that experimentation on embryos should be prohibited after day 14 of embryonic development and that the freezing of embryos should be allowed, but not prolonged for more than five years, and that standards should be developed for the creation, expansion and management of sperm and embryo banks.[67]

Advances in the area of reproductive technology resulted in the federal government appointing a Royal Commission on New Reproductive Technologies.[68] The mandate of the Commission was to examine how new reproductive technology should be handled in Canada and to identify those technologies that could be beneficial to Canadians, but also, those technologies that may result in, or arise from, misuse. In 1996 the federal government adopted many recommendations of the Commission in a Bill[68a] that imposes criminal sanctions[68b] for carrying out, offering to carry out or offering compensation to carry out any of the prohibited activities. These include: researching cloning of animal/human hybrids; altering genetic structure of an ovum, sperm, zygote or embryo, if these changes are capable of being transmitted to a subsequent generation; fertilization of eggs from female fetuses for implantation; using any medical procedures to ensure or increase the likelihood of having a child of a particular sex; using any diagnostic procedures to determine the sex of the zygote or embryo, except for reasons relating to its health; maintaining the embryo outside of the human body and fertilizing an ovum outside the human body for research; commercializing birth surrogacy arrangements and selling eggs, sperm, zygotes or fetal tissues.

No person may use ova, sperm, zygotes or embryos for research, donation, maturation, fertilization, or implantation in a woman without express consent. This prohibition does not apply in respect of sperm for the purposes of identification or prosecution in relation to an offence under the *Criminal Code*. The Canadian government has introduced proposals[68c] for the creation of a government agency that would report to the Ministry of Health to implement the regulatory regime recommended

---

[67] *Ibid.*, at 63.

[68] Canada, Royal Commission on New Reproductive Technologies, *Proceed with Care: Final Report of the Royal Commission on New Reproductive Technologies* (Ottawa: Canada Communications Group, 1993).

[68a] Bill C-47, *An Act respecting human reproductive technologies and commercial transactions relating to human reproduction*, 2nd Sess., 35th Parl., 1996 (1st reading June 14, 1996).

[68b] Prosecution can proceed only with the consent of the Attorney General and the charge may be for either a summary conviction offence with a maximum penalty of $250,000, four years in prison, or both, or an indictable offence with a maximum penalty of $500,000, ten years in prison, or both.

[68c] Canada, Ministry of Health, *New Reproductive and Genetic Technologies: Setting Boundaries, Enhancing Health* (Minister of Supply and Services Canada, 1996).

by the Commission. The function of the agency would be to develop standards for the use of reproductive materials in medical research and practice, issue licences to permit such activities and ensure compliance with the standards. The proposals suggest there should be licensing of the following: in vitro fertilization; donor insemination; use of fetal tissue; storage, handling and donation of human eggs, sperm and embryos; embryo research; pre-implantation diagnosis and post-menopausal pregnancy.

In hospitals or other health facilities in which there is ongoing research and experimentation involving patients, administrators and boards should ensure that a system is in place to oversee such activities. Many hospitals have established research or ethics committees in their own facilities or in conjunction with an affiliated teaching institution. Recently, the National Council of Bioethics in Human Research (N.C.B.H.R.) has issued a number of recommendations in relation to "research ethics boards", the basis upon which they should operate and their interaction with health facilities. These recommendations include:

- The lines of authority and reporting responsibilities of research ethics boards (REBs) should be clearly identified.
- An REB should usually review at least 50 proposals annually to maintain a breadth and depth of experience. REBs that review fewer than this number should consider combining with an REB from another institution.
- REBs should:
  - (a) require that consent forms be written so they are clearly understandable by a subject with an eighth-grade education;
  - (b) withhold ethical approval until an acceptable consent form has been received; and
  - (c) when possible, use an outcome classification — approved, conditionally approved, and not approved — for initial reviews.
- To preserve objectivity, integrity and public trust in the review process, REBs should be vigilant about potential conflicts of interest on the part of the researcher, the institution and the research subject.
- Institutions and REBs should further develop, expand and implement mechanisms for the thorough review and monitoring of human research. They should include at least annual reports on issues such as unexpected events, significant protocol changes, and termination reports. For sensitive protocols, the REB should require more frequent or rigorous review and may suggest outside monitors.
- The confidentiality of patient data should be maintained throughout the process of monitoring.[69]

---

[69] National Council on Bioethics and Human Research, *Communique*, Winter 1995, pp. 26-28.

ABORTION

There is an intricate link between abortion, health care and the Canadian legal system. At one time, more than 60,000 abortions were being performed in Canada every year.[70] Abortion interacts with a number of corollary issues: women's rights, fetal status, reproductive technology, eugenics and others.

Until 1988,[71] the performance of an abortion, except in circumstances provided by statute, constituted a criminal act. Section 287 of the *Criminal Code*,[72] enacted in 1969 by the federal government, preserved abortion as a criminal offence, with liability to imprisonment, but not if performed by a qualified medical practitioner in an approved or accredited hospital with the prior written consent of the hospital's therapeutic abortion committee once the committee had issued a certificate stating that the pregnancy would or would be likely to endanger the woman's life or health.

Section 287 of the *Criminal Code* constituted a liberalization of abortion law by permitting legal access to abortions performed by competent medical practitioners at public health facilities, but at the same time, not going so far as to permit pregnant women to have abortions 'on demand'. The object of the legislation was that abortions would be legal only in circumstances in which the woman's life or health was endangered.[73]

In 1988, the Supreme Court of Canada ruled that s. 287 of the *Criminal Code* was unconstitutional.[74] The main thrust of Morgentaler's appeal to the Supreme Court of Canada was that s. 287 of the *Criminal Code*[75] infringed the *Charter of Rights and Freedoms.* Section 287 was said to violate s. 7 of the *Charter* which provides:

> Everyone has the right to life, liberty and security of the person and the right not to be deprived thereof except in accordance with the principles of fundamental justice.

A majority of the Court accepted this argument and ruled that s. 287 was inoperable. Some judges concluded that procedural requirements set out in s. 287 created a structure that was

---

70 "Basic Facts on Therapeutic Abortions", *Statistics Canada,* 1983, Catalogue A2-211.

71 *R. v. Morgentaler,* [1988] 1 S.C.R. 30, 44 D.L.R. (4th) 385, 37 C.C.C. (3d) 449, 62 C.R. (3d) 1.

72 R.S.C. 1985, c. C-46.

73 J.P. Maksymiuk, "The Abortion Law: A Study of *R. v. Morgentaler*" (1974), 39 Sask. L. Rev. 259.

74 *Morgentaler, supra* note 71.

75 Formerly s. 251.

> manifestly unfair. It contains so many potential barriers to its own operation that the defence it creates will in many circumstances be practically unavailable. . . .[76]

The Court balanced the procedural obstacles contained in s. 287 against a woman's security of the person.

> Forcing a woman, by threat of criminal sanction, to carry a foetus to term unless she meets certain criteria unrelated to her own priorities and aspirations, is a profound interference with a woman's body and thus a violation of security of the person.[77]

The Court found that the legal mechanism chosen by the federal government to balance the rights of the pregnant woman with the "protection of the foetus" was disproportional, and, therefore, inconsistent with the principles of fundamental justice. The Court found that the administrative procedure created by s. 287 operated in a way that was unfair and arbitrary and that it impaired more of the protected right than was necessary.[78]

Madam Justice Bertha Wilson wrote a separate judgment placing less emphasis on the procedural obstacles in s. 287, and more on what she perceived to be the substantive interference of s. 287 with a woman's right to liberty in the form of control over her own body. According to Justice Wilson, s. 287 of the *Criminal Code* resulted in the woman

> being treated as a means — a means to an end which she does not desire but over which she has no control. She is the passive recipient of a decision made by others . . . .[79]

Justice Wilson also suggested:

> It is probably impossible for a man to respond, even imaginatively, to such a dilemma not just because it is outside the realm of his personal experience . . . but because he can relate to it only by objectifying it, thereby eliminating the subjective elements of the female psyche which are at the heart of the dilemma.[80]

---

76 *Morgentaler, supra* note 71, at 72 (S.C.R.).

77 *Ibid.*, at 56-57.

78 M.L. McConnell, "Even by Commonsense Morality: *Morgentaler, Borowski* and the Constitution of Canada" (1989), 68 Can. Bar Rev. 765.

79 *Morgentaler, supra* note 71, at 173 (S.C.R.).

80 *Ibid.*, at 171.

Although Justice Wilson expressed the view that the primary purpose of s. 287, protection of the fetus, was a "perfectly valid legislative objective", she concluded that the framework set out in s. 287 was an unreasonable restriction on a woman's *Charter* rights. In the result s. 287 of the *Criminal Code* was ruled invalid.

Since the *Morgentaler* decision in 1988 there has been no federal legislation regulating abortions. The activities of the therapeutic abortion committees no longer have any legal or statutory foundation.

Nevertheless, the absence of legislation under the *Criminal Code* dealing directly with abortion did not prevent further litigation. In the summer of 1989, a male applicant brought an application for an injunction in a Quebec court to prevent a woman from having an abortion.[81] The man and woman had lived together as a couple for five months. There had been a break-up. The woman was pregnant and decided to obtain an abortion. The male applicant argued that the rights of the fetus were protected under the Quebec *Charter of Human Rights and Freedoms* which stated:

> 1. Every human being has a right to life, and to personal security, inviolability and freedom.
>   He also possesses juridical personality.
> 2. Every human being whose life is in peril has a right to assistance.
>   Every person must come to the aid of anyone whose life is in peril, either personally or calling for aid, by giving him the necessary and immediate physical assistance, unless it involves danger to himself or a third person, or he has another valid reason.[82]

The application for the injunction was denied initially, but then granted on appeal by the Quebec Court of Appeal. This led to an expedited hearing before the Supreme Court of Canada. The Supreme Court of Canada, in overturning the Quebec Court of Appeal and ruling in favour of the female respondent, made it clear that the issue of whether or not the fetus was a "human being" under the legislation was, from the Court's point of view, a legal question.

> The Court is not required to enter the philosophical and theological debates about whether or not a foetus is a person, but, rather, to answer the legal question of whether the Quebec legislature has accorded the foetus personhood. Metaphysical arguments may be relevant but they are not the primary focus of inquiry. Nor are scientific arguments about the biological status of a foetus determinative in our inquiry. The task of properly classifying a foetus in law and in science are different pursuits. Ascribing personhood

---

[81] *Tremblay v. Daigle*, [1989] 2 S.C.R. 530, 62 D.L.R. (4th) 634, 102 N.R. 81.

[82] R.S.Q. 1977, c. C-12, ss. 1 [am. 1982, c. 61, s. 1] and 2.

> to a foetus in law is a fundamentally normative task. It results in the recognition of rights and duties — a matter which falls outside the concerns of scientific classification. In short, this Court's task is a legal one. Decisions based upon broad social, political, moral and economic choices are more appropriately left to the legislature.[83]

In the end, the Court was not persuaded that the Quebec legislature, in enacting the Quebec *Charter of Human Rights and Freedoms*, had intended the term "human being" to include a fetus. The Court concluded that it would be wrong to "interpret the vague provisions of the Quebec *Charter* as conferring legal personhood upon the foetus".[84]

The male applicant had also raised the argument of "father's rights" as a basis for the injunction. It was argued that his contribution to the act of conception gave him an equal say in what happened to the fetus. The Supreme Court responded:

> There does not appear to be any jurisprudential basis for this argument. No court in Quebec or elsewhere has ever accepted the argument that a father's interest in a foetus which he helped to create could support a right to veto a woman's decisions in respect of the foetus she is carrying. A number of cases in various jurisdictions outside of Quebec have considered this argument and explicitly rejected it . . . . We have been unable to find a single decision in Quebec or elsewhere which would support the allegation of a "father's rights" necessary to support this injunction. There is nothing in the *Civil Code* or any legislation in Quebec which could be used to support the argument. This lack of a legal basis is fatal to the argument about "father's rights".[85]

In the absence of any regulation of abortion at the federal level, in 1989, the Province of Nova Scotia passed a *Medical Services Act* prohibiting the privatization of certain medical services in the province for the stated purpose of maintaining "a single high-quality health-care delivery system for all Nova Scotians".[86] The Act prohibited the performance or assistance in the performance of a designated medical act other than in an approved hospital. A number of medical services were designated by regulation, one of which is

> Abortion, including a therapeutic abortion, but not including emergency services related to a spontaneous abortion or related to complications arising from a previously performed abortion.[87]

---

[83] *Tremblay, supra* note 81, at 552-53 (S.C.R.).

[84] *Ibid.*, at 570.

[85] *Ibid.*, at 572.

[86] R.S.N.S. 1989, c. 281, s. 2.

[87] *Medical Services Designation Regulation*, N.S. Reg. 152/89, Sch. "A", (d).

In other words, the Nova Scotia provincial government attempted to regulate abortion as a matter of public health law. In yet another case involving Henry Morgentaler, however, the Supreme Court of Canada held that the Nova Scotia legislation was *ultra vires* the provincial government, and therefore invalid, in that it attempted to regulate criminal law, an area of federal jurisdiction.[88]

Recent legislation, and corresponding litigation, in this area has concentrated on abortion funding. In *Lexogest Inc. v. Manitoba (Attorney-General)*,[89] a therapeutic abortion clinic challenged a regulation passed under that province's *Health Services Insurance Act*[90] that excluded payment for therapeutic abortions unless they were performed by a medical practitioner in a hospital. The majority rejected arguments that the legislation contravened the *Charter of Rights and Freedoms* or that it was inconsistent with the *Canada Health Act*.[91] The Court did rule, however, that the regulation was invalid as it was inconsistent with the intention of the *Health Services Insurance Act*, which did not authorize a regulation composing an increase in the cost of abortions for the tax paying public. As such a regulation was not authorized by the statute, it was struck down. A similar result, in similar circumstances, was obtained in a subsequent case in Prince Edward Island.[92]

AIDS

Acquired immunodeficiency syndrome (AIDS), unrecognized by conventional medicine until a little over a decade ago, has provoked intense scrutiny of patient rights and the obligations of health-care providers to patients who have been, or may become, victims of AIDS and other infectious diseases. Health administrators must recognize and deal with legal issues such as look-back programmes for blood transfusion patients, notification of provincial authorities under health protection and promotion legislation and workplace safety. AIDS has resulted in legislation in the area of infectious disease, protracted litigation and a government commission to inquire into the safety of the blood system in Canada.[93] AIDS is a fatal

---

88 *R. v. Morgentaler*, [1993] 3 S.C.R. 463.

89 (1993), 85 Man. R. (2d) 8 (C.A.).

90 R.S.M. 1987, c. H-35.

91 R.S.C. 1985, c. C-6.

92 *Morgentaler v. Prince Edward Island (Minister of Health and Social Services)* (1995), 126 Nfld. & P.E.I. R. 240 (P.E.I. T.D.).

93 Commission of Inquiry on the Blood System in Canada, appointed by Order in Council P.C. 1993-1879.

disease. For health facilities that do not meet reasonable standards in the prevention of transmission, the consequences can be enormous.

1. Health Protection and Promotion Legislation

AIDS is reportable to public health authorities in all provinces and HIV infection is reportable in all provinces except Quebec, Alberta and British Columbia.[94] Health administrators must ensure that statutory notification procedures are followed in their institutions. Failure to meet the legislative requirements may result in civil liability for the institution as well as its health practitioners.

In Ontario, for example, the reporting of communicable diseases is governed by the *Health Protection and Promotion Act*.[95] Sections 26 and 27 contain the reporting obligations of hospitals and physicians.

> 26. A physician who, while providing professional services to a person, forms the opinion that the person is or may be infected with an agent of a communicable disease shall, as soon as possible after forming the opinion, report thereon to the medical officer of health of the health unit in which the professional services are provided.
>
> 27.(1)–The administrator of a hospital shall report to the medical officer of health of the health unit in which the hospital is located if an entry in the records of the hospital in respect of a patient in or an out-patient of the hospital states that the patient or out-patient has or may have a reportable disease or is or may be infected with an agent of a communicable disease.

AIDS, in the Ontario legislation, is both a communicable and a reportable disease. HIV, as an agent of AIDS, therefore, is also reportable. The report required must contain the name, address, date of birth, sex and date of onset of symptoms of the patient. Any person who fails to make a report as required by the legislation is guilty of an offence.[96]

Some jurisdictions may have a legislated exception to the general mandatory reporting obligation. For example, in Ontario, there is a statutory exception to the mandatory reporting requirements. A physician who is providing professional services to a patient in a clinic identified in the regulations[97] is exempt from reporting the patient's name and address,

---

[94] J. Hamblin and M.A. Somerville, "Surveillance and Reporting of HIV Infection and AIDS in Canada: Ethics and Law" (1991), 41 U.T.L.J. 224.

[95] R.S.O. 1990, c. H.7.

[96] *Ibid.*, s. 100.

[97] R.R.O. 1990, Reg. 569 [am. O. Reg. 749/91].

if, before the test was ordered, the patient received counselling about preventing the transmission of HIV infection. Although considerable concern has been expressed by AIDS activists and others that a scheme of mandatory reporting, with limited exceptions, will discourage patients from coming forward for testing, the protection of patient confidentiality is not a legal basis upon which a health practitioner or a facility can disregard the legislation.[98]

Legal obligations in relation to the notification of non-governmental authorities pursuant to legislation are less clear. A patient who presents as a high risk of having AIDS based upon history and symptomology, but who refuses testing, may make it difficult to evaluate whether mandatory reporting is necessary. A patient who is wrongly identified as being HIV-positive may seek legal recourse.[99] On the other hand, even where the information is not sufficient to invoke a statutory obligation to report, the failure to warn others that they are at risk may result in civil liability. A physician who knows that a patient is engaged in high-risk, multiple-partner, sexual activity may have an obligation to warn the patient's spouse or long-term partner. When an AIDS patient is discharged from hospital in circumstances in which the caregivers know that the patient intends to engage in unprotected intercourse, the caregivers have an obligation to warn civil authorities as to the danger presented by the discharged patient.[100]

In *Canadian AIDS Society v. Her Majesty the Queen in Right of Ontario*,[101] it was held that the Red Cross had an obligation to notify donors whose blood donation had been identified as HIV-positive. The Canadian AIDS

---

[98] See Donald G. Casswell, "Disclosure by a Physician of AIDS-Related Patient Information: An Ethical and Legal Dilemma" (1989), 68 Can. Bar Rev. 225. It appears that in at least one jurisdiction a practice of "non-mandatory testing" has developed in which the patient's name is withheld from the Medical Officer of Health, though the fact that a patient has been diagnosed as HIV-positive is reported for epidemiological purposes. The practice has been developed in relation to physicians who regularly treat members of the population at a high risk of contracting the AIDS virus and on the understanding that those practitioners have experience and expertise in the treatment and counselling of HIV-positive and AIDS patients. It is questionable whether there is a legal basis for this practice. (Discussion with Ontario Ministry of Health AIDS Bureau, May, 1995).

[99] L. Priest, "Hospital, doctors Sued in AIDS error", *The Toronto Star*, June 9, 1993, A25.

[100] In Newfoundland, an 11-year jail term was imposed upon an accused who pleaded guilty to two counts of criminal negligence causing bodily harm as a result of his having engaged in unprotected sex and leaving two women HIV-positive; R. Mickleburgh "Severity of Sentence Questioned After HIV Carrier Infects Women", *The Globe & Mail*, August 13, 1993, A4.

[101] Unreported, November 5, 1994 (Ont. Gen. Div.).

Society took the position that no disclosure should take place without the express request of the donor. The Court rejected an argument that the HIV test was being done without the consent of the donor or that it was possible to conclude that releasing the names of the infected donors violated their privacy. It was held that the blood donation was a gift over which a donor could not reasonably be expected to retain control and that there was an "implied consent" to HIV-antibody testing. It was held that any right on the part of the donor to object to being told of the test result was outweighed by the need to do whatever is necessary "to prevent the spread of what has been described as an epidemic".

It has been held that the protection of the public is more important than keeping the identity of HIV-infected blood donors secret.[102] The Canadian AIDS Society had sought an injunction to prevent public health officials from obtaining the names of 13 donors who had unknowingly donated contaminated blood. It was argued that disclosure would breach the donors' privacy rights and their rights under the *Charter*. However, the Court ruled that the donors should be notified of their HIV status and their names reported to the Ministry of Health, pursuant to that province's health protection and promotion legislation.

2. Workplace Identification and Testing

The possible transmission of the HIV virus in the health-care setting has become a significant area of controversy as health facilities attempt to balance competing risks and obligations. The right of an AIDS patient to high quality, non-discriminatory treatment must be balanced against the risks to health practitioners and other patients. Similarly, a patient may wish to know whether he or she is being treated by an infected health-care worker and whether that person's treatment puts the patient at risk. The Canadian Medical Association has recommended that health-care workers who are at risk of having contracted the HIV virus voluntarily seek counselling and HIV-antibody testing. Where a health-care worker has been infected, the health-care worker is encouraged to

> . . . seek medical advice regarding the management of his or her condition, which should include a discussion of the current knowledge of risk of transmission in personal and professional life. Advice regarding occupational transmission risks could be sought from knowledgeable people such as staff responsible for Occupational Health and infectious disease epidemiology, or the Medical Officer of Health.[103]

---

[102] *Canadian AIDS Society v. Ontario*, unreported August 4, 1995 (Ont. Gen. Div.).

[103] Canadian Medical Association, "CMA Draft Position Paper — HIV Infection in the Workplace", February 13, 1992, as cited in William F. Flanagan, "AIDS-

Health facilities do not have the legal authority to test for the HIV virus without the express consent of the patient or unless a situation exists in which testing is necessary to ensure a safe health-care environment and the provision of treatment. It has been suggested that health administrators have a general duty to provide for a safe environment and may be justified, in conformance with legislation, in carrying out a general testing programme in the institution.[104] Any systematic testing of patients or residents in a health facility, however, would likely require very strong evidence of a significant danger or epidemic within the institution, and for that reason, is unlikely to be a practical solution. Mandatory or routine testing of patients or workers may offend human rights legislation.[105] The Center for Disease Control in Atlanta, Georgia has issued guide-lines for HIV-infected health-care workers:

(1) All HCWs [health-care workers] should adhere to universal precautions in the health care setting, including use of protective barriers and the disinfection and sterilization of reusable devices used in invasive procedures.
(2) Currently available data provide no basis to restrict the practice of HCWs infected with HIV "who perform basic procedures not identified as exposure-prone".
(3) "Exposure-prone procedures should be identified by medical/surgical/dental organizations and institutions at which the procedures are performed".
(4) HCWs who perform exposure-prone procedures should know their HIV status.
(5) HIV-infected HCWs should not perform exposure-prone procedures "unless they have sought counsel from an expert review panel and have been advised under what circumstances, if any, they may continue to perform these procedures. Such circumstances would include notifying prospective patients of the HCW's seropositivity before they undergo exposure-prone invasive procedures".
(6) Mandatory testing of HCWs for HIV infection is not recommended. "The current assessment of the risk that infected health care workers will transmit HIV or HBV to patients during exposure-prone procedures does not support the diversion of resources that would be required to implement mandatory testing programs. Compliance by health care workers with recommendations can be increased through education, training, and appropriate confidentiality safeguards".[106]

Related Risks in the Health Care Setting: HIV Testing of Health Care Workers and Patients" (1993), 18 Queen's L.J. 71, at 119-120.

104 Flanagan, *supra* note 103, at 81.

105 *Ibid.*, at 85-104.

106 "Recommendations for Preventing Transmission of Human Immunodeficiency Virus and Hepatitis B Virus to Patients During Exposure-Prone Invasive Procedures" (1991), 40 N.M.W.R. RR-8, as cited in Flanagan, *supra* note 103, at 111.

The Ontario Hospital Association has published guide-lines to assist hospitals in caring for HIV-infected patients and to ensure a safe working environment. The guide-lines reject involuntary testing of patients and affirm the importance of universal precautions in the hospital setting and the necessity of obtaining voluntary, specific and informed consent as a prerequisite to an HIV-antibody test. Nevertheless, the economic costs of universal precautions are significant. It has been estimated that the cost of taking universal precautions in American hospitals in 1989 was $336 million.[107]

Generally, hospitals and other health facilities must identify high-risk situations — whether the risk is from the patient or the health practitioner — and implement systems to minimize or exclude the risk of transmission. In the absence of mandatory or routine testing (which would not, in any event, be effective in identifying all infected patients[108]), the most effective, and at the same time acceptable from a legal perspective, practice is to employ techniques that assume, in effect, that every patient poses a risk to the health practitioner of an unidentified infectious disease and, therefore, should be treated appropriately.

3. Liability for Transmission of the AIDS Virus

The transmission of the HIV virus to patients and family members has given rise to intense and complex litigation. In Ontario, a class action has been commenced against the Canadian Red Cross Society and the Government of Ontario.[109] The federal government has provided a $110 million federal compensation plan[110] for victims of HIV-contaminated blood and provincial governments have provided $150 million in compensation.[111] There are several reported cases in Canada in which health facilities and practitioners have been required to defend allegations of negligence in apprising patients of the risk of AIDS transmission.

---

107 See V. Doebbeling et al., "The Direct Costs of Universal Precautions in a Teaching Hospital" (1990), 264 J.A.M.A. 2083.

108 See Flanagan, *supra* note 103, at 103:

> Testing, no matter how complete or accurate, can never substitute for universal precautions. Given the social costs associated with mandatory HIV testing, its uncertain utility, and the availability of less intrusive and more effective alternatives, the testing of patients as an infection control measure is neither an effective nor minimally intrusive public health strategy.

109 "Lawsuit Launched Over Tainted Blood", *The Globe and Mail*, December 9, 1993, A12.

110 Canada Health Protection Branch, January 6, 1995.

111 Canadian Blood Agency, January 18, 1995.

In *Ter Neuzen v. Korn,*[112] a patient entered into an artificial insemination programme operated by a Vancouver obstetrician and gynaecologist. She underwent 33 to 35 insemination procedures and became HIV-positive as a result of the last insemination procedure in 1985. Recently, the Supreme Court of Canada upheld the finding of the British Columbia Court of Appeal, which had found that the risk of HIV infection from the artificial insemination technique employed by the physician in 1989 was not well-known in the medical community and that the physician's own practice complied with the general standards of his colleagues. The Supreme Court held that the conduct of physicians must be judged in the light of the knowledge that ought to have been reasonably possessed at the time of the alleged act of negligence. There was no basis to support the argument that, in Vancouver in 1985, a reasonably competent medical practitioner would have ceased to practice artificial insemination or would have warned patients of the danger of HIV transmission. The matter was sent back to be retried on the issue of whether the physician had failed to take reasonable steps to protect his patients against sexually transmitted diseases in the screening of donors.

In *Pittman v. Bain,*[113] the patient was infected with HIV by her husband, who was unaware that he had contracted the AIDS virus through a blood transfusion. Five years after the surgery, as part of a look-back programme at the hospital where the surgery took place, it was discovered that Mr. Pittman had received blood that was contaminated with HIV. The hospital notified Mr. Pittman's family physician. Because the family physician was concerned about Mr. Pittman's heart condition and mental health, and did not wish to aggravate them, he did not advise Mr. Pittman of his possible infection. When Mr. Pittman died approximately one year later, it was discovered that he had been HIV-positive. Several months later his wife tested positive for the AIDS virus.

At trial, liability was found against the Canadian Red Cross Society, the hospital and the family physician. The trial judge found that the hospital and the Canadian Red Cross Society breached their duty to conduct an appropriate "look-back" programme. She concluded that the hospital was negligent in the implementation and design of its look-back programme. When it became apparent that it was going to take an unreasonably long period of time to achieve a need that was urgent, the hospital should have sought alternatives. Its failure to do so, and its failure to appreciate the serious threat caused by its delay, constituted negligence. The trial judge also concluded that both the Canadian Red Cross Society and the hospital were negligent in not ensuring that the family physician had sufficient

---

[112] [1995] 10 W.W.R. 1 (S.C.C.).

[113] (1994), 112 D.L.R. (4th) 257 (Ont. Gen. Div.).

information to enable him to give an adequate warning to Mr. Pittman. The family physician was also held negligent in withholding from Mr. Pittman the information that he had been transfused, in 1984, with a potentially HIV-contaminated blood component. Mrs. Pittman, her family and her husband's estate were awarded over $500,000 in damages.

4. The Krever Commission

In an *Interim Report*[114] issued partway through the hearing process, the Krever Commission has made a number of recommendations on how risks to the safety of the blood supply system in Canada can be improved. They include the following:

- That hospitals develop procedures to review the proposed use of any blood component requisitioned by physicians;
- That the hospital transfusion committee review physicians' use of blood for transfusions as a requirement of hospital accreditation;
- That hospitals be encouraged to create autologous blood programmes (donating one's own blood for one's own use);
- That hospitals, surgeons and physicians inform patients and provide written information about autologous blood programmes;
- That the risks, benefits and alternatives to blood transfusions be explained to patients in advance of surgical procedures;
- That hospitals record information pertaining to blood and blood components administered to patients and retain these records indefinitely so that they can be retrieved for look-back programmes;
- That hospitals review records to identify former patients who received blood and blood products between 1978 and the end of 1985 and that hospitals directly notify these patients that they have received a blood transfusion, inform them about the risks of HIV infection and provide counselling about the advisability and availability of HIV testing.[115]

The *Interim Report* also makes recommendations for a look-back in relation to the Hepatitis C Virus (HCV). The *Interim Report* states that 1.2–2.5 per cent of the people who received transfusions before HCV testing began were infected with the virus. Typically, Canadian hospitals have focused on

---

[114] Privy Council Office, *Commission of Inquiry on the Blood System in Canada* (Commissioner: Horace Krever). Reproduced with the permission of the Minister of Public Works and Government Services Canada, 1996.

[115] *Ibid.*, at 84-87.

the 1978 to 1985 period when the testing for HIV began. The Krever Commission asserts that there is no difference in principle between HIV and HCV infections and that direct, individual notification should be carried out for both.[116]

---

[116] On August 31, 1995, the Ontario Hospital Association published a general guide-line for programmes entitled "Establishing and Implementing Hospital Look Back Programs to Respond to Community and Red Cross Society Request". The guide-lines should be assessed in the context of the particular facility and programme being devised.

Index

D

E

N

O

P